Pic

Piccolo Santino,
My Calabrian Childhood in the 50s, Then to New York Italian Style
Copyright © Sal Mallimo 2019

piccolo santino
or
My Calabrian Childhood in the 50s
Then to New York, Italian Style.

By Sal Mallimo

Piccolo Santino

For

Nanna
November 7, 1891-February, 1987

Piccolo Santino

For

Matilda

A Maremma sheep dog bonds for life.
Our faithful dog Matilda would have swum across the Atlantic Ocean to look for us. Mamma felt it would have been too painful for Matilda to survive without us.

Piccolo Santino

Disclaimer
Compiled chiefly from memories based on actual events and Family interviews. Names and some events have been changed for story purposes.

Piccolo Santino

Prologue

This story is about my childhood from birth to age ten when my family immigrated to America. Over sixty years later, as I fly back to my hometown of Jonadi, in Calabria, Italy. I sit back and reminisce on my journey. Memories of my childhood have always bubbled inside me, and now I feel compelled to write them. I was beginning to know and love my home country when I was uprooted and moved, never again to feel those roots or cultivate the memories I thought I would complete in Italy. This change in my life left me longing and wondering what might have been.

When we arrived in America on July 4, 1958, we came to join my father, who had gone before us two years earlier; I decided to discard all memorabilia I had brought with me to make a testament, a commitment to learning American ways. I even started resenting my father singing words from Italian operas, or watching Italian programs on TV. I thought that Italian was useless once we were in America, as it contradicted my strong desire to thoroughly learn the new culture and language.

We all spoke in the Calabrian dialect, but amongst us children, we switched to English, and not with Mom and Dad. I often wondered if my parents could have become more Americanized if my siblings and I had spoken English to them and not just thought of them as settled in their ways.

Writing this book has allowed me to search inside for answers to questions about where my people originated, not simply where I came from. I had profound, soul-searching questions about things I considered to be embarrassments I tucked inside myself while growing up. I had inhibitions I wanted to lose every time I felt the shyness press on my soul. I had the type of hang-ups that suddenly strangled me when it was time to give an oral book report in front of the class. During such a moment, I would become conflicted because I could not decide if the people looking at me were with me or against me, and the doubt forced an actual internal conflict. The battle was like a racquetball bouncing back and forth. You could hear it in my voice as I tried to speak. My palms began to sweat, and my heart raced, I wanted to hide, but I was frozen in plain sight. In fear, I bowed my head in shame and walked away in despair. It had been so different in Italy, my natural turf, where a desire to succeed could, despite that fear of strangers, help me avoid such an awkward moment. In America, social situations became too complicated, and this tormented me.

We settled in Long Island, New York, and, to my surprise, we did not live in an Italian community. I liked it because it enabled me to mix with the American kids and learn from them at a better pace. In Italy, I craved an education. I loved the smell of new books and diving inside them to read and study new things. There, compulsory education was only for fifth grade, but I always wanted to keep learning. I was thrilled to discover that now, in America, there was a shining new hope. I could get a complete education. However, my father insisted on the Italian tradition for graduation. I rebelled against his plan to drop out of school at sixteen.

At thirteen years old, I found an ad in a comic book and enrolled in an animation art correspondence course at Continental Schools, Inc. in Los Angeles, California. I made the monthly payments of seven dollars by doing odd jobs. In June 1965, I received my diploma.

Because two of my sisters dropped out of school at sixteen, I graduated high school. Scholarships paid for my first year of film school at the School of Visual Arts in New York City. I exhausted my savings for the second year and received a Fellowship from the school for the third and final year. My student films garnered awards and recognition, which rewarded me immediately with finding a job in the film animation industry.

My college success precluded me from working in construction like my father had done. Still, my accomplishments did not stop him from wishing I had dropped out of school and fulfilled his hope of forming a landscaping company that would have enabled him to leave his construction job. He didn't know that I had hoped to make it big so he would not have to work anymore.

Piccolo Santino

Piccolo Santino

Table of Contents

Chapter	PART 1	Page
	Introduction	11
1	Bartolo's story	13
	Before Piccolo Santino was conceived	
2	My early memories of home	19
3	Santino's day of birth	24
4	Trip to St Catherine Church	31
5	Toddler Santino	38
6	Lillo's digestive woes traumatize Santino	46
7	My sisters make fun of my stuttering	53
8	Looking for **Papá**	60
9	Santino is denied a trip to the flour mill	65
10	Autumn 1954. School Days	75
11	Man of the house	82
12	Another sibling is born	92
13	Preparations for moving	104
14	May 1956. Moving day from the farm	119

	Part II	
	Table of contents Part II	129
	Part II Introduction	131

Piccolo Santino

Piccolo Santino

Introduction

At the airport, during my late years while boarding the plane.

    I walk to my seat before switching to a smaller plane from Rome to Calabria. I think to myself. *"How can a man be born twice and live one life to survive WWII in a Russian concentration camp? Later, be sent home in the winter of 1945, naked and blind, aboard a train with other 20,000 plus POWs. Then live to move his wife and seven children to America successfully?"* That man was my father, Bartolo Bianchi. The story of our family before I was born and when I was a baby was pieced together from family history that I learned. Thus, I describe my parents by their first names and write like a historian chronicling the story.

    Everything that follows, telling the tales of my childhood, is described from my memories. In my earliest years, I spoke of myself in the third person, as if I were "toddler Santino." However, a significant shift occurred in Chapter 6 when it jolted me from a sound sleep. I Vow to Never Talk Again, yet I became convinced to tell the story in the first person as the little boy. I hope you find this change in perspective engaging as you read my story.

Piccolo Santino

PART ONE

(Before Moving to America)

Chapter One of Part I
Bartolo's story: Before Piccolo Santino was conceived

Bartolo Bianchi, born to Massimo Bianchi and Martina Bianchi in Jonadi, Calabria, Italy, died at sixteen months. Two years later, on February 23, 1918, the couple gave birth to another baby boy. That same name, Bartolo, was given to the newborn. The second Bartolo survived with excellent health. Growing up, Bartolo became very fond of his oldest sister, Nina. Children in those days were preferred to be seen rather than heard. They had to sit at a separate makeshift table at family meals, usually the top of a trunk. Nina always ensured Bartolo's plate was neatly set and filled with food. When Bartolo was five, Nina became terminally ill, and her death at the age of seventeen crushed him.

Most people were illiterate in this part of Italy, especially women since girls were generally kept out of school altogether. If they learned to read and write, it was usually from their spouses. In southern Italy, children were lucky enough to go to school at that time. Parents would often terminate their children's education after third grade and enroll them in early adulthood by making them work on their farms. After Bartolo completed third grade, his father put him to work on their small farm with some cattle. Bartolo developed into a strong young man and gained the reputation of being the best worker around. He was always ready and performed steadily, at an even pace, stopping only for natural breaks until quitting time.

In April of 1939, at age twenty, Bartolo was drafted into the Italian army of Benito Mussolini, an army that "El Duce" promised would return Italy to the glory days of the Roman Empire. By this time, Bartolo had already been courting Anna Capari from the nearby town of Scaliti. The two had a lot in common regarding work ethics. Anna never evaded her work and was also no not afraid to speak her mind. Many men knew she had come to the defense of her younger brother Santino in a bar brawl. The husky assailant was overwhelmed and embarrassed by Anna.

Ironically, that did not stop him from seeking her courtship, only to be rejected.

Courting a lady was competitive enough, and though the siblings did not need the encouragement of an El Duce in any custom, Mussolini was offering a monetary incentive to couples who married during the time of his reign. He further suggested a bonus if the firstborn were a boy. Bartolo was very aware of his older brother Bernardo's ambition and interest in Anna, but Bartolo was not the type to worry about what others did or thought. He knew enough to always focus on his affairs. By 1939, however, after being rejected by Anna, Bernardo married Maria Grasso, a slightly larger and taller woman. However, Bernardo was satisfied that he could now qualify for El Duce's award money.

Courting in 1939 was nothing like modern-day courtship with its flamboyant attitudes and the open sexual desires of an oversexed society. Back then, girls had to be very cautious of their behavior and any display of affection. Men were all expected to behave very reservedly and distant in the company of their fiancée or women in general.

Anna's attraction placed her in an awkward predicament with her mother, Antonetta, a short, petite woman. Antonetta was almost always dressed in black and sported a black turban-like headdress. When men insisted on asking Antonetta about Anna, she always said they were wasting their time. Not until her oldest daughter Flavia was married could they come calling for Anna.

Antonetta's critical thinking continued when her husband, Arturo, often commuted to America with the seasons and sent packages home. When any shoes or dresses arrived for Anna, Antonetta would set them aside for Flavia. She would exclaim to Anna that she did not need any pretty clothes to help her appearance, but her older sister did. Flavia did marry first, and immediately multiple suitors came calling for Anna, including a wealthy landowner. She rejected them all in favor of Bartolo. When her mother and sister reacted with disbelief, she insisted that Bartolo was the only one for her. During Bartolo's courting of Anna, her older brother, Vito, escorted her. Vito, a boisterous young man whose arrogance displayed a real lack of intelligence, constantly chewed food with his mouth open and spoke out of turn. One day, Bartolo presented Anna with a brand new pair of shoes, and after the visit, her brother beat her for allowing Bartolo to help her try the shoes on.

Aware of the abuse his fiancée received at home, Bartolo could not wait for their wedding day. During a visit to Anna's family farm the day before their wedding, Bartolo argued with his mother-in-law-to-be. Back then, parents did not ask children to do things. They told them what to do. Not approving of Anna's proximity to Bartolo as they worked side by side in the field, Antonetta ordered Anna to move farther away from him. Bartolo responded that she did not have to move because they were about to be married. Antonetta swiftly and firmly replied that her daughter could not be so close to him until after tomorrow's wedding. "Until then," she loudly stated, "I'm still the boss."

Anna and Bartolo were married the next day, September 26, 1940. One of Anna's aunts made her wedding dress from white muslin material. In their wedding picture, contrary to stories, she often recalled how her mother deprived her of new things and how she had to go barefoot on her wedding day. Only then was Anna allowed to wear her brand-new shoes.

The wedding night was a frightening experience for the bride and brought the most disturbing anticipation to the groom. At first sight of her husband's naked body, Anna dashed out of the bedroom, exclaiming she had to get a drink of water. Homes had kitchens but no plumbing for running water. Anna rushed downstairs to where the jug of water was kept and began nursing the jug for a spell. Impatient, Bartolo called down to her from the top of the stairs. Anna gulped when she looked up at her husband, standing naked and looking most anxious with complete firmness. Chokingly, she responded that she needed another drink of water. Her response only succeeded in drawing a very irritable call from Bartolo. Anna slowly climbed to the top of the stairway, and off to bed, they went to consummate their marriage.

The married couple knew the day was looming when the war separated them. Since Anna had never attended school before they married, Bartolo had begun teaching Anna to read and write so they could communicate once he was away in the military. Nine months after they married, on June 10, 1941, Bartolo received his orders to report for military action.

During the first year, Bartolo was away, Anna could correspond successfully and send packages of cheese to her husband. Bartolo hated milk and milk products, but since the cheese was the only thing Anna had to send, he slowly adjusted to the taste.

By 1942, the united Nazi and Fascist armies made their push into Russia. Italy sent its 8th army, with over two hundred thousand Italian soldiers, to participate in the attack on Stalingrad, and Bartolo was one of them. When the Italian soldiers scattered to flee from their failed attack, search parties of the Russian army captured them. Before being captured, Bartolo and a fellow soldier contemplated suicide and, during their attempts, stopped to listen to voices they heard nearby. They revealed themselves when they recognized the Italian language and joined the group.

On December 21, 1942, the group was discovered by Russian soldiers and taken to a prison camp in Ukraine. With commands spoken only in Russian, if the POWs did not respond immediately, they would meet rifle butts on their shoulders. Bartolo quickly learned enough Russian to survive. Their diet consisted of boiled potatoes or boiled tomatoes. The water became a big problem, and prisoners teamed up to share their urine for drinking. Rare clandestine visits, through barbed wire fencing, by local peasant women would bring a lucky few some morsels of bread with some water. But these visits were too seldom to offer any real hope since the visits were very risky for the locals. They had to avoid being seen and could only push food through the wired fence. When my father spoke of anything about his experiences, he always mentioned this kindness.

On one occasion, Bartolo surrendered his wedding ring to a female guard for a piece of stale bread. Many died in the camp from starvation or the bitter cold. Perhaps the suicide attempt that Bartolo and his friend had once contemplated might have been a better fate. Letters from his wife were written in vain; they never reached him, and because he could not respond, she had given him up for dead.

Piccolo Santino

The war in southern Italy had its share of sorrows as the Allies performed constant bombing raids. A first cousin to Bartolo was found dead by her mother. She had died in the act of nursing her infant son. Shrapnel shot through her shoulder and pierced her heart but spared the infant, who remained in its mother's grip while sucking. After the bombing ceased, the horrified grandmother tried to free the child from its mother, but death's grip had already frozen the mother's arm around the infant. The grandmother pleaded for a long time, hoping that her daughter's spirit might still be able to hear her cry. A very long time passed with a tremendous amount of pleading when, as if by a miracle, the mother's fingers opened up during the grandmother's loudest outcry, and her arm dropped. The infant fell into his grandmother's arms, allowing her to walk away with the child. His grandmother raised Alberto, and he eventually immigrated to America and settled in Brooklyn.

December 10, 1945, Bartolo was released from captivity, and from the original 200,000+ Italian soldiers that attacked Russia, slightly over 20,000 survived. The surviving POWs were all stripped naked and packed, skin to skin, on board, a train to Poland then switched to a train bound for Berlin for another transfer to Turin, Italy. It was in Turin where they were all discovered, badly malnourished, and most of them also suffering from some form of blindness. Through the involvement of Pope Pius XII and the Catholic Church, clothes were made available for the POWs.

From Turin, the POWs were redirected to their local provinces. Bartolo was sent to Catanzaro. From there, he was taken to his hometown of Jonadi. Word had already arrived in town that Bartolo had been seen in Catanzaro, and when a close friend rushed to tell Anna of the exciting news, she responded with total disbelief. After not having heard from him for almost four years, she believed he was dead; for Anna to think of him as living was further complicated when she saw Bartolo's severely malnourished and war-worn appearance. Was this him? It was difficult for her to face him initially, but then Anna realized that Bartolo had to be led by the hand. The thought that he could be permanently blind frightened her deeply. It was about six months before Bartolo's vision returned to normal. Until then, Anna always had to guide his every step.

Another continuing thought troubled Anna; Bartolo pleaded for her to get into bed with him at night. Worried that people were gossiping about her sleeping with a stranger, she sat by his bedside each night until Bartolo fell asleep. Through all her husband's pleading, after two weeks, she finally became convinced that he was indeed her Bartolo, who had returned from the war zone.

Within the next two years, a return to everyday life occurred, at least as normal as expected in the post-war era. Finally, peace seemed possible for Bartolo and Anna with the arrival of their first child, a girl they named Martina after the paternal grandmother. It was customary to name children after relatives.

The arrival of a daughter prompted Bartolo to seek residential changes. He thought about sharecropping when he heard rumors about a small farm possibly becoming available. He had already achieved priority treatment in the job market due to his military service, but since jobs were scarce, he felt that he could do better managing a small farm to support his family. Luckily, his reputation as a rugged and reliable worker continued to precede him. He discovered this when he inquired about the rumored availability of the farm on the Fontana Di Taccuni, located on the outskirts of Nao, a locality of Jonadi.

Chapter 2 of Part One
My early memories of home

While *I am seated on board the airplane, the pilot's voice comes over the speakers, and I unbuckle my seatbelt. I lean my seat back and close my eyes as I lay my head on the headrest and think about home as I remember it.*

One main highway linked northern and southern Italy. A short distance away, just before the road surrounded our home on three sides, there was a wide crossroad at the junction of two neighboring towns, Nao and St. Constantine, known as *i quattro strati* – the four corners. We marveled at the number of strangers and some foreigners who camped along the country line. On one occasion, we witnessed a car race rip down the highway and around our home. We always felt lucky when we heard the roaring sounds from speeding vehicles and got excited when the rumble trailed off and wrapped itself around our peninsula. That day, we ran to the southern end of our property line and made it just in time to watch the race cars with fancy stripes speed away into the distance on the straightaway to the south.

On hot summer days, the blacktop was so intense one did not dare walk on the road, even with shoes. Government regulations would not allow many vehicles to travel by day, but on scorching days, one could see tire marks on the road that preceded government warnings. We rushed out from the shade of the vine arbor in our driveway to the sound of strange, motorized clanking, crawling metal, which we discovered to be a big, scary, yellow bulldozer. We stared at the motorized treads mercilessly chewing and spitting out the asphalt and leaving a long trail behind the bulldozer's path. Mamma yelled out to the driver, and he quickly stopped as she reminded him of the government ordinance. Then, the man looked back at the trail of damage and promptly drove the bulldozer onto the grassy shoulder against a natural wall. Nevertheless,

Piccolo Santino

The metal teeth ate up the road sideways well into the shade.

On the west side of our house, the terrain was populated by large orange and red poppies that seemed like bright lights on the shoulder of the road. Across the street from the poppies, rocky terrain with trees and heavy brush formed a natural wall that climbed high toward the sky. It started farther up the highway at the four corners, curved across our house, headed eastbound for about half a mile, and leveled off. Then it swerved sharply, hugged the southern side of our property, and curved again into a straightaway to the south. Above the rocky terrain across from our house lived a neighbor in a home converted from a military bunker.

Below, from where the poppies swelled in number in a shallow ravine, was the back wall of our house clinched by a thick, heavy row of brush and trees that climbed past the red tile roofline. At the end of the house, tall, black, and square-pegged metal bars formed the two gates that greeted visitors to what was known as Fontana Di Taccuni. The name referenced the natural spring on the Di Taccuni property. The farm boasted a small crop of lemons, oranges, and grapes. In time, Mr. Taccuni became so heavily indebted to Doctor Itasca that he turned the entire property over as a settlement. Although the property changed ownership, the name became so generic to the area that it remained intact.

We liked picking pomegranates from trees that grew wild in the scrub along the highway. As the hot sun forced red juice through cracking skin, we licked our chops and didn't mind getting sticky fingers as we plucked and peeled the fruit. We were eager but had to be cautious of beehives and snakes. It is hard to think which of the two scared us more, but it did not stop us from venturing further into the scrub for the wild raspberries. For fun, we ripped petals from the poppy flowers to place a petal on our left hand between our thumbs and forefingers and slapped it with our right hand to hear the loud pop as it burst.

Vehicular danger also lurked here. One day, two motorcycles careened off the road as they sped around the corner. We heard cries for help and rushed with Mamma to the scene. We saw one young man sprawled out on the ground. Two others tried to care for him while he cried out for water. I ran back to the house for the water jug and as he tried to drink, the water just poured back out from a slit in his throat.

I remember all this as our family grew up on an isolated farm that seldom had visitors, even though it was in the middle of a major highway.

Time moved slowly and added to a pleasant isolation, making the La Fontana Di Taccuni property feel like a unique, magical place. The strength of that magic forced me to believe that all natural things had human-like feelings I could identify with. I rationalized that trees, shrubs, and grass also felt the bitter cold, along with Mother Nature, who had to remain outside at night in that bitter cold and sadly could not seek shelter. I reasoned that they all shivered in the howling wind. But I, at least, had protection and could lay in a warm bed at night as the wind howled and the rain tapped against the shutters.

Papá rushed to close those shutters one night when the wind and rain blew them wide open as I lay in bed. When the warm sunlight thawed the earth and trees bloomed during springtime, they all had to sneeze like me. When plants waned during the withering of autumn, they all had to feel the change that made them recoil deep inside themselves, as I was forced to do. I was sure they all looked toward the warm summer days like I did. That was when my older sister and I pranced in the fields and visited the arriving wildflowers and vegetable patches. We ventured into the small vineyard and the orange groves as our pet dog, Matilda, a white Maremma Sheepdog, followed along. We savored mornings when Mamma treated us to ruby red cactus pears and laughed when she told us to eat figs first, as the cactus pears alone would be very binding. She told us about a boy hospitalized from eating too many cactus pears without eating figs beforehand. If Mamma had been educated, she would have been a good writer with all her stories.

When I saw snow for the first time, it felt surreal as the heavy, wet fluff clung to trees like whipped cream. It felt like a violation to trespass on such holy carpeting with the white and pristine floor. Snow was rare this far south, and when it came, the cold was very sharp and biting since we weren't in heavy clothing and unprepared. Shorts were all I could

Piccolo Santino

remember wearing, I only remember having or wearing shoes when I started school. Mamma would scold me if I didn't remove them once I got home.

I always remember Mamma in her rocking chair, swaying a baby to sleep, constantly with another one on the way. The Firstborn, Martina, was born in their home in town, in Jonadi. The rest of us were born in Fontana Di Taccuni. Papá made it our home after successfully securing an arrangement with the new landlord, Dr. M. Itasca. Papá had heard the new tenant on Fontana Di Taccuni was about to be evicted for being a laggard. About a year or so later, Papá was discharged from the military. Dr. Itasca was aware of Papá's integrity, and on their first meeting, the two sealed the usual sixty/forty sharecropping agreement. Dr. Itasca would realize sixty percent of the proceeds from the sale of the annual crop. Papá kept a portion of the grapes to make wine as part of his forty percent.

In the early days, Mamma and Papá operated a small wine and cheese eatery. Papá became known as the "Chicken Man" because of the abundance of fowl, which included pigeons he served from his farm. The restaurant attracted many people, and as some strangers began to recognize one another for past vendettas, they started carrying shotguns when visiting the establishment. Then, Papá added Matilda, the white Maremma Sheepdog, to the family. Matilda always slept by the door; not even a flea could get past her. Matilda's menacing growl was enough to scare anybody away at the sound of any noise, inside or outside the door. But when patrons involved themselves in heated arguments that came close to firing their shotguns, Papá feared for his family and thus shut down the eatery and sought employment with the national highway system. However, he still made wine for personal consumption.

In farmhouses in Southern Italy, there was neither indoor plumbing nor electricity. Women used a bedpan under the bed, and the men went outside, away from sight. Natural light was the primary source, and a kerosene lamp was lit in the evenings.

I recall how Mamma told me about when I was born, during that Easter Holy Week, early one afternoon after a short downpour. Even in

Piccolo Santino

my old age, I can envision looking between the black, square pegged metal bars that formed the tall gates of what used to be my home on the Di Taccuni property. I visualize myself staring down the long grape arbor, stretching the hardened dirt driveway's entire length and width. I picture myself listening to the screams of Mamma in labor, joined by other women's vigorous calls for hot water, the sounds penetrating the stone walls. Mamma is screaming from the pain I caused her.

I settle in my seat after the airplane hits an air pocket. I ponder questions: did I know I was being born? Do we all know what happens during our travel time through the birth canal?

Subconsciously, we must have some idea. But we must still be developed enough to put it into conscious thought. Shocked, we react by crying from the astonishment of a mighty dark inside that thrusts us through a short passage into a powerfully lit outside for a complete moment of adjustment.

Through these gates to the left, I picture a man in a jacket and a dark, weathered fedora carrying two buckets of water at the bottom of the driveway. That would be my maternal grandfather, Arturo, a tall man with a mustache in the style of John Russell, the actor from the sixties TV western *"The Lawman."* I see his walk as brisk but careful not to spill any water. I watch him walk behind the house's front wall to return to the kitchen at the opposite end of the building. I can't see into that part of the house from behind these gates in my mind, so I will let the story take you the rest of the way.

Chapter 3 of Part One
Santino's day of birth.

Grandfather Arturo entered the kitchen and placed two buckets on the dirt floor to the left of the fireplace. Over the burning fire was a large pot of water resting on a metal tripod with steam rising. Directly across in the small room, high off the floor, was a large brick oven, and seated against the oven wall on a bale of hay was my paternal grandfather Massimo, a short, stocky man with large ears and an unshaven face. The sorrows in his eyes made him look older than his actual age, sufferings he could not let go, from the death of his oldest daughter at the age of seventeen, and then, a few years after the birth of their ninth child, his wife also passed.

Arturo looked up from setting the buckets down and said, "I heard my daughter screaming as I came up the walkway. Has anything changed yet?"

"No! Nothing's changed. It's all the same," responded Massimo.

Bartolo rushed in from outside, his arms full of firewood, and the family dog Matilda panting at the doorway. He dropped the bundle of thorny rosewood thicket and other minor branches by the fireplace, brushed off his jacket, and asked anxiously, "Is the baby here? I heard Anna screaming down by the ravine. I rushed back, thinking that was the big one." His voice trembled with urgency. "No! No son, not yet," responded his father, Massimo.

Arturo walked over to another doorway, looked down the hallway, and saw his youngest daughter, thirteen-year-old Fabrizzia, walking over, recognized by many as the prettiest of his three daughters. The eldest, Flavia, the ugly duckling due to her very dark complexion, immigrated to Argentina with her husband after a couple of years of marriage in search of a better life. Anna, considered the second prettiest, was about to give birth to her second child.

Fabrizzia, held up the empty bucket. Her youthful beauty was a stark contrast to the worry etched on the faces of the others. Arturo led her to the fireplace and asked, "How is your sister doing?" Bartolo quickly interrupted, "Did the baby come yet?"

"No, Bartolo! Not yet," responded Fabrizzia as she turned back to her father and, in a grave tone, said to him, "She's holding tough Padre, but she is in pain. The midwife thinks we might have to summon the Doctor." Fabrizzia turned back to Bartolo with, "Stay here in the kitchen in case the midwife wants you to go for the Doctor. Don't go anywhere, not even for firewood. Let the others do it." Bartolo responded with curiosity. "But what's happening? Is something wrong? This is our second baby. It should be easier, no?"

Giustina, the midwife's assistant, entered the kitchen, frantically looked around, stared at Bartolo, and said, "Bartolo, come inside right away. The midwife wants to talk to you!"

"Sì! Sì! Pronto! What's wrong?" Bartolo said as he rushed past Fabrizzia as he and Giustina continued down the hallway. The midwife shouted from inside, "Fabrizzia, bring the hot water now!"

Fabrizzia explained further to the men, "Padre, the midwife thinks the baby is breeched. She wants Bartolo to get the Doctor." The front door slammed shut, and Bartolo rushed up the driveway. As he sprinted past the wide-opened gates, he listened to his wife screaming in pain and thus intensified his walk into a military trot on his journey into town.

Bartolo's father, Massimo, stopped stirring the fire in the kitchen. He and Arturo grabbed empty buckets, and both went for refills. They glanced up the driveway at the wide-opened gates as they walked by to make their way down the ramp to the spring fountain.

Inside, by Anna's bedside, her mother held a homemade cappuccino to help Anna push during the contractions. She lowered the cup to her daughter's lips, and Anna turned her head away while screaming out in excruciating pain. Antonetta, a short, petite woman wearing her black turban-like headgear, was never one to be turned down, but this time, she understood what her daughter was going through and said to her, "Be strong, my daughter, be strong. We are made for these moments."

Piccolo Santino

Moving at a frantic pace, Bartolo navigated the atrium at Doctor Itasca's house in the heart of the town. Their car was strategically parked closer to the house wall, away from the date-littered entrance, near the towering palm tree on the right, which stood a foot or so above the slate-paved ground. The cool air in the atrium starkly contrasted with the urgency that filled the space, where heavy-leaved green plants spanned to the left and right of the palm tree, joined by a circulating fountain.

Bartolo looked through the sliding glass door left ajar with curtains drawn halfway and was met by the startled eyes of Mrs. Susanna Itasca. She quickly rose from sitting on the couch by a coffee table and rushed up to him at an alarming speed as she sensed a real urgency. She promptly called out to her husband, Dr. Vincenzo Itasca, in the next room. Having heard her call, he shouted down to the lower level, and his father rushed up the stairs with his medical case in his left hand while adjusting his right arm into his jacket. Bartolo never got to express himself as the old Doctor, Michele Itasca, led the two men out the door and said to his son, "Vincenzo! *Presto, presto,* hurry. Hurry, get in the car!"

Anna's screams pierced the air, causing the men to bow their heads in concern. In the bedroom, the midwife's gaze was fixed on the baby's feet, a sight that sent a shiver down everyone's spine. Fabrizzia stacked clean towels on the table with a sense of urgency, Antonetta dabbed Anna's forehead with a cool, wet towel, and Giustina, Anna's dear neighbor, paced from the table to the front door, her steps quick and purposeful.

At the sound of a car entering the driveway, Giustina dashed to open the door. Old Doctor Itasca entered the house, looked back, and said, "Bartolo, come inside with us." Then he turned to Giustina and said, "Buongiorno!" The women returned greetings as the three men rushed to join Anna. The old Doctor stopped at Anna's bedside and said, "I'm sorry to find you with complications, but let's think that all will be well."

The young Dr. Vincenzo, concerned, called out to his father. "Please, doctor, come here!" The senior Doctor walked over to the foot of the bed, gasped at the sight of the protruding baby's feet, and called out, "Bartolo, bring the table close to the bed here, all cleared off.

Piccolo Santino

Quickly, please!"

"Si Dottore subito!" Bartolo responded. The two women hurried to help clear the table, and Fabrizzia assisted Bartolo in moving the table by the foot of the bed as the two doctors convened.

In the kitchen, the men turned their attention to Giustina as she scampered in with two empty buckets and reported that the Doctor had taken charge. A scream from Anna pierced the air in the kitchen, and the men's heads sunk further into their chests. Fabrizzia came in looking for Giustina, and the men asked for an update. Fabrizzia responded that the Doctor was trying to turn the baby by twisting its feet. Arturo looked at Fabrizzia and softly exclaimed, "Her first one arrived so fast and almost effortlessly, but now this one is giving her problems." She looked away from her father, took a bucket of water from Giustina, and both women walked out.

In the bedroom, the two doctors nodded in agreement as they looked at the birth in progress. The elder Doctor turned to Bartolo and said, "Bartolo, please come here." Antonetta moved close to the two men as the senior Doctor rose to his feet and whispered to Bartolo, "I am sorry, but the situation is grave, and we must ask you to choose between your wife and the baby." Antonetta stepped between the two men, grabbed the old Doctor by his collar while staring directly into his eyes, and demanded. "No! You must save them both. You are a doctor!" The Doctor placed his hand on hers, looked into her eyes with concern, and said, "Si Signora, I am a doctor, but this is very complicated."

They both released their hold. The Doctor turned his attention to the others and demanded, "Now I must ask that everyone leave the room except for the midwife, please!" He turned to Antonetta and said, "I am very sorry, Signora Antonetta. I can only ask for your prayers."

Then the senior Doctor turned to Bartolo, staring into Anna's eyes, and said, "Bartolo, have you decided?" Bartolo slowly approached the physician and said, "Dottore Itasca, how can I choose? Today is Good Friday. It is a decision for God to make, not me."

"Very well, I understand," said the Doctor. Bartolo turned back at his wife. The Doctor faced his son and asked, "Doctor Vincenzo, is

Piccolo Santino

everything ready?" As Bartolo walked away, Dr. Vincenzo answered his father, "Si Dottore, *Tutto e pronto,* everything is ready."

The midwife stood by Anna as the other women left the room, but Antonetta quietly stood by the exit door hidden beside a dresser and coyly dropped her body onto a chair. She grasped her rosary beads and whispered a prayer. "My Dear St. Catherine, I pray to you for the lives of my daughter and her child. In return, I vow to make the long, arduous walk through the mountains to your church and place the baby at your feet for you to see."

In the postwar era in rural Italy, there were no hospital services in these hills. Primarily, all babies were delivered at home by midwives, and only in rare cases such as these would a doctor be summoned. The young Dr. Vincenzo had just performed an episiotomy to facilitate this delivery. The senior Doctor grabbed a set of forceps and called out to the midwife, "Signora, Rosanna, hold her hands tight at her side." Then, the senior Doctor called out to his patient. "Anna, hold on tight." He placed the forceps in position and pushed them firmly inside Anna. Anna screamed, and it echoed into the countryside. In the kitchen, Bartolo cringed, as did others. At the same time, they waited in nervous anticipation. Fabrizzia turned cold as she tried to understand it all at a young age. Her father looked at Fabrizzia with deep concern, wondering if, in the future, Fabrizzia might also face a similar predicament.

Anna let out another scream, and doves suddenly reacted to her pain by darting off the roofline. Her cry rattled the red slates where the doves had rested. Bartolo pleaded with his sister-in-law and neighbor, Giustina, to check on things inside. Still, before he could finish his plea, Fabrizzia and Giustina darted to the doorway and stopped by the seated Antonetta, quietly murmuring her prayers. Fabrizzia's face turned stone cold at the sight of the baby dangling from the forceps as the Doctor threw it on the table for dead. Both women called out from the doorway at the same time. "Can we be of some help?"

The two doctors seemed oblivious to the call as they tended to Anna's wounds, but the midwife called out. "Si! Si! Fabrizzia, come here and tend to your sister. Giustina, we need fresh water." Giustina ran back to the kitchen and was mobbed by the men's wide eyes in the silence. All she could report was that the baby was out and would be right back as soon as she learned more, but for now, she must get fresh water.

The doctors began to suture the skin around the episiotomy, and as the midwife examined the baby, she became startled and hopeful at what she discovered. The heavy use of forceps left scarring across the child's head, and its face was covered by a rich mucus film commonly known as a veil, and no sooner had the midwife lifted the baby off the table than the baby let out a scream that brought Antonetta to her feet. She rushed over to look at the baby. Both doctors turned with astonishment, and they both gasped before the senior Dr. Itasca murmured, "It's a miracle!"

Antonetta made the sign of the cross as she looked at the veiled and scarred baby's face. The old Doctor looked up at Antonetta and exclaimed as he looked toward the baby, "Signora Antonetta, all is well. After all, it is Good Friday today." Antonetta replied, "Si Dottore. Indeed, it is Good Friday."

Giustina returned with the water and sighed with relief when she saw Antonetta standing by Anna's bedside and talking to her. She poured fresh water into a clean, large metal washbowl, and the midwife cleaned the crying baby. Then, she wrapped him in a white muslin cloth and brought him to his mother. Everyone greeted Bartolo as Giustina returned to the kitchen and reported the joyous news.

His sister-in-law Fabrizzia came out to inform Bartolo that he could now visit his wife and son. Antonetta, clutching her rosary beads, looked at the child's face and stared pensively at the damage done by the forceps. The nose was pushed into his face, which made the whole face look flattened. Nonetheless, she was thinking of her vow and reminded herself that as soon as her daughter was ready to travel, they would journey to the church of St. Catherine.

The midwife laid the child beside his mother, and Bartolo walked over to his wife's bedside, leaned over, kissed her on the forehead, and said, "Is it really a boy, Anna?"

"Si!" she responded, "He's a little beat up though, from the forceps." Bartolo stared at the baby, "Hey, not too bad. In time, he'll grow, and maybe everything will rearrange itself." He turned to Anna,

Piccolo Santino

"I'm happy you are both alive. Which name did you decide on?"

"Santino," she softly answered with a smile. Bartolo, taken by surprise, grinned as he looked at the child and said, "It's a good name. After your brother?" Anna nodded in agreement as she meekly said, "Sì."

"Get some sleep now. Go to sleep, darling. You look very tired." Bartolo turned to face everyone in the room and blurted out, "His name is Santino!"

"Bravo! Bravo!" responded the doctors, and they both walked over to shake Bartolo's hand as they dried their hands on a clean towel. "Grazie, Doctor Itasca, and you also, Doctor Vincenzo, you have performed a miracle here today." The young doctor looked at Bartolo and said, "The miracle is from God. We simply assisted with our work."

The senior doctor then said to Bartolo, "Make sure your wife does not get up out of bed. We will come by tomorrow." Dr. Vincenzo looked at his father and said, "Well, father, shall we go?"

"Yes, son, I'm ready." Both doctors looked at everybody and said, "Goodbye and Happy Easter!"

"*Grazie atra tanto e Anche a voi dottori,* thank you very much, and you as well, Doctors."

Piccolo Santino

Chapter 4 of Part One
Trip to St. Catherine Church

The time to fulfill the vow soon arrived, and before sunrise, Antonetta firmly wrapped a thin strip of cloth around a coin the size of a nickel and tightly tied a string around the fabric to keep it snug. She placed the flat side of the wrapped coin on Santino's belly button and then wrapped a muslin strip of cloth around his stomach to fasten the coin in place. The bandage strip was referred to as *a fascia,* a common practice by all women to secure the formation of an inner-shaped belly button. She stared at the infant's disfigured face, then whispered to him, "Today, your mamma and I are taking you on a long trip to see Santa Caterina so she can meet you."

The child showed his smile with wide eyes, and his upper lip curled under the distorted nose. His mamma then reached over to lift his shoulders to dress him in an oversized T-shirt and then wrapped a blanket around him before she placed the baby in the basket. Antonetta turned to her daughter and said, "Anna, put the basket on my head, and let's get going before the sun comes up."

"Sì Madre, turn around; the towel looks loose on your head."
Antonetta retorted with slight sarcasm. "No! No! *E buona, e Buona* It's good. I just fixed it. Now, come on, let's get going. The sun is starting to set already!"

"The sun isn't up yet, Madre! Here, here's the baby." Anna placed the basket on her mother's head. "Not so loud, or you'll wake up your husband and daughter."

"You're both crazy making a trip like this. There is nothing to worry about!" Bartolo's voice startled them as he turned up the kerosene lamp.

"*Ma fatte i cazzi tue,* mind your fuck'n business. We're in charge here," countered Antonetta. "Well then, did you at least pack something to eat?"

"Sì! Sì! We've got something," responded Anna. He kissed her goodbye and whispered, "You know you're not well enough to make this trip yet."

Piccolo Santino

"I feel fine, don't worry."

"Then good luck!" He opened the door for them, and they walked out into the cool air of the predawn darkness; he slowly closed the door behind them and listened to his mother-in-law's fading words. "The air feels damp," she said. "You think it's going to rain?"

"I don't feel anything," Anna responded as they walked down the stoop. Bartolo locked the door and walked back to bed, his eyes bulging and his head shaking back and forth as he lifted his hands in prayer.

A few sparrows scattered from trees as the two women rustled through the countryside. The terrain was hilly, with small areas of straight runs for some relief. On occasion, both women shifted hands from one knee to the other during some of the climbing. Despite the rocky terrain, Antonetta always balanced the basket, holding the infant Santino on her head without difficulty. It was a credit to all the women in that part of the country. They often carried items to and from their farms, laundry baskets from the public wash pools, or construction materials. Some of the women worked on construction sites or had other menial errands to do.

Upon finishing an arduous climb, Anna called out, "Madre, let's stop a minute. The baby needs feeding."

"We'll stop a bit farther up. I see a snake's trail here."

"Oh my god, I didn't even see it!" Anna exclaimed while she pushed forward to the stop area and sat on a large boulder. She took a deep breath, pulled a handkerchief from her cleavage, and wiped the hot sun off her brow. Antonetta approached, lowered the basket from her head, and rested it on her daughter's lap. Santino began whimpering. "Santino woke up!" exclaimed his grandmother. "Yeah, he's hungry."

When Anna took the baby out, Antonetta put the basket on the ground away from Anna's small sack of nourishment. She laid out a towel and proceeded to cut up some homemade bread, cheese, and soppressata. Then, she unraveled a smaller towel containing black sun-dried olives. "Now, the only thing missing is some red wine!" exclaimed Antonetta as she bit down on a piece of bread. She handed Anna a slice of soppressata and said, "Go ahead and eat something, child, eat!"

Piccolo Santino

"How much longer before we get there, Madre?"

"Well, we've been walking for a good hour, maybe a little more, plus half an hour or so that we rested a while back. We should arrive in another hour or so."

"Is the walk a little easier the rest of the way, at least?"

"Yes, the terrain is a lot easier, plus there is an underground spring around the bend here. We can get fresh water there."

"Good, I'm thirsty."

"Santino hadn't even whimpered this whole time. Doesn't he ever cry?"

"Oh no! He hardly ever cries unless he's hungry, and when held by another woman, he will try to breastfeed just the same." Antonetta, with laughter, asked, "What did you say? Are you for real?" Anna explained further to her Madre. "Yes, for real! One day when Fabrizzia was holding him, he tried sucking right over her blouse." Laughter broke out; Anna continued, "She is now afraid to hold him."

"You little devil, you!" said Antonetta, leaning into the baby and mother as he stopped sucking. Anna handed him over and buttoned her blouse. Antonetta asked her daughter, "And you named him Santino?"

"Well, he was born on Good Friday, no?" Teasingly, she held the baby away, looked into his eyes, and said, "Don't worry, Santino, I'll explain it all to Santa Caterina!" Then she turned to her daughter. "Come on. Let's get a drink of water so we can get going."

Anna took the baby, placed him in the basket, and the two carried the basket together to the underground spring. Around the bend, a short descent was made to a narrow walkway marred by dried wild rosebushes and raspberry bushes that waited for the summer months to bring them to full bloom. Farther away in the hills were some olive trees, a sign of land belonging to someone. The trees looked well pruned with some branch grafting. In the close distance was an old couple walking downhill, diagonal to the landscape. The man, dressed in baggy brown pants and a grey shirt with rolled-up sleeves, was guiding a calf by its reins, and they suddenly stopped when his woman, facing uphill, bent down. With a cutting motion, her hands maneuvered into the ground several times, then held up a thick harvest of dandelions to show her husband. He smiled in approval, and she tucked them with other dandelions inside her apron, which was folded upward and tucked at the sides to form a large pocket.

The man then pointed to a lower section of dandelions where the woman's backside lifted higher to facilitate the harvesting. The man cocked his head sideways, leaned down slightly, and stared at his woman's swaying buttocks, admiring the rhythm of her moves.

The sun had now sunk behind heavy clouds, and the terrain here was more forgiving. Anna and Antonetta walked a bit livelier, and the basket with Santino remained steady on Antonetta's head as it rested solidly on that soft towel. The sun played some hide and seek in the clouds. Suddenly, a runaway donkey bolted out from behind a large thicket to the right. Anna let out a scream. Antonetta reached up for the basket as she dropped to her knees in loud laughter. She safely laid the basket down, but not without an outcry from Santino.

Anna scrambled over to retrieve the infant from the basket while Antonetta laughed. In all that grief, a short middle-aged man, waving a whip, ran out from the same brush chasing after the donkey. A rope around his waist for a belt, he paused for a quick second, looked at the two women, and continued the chase while shouting an apology as his straw hat flew off his head. "Excuse me, ladies, my donkey saw the female back there and got crazy!"

Antonetta continued her hearty laughter, and the bedazzled Anna, trying to comfort Santino, exclaimed, "Madre, why are you laughing?"

"Are you crazy? Didn't you see that donkey?"

"Yeah! I saw it, but I didn't think it was funny. I was preoccupied with the baby."

"Then you didn't see anything?"

"What was there to see?" Anna rocked the whimpering Santino against her bosom. Antonetta intensified her laughter and said, "It was all dangling between its legs!"

"What was dangling? What are you saying?"

"The donkey had a hard-on longer than your arm!"

Piccolo Santino

"Damn it! In another second, my son could have gotten hurt over *un cazzo di asino duro*, a fuck'n donkey woody." Both broke out in hearty laughter as they regrouped and began their descent to town toward the church of Santa Caterina.

Growing up, Antonetta always liked it when her grandmother told her the story of Santa Caterina. She remembered hearing how a wealthy sailor was stranded at sea in a horrifying storm and, while feeling hopeless, he prayed to St Catherine. He promised that if St. Catherine brought him to safety, he would build a chapel for her. After many stormy days at sea, he made it to safety off the coast of Egypt. The sailor then settled in Egypt and built a church for her by a cliffside. When he died, he was buried inside the church, and many years later, when a bad storm caused a landslide, his tomb remained unscathed. From that day forward, throughout the years, the people spread the miracle of St. Catherine from generation to generation.

The sun felt warm on their shoulders as it peeked out from behind the clouds, and the two women walked down the final stretch of the walkway leading to the outskirts of Santa Caterina. Antonetta pointed toward the church, and both picked up their pace. A tower structured the façade on each side, and the roofline formed a triangle in the center. On the second floor, a long rectangular window guided one's eye to the wide olive-wood double doors. Doves flew above and rested on the roofline. Below, Anna led the way. She pulled open the tall, heavy, thick doors that made some people squint at the effort. Anna firmly held the handle, allowing her mother and baby to go first.

A pigeon turd dropped on Antonetta and splashed down in front of her. She quickly dashed inside. Being in a church, she refrained from using harsh words and instead reached for the cup of holy water and made the sign of the cross. In that cool vestibule, the closing doors echoed loudly, and the smell of incense was strong. The solid marble floor felt cool under their feet, revealing a far different impression from the warm grassy terrain during their journey. They slowly pushed open the second set of doors, making their way to the inside.

Piccolo Santino

Outside, the sun resumed its game of hide and seek, and the two women felt the sun's glare when its light changed intensity as it penetrated the stained glass windows and spilled inside the church. White marble lavished the walls inside, and smooth white stucco gripped the ceiling like frosting on a wedding cake. The oak benches always filled up during mass to both wings on the altar's sides. Today, one older man sat on a bench at the center-right aisle. His balding hair was thin and grey. His face was sunken from missing teeth and unshaven with more of today's salty stubbles than yesterday's darker ones. His fingers were fidgeting a cap between them as his hands rested on his lap in prayer.

Halfway down the left aisle at a confessional booth, a curtain slowly opened, and a hooded, short, husky monk came forward dressed in brown drab with a yellow ochre rope belt and a yellow tassel dangling from his waist. He stopped beside two older women seated to his right, holding their rosary beads and whispering Hail Mary. The monk stood over them from the aisle and made the sign of the cross above them, then bowed his head, humbly turned, and walked away while loosely clutching his Bible with both hands.

Antonetta and Anna proceeded down the center aisle and genuflected as they made the sign of the cross, walked to the left side of the altar, and stopped at the statue of Santa Caterina. Antonetta lowered the basket from her head and placed it by the statue's feet. She removed the blanket and noticed bird droppings on the baby's right foot. She paused for a moment to show Anna, and they both chuckled. They then looked up into the eyes of Santa Caterina as light shimmered through the stained glass window high up and poured onto the figure's sculpted reserved smile. Anna offered a handkerchief to her mother to clean the child's foot. Antonetta knelt in front of the statue and whispered to the saint as she made the sign of the cross, "Cara Santa Caterina, I thank you for saving my daughter's life, and my grandson's during the hardships they had to endure. I promised to bring the baby here for you to see, and here, I place him at your feet."

Antonetta removed the baby from the basket, and her daughter removed the knit hat from his head. She held him up for the Madonna to

Piccolo Santino

see the scars on the baby's head and face. She murmured a Hail Mary, and her daughter joined in with her. A shadow passed through a high window as doves flew outside, and the light flickered across the statue's face, creating a feeling of euphoria in the women as they looked at each other in astonishment.

Antonetta returned the baby to the basket at the statue's feet. Both women retreated to a pew close by and knelt in prayer. Rolls of thunder reverberated outside in the distance, and the two women lifted their gaze to look at each other quickly before returning to their joint prayers with heads bowed. A loud thunderclap sliced through the silence, and heavy rain danced on the church roof. The sound of doors opening was followed by quiet footsteps and rustling from a few people who had entered to keep out of the deluge.

Chapter 5 of Part One
Toddler Santino

On a warm spring day late in the afternoon, two-year-old Santino, clearly free of any congenital disabilities on his head or face, happily chased his older sister around in a circle in front of their home on the dirt-hardened patio. His mother and Aunt Fabrizzia stood nearby, chit-chatting as the two youngsters played. In the background, the grandfathers were seated on the front steps, gathering pleasure from watching the children play. Two-year-old Santino bobbled about as his older sister taunted him in a friendly tone to encourage a chase.

Fabrizzia held out her arms, walked up to Santino, and bent a few steps away to encourage him. "You look just like a doll. You are so cute! Come to your Aunt Fabrizzia, come on, come on!" Santino responded eagerly, and she lifted him into the air, then lowered him against her bosom. Santino wasted no time resting his hand inside her cleavage and pressed his mouth down onto her left breast, right through her blouse, and tried to feed at baby light speed. Weaning babies later was customary, and it was common for a child to attempt sucking when picked up by another woman.

Fabrizzia, at age sixteen and well developed, let out a burst of screaming laughter as she pulled him away and blurted out, "*Ah Dio Mio.* Oh my God! You need your Mamma, not me!"

Laughter ensued all around, and as she bent down to stand Santino to his feet, the child's grip on her blouse forced her left breast to dangle in public. Fabrizzia screamed, and hysterical laughter broke out. "You little devil!" she cried. "Get away from me! Go to your Mamma!" All the laughter swelled to a crescendo as Fabrizzia tried to button her blouse and called out. "Anna! It looks like Santino must take after his father!"

Anna, seated in a chair by the front stoop and nursing her newest nine-month-old baby girl, Stella, addressed Santino with a smile. "*Malandrino!* Little rascal! Wait until your father gets home and finds out what you did!"

Piccolo Santino

Arturo, the maternal grandfather, called out to his daughter. "Fabrizzia *andiamo*! Let's get going. It's getting late. We got a long walk home." He turned to the paternal grandfather, Massimo, who was seated next to him on the stoop and invited him to walk together since his home was along the same route. Massimo said he wanted to wait longer to see if his son would get home.

Fabrizzia kissed the children goodbye and exchanged a hearty goodbye hug with her sister. "Si Padre, let's go," she said to her father before turning to Massimo, slumped on the stoop with elbows on the middle cement step and legs stretched out over the bottom step. Fabrizzia gently waved at him and said, "Ciao Gumbah Massimo!" He returned a lazy, speechless wave by pivoting his right elbow a few times while resting it on the cement step, knowing that his thick jacket protected his skin against the hard cement. Anna called out to her father, "Ciao Padre!"

"Ciao, Anna, ciao!"

"Tell Madre I will be over to visit her!"

"*Non ti preoccupare*, don't worry." They walked away under the cool shade of the grapevine arbor that stretched the length of the driveway and stopped at the top of the exit. Arturo waved at Anna, holding Stella against her bosom, and the other two children circled her. They picked up the pace upon exiting Fontana Di Taccuni, and Fabrizzia exclaimed to her father, "I wonder why Anna's father-in-law didn't walk with us. He has to go home on the same road as we do."

"He is a sly one."

"What are you saying, Padre?"

"In a short moment, we will reach the intersection at the four corners. I think there we might find the answer."

"What do you mean?"

"Right now, you think about America. I'll take you there with me soon so you will have more opportunities. That way, after you marry, you and your husband can immigrate to America. You will be the first in the family to settle there. Your brothers will eventually follow, including your sister Anna, with Bartolo. It's too bad your mother refuses to listen to the reason for moving to America. We could have then planned to be all living there together."

A loud, tinny sound from a Vespa motor crossed the intersection at four corners. Holding onto Roberto, Bartolo saw his father and sister-in-law walking on the side of the road, turned as they slowed down, and waved. The two in-laws waved back during the brief meeting, in motion on their opposite paths. Bartolo returned, holding onto his co-worker, Roberto, as they continued motoring toward Fontana Di Taccuni.

Roberto slowly careened the Vespa around to make it through the opened gates and down Bartolo's driveway, discharging fumes when the motor began idling. The two children ran to grab onto their mother. Massimo gleefully rose from his crouched position on the stoop and wasted no time asking Roberto for a ride home.

Father Time perpetually moves at an even keel to hold life at a steady pace, at a rate often echoed by the squeak of Anna's rocking chair. Mother Nature pumps nutrients into the soil with the magic of sunlight and water for plant life to multiply so that all children and grownups worldwide can eat, drink, and enjoy the gift of life. Bartolo, like Father Time, never shunned his work on the farm, so there was always a good harvest of crops to keep the children growing. Martina, now over six years old; Santino, almost five; and Stella, at three years old, always got their share of picking vegetables or even shelling fresh peas for cooking. When the workload became overwhelming, Bartolo called on his neighbor and close friend Angelo, Giustina's husband.

Angelo, a slightly muscular man like the actor Charles Bronson, was always willing to help Bartolo. The two neighbors' working relationship was mutual whenever they needed help. One day, Angelo showed Papá how to do some tree grafting by attaching a branch from a plum tree to a peach tree. When the plum branch bore fruit, seeing plums on a peach tree felt mystical.

With his solid work ethic, Bartolo sealed an excellent relationship with the landlord, Dr. Itasca. Angelo and his son Marco, a young look-alike of Angelo, paid a social visit one night to show off their new accordion.

Piccolo Santino

They drank wine and shared homemade snacks of cheese, soppressata, and figs with walnuts. Marco and Angelo then played the accordion and sang as the kids slept in the same room, seemingly undisturbed by all the commotion. There was no electricity in these rural parts, and even if electricity were available, the poverty level could never support a radio for most families.

Later, when television arrived, doctors were the first to afford it, and most people couldn't even hope to dream about buying one. So, couples went to bed early for some personal entertainment. But we must pause here to introduce two other children and a newly conceived sixth child in the womb.

Whether through the prior effects of El Duce's doctrine, during his reign, or the results of the Catholic Church, Bartolo and Anna had become very prolific. Since Bartolo was one of nine children and Anna was one of five children, they may not need encouragement from outside forces. Nonetheless, their family had grown to five children, with a sixth on the way. The two additions were one-and-a-half-year-old Lillo and one-year-old Angelina. There were no more breech births after Santino, and in the case of Angelina, she decided on her own when to evacuate the womb. Anna's water suddenly broke as she was plowing the field one day. She had just enough time to rush onto a natural bed of grass under an oak tree. Bartolo was at work but had planned to be home early. Luckily, Anna had the immediate company of Giustina and her teenage daughter, Gianna. Both helped deliver the baby. As it turned out, possibly by suspicion, the midwife arrived within minutes of the delivery, and Bartolo was home by mid-afternoon, about an hour or so later. The baby and mother were fine, and naturally, Giustina became Godmother.

After the children came, they were the form of entertainment for Bartolo and Anna. One such evening, six-year-old Martina led her two younger siblings by the hand, circling their mother, who was in a rocking chair nursing one-and-a-half-year-old Lillo as one-year-old Angelina slept in the crib. The children sang the Italian version of ring around the rosy (*giro tondo, Gira il mondo, gira la terra, tutti giù per terra*). When Martina and Santino dropped to the floor with three-year-old Stella, she always let out genial laughter, feeling like she could not contain herself. Bartolo and Anna looked on with hearty chuckles. When the laughter stopped, Bartolo looked at the children and said, "Go on! Do it again, kids!" The children excitedly rose to their feet and, this time, ran around in the opposite direction. Anna carefully rose and said, "Bartolo, hold Lillo for a minute while I go pee."

"Why can't you put him in the crib?"

"You're not going to die. It's only for a minute."

"But he's got milk all over his mouth."

"I wiped it off already. He only spit up a little bit. Come on!"

"Yeah, but I'll still be able to smell it."

"When you play there, it doesn't bother you? But holding the baby close to you does?"

"Well, now that's something entirely different."

"Different? C*ome il culo*. My ass!"

"Hey the children are right here."

"Here, take him before I pee on the floor." Grudgingly, he said, "All right, all right." Bartolo put down his glass of wine and held out his hands, stiffened elbows tucked hard against his rib cage. "He's not gonna kill you! Don't worry."

"Put him here and go pee already!" She gently placed the infant into Bartolo's arms and ran to the side of the bed. Reaching under the bed for the bedpan, she squatted. Bartolo remained stiff as a board, waiting for Anna to return. The children again dropped to the floor in hearty laughter, looked at their father, and screamed, "Papá, should we do it again?" Bartolo turned his head toward Anna in an automated fashion and said, "How much time do you need to pee?"

"Oh, shush! I'm almost done." Anna rose to her feet and slowly slid the pan under the bed with one foot as Martina and Santino anxiously asked, "Papá, should we do it again?"

"Si! Si! But wait for your Mamma." Bartolo said stiffly. Anna stopped in front of Bartolo and took Lillo from him, saying, "See, you're still alive. How bad could that have been?"

Piccolo Santino

"You know how the smell of milk bothers me." She returned to her rocking chair as she said, "Don't forget to empty the pan. It's too dark now for me to go outside."

Asleep by the front door, if disturbed, Matilda would pick her head up, look around, and then return to her slumber. Anna resumed rocking. The children sat at the table with their Papá, and he once again began telling them the Pinocchio story about the time Geppetto had fed him a pear and was planning to eat the pear skins after Pinocchio went to sleep. But Pinocchio complained that he was still hungry and thus got Geppetto to forfeit the pear skins. The children always liked listening to that story, no matter how many times they heard it. The family had no books, and Bartolo had only gone as far as the third grade. Anna learned to read and write from him while they were courting so they could correspond when he was away in the military during WWII.

Of course, this all happened before the children came. As part of the many other stories she often told the children, Anna would tell this while Bartolo was at work during the day. After Bartolo finished telling the Pinocchio story, he looked at Santino and exclaimed, "Tino, your Mamma and I were talking about how badly the weeds have grown in the walkway down to the barn, and we thought this would be a good job for you to do."

"All by myself?" asked Santino. "Sì! You can do it," interjected Mamma. Then Papá explained, "Even though you're not quite five yet, take your time and don't worry about finishing." Mamma added, "I'll be close by should you need anything." Papá then said, "I'll leave my extra canteen for you. This way, you can drink like I do at work."

"For real, Papá? Wow! Then I can feel like I'm going to work just like you." Papá looked at Mamma and said, "Anna, make sure you fill the canteen for Tino." Mamma looked up from nursing Lillo and said, "I will."

"Now remember, son, we don't expect you to finish the whole job in one day. There's always tomorrow."

"Ok, Papá! I'll do it."

"Anna, make sure he takes his time. You know how hot the sun can

Piccolo Santino

get in the summer"

"Don't worry-Uh! Oh no! Bartolo, he keeps doing this. When will it stop already?"

"What happened?"

"You know what happened! Don't pretend you don't know."

"All right, I'll go make the chamomile tea for him." Exasperated, Anna said, "Chamomile! Chamomile! He'll just spit that up too!"

"What else can we do, Anna?"

"I wish he would hold his food down just once, that's all. Just one time!"

The following morning, Mamma handed Santino the canteen. Mamma then grabbed the small hoe Papá had left leaning against the house by the stoop, and they walked to the start of the walkway. Santino grabbed the hoe from Mamma, "Now don't forget what Papá told you about this being a two-day job." He looked up at her and nodded his head with understanding. "I'll be down the other end of the house if you need me." Santino gazed at her smiling face and said, "Sì, Mamma."

Santino placed the canteen in a shady spot and felt himself shrinking as he took a few steps into the downslope. As he turned and looked up, the ground became a horizon line, with Mamma's tall frame slowly sinking entirely from his view while he prepared to grip the hoe with both hands.

Never having held a hoe in his hands before, he didn't know what to expect. However, he felt driven by the idea of a mission administered by Papá. It made him feel exceptional, and he appreciated Mamma's reminder that he did not have to finish the job all in one day. Thus, Santino armed himself with great determination and the vision of a completely clean walkway.

Welcoming the feel of the solid wooden handle between his fingers, Santino commenced swinging the hoe with force, speed, and a growing fortitude as he saw progress. He glowed inside with a deep sense of satisfaction, a feeling that grew with each weed he cleared. He developed a natural rhythm as he kept it going into the late morning sun at a mesmerizing pace, stopping only once for a drink of water. While

Piccolo Santino

studying the softer earth with bulkier weeds to his left versus the rockier, dry terrain on the right, Santino embraced the change, which was met only by occasional weeds down the center of the path.

Mamma's loud voice from on top of the horizon line startled Santino, and he quickly looked up, stunned by the great distance between him and the summit of the pathway. He observed Mamma's studious, slow descent from the high horizon and took glee as she occasionally stopped to admire individual sections with pride. Santino turned to look behind and felt disappointed. He feared Papá would be dissatisfied if Santino did not leave any work for tomorrow.

That evening, Mamma ran up to Papá as he arrived home and rushed to break the news. Papa's face beamed with pride and awe as they all stood at the top of the path and gazed at the pleasing results. He was so proud to invite the landlord to witness Santino's handiwork. The next day, disappointment followed, but Papá assured Santino the landlord would come the following day.

The landlord, Il Dottore Itasca, arrived the next day and brought his son. As Papá stepped out of their car, he led them down to the walkway. Mamma and Santino followed as they inspected with elongated faces and lifted eyebrows. Santino savored every moment as they admired the sight. The doctors then turned to Santino, and both exclaimed, "Bravo, Santino!"

Standing there awkwardly, Santino absorbed all that praise. His heart swelled with excitement and pride, the landlord's words echoing in his mind.

Chapter 6 of Part One, 1953
Lillo's digestive woes traumatize me

Some of this I recall. The rest was told to me

It was late afternoon, toward the end of a warm summer day, developing into a clear evening. And there I was, five-year-old Santino, dressed in shorts and suspenders, with shirttails out and barefoot, seated on the ground pouring water from a tin can onto a small heap of dirt. In front of me, sitting on the stoop, was Mamma, showing another baby on the way and nursing her one-and-a-half-year-old son, Lillo. The youngest daughter, Angelina, was sleeping in the crib, and her two daughters, Martina, now six, and Stella, age three, were seated next to her. Martina was busy knitting with white yarn, which she thought was learning how to make a blanket, but unknown to her, Mamma created part of her dowry. Mamma expected to complete it by the time Martina came of age.

Mamma kept wiping Lillo's drooling mouth as he fed on her right breast. Stella stared at her sister's fingers in wonder as Martina studiously navigated the needles back and forth, wrapping the yarn around to start a new row of stitches. I had my concentration turned to the ground in front of me, and having created enough mud, I began shaping it into meatballs. Like the speed and agility of an experienced chef, I arranged six mud balls as if they were on a plate, then leaned back and stared at them in a hypnotic trance.

Coming up the pathway from the barn after feeding his animals, Papá said, "Tonight we're all going to eat well! Santino has made meatballs for us!" Startled by Papá's sudden voice, I quickly said, "No, they're not for eating Papá, they're for playing." Mamma pulled Lillo away from her breast as she leaned forward to look at me. She quickly yelled out as I wiped my hands on my t-shirt, "*Figlio di Buona mamma*, (often used as slang to represent the phrase 'son of a bitch') son of a good mother, he ruined his clothes!" I held up a mud ball. "I can make more Mamma."

Piccolo Santino

"*Ora te batteró,* now I'm gonna beat you!" Papá interjected, "Don't worry, Anna, it's nothing!"

"Nothing you say? I'll take a beating to you, too!"

"I'll help him get cleaned up. Calm down."

"Calm down, nothing. I'm the one who does the wash around here." Lillo vomited all over Mamma and Martina, and Stella moved away quickly as Mamma scrambled to her feet. "Not again! Bartolo, what are we going to do about this? He never holds his food down. I feel helpless. I don't know what to do anymore!" Lillo began wailing amid the vomiting spells, and Papá reached out to their two daughters as they cautiously gathered by him. I continued in my world of mud pies but at a slower pace.

"Bartolo! I fed him some *panecotto*, cooked bread with sugar earlier, and he spits that up. Now I was hoping he could hold down my milk, but it all feels hopeless!"

"All right, I'll make some chamomile tea for him with a little sugar. Perhaps that will help. "All right, go make the chamomile then."

"Santino! Come with me, son. We need to get you cleaned up."

Before I drifted into sleep, I was struck by the sight of two doves' heads, glowing in the moon's gentle light. They then retreated, finding solace in the comforting darkness of the shadows cast by a nearby tree on the red tiles that adorned not just Papá's modest home, but also the curved, convex tiles that once graced the rooftops of Apollo and Poseidon's dwellings. These terracotta tiles, the first to replace thatched roofs in ancient Greece, now sheltered us under the same moonlit shadows that had embraced our ancestors, a testament to the enduring legacy of our ancient traditions.

The shadow of a pigeon expanded its wings and animated out from within a tree's shadow on this roof. Down below, another shadow rested on the dirt patio before the front door. Like a weightless stalker, it crawled forward and upward to the front door. The silhouette of leaves knocked gently against the solid olive wood door from this evening's breeze. Inside, our sleeping watchdog, Matilda, could not hear the shadows nor

Piccolo Santino

see the sharp contours of the rosebush thorns in the soft moonlight behind the locked door.

The melodic sound of crickets had penetrated the locked front door and joined the ticking of time from a wind-up clock. Both were subservient to the sound of Mamma rocking Lillo in her rocking chair. This modest home had no separate bedrooms, and all the furniture was contained in this one large family room with a cement floor. Against the left far corner, opposite the entrance, was the master bed. To the right of the access was a smaller bed where the children slept. The girls slept at the head of the bed, and I slept at the foot. Close by was the baby's crib, where Angelina slept quietly and never seemed to be a bother to Mamma. The last piece of bedroom furniture the family owned was a large dresser situated to the side of the master bed.

Papá was seated at a small dinner table and nursing a glass of homemade wine. Away from the table facing the entrance was a large metal tub to burn wood on cold nights. At a fixed pace, situated between Papá and the sleeping children, Mamma routinely rocked Lillo, even though he had been asleep for about a good hour or so. As Mamma lifted the baby blanket, tears silently dripped from her eyes as she studied the half-naked, scrawny body of a preemie-looking baby, a condition she could not understand since Lillo was almost two years old.

Mamma could not fathom how her son had survived thus far and now feared for his future. She looked at Papá as she rose from her chair and approached him. Standing before Papá, she held the child out for him to see. He looked down at the child and thought about his sagging skin looking all wrinkled and loose— the actual image of a malnourished infant. Mamma shoved the baby toward Papá and, with a loud voice, angrily demanded, "Here, take him and go dump him in the ravine by the four corners so he can die already. I can't stand to look at his skinny body anymore. He's so ugly!"

Jolted from my sleep, I quietly lifted the covers over my eyes. *I could be next because they kill you if they think you are ugly!*

Papá looked up at her and said, "Here, let me have him." Mamma, frustrated and angry, loudly said, "Go on now. Go already."

Piccolo Santino

I listened to Papá's steps and the sound of the door opening and closing as he went outside. In the silence during Papá's absence, I felt helpless about what to do if Papá returned without Lillo. Afraid of Lillo's life, I decided never to talk again. Anticipating Papá returning without Lillo, I remained awake, holding the covers over my face. While waiting, I imagined Papá's walk to the four corners and back to simulate the space of time during that silence. Then the front door clicked, and, too afraid to lower the covers for a look, I listened to the slow swoosh of Papá entering and closing the door, then completing his way to Mamma. I waited to find out if Papá had obeyed Mamma.

"I couldn't do it!" Short pause. "I was afraid somebody would see me and call the *carabinieri* police."

I tried to understand the blow gripping me and sensed the smoldering feeling of a severe letdown, and I thought Papá should've said he couldn't do it because he loved Lillo, not because he was afraid of the police.

The following day brought the screeching, loud voice of Caterina Malaferma, a plain, tall, lanky widow in her thirties who walked with a limp, the result of a shrapnel wound in her left hip during an allied bombing raid. Her husband did not survive the war, and, as a result, she now lived alone. Caterina pushed the metal gate that felt warm to the touch from the sun, even at eight o'clock on a hot day.

She eagerly limped down the friendly slope from the top of the drive while shouting, "Donna Anna and Bartolo! Where are you? May I enter? She turned her head from side to side as she continued shouting, stretching out Mamma's name, "Yoo-Hoo-! Donna Ah-nnah!"

From down below, behind a heavy barrier of low trees and heavy brush, Papá came out of the barn and walked halfway up the ramp leading to the drive. He stopped short as Caterina spotted him. He quickly brought his finger to his closed mouth and then pointed for Caterina to keep walking to the other end of the house. Then, he coyly turned around and walked past the barn toward the orange grove.

As covertly directed by Papá, Caterina headed in the opposite

Piccolo Santino

direction and called out again, further asserting, "Donna Anna, where are you?"

Mamma leaned out of the kitchen doorway and yelled, "I'm over here! I'm over here!" Caterina looked up and said "Oh there you are Anna!"

"Oh, it's you." Mamma stepped outside, made eye contact, and jibed at her, "I'm right here, *ma che cazzo vuoi?* What the fuck do you want? So early in the morning." Caterina picked up her pace and limped over to Mamma with a slightly heavy breath, "Oh Anna, I came over to make you a present this morning." Mamma looked puzzled, "What present, what you are talking about, Caterina?"

"Did you forget already?" She reached into a sack she was carrying and pulled out a young adult black cat. "What! *Un cazzo di Gatto?* A fuck'n cat?" Mamma blurted out and continued spewing words with expletives. "What happened? You didn't have anyone to dick around with this morning?"

Both her daughters, six-year-old Martina and three-year-old Stella, rushed out from the kitchen in excitement to hold the cat. Caterina placed it in Martina's small hands against her body. "Mamma, she's black as coal," Martina said. "I think that should be her name, Carbone."

"Si! Si! That's her name, child. That's it! Carbone," exclaimed Caterina as she looked over to me, standing in the doorway looking sheepish. Mamma asked, "Caterina, where did you get this fuck'n cat?" While staring at me, Caterina said, "My aunt and uncle came to visit me. They brought it down from Nicastro on the bus."

"*Dio Mio.* Oh my God!" exclaimed Mamma. "Please thank them for me!"

"Ah, that's not necessary, but I will. Anyway, you're welcome!" Caterina turned back to me. Santino, why won't you come over and pet the cat?" I humbly shook my head, "No," and stayed put. "My dear godson! You don't have to be afraid of the cat, child!" Caterina reached out and signaled with her hand. Mamma said to me, "Come on, son. Come over here." I looked up halfway and struggled to speak, but the words came out with a long stutter, "N-n-n no, I-I-I'm a-a-afraid."

Piccolo Santino

"So it was you! *Cazza di Caterina!* Fuck'n Caterina, causing all the ruckus so early in the morning." Papá called out. Caterina turned as Papá stopped in front of her, and Mamma looked up to watch her husband holding a few oranges pressed against his chest. "Gumbah Bartolo, I brought you this cat to catch the mouse."

"Look at my wife. Can't you tell that we have already caught the mouse?" Caterina glanced at Mamma's bulging stomach and said, "Your husband is a real comedian this morning." Papá lowered five oranges into the sack that had carried the cat. "Here, take these home with you." Caterina looked into the sack and said, "Oh! Grazie! Grazie so much, Bartolo. But I also came to tell you both something."

"What is it you want to tell us?" Mamma asked. "Well, this is something you should ask Doctor Itasca about. My aunt Peppina just came to visit from Nicastro and said that the government is to set up a special visiting nurse to help the children of this region." In the kitchen doorway, I blushed as I rested his head against the doorframe and stared outside. Mamma and Papá both exclaimed, "For real?" "Sì! Sì! *Per davvero* for real!" Exhilarated, Mamma spoke over Caterina and poured out her emotions. "*Benedica,* God bless."

Caterina continued. "The program is scheduled to start sometime soon. Dr. Itasca will probably contact you himself. When you're in town, you should stop in and ask him about this."

"Oh, bless your soul, Caterina, for coming here this morning," said Mamma. She then turned to Papá but didn't even have to think anything as he already had the words for his wife. "Sì! Sì! Anna, I understand. I'll be going to the smoke shop one day next week. I'll talk to the doctor then. Don't worry, Anna."

"*Bene tutto a posto*, well all right then." Caterina said as she straightened up. Mom looked at her, "Sì! Sì! *Molte Grazie.* Thanks a lot, Caterina."

"I gotta go now. You guys, take care! Ciao."

"Ciao Caterina," they both said as they watched her limp away.

Papá looked at her with his head cocked sideways. As Caterina was about to turn the corner of the house, he jokingly shouted to her, "Thank you for the fuck'n cat, Gummah Caterina." Caterina stopped, looked back, lifted and raised her left arm, slapped her bicep with her right hand, and jerked it toward Papá as she jokingly yelled in laughter, "*Ma va fahculo!* Up yours!" They all laughed, and Papá shouted, "Go on, get out of here."

Caterina resumed limping away, out of sight behind the house, up the driveway. Mamma turned to Papá and demanded, "And why were you looking at her sideways?"

"Nothing! I just get at kick at how fast she moves with that limp. That's all."

"Oh yeah? What were you doing down there all this time? I thought you were bringing up hay to re-stuff the mattress."

"Yes, I was getting it ready, but then I heard Caterina," Mamma interrupted him. Don't tell me. You heard her limping, I gather, huh?" No, I went to get some oranges for her." While wiping his brow haltingly, Papá responded, "I have two big bundles ready for you in the barn." He walked away toward the barn as he spoke, "Go get the bed ready, and I'll bring it up."

Piccolo Santino

Chapter 7 of Part One,
1953 My sisters make fun of my stuttering

Mamma, holding an empty galvanized metal bucket, was slowed down by a menstrual cramp. She leaned over and held her stomach with her other hand as she quickly breathed. Mamma recently had a miscarriage and was now beginning to get back to normal. With the pain gone, she resumed her walk down the hall toward the kitchen.

Papá tied a rope around the neck of his hog and led it out of the barn and up the ramp by a tree across from the kitchen area. Three other men awaited their arrival. Mamma walked out of the kitchen with the galvanized bucket and handed it to Angelo, a hefty-built man with muscles hidden under his shirt.

Mamma walked over to Angelo's wife Giustina, holding Mamma's fifth child, eighteen-month-old Angelina, and said, "Gummah, put Angelina down. You don't have to hold her."

"Oh, don't worry, Anna, she's not heavy. Besides, I want to hold my godchild for a while."

"Gummah Giustina, she can stand on her own. This one was walking already at six months!"

"Yes, I know." She looked Angelina in the face as she held her away and happily said, "That's because she's my godchild." Giustina and Angelo also brought their two children, Marco, who was in his mid-teens, and their youngest daughter, eleven-year-old Lola. They had come to help with the work during the hog's slaughtering and butchering. Angelo and his son Marco propped a ladder against the tall tree, which natural causes had almost entirely defoliated. Some foliage remained, but only in the highest branches.

Lola and Mamma's sister Fabrizzia were off to the side with her husband Nicola, a thin and very kind-looking man with wire-rim glasses. They had a large pot of water over a fire as the sound of the hog's grunting intensified. Marco climbed the ladder while holding one end of the thick

Piccolo Santino

rope, flipped it over the top of a large bare limb, and called down to his father to grab the end as he slid it down. Angelo pulled it down and then, with Papá, rolled the hog on its side on the ground and tied its hind legs together—the sound of the hog grunting escalated. Angelo remarked, "He looks very well developed, Gumbah!" as he removed the reigns from the hog's neck. "For real!" exclaimed Fabrizzia, then turned to her husband and said, "Nicola, look at those ribs!"

"Today we are going to eat well, everybody!" shouted Nicola. That brought out hearty laughter from everyone. He leaned over the thick table to visually inspect the sharp skinning and boning knives, then lightly ran his fingers over the meat saw to feel the sharpness of the blade. He rested his hand on the handle of the meat grinder and turned it counterclockwise, then reversed direction to feel its smooth motion. A large galvanized tub was directly under the meat grinder where the ground pork would drop to make sausages and soppressata.

Sitting next to the galvanized metal tub were Martina, me, and Stella, whose hand slid off Matilda as she got up to walk away. Martina leaned over to me and said, "Everybody makes fun of you when you talk."

"So what! I-I-It doesn't ha-ha-happen all the t-t-t-time." Stella let out a peal of grinning laughter, and Martina joined in to taunt me while pointing their fingers. I shouted back, "b-b-b-b-b-Basta! Basta! Basta!" The girls laughed harder and exclaimed mid-laughter, "You did it again! You did it again!" Nicola leaned over the meat grinder and calmly reprimanded the children, "Basta! Kids, that's enough now!" Both girls turned to me and, in a questioning manner, mimicked their uncle's words. "Basta. Basta. Basta." I shoved Martina into Stella, forcing her to fall into the galvanized metal tub. Stella cried out. Uncle Nicola reached down, lifted Stella, and consoled her. Stella broke free from Uncle Nicola, pushed me to the ground, and ran over to Aunt Fabrizzia. "What happened?" asked the aunt.

At that point, Mamma reached down, lifted me by my ear, and yelled, "How many times do I have to tell you to leave your sisters alone?" Lola turned to Mamma and said, "No, Gummah, the girls were making fun of his stuttering." Lola knelt and wrapped her arms around

Piccolo Santino

me with a gentle hug and asked, "Were they making fun of you, Santino?" With my head buried against her body, I nodded. "Yes." She rubbed my head, lifted my chin with her other hand, and softly said, "Don't worry, Santino, you're still a baby, and you'll be okay when you grow up." Mamma looked at Lola and responded, "*Speriamo che sì*, let's hope so, for his sake."

A fierce supernatural outcry from the hog burst into the sky like a cannon blast as Angelo and Bartolo pulled on the rope and hoisted the creature by its hind hooves so high that its toes almost touched the branch above. In its remaining violent breaths, sudden shock inside the dangling animal reverberated from its core to its outer skin and toes. Its remaining energy shook the tree in a desperate effort to free itself. The poor creature helplessly wiggled like a storm at sea, and its sharp cry sped into the clouds and beyond, like the continuous sound of a train braking to a stop.

The hog was trapped, dangling in mid-air, with complete fear for its life; its eyes bulged as it stared down into the large empty bucket under its head. The poor pig jerked its head from left to right, but Angelo quickly and mercifully slid his large knife across the beast's throat. The knife's action reduced the turbulence to a slow quiver, and the animal quietly emptied its life's blood into the bucket below as its cry was replaced with the outpouring of blood. Papá and Marco steadied the dangling carcass as Fabrizzia gasped at the flow of blood and lamented, "*Ah, Dio Mio!* Oh my God!"

"*Che spavento!* What horror!" called out Giustina. "What an amazing show of fear. The poor thing!" cried out Fabrizzia. Nicola justified the slaughter of his wife by being philosophical. "Horrible, yes! But God does want us to eat." We children peeked out from the kitchen doorway, where we had run to hide at the first sound of the animal's cry. The hog's blood stopped draining out before it lowered its body into a large metal tub. Hot water was poured over the carcass to soften the skin. The corpse was then laid on a table, facilitating the removal of hair. Once the hair got cleaned off, body parts got dissected, and some, while boiling, gave off a dirty, personal smell. We ran to the other end of the house, away from the kitchen and butchering area.

Piccolo Santino

Some of the meat got fed through the meat grinder. After the gut was well cleaned, it became casings for making sausage, soppressata, and capocollo. My sisters and I ran to sit on the front stoop because the smell of boiling body parts made us feel like vomiting.

Matilda returned to sit with us, and Martina explained that she probably smelled food cooking from far away and thus felt that if she hung around, she might get some. Lola brought a plate of boiled blood and some bread no sooner than spoken. We took turns dunking bread into the paste-like substance of the cooked blood that tasted like liver. Matilda looked up at the kids from the bottom of the stoop as she smelled the aroma of the liver. I threw her a piece of bread moistened in the cooked blood, and she couldn't stop licking her chops.

That was the end of the summer in 1953, and this type of excitement was not something we kids would witness again, but it was unforgettable. A few days or a week later, Mamma insisted that Martina and I go with her as she grabbed hold of our hands and had us walk alongside her. Martina looked at her and asked, "Mamma, where are we going?" Firmly, Mamma responded, "Just come with me!" Mamma's walk was firm and exact as we exited the gates from our home and walked past the bright orange poppies that grew wild on the wide shoulder behind our house. Farther up, the poppies were sparse as the shoulder became narrow, and the terrain was riddled with gravel on the dried grassy earth, which made it harder to walk on. The shoulder remained thin enough for two people to walk abreast to the four corners.

I walked on the flat highway under Mamma's constant grip. Though vehicles did not travel much in these parts, the noise made by the occasional auto was enough of a warning for one's safety. As we reached the four corners, the ground became level. We turned left toward Nao. I looked to my left into the ravine, and fear ran through me. This ravine was the place where Mamma had asked Papá to dump Lillo.

A few steps further to the left was the *sigaria,* the sawmill. I stared into the mill as a colossal log outside was slowly pulled by a conveyor system under a large wooden canopy where a giant circular saw with

Piccolo Santino

sharp, thick metal teeth awaited.

One man lowered a big handle switch on the wall, and the saw became almost invisible as it spun and screeched at a speed I had never seen. Two other men guided a massive log closer to the whirling teeth of the steel blade. Dragging my feet, I leaned back to get a better view. I heard Mamma's harsh scolding and felt a hard tug on my arm. She pulled me away from witnessing the dramatic push of the giant log into the enormous, gyrating, circular saw waiting to rip the trunk in two halves.

I skipped a step to catch up to Mamma, and although I could not see the log and saw meeting and departing, I could smell the cherry wood sawdust the instant the saw blade screeched and ripped through the colossal tree log. That smell of cherry sawdust flashed a picture of the big, dark red, luscious cherries from Nanna's farm.

Mamma released Martina's hand and demanded we kids both make the sign of the cross as we walked past a religious station. I looked at the partially weather-beaten station displaying a Madonna statue with wilted, dried flowers at its base and a small basin built into the sanctuary for holy water. I wondered if rain added to the sacred water or diluted it.

The hard dirt road we walked on began to show cobblestones sporadically pressed into its surface. As we approached the beginning of town, the cobblestones became more densely populated and covered the street altogether. We had to adjust our walk to the more rigid, bumpy surface.

The cool shade created by rows of buildings on both sides of the road evoked a slight chill on my shoulders that had me craving the sunshine as we stopped. "This is where you two will be going to school," Mamma said as she looked inside the courtyard sealed by tall black metal gates with rounded pegs. "You two will be coming here every day for kindergarten." We, kids, stared at each other with stunned faces as Mamma peered into the courtyard and called out through the locked gates. "Buongiorno! Sorelli! Sisters! Buongiorno! Sorelli!" Martina exclaimed to Mamma, "We don't need to go to school, Mamma." Mamma responded humorously, "That's what you say." From the depth of the courtyard on the far right, two nuns dressed in white habits walked out

Piccolo Santino

from a doorway and approached us while speaking to Mamma, "Ah, you have arrived."

"Sì, we're here." The nuns looked at us kids, and one said, "These are your children?"

"Sì, they are Martina and Santino."

"*Sono così Belli!* They are so beautiful!"

"*Grazie sorelli!* Thank you, sisters." The nuns reached to open the gates, and one said, "Please come inside, children." The gates opened, and Mamma pressed her hands on our backs and pushed us forward, forcing us to walk to the rear of the courtyard.

Feeling frozen to the slate stones under our feet, we shook in a cold fright that brought a response from the older nun as she leaned down to us and softly said, "Don't you want to stay here with us in school?" We fiercely shook our heads. "No," and Mamma said, "You kids stay here, and I'll come back for you after school." Martina, not wasting a breath, answered, "Why didn't you stay here, Mamma, and we'll come back for you after school?" Laughter ensued amongst the adults, and the older nun suggested we kids might be hungry. She sent the younger nun inside for snacks. The older one turned to us and said, "You'll like it here. Look inside; there are other *Bambini,* children here like you."

We looked through the opened doorway and saw other kids walking about. I was only frightened more by the thought of being trapped in the company of strangers, but my sister and I shook our heads. "No."

The young nun returned with a small plate of yellow chunks of cheese, and Mamma insisted, "Why don't I watch you both from outside the gate for a few minutes until you get comfortable with my absence?"

"That's a great idea!" exclaimed the older nun as she handed out pieces of yellow cheese from the plate. As the younger nun said, "This cheese comes from America. It's delicious!"

We slowly sampled the stuff without swallowing, and as Mamma peered at us from behind the wall bearing the hinged gate to the right, we spit out the yellow, awful-tasting cheese. From behind the gates, Mamma leaned out of sight. Martina and I began a wailing tirade and ran for the exit to discover that not only were we locked in, we could no longer see

Piccolo Santino

Mamma. We cried louder as our wet faces pressed against the steel bars in search of our mother. The crying moved the nun to pry my hands away from the steel bars, and in retaliation, I bit her left wrist through her sleeve. She vociferously called out to Mamma to take us home. The sister quickly opened the gates.

Feeling like we could breathe again, we dashed outside and realized Mamma was pretending to have left. We saw her leaning against the wall. We walked home hand in hand with Mamma, and she only let go of my hand long enough to slap me hard on the back of my head.

Piccolo Santino

Chapter 8 of Part One, 1953
Looking for Papá

Mamma put the handful of spaghetti back down on the small table. She grabbed the jug of cold water and poured some into the pot of boiling water on the wood fire tripod. Steam rose in front of her face, and she pulled back quickly. "I'm sorry, father, I don't know what's keeping him. He said he'd be back in time for the holiday dinner."

"Don't worry, daughter, we'll wait a bit longer."

"No, that's not right. Bartolo told me where he was going. I'll send Santino into town to get him. It's been long enough."

"But he's just a child. Don't bother. I can eat something when I get home."

"Oh, he'll be fine. He is going to be six in a few months, and he knows the way. Besides, you came here to visit for a holiday dinner."

"Santino, come over here. I need you to go to Jonadi and tell your father to get home right away."

"Si, M-m-m-mamma."

"First, go to Don Filippo's and Yolanda's house." I nodded, "Yes."

"Then go to the bar behind your grandfather's house in Jonadi." I nodded my head again. "And last, stop at the last bar in the center of Jonadi on your way home."

It was a lovely sunny late afternoon. I hadn't expected to go to Jonadi at all on this holiday. With my head back, I was all dressed up in socks and shoes. I moved swiftly with suspenders, buttoned to my old shorts, feeling snug even though my shirttails were slightly out. I dreaded having to talk to strangers on this mission, face Don Filippo, and then go to two bars filled with total strangers all on my own. I was so terrified of having to talk that my heart was choking just at the thought of it. But I was more frightened by the idea of failing, so I told myself, *keep moving your legs to those places, and things will happen on their own once you arrive.*

Piccolo Santino

The path was the same as usual, a left turn at the four corners where the deep ravine lay, and I rushed past it at the thought that Lillo could have died there. Instead, I thought of the Sawmill next to it. The smell of sawdust always attracted my attention here, even though no one was working today. When I came to the holy station, I admired the fresh flowers somebody had placed for the Madonna. I made the sign of the cross as I remembered Martina's words that God was always watching and our sins never go unnoticed.

I felt the cobblestones in the streets of Nao and rushed past the black iron gates to the kindergarten school Martina, and I refused to attend. Between Nao and Jonadi, the road was hard dirt and void of buildings on either side. God's original landscape filled my nostrils with natural perfume every spring from the growing flowers and blooming wild fruit trees, except when I walked past the olive oil factory. The waste extract from the olives had a pungent odor that raked your nostrils deep into your throat even if you held your breath. I rushed past it.

I stopped for the panoramic view to admire the red slate roofs on the stone-built homes overlooking the countryside from a hilltop in Nao. I turned onto a bridge wide enough for a bus to pass over a small natural gorge at the bottom of the mountain. About a hundred meters past the bridge, cobblestone began to form the road. Buildings shaped Jonadi on both sides, much more so than in Nao, where the town was much smaller.

Upon reaching the smoke shop across from Dr. Itasca's house, memories of accompanying Papá once when he purchased tobacco and cigarette wraps. I recalled marveling at the smell of things in the shop, especially the nougat candy and other Perugina chocolates that I could not wish for. Papá also asked the keeper for spaghetti, and the clerk looked behind into wooden concave shelves resembling a honeycomb containing many varieties of pasta. The storekeeper placed a sheet of blue parchment paper on the scale, and Papá asked for perciatelli.

I continued farther up the street to a T intersection. The bar Mamma advised me to visit on the way home. I thought about going there first to avoid facing the other people but felt guilty about not following Mamma's orders to the letter. Directly across was the street leading up to Don

Piccolo Santino

Filippo's house, located at the top of the hill. I trekked the uphill road and noticed some of those homes had rows of thick pipe railings held up by brick posts along the front, with some plaster dried up and broken off. I stopped at the top, where the road bent to the left, and climbed into a huge piazza filled with many people and joyful noises.

This place was the piazza hosting the Madonna's celebration festivities. I turned into a walkway featuring many other homes and remembered that Don Filippo's was the third house. I listened to voices inside and hoped to identify Papá's voice from outside. But the voices were too chaotic, and it became impossible to distinguish who was talking. Left without a choice, I paused to conceive a way to best manage with the least amount of talking. I knocked, hoping the person coming to the door knew I had sought Papá.

I knocked three times, and a voice yelled inside that someone was at the door. After a short pause, a tall, thin man, Don Filippo, opened the door and greeted me, "Hey, it's Santino!" He looked behind him and yelled to his wife, "Hey Erica, Santino has come to wish us a Happy Holiday!" I entered, thinking, *oh, Don Filippo didn't ask me if I was looking for my papá. Now, what do I do? I don't want to talk.*

Don Filippo closed the door and escorted me into a large room with many strangers. I kept looking down, hoping to recognize Papa's shoes; then I raised my view to observe the host of legs. Don Filippo asked me if I would like a cordial and didn't even wait for my response. Don Filippo just called his wife over with a tray. I hoped for a shot of Marsala, I hesitantly stared at the tray of cordials without any Marsala. Don Filippo handed me a shot glass of Anisette and asked me to sit down. I sat on a straw-laced wooden chair against the wall, making it my lookout point for Papá.

Since Anisette had a potent taste, I sipped slowly and surveyed the room carefully. I listened for Papá's voice. Convinced that he was not there, risking a burn in my throat, I downed the Anisette. Feeling guilty as I planned my getaway, I thought of waiting a little longer to make it look like I had indeed come for a holiday visit. Needing to lose the shot glass, I looked around and saw a small table on the way to the exit point.

Piccolo Santino

When the crowd noise surged with laughter, I smoothly made my way to the exit, put down the shot glass on a small table, and rushed to the door unseen.

Sensing instant relief outside, I stared at the skyline as the twilight was preparing to usher in the night. I walked to the bottom of the hill and thought about just going into this bar right there, but the guilt about not following Mamma's orders led me to make the quick right turn toward the bar by Grandpa Massimo with trepidation. My heart was still pounding from the previous experience, and when I reached the closed front door to the bar, it gave me a feeling this was more like a private club. The thick olive wood door emanated such taut feelings of a forbidden zone that didn't need to prove anything further to this feeble self-esteem. Overcome with fear, I waited for someone to come out or go in so that I might hear Papá's voice. Neither one happened, but the laughter inside through the large window above was loud enough to say that Papá was not there. I turned back to visit the previous bar.

This place was like a bar and convenience store with wide double doors, and it instantly felt friendly. It felt like I could float in with the air and not stick out like a sore thumb with the doors so wide open. I walked inside the convenience section of the establishment and turned left into the bar area, and no sooner than I turned, Papá's cheerful voice called out. "Ah, your Mamma sent you to get me! Come over here, son."

He was playing cards with three other men. They were seated at the first booth directly to the left. I squeezed past the man seated on the outside. Papá sat me between him and the wall on the bench. The card game was hours long, and this round was close to the end, as the wine glasses were all empty. Papá said, "We'll leave soon. This game is almost finished."

The game did end quickly. But now, the boss and underboss had to deal with dividing a new bottle of wine. That routine sometimes lasted longer than the game itself, but it was often the source of countless long-lasting feuds between family members, friends, or strangers. Some got so serious it would result in physical fights or stable formation of vendettas where ties would be severed entirely. In this case, the bickering remained

Piccolo Santino

mild enough to agree on one more game to settle the score. I had hoped they would be leaving, and thus, between my nodding off, I listened to bits of bickering until I found myself waking up the following day in bed and recollecting.

Mamma was braiding Martina's hair as I put on my pants, and she began telling the story about what happened with Papá last night. "Ah, you're up," Mamma said to me. "Wa-wa-what-hh-happened?"

"I don't know how your father managed to get you both home last night, let alone get you safely to bed."

"Why w-w-where is he?"

"He was puking his brains out."

"Is he okay?"

"He was in the barn puking his brains out if he has any left in him." In a laughing manner, Mamma continued telling the story about Papá. "I tried to wake him up around midnight to get him to come to bed, but he was too far gone. He kept caressing the cow's udder and calling the cow 'Anna'!" We all laughed, and Martina asked, "And then what did you do, Mamma?"

"He thought he was talking to me. He kept calling my name and asked me to get closer to him as he tugged on the cow's udder!" We broke into so much laughter that we woke Angelina up in her crib, and then she began crying. Mamma finished braiding Martina's hair and ran over to get Angelina, "So I just left him there to sleep in," Mamma said as she consoled Angelina and checked her diaper. "The whole night?" We asked. "Let's go see Papá!" shouted Martina."

"Yeah, let's go!" we shouted, and Mamma retorted, "Don't bother!"

"I heard his friend Roberto with his Vespa early in the morning, picking him up for work. I don't know how he was even able to get up, let alone go to work."

Piccolo Santino

Chapter 9 of Part One, 1954
Santino is denied a trip to the flour mill

Papá loaded the fourth sack of wheat on the mule, and Mamma held it in place for Papá to secure it with rope. I pranced side to side in front and around the mule, pretending to be checking the action, prepared to call out anything wrong with the security of the sacks. Martina was standing with her hands at her waist, and I suspected she already knew she would be making the trip to the mill with Mamma. I was eager to see how the wheat ended up into flour. From having once walked past the mill with Papá, I remembered seeing a big round stone that somehow turned to crush the kernels.

I grabbed the reins off the ground and tried to remain inconspicuous by staying under the mule's neck out of Mamma's line of vision as Papá said, "Take Martina with you." I felt a lump in my stomach as Papá did not mention my name, so I stepped back and tugged on the reins. Papá explained further details of the swap with the mill owner to Mamma. I hoped Papá could keep talking, and Mamma would follow as I started the mule. And to my surprise, with the second tug of the reins, the mule started walking, "No! No! Son, you're not going; your sister is going with Mamma."

Papá already had said Martina was going, and then I tried to see the adults' logic in the scenario and thought it was because Martina was the oldest. It also seemed more fitting and sensible for Mamma to have her daughter with her. Then I tried to see it from an outside perspective, figuring Mamma and Papá didn't want to impose on the mill owner by being too intrusive with two children. But I wanted to see how the hard wheat kernels changed into soft flour. And I did not want to miss this opportunity. "No! No! I want to go!" I shouted. Mamma walked toward me, and I held the reins hard. "No, you're staying here. Your sister is going!" Mamma reached for the reins. I stepped away from Mamma with the reins firmly in my hands. "I want to go too! I want to go!" Mamma

Piccolo Santino

moved closer, and I lifted the reins in the air. As Mamma reached up, I slammed them back down, only to be met by Papá's firm grip. He pried my fingers open and handed the reins to Mamma. With tears in my eyes, I began wailing, "I want to go! I want to go!" In a calm tone, I continued bawling, and then Mamma said, "Two of you kids can't be at the mill at the same time. You have to stay here." I became disillusioned and sullen, and Mamma said, "Tino, you can help Papá here with supper."

"That's right, son. Come with me now." He signaled to Mamma with a nod as he pulled on my hand. I turned my head, and with wet eyelashes, I watched the donkey follow Mamma up the ramp. My crying transformed into heavy whimpering, and Papá walked me by my hand and said, "Come on, son, we are going to cook a delicious meal for supper. Now stop your crying."

"B-b-but I-I-I wanted to s-s-see the m-m-mill Papá!" I lamented. "I have potatoes with peas and onions cooking in tomato sauce for a nice dinner. Come, you can help me prepare a wonderful supper for Mamma." I was still whimpering as we stepped into the kitchen, and I got an instant whiff of a delicious aroma and staring eyes from Stella, Angelina, and Lillo seated on a bench. "Come on now, stop crying," Papá said as I looked to see if I could sit on the end of the bench next to Lillo. Facing Papá while standing sideways, I watched him stir the fire with a metal poker, and he said to me, "Get that block of wood for me right behind you, son."

I saw Stella's curious face as I turned to Papá and took two steps to reach for a small log. I turned to make a long stride, and my right foot slammed into protruding wood from inside the tripod. And the entire pot of steaming tomato sauce with the contents poured onto my right foot. My sisters and brother gasped and leaped from the bench as I let out a screeching wail at full blast. "AHHHHHH!"

In an instant, Papá scooped me up, sat me on the bench, and struggled with my shoe as he talked to himself over my excruciating cry, "What am I supposed to do now?" He then ran into the family room while mumbling in a frantic tone. *"Mannaggia i diavoli, poveraccio,* Damn devils! The poor kid." He ran back as fast as he left and said, "I couldn't

Piccolo Santino

find anything to put on your burn, son! But here! This is good!" He poured a bottle of blue ink on the burn, and the cooling effect of the cold ink evaporated instantly, and the burning sensation pierced inside me as I continued screaming.

"Hang in there, son. Your Mamma will be back soon. Then we'll put you on the donkey and get you to the doctor." The wait felt endless, and at that moment, Mamma returned. Her face dropped at what she had learned. She stared at me solemnly, and I could read what I had wished for earlier in her eyes. They quickly unpacked the mule and sat me on it, and seven-year-old Martina was left in charge of the three younger children as Papa and Mamma took me to Dr. Itasca in Jonadi.

As we traveled, I wondered what the ink was supposed to do for the burn, for it wasn't soothing the burning sensation anymore. I felt delirious, and for a short moment, I thought of the story Papá would often tell us about Joseph and the Virgin Mary traveling with their mule looking for an inn. I hoped the doctor would have a better solution, but instead, he just yelled at Papá for pouring ink on the burn and told us to go home because there was nothing he could do.

I became bedridden and slept on top of the covers at the foot of the bed, with my foot sticking out. A light towel covered the injured foot. During the day, the door was kept open, and I liked how the sunlight rolled inside. I liked how the sunlight rolled inside. Stella came to check on me. "Did you want anything?"

"Yeah. Tell Papá I need to go." She would fetch Papá, and he would scoop me up in his arms and carry me to the side of the house. I stretched out my right leg to squat and balanced myself off the ground with my left foot and hands planted. Indoor plumbing was not a reality in homes in these rural towns. So, a secluded section of the house was commonly used. While bedridden, I thought a magical healing process would occur since the doctor could not help and nothing was being applied to my wound. I hoped that as the days passed, the magic would happen.

"Papá is at work, son, and he suggested you try walking with a stick today." I looked at Mamma as she showed me a thick walking stick, and

Piccolo Santino

I lifted myself and swiveled my body sideways on the edge of the bed. "Here, son, let me help you," she said. Mamma reached out and handed me the stick, "Okay, now try taking a step with the stick." With both hands on the stick and my weight on my left leg, I slowly lowered my right foot and planted it on the cement floor, but to no avail. Even the slightest pressure made my foot feel like a soaked sponge, and the pain was like razor blades slicing through nerves. I looked at Mamma and saw more pain and sorrow in her eyes than what I was feeling. I said to her, "Mamma, I have to go again."

"How are you going to get outside? I can't carry you."

"Mamma, I can probably crawl." I leaned against the bed, slowly lowered myself, maneuvered into a crawling position, made my first stride, and felt pain from the right toe. I learned that the toes could drag on the ground in the crawling process, so I always had to raise my right foot as I maneuvered. I turned my body around at the doorway and crawled down the steps backward. Once I planted my knees and palms on the warm, bare earth, it became more manageable than the hard cement floor. While crawling, I was conscious about keeping my right foot raised, but I cringed during several failures. Once I got to the secluded area, I already had my balancing act down to a science. But I kept looking over to my right, where once I tossed a big rock high into the brush at a beehive. I noticed the bees had resurrected the hive as they hovered around it.

Time felt measured each day as I lay with my foot hanging off the bed. I couldn't even look down at it. I thought about school. I was supposed to start in a month or so and wondered if I could ever go at all. In midmornings and afternoons, I listened to the noise of flies and tried to follow their paths with my eyes. When my brother and sisters played outside, I would listen to their chatter. I felt spirited by the occasional interruption from one of my sisters when they came to check on me.

I liked when new sunlight launched through the wide-opened door and how each visit landed on the cement floor on sunny days. When it rained, I loved listening to the raindrops and somber feelings brought on by thunder, and I felt snug in bed.

Piccolo Santino

One day, I heard a woman's voice, which I needed to familiarize myself with, talking to Mamma outside. "Signora Anna, Gummah Giustina explained to me about your son, and I came right away."

"*Oh, Dio Mio,* God Bless you! You must be Gummah Catarina?"

"Si! I'm Conzini Catarina."

"Please come inside." Mamma lifted the towel from my foot and showed her my wound. The woman leaned backward, dropped a sack she was carrying, and pressed her right hand against her bosom while gasping. Mamma explained, "He's been like this for days already, and the doctor is useless!"

"Days?" she asked as she gasped again.

"Si Signora Conzini, six days!" Transfixed in anchored silence while waiting to see what would transpire, I turned my head toward the stranger as Mamma said, "Santino, the Signora is here to fix your foot." I nodded "Yes" as I looked at Signora Conzini, leaning over for a closer look. She grimaced and shook her head in disbelief, which induced a knee-jerk reaction in Mamma. I studied her middle-aged appearance, which emitted a consoling aura of confidence, and I felt immediately at rest with her. "Don't worry about a thing, Gummah. Everything will be fine."

I tried to observe what she was doing but was glad the rolled-up covers blocked my view. In an instant, a shocking cold sensation soaked into my ankle bone. Ultimately, almost freezing my right foot made it feel like a solid block of ice. Next, a pungent rotten odor I could not identify but felt familiar gripped my nostrils and forced me to welcome its presence because of the relief I was experiencing.

I stared at the Signora's arms, navigating the space above my foot. My body grew fond of the cold sensation and fully accepted the invasion. I could see the Signora lift a white enameled bedpan as she scooped out more gooey stuff and meticulously applied another layer. The cold sensation began to shift as she moved the spatula from the instep of my foot to the top. Thus, I was starting to get a notion of what she was doing.

She laid down her pan and spatula, turned to Mamma, and said, "Now, we need to wait a bit for the medicine to take effect."

Piccolo Santino

"Signora Conzini, will you excuse me for two minutes? I will be right back."

"Si, go right ahead, Gummah." I heard Mamma scream as she stepped outside. "AHHHH!"

"What happened, Gummah?"

"Cazzo di Piccione! Fuck'n pigeon! A pigeon shit on my left breast." With a burst of slight laughter, Mrs. Conzini said, "That's a sign of good luck, Gummah."

"Speriamo! Let's hope so," said Mamma as she walked away, mumbling to herself, *"Cazzo di Piccione,* Fuck'n pigeon. Got me on my head, too!"

I heard pigeons rustling on the roofline outside, and then I listened to what I could not see Mrs. Conzini doing by the sound of light metal clanking. I gathered she was reaching down inside her sack. I also sensed the cold paste that made my foot feel like a solid, hard block was drying somewhat. Then I recalled a smell of penicillin from the doctor's office that I related to this odor. There was also the odor of feces. Later, Mamma explained that Signora Conzini visited people's homes, collected mold from their bedpans, and cultivated penicillin from the mold scrapings.

Mamma returned with a bundle inside a towel and carefully offered it to Signora Conzini. "These eggs are for you, Signora Conzini, a way of my thanking you." Surprised, she said, "That's not necessary, but I appreciate it. Grazie."

"*Nemmeno lo pensati,* don't even think of it."

"Now I think it's time." She picked up a utensil that I couldn't see. I felt scraping on my foot, and the sensation between my toes felt like a wooden spatula. The scraping continued as if tissue or muscle was missing, and then I felt a cool, wet towel lightly navigating over my ankle bone. I did not see the final results but hoped to walk normally again. Mamma listened as Signora Conzini explained that she would return next week for another visit.

On the second visit, the rancid odor returned as the Signora Conzini applied more of that gooey mixture. This cold sensation seemed reduced and somewhat sharp and thin, as if frozen needles were pricking me and

Piccolo Santino

making deep pinholes into the bone. However, unlike the initial solid shock, it was a more serene, comforting sensation. I recognized the Signora's scraping away the gel-like substance, and with that comfort, I now wondered if I could genuinely walk again.

Days later, I tried walking with the aid of a stick and felt a friend in Mamma when she encouraged me to try without it. I hesitated initially, then sensed a pang of guilt in Mamma as her eyes gave her away. I handed her the stick and limped slightly. After several more attempts, I was walking well again.

A week or so later, Martina took me for a walk into the grapevine field, and I hoped we could find some ripened grapes we could snack on. Matilda positioned herself between us, and we walked past the side of the house where the smell of fertilizer was prevalent. Below that heap to the right were six large fig trees, two very tall ones that yielded jumbo white figs. The other four produced the big dark red ones. When they ripened, the juices bulged the fruit until the sugar pierced the soft skin and clung, droopingly to the outside, especially the green ones, waiting for someone to reach up and carefully pull on the stem, careful not to squash the delicate, moist bulb. With care, you could then hold the bulb by the stem with your thumbs and index fingers. You could softly squeeze and gently pull apart the two halves with both hands. Your eyes would instantly feast on that delicacy as your tongue rushed inside the soft, fruity pulp drowned in sweet, juicy, natural sugar. As your mouth pressed on that bonne bouche, your taste buds would then catapult you into the stratosphere and slingshot you back to earth-heaven for more ripened figs. But we had to wait another month or so for the pickings.

We continued down the grassy slope toward the vineyard, searching for what might have looked like sundried raisins on the vine. Martina began a conversation. "Papá went to pick up a package from America at the post office today."

"How does he get a box from America?"
"Uncle Gustavo mailed it to him."
"You mean people can send things from far away?"

Piccolo Santino

"Yes, by mail on a boat or airplane."

"Who is Uncle Gustavo?"

"Uncle Gustavo is his brother in America. He's sending him things he might need. One day, we are supposed to move there."

Matilda chased after something she heard rustling in the grass, possibly a chipmunk or field mouse. We would have heard it and seen its flight in the brush if it were a sparrow. "How do you know all this?"

"I heard them talking when Papá got a letter from Uncle Gustavo one day."

"When are we going to move there?"

"First, Papá will move to America alone, and after two years, he will send for us." I threw a stick for Matilda to fetch, and she rushed toward the sound, looking for something else. "You'll probably be in fourth grade when we can move, and I'll be in the fifth grade." I liked moments like this with Martina because, for the most part, she informed me of family activities that that I usually would find out about on the day it happened. Somehow, Martina always managed to get the inside information. "But I didn't even start school yet!"

"Well, you're going to start in two weeks, and when you finish second grade, Papá will leave for America."

"If I'm gonna start school in two weeks, it's gonna take a long time for me to get to second grade, so why worry now?"

"Well, first, he has to go to Naples to make his papers. After the second trip to Naples, he leaves for America." After walking past many rows of vines, we reached the far end of the slope and only got about a handful of each of the ripened grapes. We were afraid to venture farther into the right side of the field. "So when does Papá make the first trip to Naples?"

"He has to get the letter from Uncle Gustavo to tell him when."

"Could it be in the box he's bringing home today?"

"Let's go back to the house and see if he's back!" exclaimed Martina. As usual, Matilda ran off on her own somewhere in the field. We never had to keep track of her, as she always managed to get what she

Piccolo Santino

needed and always returned. "Can you run now?" Martina asked, "I think I can. Let's race back!" And I took off before I finished my words, and Martina followed. We both reached the house simultaneously, with me limping slightly. We walked to the front entrance to find Mamma listening to Papá finish reading a letter from Uncle Gustavo with the words, "You, should be able to make the first trip to Naples sometime in November."

"Oh, that's good news, Bartolo."

"Yes, for real. Now let's see what's in the box." We ran into the family room to join Stella, Lillo, and Angelina, all cheering in unison as Papá ripped the top of the box open. He handed Mamma a small dress, reached into the box, and lifted a white T-shirt. "This is for me," he said, then flopped it on his shoulder. He removed small items and laid them down on the table, including a small hammer that caught my eye. But Martina's hand was quicker as I reached over. A tug-of-war with a shouting match developed. Martina shouted, "That's mine!" I said, "No, it's mine!"

"No, mine!"

"I saw it first!" I said enthusiastically, tugging the hammer away from Martina and forcefully twisting the handle. In the same motion, I lifted it and smacked her on the head. She cried out, and Papá took the hammer away from me. I shot a moping glare at Martina as she rubbed her head and leaned against Mamma. I then picked up a small nail that had fallen from a container. I held it to my eyes and became fascinated with the small round head. I studied its shape as the top made me think of a hat on a person. I pressed it against my lips to feel its smoothness and wondered if the underside was just as smooth. I placed the underpart on the inside of my lips. I found interest in how the underpart molded itself into the stem. Then, I slid the nail from one side of my mouth to the other before arresting it again with the center part of my lips to further study its shape.

I then blew on it several times to get a different feel of its structure. But after retrieving more air, I inhaled too hard and boom! Swallowed it. I gulped and wondered if I was going to die soon. Unknown to others

Piccolo Santino

around me that I had eaten the nail, I decided not to panic and, instead, very quietly, walked outside, hoping to hatch a plan of action. Unable to invent anything, I thought I could wait twenty minutes, and if I didn't die, then I should be convinced that I had nothing to worry about.

Piccolo Santino

Chapter 10 of Part One
Autumn 1954, School Days

On the first day of school, Papá walked us to Jonadi along the usual path up the highway, turning left by the four corners past the sawmill and through Nao. We walked past those haunting gates to a kindergarten we had never attended. Martina was in second grade and was dropped off at a schoolroom above the smoke shop. Her teacher waited outside to greet his students, and Papá greeted the teacher with two large oranges from our farm. The man smiled from ear to ear, leaving me with the impression of a tailor because of his neat attire. Papá repeated the gesture with my teacher, who greeted his students outside three buildings diagonally across Martina's school. I likened my teacher to a tall, skinny, out-of-place insurance man in a baggy suit.

Papá approached him like he did Martina's teacher and said, "*Scusati, professore.* Excuse me, professor. I am Bianchi Bartolo. Here's a couple of oranges for you." The teacher did a double-take at the large oranges, his expression like that of a glutton whose eyes seemed to pop out of their sockets, as he responded, "Ah, Grazie! Grazie! Signore, my name is Petrozzo Gaetano. But call me Gaetano!" The two shook hands and engaged in a quick conversation, and I walked away feeling assured that I would undoubtedly receive some special attention from the teacher.

In class, we were to refer to the teacher as professore without using his name. Between students, calling each other by their last name was most common. Culturally, last names always preceded first names, and we used first names only between close friends outside of school and, of course, within the family.

I enjoyed school tremendously from the first day and always worked faster than most students. The teacher noticed, and I soon became a favorite. He always stopped to look over my work and exclaimed, "Bravo, Bianchi! Bravo!" On the second day of school, my father did not come to pick me up. Instead, my cousin Simona was there waiting for

Piccolo Santino

me. Simona was in her teenage years, and although we hardly saw each other, I felt immensely comfortable in her presence as she greeted me kindly. "Ciao, Santino. Did you like school today?"

"Sì."

"Did anybody bother you?" I nodded my head, "Yes."

"Oh, what happened?"

"A kid stole my pencils."

"Did you see who did it?" I nodded my head "Yes" again. "Who was it? Point him out to me." I looked into the crowd for the kid with the broad face, who sat next to me and spotted him staring into my face. "There he is." I pointed him out, and Simona dashed right over. He tried to move away as he saw her going toward him, but Simona grabbed his collar and stopped him. "You give back the pencils you stole." He held the pencils and said, "I didn't take these from him." Simona ripped the three pencils from his hand, turned toward me, held them up, and said, "Are these the ones?"

"Sì," I said and also nodded my head twice. Then Simona released her grip on him, and from that day on, I was always grateful as Simona made me feel that I had a special friend in the world.

The winter months brought new births, the first one I can recall in our family. It was a cold, misty day in February. We were keeping warm in front of the fire as Papá and both grandparents maintained it for the supply of hot water needed by the women tending to Mamma screaming in labor. I liked the presence of friends and family members and the help of Gumbah Angelo's wife, Giustina, and her older daughter, Aida. But most memorable to me was the midwife when she yelled out, "It's a girl, it's a girl!" Both grandfathers shook hands with the new proud father. "Congratulations, son, congratulations."

Papá looked at us children seated on the bench by the fire and said, "Later, you kids can come in to see the new baby." Giustina came out through the hallway into the kitchen, looked at Papá, and said, "Gumbah, you may come in now to meet your new daughter." Papá went right over, and we stayed seated on the wooden bench as both grandfathers minded

Piccolo Santino

us. A soft wind blew in a thin sheet of misty water on me as I was sitting at the end of the bench closest to the door. I felt sharp bites on my face and legs. Misty drops quietly dissipated by the glaring fire as it flared up from the rush of wind that sent heat over and caressed my body.

Papá soon came out and announced our new sister's name as Fabrizzia Petrosina. Somehow hearing the title made me feel proud, and I couldn't wait to meet her. Our maternal grandfather grinned from ear to ear as that was his daughter's name also. You could tell he missed her since she had just left for America a few weeks ago. I was happy Papá brought us inside, including the grandparents. He walked us over by Mamma's bedside as the baby lay next to her. One by one, Papá helped us children lean over and kiss Fabrizzia on the forehead as everyone observed.

Our paternal grandfather, who hardly ever said anything, then exclaimed in a low tone, *"Che Bella,* she is very beautiful." Our maternal grandfather joined in, *"Sì è Bella,* Yes! She is really beautiful." The paternal grandfather looked to Bartolo and said, "Thank God all went well."

"Si. Grazie Padre." I looked at Angelina as she kept staring at the new baby, and then she asked, "Mamma can she play with us later?" A peal of loud laughter broke out, and Mamma tried to maintain herself as Papá responded sarcastically, "Just wait here a spell, and she'll grow right away." All broke out in hardy laughter. "Well, I think we best be leaving now, son," said the maternal grandfather. He turned to his in-law and asked, "Well, should we go together, Gumbah Massimo?"

"Si, si, Andiamo Gumbah, let's go," replied Massimo. Bartolo looked at them and said, "Padre. Wait! We can make something to eat before you both leave."

"No! No! You have enough to do, son." Both walked out together, saying their goodbyes.

The school continued well after that initial day, and I was glad that school always ended at one o'clock every day. Only the major subjects were taught, including Catholicism. There were no lunch breaks, and

Piccolo Santino

when we asked permission for bathroom breaks, the guys usually would go out the back door into a secluded area for the number one, and the teacher gave the girls a urinal pot to bring outside in the private space. The teacher would then go unseen by anyone and dispose of the contents. There were more girls than boys as they occupied more desks on one side of the room, and rarely would one wander over to the other. One day, the teacher had to go out and left a student, Federico, in charge.

Federico was a chunky kid with thick, rosy legs. Since the teacher was not around, a beautiful girl raced to the blackboard and wrote, "Federico is my boyfriend." The boy got all red-faced, and everyone giggled. Then a skinny girl with buck teeth ran up and replaced it with newer words, "No! Federico is my groom!"

Now I wondered if another girl would go up and write me a note like that. I trembled at the idea, and we heard the teacher's voice outside as I entertained the thought. Between the outside door and the classroom was a vestibule with another entrance to the left of the entry. The upper half of the vestibule had frosted glass that blurred the vision of any onlooker. We could see our teacher's tall, lean silhouette slowly climb the steps from outside as the girl who wrote on the blackboard raced back to it. The teacher stopped outside a moment to finish his conversation. After he climbed into the vestibule and paused to turn his head for a final goodbye, the girl erased the message and returned to her desk safely. The teacher walked in, surveyed our heads, and recessed into our assignment, which was writing a one-page composition on any topic.

No sooner had he sat down than he cleared papers before him and called out, "If you finished your assignment, please bring it up here." I had been finished for a few minutes and rushed to hand him the paper. He quipped, "*Grazie*, thank you, and please wait here." I watched him make corrections and liked the red ink he used to correct my errors. Then, the shocker came as he crossed over a small section. I watched him draw a baby in a diaper, hanging from a giant bird's beak, flying on the top margin of my paper. Then he drew a red line with an arrow pointing down as he crossed out my words and wrote while he yelled out, "No! No! The baby was brought to you by the stork!"

Piccolo Santino

I had been so proud of my paper, but I could not understand what a stork had to do with my sister's birth. I stared at the nice drawing he did, and I thought for a minute. And neither my Papá nor anybody else chased after a bird for my sister to arrive. It was the midwife who did all the work. My classmates reacted by giggling softly at their desks, and when he finished, I was at least able to feel some consolation by the high grade and his kind words of "Bravo, Bianchi."

The following day, when Papá dropped me off, the teacher hurried over to him and congratulated him. Then he discussed my composition, and as they began laughing, I rushed inside.

In the spring of that year, Matilda seemed listless and dragged her paws as she walked around with her head down. Mamma had suspected something and kept watching her. Even Papá was concerned, and as he spotted the bitch coyly walk down to the barn, he followed along. Matilda had scratched out a hole through the hay wall in the side rear of the barn and created a bed with the loose hay. Papá saw Matilda lying down on the bed outside the barn. And from inside the barn through the hole in the wall. Five puppies scuffled out and rushed for her teats.

Mamma was in the house in her rocking chair nursing Fabrizzia, and we were sitting by the front door on the steps when Papá walked up the ramp from the barn and said, "Hey kids, look what I brought you." We all turned to him but couldn't see what he was hiding in his arms. He came closer and dropped three puppies at our feet, and we all scrambled to grab one. "There's more. Don't fight. I'll be right back."

Martina reached for the white puppy, Stella chose a brown one, and I got a mixed brown and white puppy. Papá returned with two more white ones, and Lillo sat beside Angelina on the ground. Papá laid the puppies on their laps, and they immediately began to pet them. Martina and Stella held them to their chest. I held my puppy out to look at its big eyes, and it peed in midair. Hearty laughter followed, and after a short spell, Papá said, "Playtime is over, kids. The puppies need to go back to their Mamma." Stella rocked the puppy against her chest and said, "Mine is the cutest! I don't want to give him back yet, Papá!"

Piccolo Santino

"Come on, kids, let me have two now, and I'll return for the others."

"Papá, why can't we keep them with us?" cried Stella. Then Angelina called out to Mamma in her rocking chair, "Mamma, I wanna hug mine when I sleep." Mamma quickly snapped, "Bartolo, get these, *cazzi di cani*, fuck'n dogs, out of here right now, or I'll take a stick to all of you!"

"Oh, but they are so cute," answered Angelina. "Papá, we want to keep them! Please?"

"No, that's it. Mamma said no." Papá looked at me, and I handed my puppy over to him. Then he reached for the two puppies on the ground, about to escape Angelina and Lillo. He scooped them both up by their necks, then suggested that Martina and Stella go with him so they could bring their puppies back to Matilda. They obediently followed. I thought this would be another composition I could write about in school, but I decided against it since I did not want to be corrected about a stork again.

But the next assignment was reading, and on that day, Tulio, who sat next to me, was not paying attention. When he spotted the teacher making the rounds, he leaned over to see what page I was on. I let him look, knowing he would be on the wrong page when the teacher arrived. The teacher looked at my progress, leaned over to Tulio, and slapped his ruler on the desk, creating a loud slapping sound, and he yelled out at Tulio, "What are you doing reading way ahead of the class assignment? You should not be reading that far ahead!" Tulio answered back, "But Bianchi is reading ahead, too!"

"I can excuse him, for he is a much faster reader than you, and I am positive he read from the assigned page already. Now go back and start at the beginning!" I felt vindicated, as my trap of personally paying Tulio back for stealing my pencils on the first day of school worked. I kept on reading as Tulio stared at me, red-faced and snarling. Although he was my nemesis, he could also stimulate my good nature, as his family seemed to have even less than we did. His slow learning habits became understandable, and I did come to feel sorry for him.

Piccolo Santino

Sorrow was a feeling that surfaced unexpectedly one morning as I was dressing. The early morning sun was warm and friendly as it angled inside through the doorway. I liked its feel as I finished dressing in that new light. I never dreamed that a cold chill could cut so deep with such abruptness by a languid Matilda walking into my view frame as I looked outside. My body and soul quickly drooped at even keel with that of Matilda.

With a dead puppy dangling from her mouth, she slowly drifted past my view. There wasn't enough sunlight in the world to erase that moment's anguishing chill, which only escalated as I thought of the part we played in bringing this pain to Matilda. Yesterday, Papá had tied Matilda to a secluded tree far away from where he was digging a grave large enough for all the puppies. We stood by watching Papá dig the large hole, and then he demanded we hand over the puppies one at a time. He individually took a puppy from us, dropped it into the grave, and covered their living bodies with dirt. Killing the puppies was a primitive way of dealing with the newly discovered overpopulation of canines on our farm since no one showed interest in adopting them.

I went to visit the graveside after seeing Matilda carry off that dead pup. She had dug up the grave entirely and was returning to retrieve another one. I stared at the exposed dead puppies as Matilda walked away with the tiny corpse dangling by its neck from her mouth. She took the dead pups to her secret place of mourning, and I did not dare follow her.

Piccolo Santino

Chapter 11 of Part One, 1955
Man of the house

Mamma had tied a towel from my head to my jaw. I pressed on the tooth with my tongue and stood the pain for as long as I could. "Wait until the tooth is very loose, then you can pull it out, and the pain will go away." Papá said to me, but the pain was throbbing, and I looked up at him and said, "Goodbye," with my eyes as he leaned down to kiss me on the forehead. "Ciao, I'll be back in less than a week, son." I couldn't wait for sleep to take my pain away.

I woke up with my tongue pressing on the very loose molar. I reached in with my fingers and pulled it right out with minimal pain. At Mamma's voice, I looked up. "Is the tooth still bothering you?" I stuttered out some of my words and handed her my tooth. "N-n-no, where is Papá?"

"He left early for Naples."

"Do you think an animal will eat it, my tooth?"

"I'll see that it doesn't happen."

"Mamma, I don't want a cow's tooth to grow in my mouth." She looked at me with laughter as she walked away, saying, "And I'll keep it in a safe place then."

In the dusk of a beautiful, clear August evening, we watched Mamma make poached eggs in a large frying pan over the fire. I thought we must be out of olive oil; otherwise, she would be frying those eggs. I liked how she scooped bubbling water with a large spoon and then poured it over the yolks until they turned white from cooking—the same way Mamma did with olive oil, which resulted in a different cooked effect.

She had us line up with our plates and placed an egg on each plate next to a chunk of homemade bread. We ate seated on the front stoop, and we watched Mamma pull the dried clothes off the line down by the other end of the house. We ate the eggs slowly to savor every bite, and we dunked our bread in the yolk and wiped our plates clean. We even talked about not having to share our food with Matilda since she was not around. When Lillo ran out of bread, he licked his plate clean. Mamma entered the house down the hallway from the kitchen, carrying a basket of dried clothes and an empty kettle. She said to Martina, "Put the dirty dishes in this kettle, Martina."

"Sì Mamma."

"And you, Stella, fill it with water." Martina walked over to Mamma to take the kettle from her. As Stella reached for the water jug, Mamma stopped her. "Never mind, Stella, we must go to the spring for more water. We'll do it tomorrow."

It was getting dark inside as Mamma tried to fold clothes. She paused momentarily to light the kerosene lamp on the table, but the wick was not holding the flame. She unscrewed the cap to check the tank; it was empty, as was the supply container. Mamma's eyes showed the panic that surfaced from her heart at the thought of her family being in the dark for the night and Papá far away in Naples. "Santino!" she cried, "You are the only one that can go into town to get the kerosene."

I looked at my sisters and brother and wondered *why we couldn't all go.* They seemed lost at the thought of being in the dark. I thought of the path that made me most comfortable for this mission and asked Mamma, *hoping to avoid the country path.* I stuttered, "I just walk up to the four corners and turn right and go that way, right?"

"No! No! Son, it's shorter if you cut through the countryside. It will be too dark to walk back alone through town and down the highway." My face froze when she mentioned the countryside path. I recalled a time when Martina and I were robbed in that area. Papá had sent us on an errand to that same store, and we took the path through the ravine to stay out of the hot sun. Luckily, our uncle, Nicola, was visiting that day, and he insisted we show him where we got robbed. The kids were still there when we returned, and Uncle Nicola reprimanded all those kids and retrieved the money for us. Blank-faced, I looked at Mamma, and she pleaded, "For the love of God, son, you must do this for us!"

"Sì Mamma, all right, I'll go."

Piccolo Santino

"Wait here. I'll be right back." Frantically, she returned holding a towel with stuff inside and said, "Here, take this. I wrapped up eggs in this towel to pay for the kerosene. Be careful you don't break them. We'll all walk down the trail with you to see you off." With a desperate look, Mamma held out the metal container for the kerosene, and I reached for it with my left hand.

She led us all down the walkway. I had enjoyed cleaning, but this was a different kind of job now. To get this job done, I would have to talk. Mamma did not even know how I trembled inside just at the thought of talking to strangers, but she said nobody else could this errand. So, I had to get this done. In an Italian family, the eldest boy is supposed to be the man of the house when the father is away.

We turned right at the bottom past the barn and carefully steered away from the mud created by the overflow of water from the laundry pool. Tomorrow, the pool would be emptied so the crops could be watered, and Mamma would do that for Papá.

We reached the clearing at the bottom of our property line, where the grass grew thick. Its tallness was windblown flat and felt soft under one's feet. "I know it will be dark for you on the way back, but Papá is not here, and we are all counting on you, son."

"Bene," I said while nodding "yes" with my head. As I walked away, I looked back only once and saw Mamma holding Fabrizzia against her bosom in her right arm. Angelina stood next to her, holding her left hand. The rest of the kids stared in my direction while silently waiting there. "Go ahead, son. We'll all be waiting here for you."

The air was warm on this summer night. I marched forward in the twilight, through that field sparsely populated by trees and tall, thick perennial grass. The colors clung like temporary glue on the landscape. In the sky, the colors had texture. The dark sifted through the different layers of atmosphere that made the night feel like the weave of a thin layer of paint-stained cheesecloth.

The tall grass stung my shins as I plowed through the warm evening air, and the sky was dimming. I thought I would arrive in town with ample light glowing, but I became apprehensive about the return trip. When the

Piccolo Santino

grass was tall, I lifted the eggs so they wouldn't break. While my heart was thumping my mind still wished I didn't have to do this. My legs kept at an even keel to my feet as they stepped forward with force inside me that felt foreign. I marched on, mainly looking down; I figured I would know when to look up. I looked up and saw the rear corner of the building and anticipated the imposing aura of strangers that might be inside. People I didn't know and needed to talk to but lacked the courage.

Nonetheless, I continued up the natural ramp, which showed that visitors had trampled on it many times. I made it to the top, stepped down onto the street, and turned right to the entrance a few steps from the corner of the building. I took a deep breath and pulled open the screen door. I walked straight ahead, feeling crowded by merchandise hanging from the ceiling and shelving on both sides of me. I stopped where an older woman and two young boys a little older than me stood in front of the store counter. She had soft grey hair that made me think she was grandmother to the two boys, suggesting the woman had an honest way about her. She studied the towel and tin can I was carrying, then looked at me as I stopped before her. She abruptly asked, "What do you want?"

I was happy she got right to the point but wished she could guess so I didn't have to talk. My heart pounded, and with my conviction to accomplish my task, I reluctantly began to speak. "A liter of-" The first three words shot out like a cannonball, and I felt proud and lucky at the same time, but then I felt her eyes growing in front of me, and the two boys just stood there waiting patiently. Fearing that I would stutter, I opened my mouth anyway. I hoped the word kerosene would fly out, but the letter "k" got hung up. "k-k-k-k-k-k-k-k." It felt endless, and finally, the word made it out. "Kerosene," and I wondered why they were not laughing at me.

I held up the towel containing the eggs, then the tin can, and she asked. "Are they fresh?" I nodded, "Yes," she took the eggs and carefully unraveled the towel on the countertop. She inspected each egg by holding them individually up to the ceiling light. I didn't expect that, but as she laid each one back down on the towel, I wondered, after all the anguish, if this would be a real hindrance and precipitated failure in my journey.

Piccolo Santino

She put down the last egg and made a wide grin of approval. The woman took the can from me, handed it to the boy beside her, and said. "Go fill this up."

I breathed a sigh of relief, thinking I could now be on my way home as soon as the boy returned. I reveled some more in the thought of having succeeded despite my handicap. The boy came right back and handed me the filled container of kerosene. Delighted about fulfilling the most challenging part of my mission, I darted out of the store, not even looking at the people staring at me while I rushed past them. I listened to the screen door slam behind me while my feet hit the pavement and turned left at the corner of the building down the dirt ramp into the field toward home.

I saw the remaining sunlight passing in front of me, even though I had hoped there would be more of it when I walked into the store earlier. As I advanced inside the grassy field, it had already begun to reflect some of the moon's glimmer, and I befriended the sweet smell of clover and alfalfa as my feet moved rapidly and steadily. I kept telling myself that Mamma was waiting at the end of the path and that I accomplished my mission. It was just a matter of bringing the kerosene home now; the hard part was over, and there was no need to look back at the thought of something evil possibly lurking behind me.

I kept telling myself never to look back as an owl hooted in a tree, and the sound of brush moving off to the rear gave me a sudden fright. Because of the sound, I speculated a small animal was stirring back there; it felt like a young pig. I questioned if I would be accosted again by those same bullies. I even speculated if the boys in the store were part of the group that had robbed Martina and me. But I quickly reminded myself I was not traveling the same path where the robbers lurk. This path was a safe distance away, in the open country, from where we got bullied. And the moonlight was a friend as it lit the night for me. I kept telling myself not to look back as the thought of looking back made me afraid of the unseen. As much as I wanted to turn around, I kept repeating the exact words "don't *look back" – don't look back.*

Piccolo Santino

I heard Mamma's faint voice call out to a nearby neighbor on the mountaintop to my right. "Gumbah Ciccio, I sent Santino to the store for kerosene. He should be walking around by now. Let me know if you can see him!" At first, I resented her calling out, as I felt it was a way of telling potential bullies where to find me. Mamma called out several times, and even though the human voice traveled far in the open country, it could take a while for the receiver to get in position to respond. Still, Gumbah's voice responded to Mamma's almost at the exact moment I thought of it. "Gummah, Anna, don't worry. I'll watch out for him!"

"Grazie, Gumbah!"

"I see him!" I turned slightly toward the mountain top to my right, just enough so that I would not see somewhat behind me. I saw the silhouette figure of Gumbah Ciccio with his wife and two kids up on the mountaintop, and he responded. "He's coming back."

"Bene! Grazie, Gumbah!"

"He's on his way back. I can see him! He's coming back!"

"Bene! Grazie, Gumbah!" The voices then stopped, and if I gained any composure, it was from knowing that now I was within reach of Mamma's voice, and I would be there soon. Ignoring the sharp sting of grass slapping my shins, I forged straight ahead and was relieved when I saw my family in the distance. I sensed Mamma's concern lifting from her as she shouted back at our friend in the hills. "He made it back, Gumbah. Buona sera!"

Now, I relished the sound of the wild grass against my shins as each step forward brought me closer to my family, and the darkness began to feel less ominous. Once separated in the moonlight by distance, we were joined in the same space under the same light, and with everybody smiling, we walked home together on the friendly moonlit night.

The last few days of August breezed by, and September brought Papá home from his trip to Naples, and he surprised me with a *Lone Ranger* comic book. I was thrilled and brought it to school to show my best friend, Franco. He told me to watch out and not leave it on my desk, for it would get stolen, so I heeded his words and took it back home that same day. Also, on that day, the teacher had to go out on some errand and left me in charge, and as much as I shunned the attention, I also savored it. I felt it was safe to speak in school as long as I didn't have to elaborate; then, I could control my stuttering. Knowing I was there to learn, I hoped to accomplish something, and perhaps my stuttering could vanish. Even with my friends, I did not have a problem, and if I felt it coming on, I would pause and wait for the right time to speak. When the teacher left somebody in charge, we sat at his desk and did classwork there. We heard the door open outside and saw a man's silhouette behind the vestibule's frosted glass. The class observed the man as he entered and stopped short when he saw me at the teacher's desk. "Buongiorno, where's your teacher?"

Since I was in charge, I put on an aura of importance to control my stuttering and quickly responded, "He'll be back soon. He had something to do, sir."

"Grazie!" he responded, turned around and I quickly rose to my feet, faced the class, and called, "*Tutti in piedi,* everybody rise!"

The man stopped and turned around to see the students all on their feet. He looked at me, nodded, and proudly said, "Bravo!" He then politely walked away and closed the door. The class sat down and resumed their work without a whisper. When the teacher returned, one of the students described what had happened: "Professore, you had a visitor."

"Ah yes, I saw him outside, thank you."

"And while he was leaving, Bianchi told us to rise, and the man said, "Bravo!" The teacher looked at me as I left his desk and proudly exclaimed, "Bravo, Bianchi!"

Feeling elated that day, I began to question the Italian dialect we spoke at home, which could equate to a version of an Italian Ebonics. Compared to the grammatical Italian we were taught in school. I wondered why we didn't speak that way at home, too. It just happened that Papá was conversing with one of his friends in front of our house. I was sitting on an ample supply box containing two small barrels inside. The top lid was hinged and constructed to slant downward toward the

Piccolo Santino

front. Papá and his friend leaned against the container with their back toward me.

I was afraid to ask Papá why they weren't talking in proper Italian. I thought it was best to articulate their conversation using grammatical Italian and hoped it would convince them to switch to how I was demonstrating. I repeated their lines aloud, expecting Papá or his friend to change to the grammatical Italian. I also hoped they would approve by giving me a "Bravo, Santino." I heard a loud slap on my face after the third line without seeing Papá's hand move. The sting felt everlasting as I rubbed my face, and I felt bruised more in pride than in body. I became stupefied since I could not understand how I didn't stutter on their lines.

On the last day of school before Christmas break, we took a test, and as we finished, we brought it up to the teacher for him to include in our final grades. We were all anxious, not just to receive our grades. But every year, the teacher would compose a traditional Christmas letter on the blackboard for us to copy and bring home. Some students were so slow we wondered if we would get our final grades and write the traditional Christmas letter. Other students had already asked the teacher about it since dismissal was approaching. Finally, the last student got his grade, and the teacher got up from his desk and rushed a short composition on the blackboard. A man wearing a trench coat walked in, and we immediately all rose to our feet as usual.

"Ah, buongiorno, Crisafulli. Make yourself comfortable at my desk."

"Ah, buongiorno, professore. Grazie, I will."

"I'm almost done here." It became apparent our teacher had been expecting him, and we learned the situation as the two spoke. "As each student has finished copying this letter, you can send them home." Our teacher grabbed his hat, coat, and suitcase he had under his desk, turned to us, and said, "You can all leave when you finish copying your letter. Have a good vacation, a Merry Christmas, and a Happy New Year!" He then turned to the substitute before he rushed out like a lightning bolt. "Crisafulli, Grazie. Have a good holiday and arrivederci."

"Arrivederci, Professore Petrozzo and happy holidays to you also."

Piccolo Santino

We all rushed to copy the letter, but some ran late past the dismissal time, and to our disappointment, the substitute needed to dismiss us. The teacher then looked up and exclaimed. "I see everyone finished writing. Well, then you can all go. Arrivederci and happy holidays, kids."

We all got up, cheering, and ran for the exit. I asked my best friend Franco, a friendly kid, about my size and height about the letter assignment. He was very sympathetic and quickly explained the purpose of the Christmas letter. He explained that we should sneak the letter under our father's dinner plate on Christmas Eve. That way he would read it after finding it and give us a present. I sensed instant discouragement since I felt this was a pointless idea in our home, but I decided I'd do it since it had a good purpose, regardless of a gift.

I walked up to Papá, as I spotted him waiting for me. I grabbed his hand while I yelled goodbye to Franco. On the way home, Papá stopped by some people's houses to wish them Merry Christmas. Wherever we went, Papá was always greeted with respect. I offered a shy smile, thinking of Papá's orders to never ask for anything, and if something was offered, I was to refuse it unless they persisted.

I had noticed the richness of Christmas in the homes of people in town with their assembled decorations. I specifically enjoyed watching one person create a manger display with statues of Joseph with Mary, baby Jesus, and the three wise men. I marveled at the man's handiwork, creating a landscape, decorating it using straw and actual moss, and then painting wardrobes on some statues. It all made me want to go home and create such a display. But I knew there was no room in Papá's pockets for such extravagance. So, I stopped dreaming. After seeing all those Christmas decorations, I realized how much we lacked in our family, for such ornaments felt unattainable. Thus, I thought that the letter I wrote in school for Papá wouldn't reap anything for me, and even if it did, how would my brother and sisters feel left out?

Christmas Eve arrived, and dinner was about over. I recall snacking after dinner on desserts of dried figs filled with hazelnuts, tangerines, oranges, and nuts. I considered placing the letter under Papá's plate but missed the opportunity. Then, I also thought about my brother and sisters being left out. I wondered if I should keep the letter and later tear it up, but I was concerned about writing it and not using it. Quickly, I grabbed some plates from the table and handed them to Mamma; I then reached into my pocket, palmed the letter, and in the same motion, grabbed Papá's plate, leaving the note on the table, and I said, "Look, something was at the bottom of your dish, Papá." Papá unraveled the letter, read it softly, and said, "Bravo!"

"Tino did that so he could get a present." My sisters and brother quickly commented. I thought of the words in the letter and blushed as I quietly sat there. I didn't know I would get a gift, but I did get a small coin.

On the evening of January 6, Mamma and Papá urged us to hang our socks in the kitchen so the good witch could surprise us with gifts for the feast of *La Befana,* the Epiphany. Mamma also explained that the witch could leave coal in our socks if we were terrible. We all rushed out of bed early on the morning of the Epiphany. We ran to the kitchen to check our socks. In all the excitement, we confused Lillo's cry for help for the enthusiasm of the La Befana celebration. We turned to Lillo screaming and standing stark naked as our cat Carbone dangled from his wiener!

Quickly, Mamma lifted Carbone by its tail, which forced a whining cry from her, and then she tossed her aside. In laughter, we watched Carbone sprint into the hallway and out of sight. Mamma checked on Lillo and then got his socks for him. In all that unexpected laughter and excitement, we raced back to the family room as we pulled out the nougat candy that stuck out from our socks. We settled around the family table and proceeded to find more surprises inside. We were delighted to find biscotti and *Perugina* chocolates. I was most amazed to see a small penknife. We all celebrated with added laughter as Lillo's stocking received some coal and ashes, candy, and chocolates. Seeing the world come through so magically for us was a good feeling.

Chapter 12, of Part One, 1956
Another sibling is born

It was a balmy winter day toward the latter part of February. The chill bit my legs like sparks spitting out of a bonfire. I was introduced to long pants later, and my socks only covered up to my calves. My shins felt frozen, but they did not feel the bite of the wind like my thighs did as we walked up the hill from Jonadi toward home. The wind circled down from the hilltop with a downdraft that felt like pine needles pricking my skin. Martina was lucky she wore knee socks under her long dress. Since she was in third grade and I was in second, we were allowed to walk alone. Sometimes in the winter, Papá did accompany us in the morning.

On the hilltop, the road around the bend by the religious station was more forgiving, and as we came toward it, we saw a bicycle parked against the shrubbery but not chained up. We looked at each other in wonder, and I exclaimed, "Now, why would anybody leave a bicycle unlocked like this? Someone could steal it very easily."

Before my sister could answer, a man shouted from above the religious station. "What are you going to do? I'll come down there and break your horns. You son of a bitch!" Scared and misunderstood, my sister and I ran so fast it knocked the cold out of my legs. Martina, while making the sign of the cross, said. "We forgot to make the sign of the cross by that station."

"What good will it do now?" I said. She responded, "We better do it at the next one."

"Why? Mamma is not with us."

"I told you God sees everything."

"Yeah, but we didn't do anything wrong."

"It doesn't matter. You're supposed to make the sign at all religious stations." We came to the next station at the outskirts of Nao and made the sign of the cross. And my thighs began to feel the cold again.

Piccolo Santino

Giustina came to the door as we tried to enter and told us to go down to the kitchen, as Mamma was having her baby. We saw Papá pouring water into the large pot on the fire and our maternal grandfather feeding the fire. Seated on our favorite bench were our younger sisters Stella, Angelina, and Fabrizzia. Our younger brother Lillo was standing by our paternal grandfather Massimo, who was sitting on a chair.

Lillo was munching on a hunk of bread and picking olives off a plate resting on grandfather's lap. We stood by the fire for a minute to shake off the chill, and Papá told us to sit on the bench and we could have some bread and cheese to eat. Mamma screamed from inside, and Giustina ran down the hall and through the doorway with an empty bucket. "Gumbah, we need more hot water." Papá answered quickly, "Si! Si! Pronto Gummah." Papá handed her a new bucket with warm water, and Arturo, the maternal grandfather, said to Giustina, "I guess it's still too early to know anything, Gummah Giustina."

"*Ah, Si! Si troppo presto Compare*. Oh yes! Much too early to tell Gumbah," she responded while walking back down the hallway. Grandfather Arturo turned to Papá and said, "Bartolo, I'll go with you. Where's the bucket?"

"Over there." Grandfather Arturo took the other two empty buckets and said, "Okay, let's go." Papá turned to us and said, "We'll be right back; you kids behave for your grandfather." We all answered, "Si! Papá."

Stella and Angelina began teasing each other with straws of hay. One poked the other in the neck, causing an itch, and then innocently looked the other way. Lillo pulled a thick alfalfa straw from the woodpile, sneaked behind Martina, and poked her behind her ear as he whispered, "It's a mouse! It's a mouse!" Martina was not fooled and reached over and snatched the straw from Lillo and said, "I saw you, you rascal." Lillo then pointed to our paternal grandfather, asleep and snoring in the chair with his chin to his chest and hat loosely on his head. I took the straw from Martina and put my index finger over my lips. I looked at everybody as I quietly sneaked next to Grandpa. I slowly rubbed the back of his ear, and he moved his head as he snored, and I pulled back. I waited for him to settle down before I repeated the same act.

Piccolo Santino

He swiftly swiped his right ear with his hand, and then I inserted the straw inside his ear while I whispered, "A mouse! A mouse!" Wide-eyed and dazzled, he promptly shook his head, straightened himself up while losing his hat, and yelled out. *"Che cazzo è successo*? What the fuck happened?"

We all laughed hysterically at Grandfather as he rubbed his ear, and I contained myself with an aura of seriousness as I looked at him with his hat in my hands. "Your hat fell, Nonno." He looked at me, snatched the hat from my hands, all shook up and raced outside while mumbling. *"Ma queste sono cose da un altro mondo.* These are things from another world." I followed him to the doorway and poked my head out. He then walked around the side of the house into a private area. "Where did he go?" Everybody asked. I whispered, "He's on the side of the house."

"What's he doing?"

"He is doing la pee-pee." Lillo laughed and mimicked peeing by prancing about as he repeated the words. "Fa la pee-pee! Fa la pee! Fa la pee-pee." The girls giggled and then laughed loudly. I heard the tinkling sound slowing down, and from inside the house, Mamma let out her loudest scream of the day. The girls stopped giggling and stared in the direction of the scream, and Lillo ran to sit back on the bench.

Grandpa haphazardly rushed out from behind the wall outside while buttoning his pants. I ducked my head inside and was startled by Papá's sudden voice as he said, "What are you doing over here?" Seeing Papá and Grandfather Arturo carrying the buckets of water, I felt a surge of unity. "Papá, Mamma screamed!" I blurted out, knowing they would understand. Papá rushed over carefully to avoid spilling the buckets and said to me, "Yes, son, we heard her. Now get inside."

"I heard her, too," said Massimo as he finished buttoning his pants and followed inside. At the same instant, Giustina emerged from the hall doorway. "Bartolo, we think this is the moment the midwife says you should wait here." She stared at Papá, "Sì, sì of course."

Mamma let out another scream, louder and longer than the previous one, which brought back memories of Fabrizzia's birth. Before Fabrizzia, Angelina managed to skip this type of drama inside the house as Mamma

Piccolo Santino

would tell us how she was in the field plowing when her water broke. She had just enough time to lie down in the shade, and within minutes Angelina was born outside under a large oak tree. Five of us were born in this house, and Angelina was born out in the field, and Martina was born in town in the first house Mamma and Papá had moved into right after they got married. Now it was number seven with Enzo, last to be born in this house. It was we boys who caused Mamma the most hardship at birth or post-birth here in Italy. Except for Angelina, none of the other girls were a cause for concern during their arrival.

    I liked experiencing the seasonal changes here on the Fontana Di Taccuni farm, from the splendor of summer's harvests in the fall to the warmth indoors by the fireplace in winter, listening to the battering rain against the shutters at night with the howling wind. The occasional snow made the arrival of spring much sweeter when the fruit trees blossomed and shed their fragrance. It all made me speculate if I would like it living in town. I immediately thought being closer to school and meeting with my friend Franco for companionship on the way to school would be fun. That thought became my sanctuary, my place of retreat at the idea of leaving what had grown to be a magical place during the years we lived here. Except for the one tragic motorcycle accident that led to the death of that young man, we were never afraid of anything here.

    On the other hand, Mamma would tell us of a woman's voice that used to call out to her at night for help during her first months here. While she was in a sound sleep, Mamma kept ignoring the pleading calls, and on the fifth night, unable to sleep anymore, she decided to go outside to see what the woman wanted. Mamma looked up from the bottom of the drive and saw the woman calling her from outside the gates. "Anna, please come. We need your help!"

"What happened?"

"Please come quick!" Mamma rushed up the drive, opened the gates, and followed the woman in white down the highway in the moonlight for a few minutes. Then, she saw her vanish in front of her eyes.

Piccolo Santino

The next day, Mamma was going into town to pick up the new bedsheets her aunt had weaved for her with her loom, and Mamma described the woman in white to her aunt. "Why, you just described a cousin of your mother's and mine. Her name was Adelina." The aunt gasped. "What do you mean? What are you saying?"

"What I'm saying is that she died in a car accident at that very spot ten years ago."

"Oh, how frightening!"

"Oh, stop. You can make the ghost go away."

"Yeah! Make it go away! How?"

"Just sprinkle salt around your house; ghosts will never bother you, my dear niece."

That formula worked on ghosts but did not deter a wayward stranger as he woke some of us up from a sound sleep one night. I heard knocking at the door and could barely see through my sleepy eyes and the dim light of the kerosene lamp. Mamma whispered to Papá, "Bartolo. Put something on! Santino can see you. He sleeps right here at the foot of the bed."

"I'm using my hands to cover myself." The knocking happened a second time, and when I opened my eyes, I saw Mamma in her nightgown and Papá with his back to me naked. I thought men must have big ones and women had smaller-sized ones. That had to be the difference between the boys and the girls. Papá called out to the knocking outside, "Who are you? What do you want?"

"I am a stranger. I thought this place was an eatery. Can you let me in?" A man's voice answered. "No, it's not an eatery. I closed it down years ago!" Papá reached for the broom against the wall near where Matilda slept. "I'm just passing through and was hoping to get something to eat."

"You can keep going. There is nothing here." Papá militarily held the broom like a rifle with a fixed bayonet.

Outside, the stranger shook the door by the doorknob, and Matilda gave a menacing growl. Almost instantly, we heard the release of the doorknob, and a long silence followed. Matilda rose to her feet and stood

Piccolo Santino

next to Papá. The stranger must have been scared off by the growling as there were no more sounds from outside. Mamma whispered to Papá as he put his ear to the door, "Did he leave?" Papá whispered back, "He must've. It's very quiet now. I heard him step away." Matilda returned to her sleeping post by the door and lay back down. "It's okay now. Let's go back to bed."

Papá needed money for his trip to Naples before leaving for America, so Mamma arranged to rent out the brick oven to a small group of women who banded together to defray the rental amongst themselves. One morning, one of the women, with wiry curly hair, in a dark floral print dress well below knee length and black shoes with thick heels, arrived to inspect the oven and seal the agreement. I watched Mamma and the woman debate back and forth from a short distance, no doubt discussing a price or plans for using the brick oven. From a distance, I observed their animated gestures during their conversation that I could not hear.

Mamma shook her head, saying no, with lips wide shut. The woman clutched her fingers and raised both hands before her face. She shook them back and forth at Mamma. Mamma shrugged her shoulders together, grasping her elbows against her rib cage while holding her palms up in front of the woman. She leaned her face in a bit as she moved her lips in a lively manner. The woman lowered her arms, smacked her hands against her sides with a slight sign of disdain, and looked down and shook her head back and forth.

Calmly, Mamma crossed her arms against her bosom as she smacked her lips and shook her head left and right. The woman scratched her head with her left hand while moving her head back and forth and placed her right hand on her hip. She stopped scratching and slid her fingers to her forehead, pausing momentarily, then softly rubbed her forehead. Mamma gently uncrossed her arms and pointed toward the kitchen.

The woman sighed with relief, and they walked away, chattering and turning their heads back and forth. Martina was seated on a stool,

Piccolo Santino

knitting inside the house away from me on the stoop. When Mamma and the woman turned left up the driveway and began chattering again, I was able to make out one line from the woman. "The holiday is in a few days. We need to do our baking before that." I then heard the sound of the metal gates closing, and Mamma scurried back, seemingly annoyed. She continued toward the other end of the house and into the kitchen. Martina put down her knitting and witnessed as Mamma huffed and puffed.

Yesterday, Mamma had decided to roast the entire hot pepper plant harvest. Usually, she would wait a week for the toxic fumes to subside before separating the red peppers from the burned plants. But now, it looked like she was forced to clean out the oven immediately. We heard Mamma coughing violently, so Martina and I hurried to the kitchen and saw Mamma's face and eyes severely irritated and tearing heavily. Upon seeing Martina Mamma reached out, arrested us, and pulled us toward the oven. "No, Mamma, No!" we both cried out. "You two get inside and rake those red peppers out right now!" She pulled on my arm with her left hand and, with her right hand, forced Martina up on the ledge. She then forced the both of us inside head first as we resisted. We had just witnessed what happened to Mamma from the outside, being close to the oven. And for us to go inside seemed suicidal. Having been forced to yield to her shoving, we tried turning around for a gasp of air as the fumes were overbearing. "Get inside right now, the both of you!"

Trapped into submission with our knees planted on the ledge, we slowly crawled forward. Instantly, our eyes burned and teared up as we inched inside in two short strides. The gagging forced us to turn our heads toward the outside for a gulp of fresh air. With a metal rake, Mamma pushed us farther in. Feeling bound to her command, I grabbed the rake after Mamma threw it in, and Martina used the one already inside. But it was no use. Our eyes teared heavily, and then the gagging forced us to drop the rakes and hurry toward the exit.

Mamma blocked our escape. I learned to my right, and Mamma pushed me back in. As Martina moved to her left, Mamma stopped her. During the struggle, Mamma breathed more fumes, and her gagging resumed. We then gained just enough leverage to jump down. As Martina held herself up by the ledge, Mamma grabbed her by the hand and shouted, "You're not going anywhere."

"No, Mamma! No!" I cried out. Get back in there right now!" Mamma yelled back. A tug of war developed. Martina resisted Mamma's pulling and had gained some leverage, then. As Mamma's coughing subsided, Martina slid toward Mamma a bit. Afraid for Martina, I grabbed her other hand and pulled her toward me as I pleaded, "No, Mamma! No!"

"You both get back in there right now!"

"No, Mamma! No!" I yelled back as Martina's scared eyes stared into mine. *"Cornuto*, you cuckold! Let go, or I'll take a stick to you!" The added pressure exacerbated Mamma's gagging fit, forcing her to reach inside her apron for her handkerchief. She coughed violently again, covering her mouth with both hands on the handkerchief. Forced to let go of Martina's hand, we raced down into the vineyard. In a raspy coughing voice Mamma's, yelled out to us, "Both of you, come back here right now!"

We ran away deep into the safety of the vineyard with our heads down to avoid direct sunlight, and Matilda followed us. We got down on our stomachs on the grassy walkway between rows of grapevines when we heard Mamma talking, "Where the hell are they?" Furtively, we looked up and watched her walk down a short way looking left and right as she shouted out, "Come back here, you two! Right now!"

We laid silent as Mamma stared down to our area, then as she turned back, we breathed normally again. Martina explained how to deal with the situation. "I told you we are just property to adults."

"What do you mean?"

"Children belong to adults, and they can do what they want with us."

"Yeah? You mean they could sell us, too!"

"It doesn't matter. Parents can force us to do anything they wish."

"So who can we complain to?"

"There is nothing we can do until we grow up, get married, and

Piccolo Santino

move out on our own."

"By then, it's too late."

"At least then you can pay them back by holding a grudge for a few years."

"Hold a grudge how?"

"That's what people do. They wait until they get married to get even."

"So how do they hold a grudge?"

"They don't talk to them."

"Forever?"

"Not just for a year or so."

"What does that do?"

"That punishes them for being mean." We remained out of sight for the remainder of the afternoon, hiding in the vineyard and occasionally sneaking up to see if Mamma was still looking for us. We spotted Papá and ran up to him, shouting, "Papá! Papá!" We clung to him, and he quickly asked, "What's wrong, children?" Mamma pushed us into the oven to rake up the red peppers.

Then we started choking and got scared and had to hide all day!" Papá stared at Mamma, and she shamefully shook her head in denial, and he then said to us, "That can't be. I would think she was punishing you for something. She loves you." Martina and I looked at one another, and both thought back to the conversation we had.

The next day, the woman returned with her entourage of workers and began setting up outside the kitchen area for their bake fest. Mamma approached the woman, and both were having a seemingly cordial conversation. They walked into the kitchen, and surprisingly the toxic vapors inside the oven had dissipated entirely. They walked outside, and I watched as money exchanged hands and Mamma stashed it inside her bosom. The woman walked over to where the table preparations were being made.

Mamma made it a point to walk over to the front stoop where I was

Piccolo Santino

curiously observing all the activities, excited by it until Mamma admonished me, "Now, don't be a pest to these people."

"Si." I answered, and she continued, "I don't even want to catch you looking over there." Feeling chagrined, I looked up at Mamma and hoped she wouldn't tell me to move away. I figured I could safely observe some of the activities. She continued with her warnings, "Now, don't you talk to them or ask for anything." She didn't have to worry about my not talking to anybody. That was easy, but to be expected to control the sense of smell was like asking me to snare one's soul with a mousetrap. "If anybody offers you something, refuse it unless they insist!" With sad eyes, I looked up at her and nodded, "Yes."

"They are not baking things for us. They are making bread for themselves. You understand?" I nodded "Yes" again and kept my head down as I brought my knees up to my chest and wrapped my arms around them with my eyes lifted and, head down, I looked out into the valley beyond, at the long-empty highway as Mamma walked away.

I enjoyed the feel of the hustle and bustle of the people, running in and out of the kitchen, setting up tables outside in the warm sun on this clear spring day. It all felt euphoric, a big contrast from when they slaughtered the hog in that area. Mamma had already shown them where the spring was for their water supply. And three women smiled at me as they walked by with vessels for water. It seemed that there were three parties in the large group as each set up its table on wooden horses. I counted only two older men in the group as I looked at the heap of wood supply Mamma and Papá had stacked for them by the large tree where our hog was slaughtered a while back. Some of the lighter branches had already been placed on the kitchen floor, there to get the fire started in the oven. Then two men carried big sacks filled with charcoal into the kitchen.

Outside, the women began mixing some dough and then covered it with large white towels and set it aside for it to rise. But they also worked with some pre-mixed dough and began to shape it into various sizes that I could not identify.

By late morning, the aroma of baked bread traveled into the infinite

Piccolo Santino

sky, and its magic made me think that something so precious could not have been an exclusive creation of these people alone, here today. These people had to be simply perpetuating what originated in the vastness of a past time, somehow, after the discovery of fire. For today, those who directly farmed the wheat for this aroma harvested it, milled it, and must share in the credit. The workers who built the oven had to be affected by those who discovered fire and the idea of making flour to mix it with water. They all had to count, too! That is why ancient spirits come from hiding behind clouds in the sky as bread was baked that day—sniffing this air because the earth's most heavenly aroma was rising and free-floating high above for all to share past and present. You cannot help but love bread just for its aroma during the baking alone.

"Is that your son, Signora Anna?" I heard one woman ask *and wondered if Mamma might be here.* Then Mamma's voice floated through my ears. "Si, he's my oldest boy."

"He's been sitting there so quiet all this time." *I listened with interest.* "Oh no, he hides it all very well, that one." *That made me feel bad.* "Oh no! It can't be! He seems like a little angel." *Why can't Mamma feel this way about me?* "Maybe when he sleeps." Loud laughter ensued, and Mamma addressed the women, "Let me know if you ladies need anything else."

"All is good, Signora, grazie." I turned my head toward Mamma as she descended the walkway to the barn. Because I was now paying attention to her walking away, I was able to come out of the hypnotic trance from that magical aroma and realized I had been confused as to how I could hear Mamma talking when I didn't see her walk back here in the first place.

A new aroma suddenly drifted under my nose. I turned back and stared at the women handling a new kind of bread I was unfamiliar with. I wondered if they used yellow flowers to make that bread look yellow. As they brought more of it out from the kitchen, the hot aroma reached me faster than I could handle. I had no defense against its power; my nostrils expanded on their own, and I wished terribly for a piece to absorb its aroma and then hoped to discover how its form would crumble in my

Piccolo Santino

mouth. But Mamma's orders prevented me from walking over there.

Hoping to get my mind to concentrate elsewhere, I stared out onto the empty highway down the valley in search of the car sound my ears were following. "Here you are, son. Would you like a piece of cornbread?" Two women stood by me, and one of them was holding a piece of that yellow bread, and my eyes burst out. I stared at the bread while Mamma's voice reverberated inside my head. If *they offer anything, refuse it until they insist!* But I thought to myself, *how can I refuse this delicacy?* I stared intently, and the woman lifted the bread toward me. They both said, "*Vai, Mangia figlio. Mangia!* Go on, child, eat. Eat!" I smiled with moistened eyes as I cupped my hands to watch the woman rest the soft, firm creation on my palms. I was compelled to speak. I softly said, "Grazie!"

Piccolo Santino

Chapter 13, of Part One
Preparations for moving

"What are you doing with all that hay over here?"
"We'll put the cow to bed here outside the kitchen every night until she gives birth."
"What happens if the heifer runs away while we're asleep?"
"I'm going to tie her to this stake with a rope."
"*Veramente!* Really? Just because you are going to Naples, suddenly you got smart?"
"I see a piece of hay on your chest. Come over here. I want to remove it for you."
"*Tu sei troppo Furbo*. You are too clever!"
"I served in the military, remember?"
"You'd better hurry and finish before it gets dark."
"Sì, Sì! If she gives birth while I'm gone, call on Gumbah Marco."
"I will, but you'll still be here for two more nights. Who knows, maybe it will happen before you leave."

Papá had left for Naples, and the heifer hadn't given birth yet. Then, early one morning, Mamma's voice penetrated the predawn hour outside. I was still in my bed on what felt to be a warm day. Her call percolated in my senses and told me I heard her voice. Yes, of course, Papá was gone. It was all coming together now. She's calling Gumbah Marco. I listened some more, my eyes still closed and my thoughts lucid. She stood outside on the hill overlooking the country from our house, projecting her voice toward Gumbah Angelo's farm.

The rooster, with his early morning crow, joined the symphony, vying for dominance of the airwaves with Mamma. I couldn't help but chuckle at the rooster's confusion, thinking that Mamma had risen before him, and the sun had yet to grace the sky with its light. "Gumbah Marco! Gumbah Marco! The heifer is giving birth! Come! Come quick!" She repeated the words several times.

Piccolo Santino

I could visualize her calls taking flight down to the valley past the edge of our farm, crossing the highway fast beyond the meadow and across the railroad tracks over a short hill into the neighbor's barn, sifting through the thatched roof and walls without a knock. Like water on a tissue, Mamma's voice swiftly filtered into the ears of Gumbah Marco. She called because the heifer was giving birth, and Papá was not back from Naples yet.

With sleepy eyes, I saw Angelina, grasping Mamma's dress, standing by my bedside. I lifted my head as Mamma tapped me on my shoulder. "Tino! The heifer is having the baby. Come and watch."

"*Per davvero*? For real? I want to see."

"*Si, dai, dai.* Yes, come, come."

I reached down on the floor for my shorts and put them on haphazardly as I followed them down the hall. The predawn lighted the outside on a hot spring day. My brother and sisters were seated on the ground. Watching the heifer on its bed of hay with its legs stretched out—a lot of wetness by its rear. I sat beside Lillo as Mamma put Fabrizzia down between Martina and Stella. Then she walked around behind the heifer, and I looked at the cow's eyes, following Mamma's every move, and felt a deep sense of gratitude from the animal.

Mamma looked down at the cow's birthing area and exclaimed, "Look, kids, it's happening!" We gazed as we yelled out, "Oh look, look, you can see the head." Our excitement was infectious, filling the air with joy and anticipation. We saw the calf's snout and then its head, and slowly, the front hoofs extended out as the newborn curled them and pointed toward outside. We watched for fifteen minutes or more, but it was long enough for Mamma to look worried as the calf and heifer looked stuck in suspended spirits and animation.

Mamma, with a look of relief that instantly replaced her exasperation, let go of the calf and turned to look behind us. She had been tugging at the calf's front legs, causing the heifer to lift its head, in a bid to assist with the delivery. Her efforts had paid off. "Gummah, I'm here. I heard you calling me."

"You arrived just in time, Gumbah! Grazie," Mamma exclaimed,

Piccolo Santino

acknowledging the crucial role Gumbah had played in the birth.

We all turned around to gaze at Gumbah Marco, walking steadfastly in his straw hat and short-sleeved red and black checkered shirt with baggy pants and a long, thick rope flung around his shoulders. He rushed over to the calf, tied the rope around its protruding hoofs, and stepped back, holding on to the rope with steady hands and bursting arms of strength. The first effort was slow and forceful, and then Mamma joined in, and with both pulling, the calf slid out steady and smoothly.

Gumbah Marco untied the rope, and the calf slipped and slid as it tried to lift itself. After several attempts, it sprung up on all four legs for a first stretch, and it teeters tottered several times, then suddenly fell flat with all four legs stretched out. Then, the heifer rose and looked at its offspring as it struggled on the ground. With its legs spread apart, it began to inch those brand new legs closer together, and despite their wobbling, they finally sprung up, and the calf stood still for the first time. Slowly, it swaggered closer to its mother for a face-to-face meeting. The heifer immediately began licking the calf on the head for the formal introduction and cleaning of the face. With the greetings and cleaning completed, the calf turned around and wobbled for its first feeding.

The early morning felt like popcorn on an open fire as things seemed to sprout suddenly, moment by moment, at the sound of Papá's voice. We all turned around when we heard him call from the other end of the house as he rounded the corner. "What's going on?" Screaming with glee, we all ran up to him. "Papà! Papà! Papà! The cow made a baby!"

"Ah Gumbah, Bartolo, you returned from Naples."

"Yes, I see the heifer has given birth."

"Yes, Gumbah, she just gave birth. We're just cleaning up now." We pulled Papá along by his hands and said, "Papá come and see the calf."

"Yes! Yes, children, let's go see the new calf."

After the sun had illuminated the entire landscape, Papá brought the heifer to our front door, and we all gathered to watch him fill a big bowl with fresh milk from the heifer's udder. Then Mamma dropped pieces of bread into the milk, and we all gathered on the front stoop with spoons in

Piccolo Santino

our hands and ate from that large bowl. When it was all gone, Lillo was not satisfied, so he went under the heifer and squeezed milk directly into his mouth from a teat. It then became a free-for-all. We all competed for a turn at the milk source until the heifer slapped us around with its tail. And Papá put a stop to our wildness. We felt rich and figured that we had something good, and we thought this was everlasting. But Mamma and Papá had to liquidate their stock in preparation for the big move.

"*Dai Andiamo! Asino,* Come on, move! You jackass!" The donkey remained lifeless as if made of stone, "Move it, I said." Looking as if he was pulling on a mountain, Papá gave a long, hard tug on the reins, then a few short tugs with a tongue clicking, but the donkey refused to budge and continued posing like a marble statue. "Come on, go drink your water." The donkey shook his head as if trying to shake the reins away, and Papá looked puzzled, so he made one violent tug of the reins that shook his shoulders towards the donkey. "Come on and move your ass, you stubborn mule!" The two stared at each other with mutual firmness to make a bitter standoff, and Papá shouted, "*Pezzo di merda!* You piece of shit! Move your ass."

Papá dug his heels deeper into the soft ground and pulled hard and steady on the reins. He slid forward on his heels and almost fell face down. Papá stopped to steady himself and began a series of short, hard tugs, but the donkey remained frozen. Papá raised his voice with each new expletive as Mamma, and I walked down the ramp toward Papá. "*Cornuto! Bastardo! Figlio di puttana!*" Cuckold, bastard, son of a bitch!" Mamma tried to appease Papá, "Bartolo, why don't you leave him alone? Can't you see he is not thirsty?"

"*Ma fatti le cazze tue va*. Mind your fuck'n business. Go!"

"*Adesso Basta*. Enough already; he's not listening to you."

"I'll show him who's in charge here!"

"*Ma tu sei pazzo*! You're out of your mind!"

"You'll see who the boss is." He looked around and saw his whipping cane against the bottom edge of the pool. He stepped over to get it while he continued berating the animal. "*Ora ti batto il Culo!* Now

Piccolo Santino

I'm going to whip your ass!" He picked up the long cane and waved it in front of the donkey's sight as he continued taunting him. "Ass that you are! Listen up. If you don't move your feet, I will split your skull with this." Papá whipped the mule with force and extreme anger many times, but the donkey remained motionless. "Bartolo! Leave him alone. You're making yourself crazy." Papá ignored Mamma. "I'll show him." He waved the cane in both hands and walked around to the mule's rear. Bartolo whipped him with continuous blows to his back and hips.

"Papà, maybe he is full. Look! Something is growing on the bottom! Look, Mamma."

"Bartolo, take a look. Tino is right. It's starting to all hang down on him!"

"*Ma è impossibile.* That's impossible. I whip his ass, and he shows me a hard-on?" Papá lifted his arms in despair and shook his head as he looked down at the donkey. "Papà, what's that thing for?" Exasperated, he slammed his hands to his sides with the cane in one hand. "Ask your mamma. I've had it."

"*E 'per fare la pipì figlio,* It's for peeing, son." Mamma said.

"That's why the donkey doesn't want to drink, Papá," I said. "He looks really full."

In complete frustration Papá slammed the cane down while saying, "Here, you deal with this ass; I've had it." Defeated, Papá turned away but not before having the last word. "Ma v*a fa in culo testardo, tu e Cristoforo Colombo!* Up your ass, you thick-headed beast, you and Christopher Columbus!" He rushed up the hill to the house without even looking back. Mamma took the reins, looked at the donkey, then clicked her tongue twice, and the donkey quickly followed her into the barn.

The next day, Antonia and Rocco, the couple that lived on the mountaintop in the converted army barracks, came to take the donkey. They needed many things; if anyone could use the animal, it was them. I was sure they had scraped bottom for whatever price they were paying Mamma and Papá.

Piccolo Santino

In return, the wife, a short, stocky woman whose head barely reached the backbone of the donkey, offered to perform a ritual to protect Papá from the *Malocchio* evil eye during his journey to America. Papá gave a slight laugh, Rocco, only a few inches taller than his wife, walked over to Bartolo to assure him that it would be a good thing even if he doubted the evil eye. "Bartolo, even if you don't believe in the malocchio. You should do it. You're going to America. You never know what can happen along the way."

"Oh, leave me in peace, will you. There are no devils here."

"Bartolo, I let her do that to me whenever we go to market. I don't like strangers staring at me." Antonia raised her arms and turned to Papá as she exclaimed, "He's a sly one! It's him that looks at the girls." She turned to her husband Rocco, who was turning red. "I tell you all the time *non puoi fottermi. You* can't fuck with me." They all laughed, and Antonia said, "Laugh all you want. Next time I'll just let the evil eye fuck your head up."

"Si! Si, but the women were looking at me first. They can't resist me."

"That's because it was all hanging on you. You were walking around with your pants torn at the seam." Everyone laughed more, and Antonia turned to Mamma. "Come on, Anna, get me a dish with water, bring some oil, and let's do this.

Mamma entered the house and quickly returned with a deep water dish and a small olive oil cup. Papá looked at Mamma and sarcastically exclaimed to Antonia, "You are serious about this?" Antonia insisted, "Just sit on the step there and be quiet!"

"Are you planning to dump the water on my head?"

"Bartolo, standstill as I do this, or I will." Papá sat down on the lower step to accommodate Antonia's vertical challenge as she moved close to him and held the dish over his head. She whispered inaudible chatter as she pushed the dish in slow circles, then brought the plate close to her and sprinkled drops of oil into the water, which coagulated into a cluster. Antonia repeated more chatter as she returned the plate above Papá's head and slowly moved it clockwise several times while

Piccolo Santino

whispering more seriously. Then she sped up the rant, and the water began to undulate. She brought the plate closer to her, sprinkled a few more drops of olive oil, and repeated the secret chatter faster. Papá remained calm. Antonia hovered to look into the dish, and the oil drops began to repel from each other and scatter. Antonia then carefully brought the plate to show Papa and said, "Now you can travel without any worries, Bartolo." Antonia turned to Mamma and said, "Did you see how the oil moved?"

"I saw it! That was scary." Papá stared at Rocco with a curious look, and Rocco responded with credulity, "I saw it too, Bartolo!"

"I think I felt rain on my head, not your shenanigans." Papá said. *"Va cacati va!* Go take a dump, Bartolo." Retorted Antonia. Rocco extended his arms and exclaimed, shaking his hands, "*Sporca miseria!* Good grief! The oil moved like waves in a storm at sea! What are you saying, Bartolo?" Antonia quickly and intentionally cleared her throat to interrupt her husband." Ahem. Let's go now, Rocco. What do you say?"

"Oh! Yes! Yes, let's go, now that we have a new ass to feed." Antonia, with sarcasm, said to Rocco, "Go on! You're the one being the ass now!" Rocco turned to Papá and asked, "Bartolo, *a proposito*; by the way, what's the name of the ship you are traveling on?"

"It's The Andrea Doria." Antonia interrupted again, responding, "Don't you guys worry anymore; all will be fine!" Mamma hugged Antonia, saying, "Thanks for getting rid of the malocchio, Antonia."

"It's the least I can do. You were kind to us also." Rocco grabbed the donkey's reins, and Antonia moved to join Rocco as she said, "Bartolo, we'll see you before you leave."

"*Va bene Antonia,* Very well, Antonia. Go home and feed your ass now."

"Ooh, you're as bad as my husband." Rocco looked back while pulling on the reins and said, "Arrivederci!"

"Go already, will you. Watch out! Your ass is taking a leak!"

"Ah! *Ma che cazzo!* What the fuck!" shouted Antonia as she stepped away from the splash of donkey urine and rushed to catch up to her husband while yelling, "*Aspettami,* wait for me, Rocco." Papá and

Piccolo Santino

Mamma laughed, and Papa shouted, "Maybe you can practice some of your magic on the donkey now."

"Come on, come, Rocco, let's get out of here. *Lui e pazzo,* He's crazy."

I lay on lush green grass that felt like fur underneath me. Like dying simmering coals, the heat from a sky filled with a tremendous volume of light. And infinite space spotted with prodigious bodies of pristine white foamy clouds, as if I laid on a blanket of warm ashes. I couldn't even sense the vast hardness of the earth underneath me as I lounged on its warm fur. This rural area behind the above-ground laundry pool where Mamma had just finished washing clothes felt alien and so new. I couldn't remember ever being there. It all felt so secretive, so hidden. I never understood why I had never been there before, all surrounded by brush with only one exit point by the poolside. I perceived this to be a secret corner at the end of the world. The spell was immediately broken, practically numbed by it all, and simultaneously glad that I could now imagine it at any time in my life. "Here, get up!" Mamma's voice cut through my quiet moment like a giant boulder falling on a cup. I lifted my head to see her hand holding the end of a rope as she continued talking. "Here, hold this rope while the cow grazes. You won't need to do anything else."

I sat up and took the reins from Mamma as she said, "Just hold on to the rope while you sit there." I sat on a small boulder and watched the heifer graze. I now remember seeing Mamma when she juggled the reins in her hands as she tried to hang clothes simultaneously before she asked me to help her. I could've take the reins from her but had concluded I was too young to control such a big animal, and the line was too high for me to hang clothes for her. She could have tied the cow to a tree, but there weren't any trees in this section, and then the heifer would be limited to a confined area. I clutched the rope tight, and it didn't feel heavy. So, it was an easy enough job for an eight-year-old. The heifer seemed pretty docile as it grazed on what appeared to be a delicious grass meal. As Mamma hung the laundry, I observed the construction of the line. The

Piccolo Santino

pole to the right was sunk straight into the earth, and the other was leaning backward. But it held up the weight of the wet clothes even as they gently fluttered.

Then the heifer suddenly took off, and I squeezed the reins tight and did not release for fear of defeat. I stayed silent, hoping I could regain control. But the heifer pulled me down and introduced my face to grass surfing as the heifer sped along. Earlier, I had thought of the grass as soft and fluffy. Now, its blades revealed another side, very sharp and stinging when they slapped me in the face. I felt tenacious and stupid as I refused to let go of the rope for fear of losing the cow and swallowing the sting of failure. I yelled loudly, and within seconds, the surfing stopped. I saw Mamma twisting the cow's head by its ears with such an exhibition of strength and determination that it opened my eyes wide and startled my thoughts to a standstill as I watched the heifer succumb like a bashful giant.

"Anna, where are you? Anna! Anna."

"I'm over here behind the pool." Papá came around and didn't look at my face. But I guess the grass did not scratch; otherwise, he would have said something, so I listened to their conversation. "I put the calf in front of the house, away from the heifer."

"I'm almost finished here."

"When you leave, take Tino with you."

"*Va bene*. All right, I'm all done. What do you want to do with the heifer?"

"I'll put her in the barn for now."

"*Andiamo Tino*. Come on, Tino. You are coming with me!" I didn't know where we were going but began to understand as Papá explained the price to Mamma. "Now, Anna, don't settle for a low price, alright?"

"*Va bene! Va bene!* All right, all right." To avoid the heifer seeing her calf, we left out the front gates and walked around our property line on the highway until we reached the straightaway heading south. After about a half hour's walk, Mamma cut into the country landscape for the occasional shade from the trees on this hot day. We came across a very shallow part of a stream and stopped to rest. A woman there finishing her

Piccolo Santino

laundry talked with Mamma as she thought we might also be there to do the same. The conversation was friendly, and it felt unusual as it all sounded like a very friendly chit-chat amongst strangers meeting for the first time.

It soon became evident she was being warm in trying to find out if we could be new neighbors. The woman placed her laundry basket on her head and said goodbye as she left. Mamma handed me the rope to the calf as it drank in the stream, and she walked over to a brush and came back with some blades of sugar cane to snack on. The taste was tender and sweet, and I wondered why we seldom ate them if they grew so rampant in the countryside.

We reached the outskirts of the market square in what felt like hours after leaving the house. I looked around, as the outskirts seemed pretty sparse with vendors, but once we got inside, the area was well populated by merchants with their stands and a swollen atmosphere of people that made for the feeling of a traditional feast but lacking the religious paraphernalia. Still, this gathering exposed me to many more vending sights and a more business atmosphere than a usual feast.

I looked around for a cow section, and then Mamma led the way behind the façade of a stand. However, my attention became glued to the glimmer of toys on shelves, the likes of which I never dreamed. Now, here they were, all in front of me. As Mamma engaged in a seemingly animated conversation about a potential sale, my interest remained fixed on a black and white checkered soccer ball. But I also thought about its probable cost, possibly about half of what the calf could garner, and then I sensed that Mamma didn't come all this way to trade a calf for a soccer ball. "The calf is too young to be sold, Signora. I can't give you that much."

"Oh, can't you do a little better?"

"I tell you what. If you don't get a better offer, you can return."

"All right, fair enough." I was glad we were moving on because this failure provided another opportunity to convey my thoughts to Mamma. I dallied and stared into stands as we passed them. "What are you staring at? Come on. We don't have all day!" I rushed to catch up, and Mamma

Piccolo Santino

turned next to a small corral and stopped in front of two men exchanging money. The man with the most money in his hands turned to Mamma. "Buongiorno Signora."

"Buongiorno *Massaro,* herdsman, will you make an offer for my calf?" The man took a few steps toward the calf, thought for a moment, rubbed his chin with his left hand, and said, "That calf seems much too young for the market, Signora."

"What do you mean too young?"

"I can't possibly make you an offer. This calf will still look for its mother for at least another six weeks or more!"

"Ah, you don't know what you're talking about."

"All right, I'll give you a few hundred lire then."

"A few hundred lire? You gotta be kidding!"

"Take it or leave it."

"Go stick it in your ear!"

"Va bene," said the man. Mamma took a look nearby, then turned the calf around, and we headed back the other way. I hesitated, and Mamma pulled on my arm, and I almost tripped. She hollered out, *"Che cazzo guardi?* What the hell are you looking at?" I regained my balance as we raced back to the first vendor. Even though the calf was too young for a good sale, this guy was at least nice about it. Mamma took the offer, and I saw hope for my soccer ball. The only problem was getting Mamma to read my mind, for indeed, I didn't dare speak out.

Mamma put away the money inside a snapping purse and immediately rushed me off. I kept looking back to the stand with the soccer ball, and as Mamma increased her pace, I began whimpering and dragging my feet. I then spotted the same ball at another display next to us and raised my whimper to an annoying cry, but Mamma kept walking, so I let go of her hand, planted my feet, and intensified my crying. Mamma turned to me and asked, "*Cosa hai?* What's the matter?" I cried some more, hoping she would get the message. "But what is it?" she complained.

I realized I'd have to say something, so I blurted out, *"A palla.* A

Piccolo Santino

ball." She stared into my face with stretched disbelief and said, *"A palla? A ball?"* Mamma looked around and then back to me, asking, "You want a ball?" I nodded my head, "Yes," but my heart told me it wasn't going to happen even though Mamma ushered me to the stand. She looked about, picked up a pink handball, and held it up close to my face. "Is this what you want?" I shook my head, "No," and cried harder. "Then tell me which ball you want!"

I pointed to the soccer ball, and as if her eyeballs sprung out of her head, she said, "No! Not that one. If you want it, you can have this one." I shook my head "No" real fast. "No? *Va bene!* Well then!" She handed the handball back to the vendor. *"Dai Andiamo!* Come on, let's go." I intensified my crying and refused to move. "If you want to cry, then cry over this!" Mamma slapped my face so quick and complex that it not only stung my cheek but stopped my crying and left me practically brain-dead all the way home.

Gumbah Angelo's family and ours gathered for a family picnic one last time on his farm. White tablecloths were laid out in the field, and we all shared food and wine on a hot spring day. The crops had all been sown weeks ago. And much of the corn and wheat crop had begun to sprout. Today, we all helped cultivate the potato plants and tomatoes. After everybody finished eating, Gumbah Angelo handed Lola a bucket of plant roots to bring to the barn to feed the hogs. I liked Lola as she was friendly, and I remembered her best for coming to my defense during the pig slaughter when my sisters were making fun of my stuttering. Now, she invited me to walk up to the barn with her. The barn was a good walk away, and after a reasonable distance from the picnic, Lola began asking me questions. I spoke my words carefully, hoping to avoid stuttering, and I felt lucky as I rarely stuttered with Lola. "Your Mamma told you that long thing under the donkey was just to pee with?"

"Ah si, but how did you know about that?"

"My parents were talking about it the other day. We were all laughing hard."

"Why was everybody laughing?"

Piccolo Santino

"It gets that big on donkeys and even bigger on bulls. But not on men!"

"Is that why mine doesn't get big like that when I drink water?"

"Ah, hah, hah, you're funny! When that thing gets like that, it's for other things! Not for peeing."

"What things?"

"Things grownups do on their wedding night." Lola got my attention fast. "What are you saying? What do they do?"

"I can show you inside."

"What's inside the barn?"

"You want to see what grownups do when they're alone?" This sounded like an excellent learning time since I sometimes wondered about the sexes. But it felt sinful, and I became concerned that I would lose a power I might never get back if I surrendered. But the idea of learning such a big secret was too alluring to pass up. "Yes, I want to learn." I said, "First, help me fill another food bucket for the hogs."

"All right then." We went to the side of the barn, and Lola lifted a thatched straw lid to a storage compartment constructed as an attachment to the barn. Inside was a heap of corn husks, and we filled the bucket. "*Be tutto è a posto!* All ready! Now let's go inside."

She carried both buckets to the entrance and put them down to undo the rope latch that had secured the door; I held it open for Lola so she could manage the buckets and followed her as the door closed. I felt my way through the dark using the different smells and grunting of the hogs and the cackling of some chickens scattering about. The darkness felt eternal for the eyes to adjust. Then, the rush of Lola dumping the bucket of corn husks and plant roots over the wood railing brought on louder grunting from the hogs that prompted my ears to help my mind picture where the noise was in that murky atmosphere.

I could hear the few hogs rush toward the scattered food as if fighting each other for a bite. That's when Lola held my hand and pulled me close. I very much preferred the smell of her sweat through her clothes to the barn smells. The warm feeling of her hand tingled inside me as she led me deeper into the dark.

Piccolo Santino

I was just eight years old, and she was fifteen, and now I was going to learn secret things from her. She let go of my hand, and I breathed the wind of her motions as she climbed the stable railing and leaned over to the wall. I listened to her sounds and then heard rattling against the wall, and the light peered through a crack. Like a radiant flame, the sunlight burst into the room, creating a mesmerizing display of sun rays that danced through the open window. They formed a large, cone-shaped pattern traveling to the floor, capturing millions of specks that twinkled like stars in a night sky. The simple joy of the scene was so dense and yet so weightless, it seemed to be held in a friendly, transparent embrace. "Santino, what are you doing?" Lola said as I listened to her rustling on the heap of hay by my feet.

Overwhelmed by the unique quality of the sunlight that entered through the window, I found myself staring at the heavenly strings as they gently vibrated, like the strings of a harp. It was a burn that passed through time, a silent melody humming within the arresting cone shape, as if an angel had suddenly appeared. The light, so new and impossible to touch, seemed to be saying, *'This is what the sun hides outside in total light, but you need a window into a dark room to reveal the soul of that light.'* It was as if the light of movies was coming through the movie machine, but this light was alive, arriving in the color of egg yolk sifted through an invisible strainer. It made me forget about Lola until I heard her calling again.

"Santino, look down here," But I was transfixed in that aura of light. My eyes kept following the path of those flimsy strings dangling from infinity, traveling so mystical and swift to shine on these strands of hay in a heap on this barn floor. I remained awed, watching millions of dust particles dancing inside that euphoric yellow cage, continually capering at lightning speed. Like sparks in an open fire, and yet, at the same time, all feeling like swelling in slow motion. However, my eyes feasted on the light. I was humble as battered lint in a hurricane and yet felt the weight of a glacier inside me. I felt frozen with reverence for the origin. "Santino, look here, come down by me!"

I looked down at Lola. She was without underwear as she lifted her

Piccolo Santino

dress to her waist for a different revelation about where legs converge and what clothes hide. I felt my body sink to the floor with my shorts as she pulled me down and guided me between her thighs. She pulled me toward her, and I knew not what to do, so I lay there in the warm feeling of her body as she said, "This is what big people do on their wedding night." She reached for me down below. And this moment might be a spell of warm rain falling through the window from a sun shower. During that spell, my eyes remained closed, and then I heard her move away, so I rose to my knees and sat on the back of my heels as she got up. Without warning, I heard the light go out at the sound of the window closing, and then Lola's voice, "Santino, get up! We gotta go now." Feeling somewhat incoherent, I slowly got up while pulling on my shorts. In that dark, I opened my eyes as my lips spoke back, "That light was beautiful, Lola!"

"*Dai! Santino andiamo.* Come on! Santino, let's go!"

The sweet voice of her calling caressed me, making me feel like a baby in a cradle. I thought about the light that had entered through the window and also what I had learned from Lola. I said to her, "Lola! It's so dark again?" She grabbed my hand and said, "Santino! Come on, let's go!"

I stared into the darkness, thinking that what I had just learned about light could not lift the guilt about what I had given up today just to learn something from Lola. I wondered if I might have been better off waiting to know it, on my own accord, later in my life. I thought, for now, I could hate myself to make the guilt go away. Then she pulled me forward into the light outside.

Piccolo Santino

Chapter 14 of Part One
May 1956, Moving day from the farm

Moving day arrived abruptly, and we found ourselves loading our furniture onto a large wagon, now hitched to two cows, the second heifer Gumbah Angelo purchased from Papá. The thought of visiting Lola and her family from Jonadi during our two years before leaving for America was a futile attempt to console me. The reality of our shared farm life coming to an end, and the realization that brief visits from town could not restore what we once had, hit me hard.

Marco was on top of the cart, placing one of the new chairs inside a barrel. Mamma insisted on hiding it so that the mayor would not come for the sales tax when we rode through town since his office was indirectly across from our new home. Papá and Gumbah Angelo wrapped a rope around the contents to secure them, and I watched his wife and daughters cry into their handkerchiefs as they waited to say goodbye. I looked at Lola, sensed her absence, and hoped she would occasionally visit us. We all said our goodbyes with all the furniture loaded, and I particularly liked when Lola kissed me on the cheek.

As Mamma and Giustina wept and embraced, I felt the weight of our departure. The late morning sun cast a somber light as Papá settled us on top of the wagon, Mamma and Papá following on foot, taking turns holding Enzo. I felt a mix of anticipation and anxiety as I sat next to Gumbah Marco, the driver, and listened to his call, 'Are we all ready?'

"Si Gumbah, we can go." Gumbah Marco cracked his whip, and the two cows pulled the cart up the driveway. I watched Lola and her family wave a sullen goodbye before they turned down the walkway for their walk home through the land where we once lived.

Up the driveway, we went through the opened iron gates onto the highway headed toward Jonadi. At first, I wondered if everything would slide off the wagon, but once we were rolling on the paved road, I felt more secure yet frustrated as the contents blocked any view of the

Piccolo Santino

shrinking past.

I looked down at the laboring cows. I became fascinated with their hips and shoulders up and down motion—the motion as their legs alternated between lifting and planting their hoofs. I looked to my right to see if the landscape would show the same stop-and-go action. I glanced back down and surmised it had to be the unyielding, steady commitment of the cows, acting in unison with the rolling wagon wheels that made the landscape pass by so smoothly. It is combined into a balanced mixture of fundamental contradictions that act in concert to move us forward.

It made me think of the movie machine I saw in the square when Papá once brought me to the feast. The device also had two wheels that turned with a loud noise. Then, a light came on, and black and white pictures moved on a large sheet that hung between two balconies across from each other in the square. I looked back at the source of that large cone of light and saw changes in light density that flickered fast as if it was stopping and starting, just like the cow's hoofs stopped and moved but at a more unhurried pace than the movie light.

My anticipation grew as we approached the corner by the sawmill. The cows, sensing the turn, began to slow down. I observed the contrast in their movements, the inner cow restless, the outer cow moving with a more coordinated pace to negotiate the left turn. The softer sound of their hooves on the dirt road was a stark contrast to the previous hard clanking steps on the highway. In less than half an hour, we arrived in Nao. As we rode through, I couldn't help but feel self-conscious about our personal belongings stacked on top for all to see. I focused on the sound of the cow's hooves hitting the cobblestone street, the distinct sound of the wagon wheels, and the frustrating rattle of the stones against the wagon. Gumbah called out to Papá. "Gumbah, is everything okay up on top?"

"Don't worry, everything is fine!" Once outside of Nao, the ride was smooth again, and the sun had been warm, not overbearing, as we rode off the cobblestone and onto the hard dirt road. We were on the hill approaching the small bridge of the inroad to Jonadi. Marco was now applying the brakes on and off for the first time. It scared me a little each time I heard the loud rubbing against the wheels. We made it safely to the bottom, and this turn was more cranky and sharp than the turn by the sawmill.

Past the bridge was a repeat of the bumpy-noisy ride from the cobblestone street. We rode past my school, and I was glad the kids were absent. The wagon had to make another sharp turn at the bend just past the school, and this time, the cow on the right did the haphazard work as the turn was short and tightly flanked by buildings. Beyond the bend was a clearing to the left with a small square, and a few people gathered at the public water fountain, filling their pitchers. One woman washing a few clothes looked up at us. I decided to get used to it because this is where we would be coming for our water supply, and I could also wash my face and ears on the way to school in the morning.

As we rode past the mayor's office that Mamma was worried about, Papá ran ahead of us, rushing his stride. I felt the end of our trip as he reached into his pocket for the key. He opened the door to our new home and called out to Gumbah Marco: "Gumbah Marco, you can stop the cart here close to the house."

"*Va bene Gumbah*! Very well, Gumbah." Gumbah helped me down, and then my sisters and brother. We moved some small items off the wagon, and then Papá came out of the house cursing. "*Cazzo di Macellaio!* Fuck'n butcher! He didn't move his stuff out." Mamma reacted quickly. "C*azzo di cornuto!* That fuck'n cuckold! Now, what do we do?"

"Let's get all the stuff inside the main room first." The oversized items were the main bed, the small bed, a crib, a dresser, the giant metal round portable fireplace, a small family table, and four chairs. Two of them were new.

Mamma was funny. As Marco and Papá carried the chairs in, she called out to them, "Hurry with those chairs. The mayor's office is right there." After Papá and Marco set up the big bed and furniture, there was no space left for the small bed in the main room. So, Papá propped the frame and mattress in a corner. Papá and Marco carried the two big barrels downstairs from the outside stairway to the right of the house. Marco bid us goodbye at that point, and I watched him climb the cart and

Piccolo Santino

guide the cows into the turn for their way back.

A man with a large body and broad, unshaven face sporting the attitude of a riled bull rushed up to Papá and started sputtering words. "You can't just throw me out like this!"

"I told you and the carpenter when I moved back into my house three months ago. You were supposed to be out of here already. The carpenter didn't have a problem understanding me."

"My new place isn't ready, yet I need a few more weeks."

"You get your stuff out of here by tomorrow. I need that room for my family!"

"*Dove cazzo vado?* Where the fuck do I go? You can't just do this to me!"

"You think so? The carpenter had no problem vacating. This is my house, and you were given plenty of notice."

"But why can't you be reasonable with me!"

"You are the one that needs to be reasonable. I have a wife and seven children to take care of."

"I can't believe this."

"Now, you either clear out your stuff by tomorrow, or I'll get the marshal!" As the butcher left, his anger still palpable, I followed Papá inside the house where Mamma was seated in the rocking chair holding Enzo. The unity of our family was evident as Papá stood over Mamma and Enzo, so I went back outside. Within minutes, Papá rushed down the street in a real hurry. I walked down the stairway to check out the dirt patio overlooking the bottom of the hill where a row of houses was clustered together, and I saw a door under the butcher's room, but it had a padlock on it. I also saw a door under our main room, and that was locked, too. Upon returning upstairs, I saw Papá rush inside behind the old Doctor Itasca, and quickly, my brother and sisters were all asked to stay outside.

Martina came out with a blank look on her face, and the other kids followed behind. We assembled away from the door. Dusk approached, and two women walked toward the house, one older and the other in her

Piccolo Santino

early twenties. The younger woman began talking to Martina and me. "You two must be Martina and Santino."

"Si," we both responded. "I am your cousin Stefania, and this is your aunt Ernestina. Tell me, is Uncle Bartolo inside?" Martina answered quickly. "Si! The doctor is in there, too. Papá told us not to go inside."

"*Oh, Dio Mio!* Oh, Dear God!" expressed Aunt Ernestina. Stefania turned to her mother and said, "What do you say, Madre? Should we go inside?"

"*Perché no?* Why not. The poor baby! We should go and see. Come on." They entered the house, and moments later, the doctor came outside and turned to Papá standing in the doorway. His words hung heavy in the air as he quietly said, "You might as well dress him in his death clothes. Come morning. I don't think he will see the light of day."

The old doctor walked away in solitude, and Papá signaled from the doorway for us to go inside. Once inside, we saw Aunt Ernestina and Cousin Stefania solemnly standing beside Mamma. Mamma was holding Enzo close to her chest in her rocking chair, surrounded by the unwavering support of her family. Aunt Ernestina leaned down and whispered to Mamma, "He said for sure it is meningitis?"

"Yes, he's sure!" Mamma cried, her voice trembling with fear, as she held Enzo close to her chest. "The doctor is coming back early in the morning. He said everything would be fine if the baby is still alive by then." The uncertainty of the situation hung heavy in the air. Papá stood in front of Aunt Ernestina and Stefania and said, "Then it's okay for Martina and Santino to sleep at your place for one or two nights until the butcher moves out?"

"Si, Bartolo, don't even think about it," responded Aunt Ernestina. "Uncle, we are only happy to help you," said cousin Stefania. Aunt Ernestina said to Mamma and Papá, "We will pray for your son tonight. And Bartolo, we will pray that all will go well for you also. God knows how much you have done when you were away at war."

Martina slept in the same bed with Stefania and Aunt Ernestina. I could have slept in the same makeshift bed on top of a trunk like this at home, but now I wonder if that was a ploy to keep us away for the night

Piccolo Santino

in case Enzo did die. Early the next morning, Aunt Ernestina and cousin Stefania accompanied us to our new home. We witnessed the doctor walk out of our house with his medical bag, exclaiming in total bewilderment, "It's unbelievable! This is a miracle!" While looking up to the sky and shaking his head in disbelief, he rushed past us without eye contact. We entered the house, and Mamma was in the rocking chair nursing Enzo. We learned she never got up even once all night.

The butcher returned early the following morning with his broad sulking face, and Papá turned to him as he unlocked the padlock to his enterprise. Two other men and a woman accompanied him, and they began loading wooden wheelbarrow-type carts outside with various items out of our soon-to-be bedroom. Within ten minutes, they evacuated the entire room. The butcher left with a lasting stinging comment. "You have managed to evict me. Goodbye!" Papá responded, "Yeah, all right! Now go!" Papá scrubbed that room to get blood stains and odors out, and by midday, the bed was all set up for Lillo and me to sleep.

The first night in my bed again, I felt strange but comfortable after sleeping at my aunt's house. It wasn't the old house with the familiar quiet at night. This new home hosted so many local sounds that sleep became laborious. Loud voices called out inside other dwellings, "*Ora Cosa stai facendo?* Now, what are you doing?"

Or a person was sneezing, and a child was crying loudly. Then, there was the sound of a door banging from across the street, with a thick silence afterward or the occasional noisy passerby. These noises reverberated my loneliness, making the new surroundings feel like an intruder. One that reality is woven with fate to ring in the change. But there were also soothing sounds, such as church bells or the late commuter coming home from his farm on his mule or cow-drawn cart. I liked best waking up to the sound of hooves clip clapping, with the rolling of the squeaky wheel on the cobblestone street. Sometimes, there was even the familiar sound of a rooster crowing down the hill across from us. But it was no longer the constant as it once was in the country.

On cold nights, we sat around the fireside and told stories that would be interrupted by church bells, and Mamma reminded us to make the sign

Piccolo Santino

of the cross. If the death toll rang, everyone in town could hear it, no matter what church it rang from. Then, we would talk about how the shadow of death could crawl under our door and sneak up behind us. We kept the conversation until one of us worked up enough courage to go and lock the door. Then, we felt comfortable and quickly changed the subject.

Our cat, Carbone, found a new place to rest her body at night, and although my feet liked the warmth, my mind could not deal with the sudden gripping sensation that forced my feet to jerk upward quickly. I preferred waking up to squeaking wagon wheels, with the plodding of hooves and or the church bells. I even liked the sound of splashing water when a neighbor emptied the wash pan by tossing the water onto the street, followed by a greeting of *Buongiorno*. But it bothered me when Mamma emptied our pan and hoped that the neighbors would engage her in a long conversation because I knew she would force me out of bed when she returned inside.

I took walks and liked seeing how the town unfolded in the morning. Doors opened and closed with people exiting. The sight of a woman wrapping her house key in a towel. Then I watched her hide it under a removable stone, inside a hole at the base of the doorframe—the flapping of a bed sheet or tablecloth from a balcony or emptying a urinal pot. I once witnessed a passerby scream as a woman accidentally dumped her urinal pot on his hat while he passed under her balcony. His screaming was most animated, and her response was very nonchalant as the man scolded her. In her retort, she called him stupid for walking under balconies. She squared her shoulders, lifted her nose, swayed her body back inside, and slammed her door.

I liked the gushing sound of water from the public fountain. But when I encountered a crowd by the public fountain, it often disturbed my composure. As I waited my turn, I pretended to make the people magically disappear by blinking my eyes. Then, two women washing clothes apologized and stepped aside so I could drink from the spout. I felt guilty as I walked away without thanking them because I could not gather the courage to speak to strangers.

Piccolo Santino

Papá was to embark on the *SS Andrea Doria* in June and was in town with us for only a week or so. As I watched him pack his trunk, I tried ways to prepare myself for his absence. The night he left in late May, one of Papá's cousins who lived across from us would accompany him to Naples. We were all seated in the main room. Mamma was in her rocking chair with Enzo in her arms. I was sitting on a small step stool, and my brother and two sisters were on the long bench. Stella was seated in a chair, and our youngest sister, Fabrizzia, sat on another chair beside Mamma. Papá gathered his suitcase and trunk, and his cousin Eugenio helped him carry it outside into a car.

I thought about Grandpa not being around to reward me for my name day. After the familiar tugging of my ear, I felt obligated to inform him that he would be missing out on the opportunity. "Nonno, now you can't pull on my ear."

"*Che dici?* What are you saying?"

"For my name day."

"*E perché no?* And why not?"

"Because you're going with Papá."

"Don't worry. It's only in a couple of days from now. I can still do it." He hesitated and waited to sneak up on me, grabbed my left ear, and at once said, "*Adesso!* Now!" He tugged on my earlobe so hard it created a sharp and lasting pain. I then wished I had kept my mouth shut and debated if the small coin he gave me was worth the pain.

Papá came back inside, and Mamma got up from her rocking chair. "The time has come, Anna."

"*Si veramente.* Yes, for real. You be careful and make sure you send me a telegram as soon as you arrive in America."

"*Si cara.* Yes, dear. Don't worry, I will." They hugged with a hearty kiss, and then Papá made his round for kissing all us children one by one. I looked up at him as he spoke to me, "Ciao Tino. Figlio Mio. Bye Tino. My son." I watched him turn away and go out the door. I felt numb from emotion as I thought back to all those days we waited for this moment, and it all felt anticlimactic. I kept thinking, now we wait the two years until we see him again. Mamma told us to stay inside. This way of saying goodbye didn't feel so bad, and I found comfort in the solace of the situation.

Piccolo Santino

Piccolo Santino

Table of contents

Chapter	PART II	Page
	Introduction of Part II	**131**
1	Life without Papá, the first 30 days	132
2	Getting used to the carpenter shop	159
3	Exploring the old barracks	165
4	Anguish befalls best friends	190
5	Last year of school in Italy	204
6	Building a Baby Coffin	234
7	The final preparations for America	245
8	Move to Nanna's and on to Naples	256
9	Eight days on board the MS Giulio Cesare	279
10	Our new home in America	287
11	School in America	305
12	Outside and playing Damsel in Distress	311
13	Going to work early in life	318
14	Trouble can follow good work too	325
15	Fifth grade in America	335
16	Return to Fontana Di Taccuni	355
	Acknowledgements	357
	About the Author	358

Piccolo Santino

Piccolo Santino

Piccolo Santino
Part II

The flight attendant walked over to my seat leaned in and said "Excuse me sir, would you like a beverage?" I politely refuse, "No thank you." I turn my head and gaze at the sunset.

Piccolo Santino

Chapter 1 of Part Two, 1956
Life without Papá, the first 30 days

Morning arrived with the weight of Papá's absence on my mind. As I was getting dressed, I worried about how Mamma would provide for us and not get crazy. I figured it would unfold one day at a time, and once we made it past the first day, the others would unfold. This thought brought me some peace.

A foul smell hit me in the face just as I turned right after stepping out the door. Today, I planned to explore what was about the top of this mountainous street up ahead to my left that got my attention that first day we moved into Jonadi. I bit down on a chunk of bread I had grabbed from the breadbox, but the foul smell in the air forced me to put it back in my pocket for later. I slowly made my way into the small crowd gathered around a trench dug up at the end of our house, right at the corner where I needed to turn left. A long terracotta sewer pipe from the bar had burst, and it joined with a thicker, longer line partially exposed in the trench. Workers were digging around it as onlookers held handkerchiefs over their nostrils.

Some women had lifted their aprons over their mouths to filter the smell of human waste floating in the trench. I guessed that whatever it was inside that they used to squat on, for those fortunate enough to afford it, was what drained into these pipes. But this was a bar, and they could undoubtedly afford indoor facilities. I wondered what a price for all to pay with such a fate. I then considered how I enjoyed the lack of indoor facilities back home on the farm we just moved from. We used to go outside on the side of the house, exposed to the world yet feeling secluded and private despite the vast openness. Suddenly, I felt special because I had such privileges in the open air. Papá used to rake the waste and mix it with freshly dug soil to help it decay into usable fertilizer. Somehow, that appeared more practical than risking a broken sewer pipe by exposing such a smelly secret to so many people, all watching

Piccolo Santino

simultaneously.

This stinky atmosphere all seemed so embarrassing. I observed the workers in the muddy trench. At least they portrayed an aura of humility and respect. I wondered if God could have come up with a different way for the living to process their waste. I walked away and turned left for the uphill climb, leaving the situation to the crowd of people still observing. Mamma had once sent me to look for Papá at this bar. Although I didn't find him at this location, I remember going in there with him once.

I looked toward the top for the steep climb and decided to make a game of my steps by walking only on the cobblestones and avoiding the joints. After a short rise, the effort became too laborious, and I abandoned the idea as I became fixed in the mystery that lurked on the hilltop. I studied the road as it bent around behind a cluster of buildings like it was sinking into a secret place. From behind those buildings, long, hard shadows of two people seared down on the cobblestone-like a slice of theatrics, accompanied by the melodic sound of small hoofs echoing as they clip-clapped and bleated into view.

Two women walked out with a goat and descended as I ascended toward the top. As we crossed paths halfway up the hill, I noticed rosaries dangling from a partially torn pocket on the older woman's apron as she balanced a basket on her head. The younger woman was leading the black and white goat by a rope. I kept to the right of the street as they kept to the center of it. They seemed preoccupied, and I figured they must be going to their farm. The rosaries slid down, and I tried calling out to them, but my fear only permitted me to utter a stutter.

When the woman turned, she noticed my pointing at them. But the goat was lifting the beads off the ground with its tongue. I pointed to the goat, and the older woman looked down and gasped, *"Dio Mio!* Oh my God! The goat is eating my rosaries!" The younger woman gave a sudden jerk on the rope, and the goat inhaled most of the beads as others rolled down the street.

"But how did it happen?" asked the young woman. "They must've fallen out of my apron." She put her hand in her apron, and her index finger stuck through the torn pocket. The younger woman forced open

Piccolo Santino

the goat's mouth to look inside but came up empty and said, "Now, what are we going to do?"

"What are we going to do about what? The goat or my rosaries?" said the older woman. "For both, I guess," answered the young woman. *"Cosa possiamo fare?* What can we possibly do? We can't even pray for the goat since she ate my rosaries!" The younger woman asked, "What do you think will happen to her?"

"What can happen? Except I guess she will be taking a holy crap," said the older woman. The younger one responded, *"Non parlate così!* Don't talk like that!"

"Vieni, andiamo. Come on, let's go," the older woman said. She looked toward me while they walked away. "But why didn't that little boy say something right away instead of just pointing with his finger?" The younger woman looked at me, quickly turned to her companion, and whispered, "He seems deaf and dumb to me!"

I turned away and thought this incident would have ended differently if I had been bold enough to call out. But I was always too afraid to show my voice. I kept at a silent traveling pace from this chance meeting and separation of us strangers. I mumbled under my breath several times over while holding my head down. *"Sei stupido! Stupido!* You stupid! You stupid idiot!" Embarrassed, I waited for their voices to trail away and then ran to the top of the street behind the buildings and felt swallowed up in cool air by the shady street. I paused and reached in my pocket for my bread as I moved to the sunny side of the road, still ashamed of not having dared to speak. With my arms in the air, I decided to prove that I could talk problem-free by exclaiming, "Excuse me, Signora, your rosaries are falling out of your apron!" I bit down on my bread.

"E! Cosa hai detto? Huh! What did you say?" A male voice startled me from inside the shade across to my right. I saw an old man clinging to the wall as he hopped out from his doorway on one leg. With my mouth full, I stuttered two words in his direction, "N-*n-n-Niente s-s-s-signore! n*-n-n-nothing s-s-sir!" he looked stupefied at me and responded, "Ah, you're eating bread, and I have nothing." A woman came out with a chair

Piccolo Santino

and placed it by his side so he could sit. I gathered the poor guy must have been a victim of the First World War, and the younger woman, somehow, perhaps a victim of the Second War, as her black drabs suggested. I lingered on my journey past this house as my thoughts about these people weighed me down more than my issues.

Someone up ahead in the next house must have been cooking kale. I could smell the water they discarded in the gutter. I crossed over to avoid the stench, only to be confronted by the urine smell. The smell forced me to put my bread back in my pocket again and looked up at the balcony above, and I saw water dripping from hanging plants, a sign somebody had just dumped their piss pot, then overflowed their plants to camouflage the act. I decided to keep to the middle of the street. I realized this was a cross street to the other side of town.

I liked how the mystery unraveled through this tight, chilly street, with its shadows reminiscent of the tunnel-like ravine back on the farm where Martina and I were once accosted. Only this place had no such danger, and instead, I was led into a wide-open square up ahead, and of course, where there was a square, there was usually a church. This site was the piazza where Papá brought me to a feast for the first time one night. I remembered the orchestra playing on stage in the center of the square. That time, Papá conversed with musicians walking about and asked them if they would perform "La Traviata." They retorted, "Perhaps, maybe The Barber of Seville!" and all broke out laughing.

I looked at two mannequins on a shoe stand. One was headless and wearing an unfinished jacket in front of a tailor shop. They both seemed to be staring at me as I walked past them. I ventured further out into the hot, open space of the piazza, which was lit by sharp sunlight. I stopped at the spot where I tasted watermelon for the first time. I looked toward the church across the square and watched its elegance rise into the hot sky with extra-wide marble steps below looking inviting. This church was also the last stop for the dead as it stood in the path to the cemetery beyond another hilltop populated by rows of poplar trees. I poked about as the aroma of watermelon haunted my senses. I also reminisced about Papá's tobacco when he rolled a cigarette here. I liked how he greeted

Piccolo Santino

Strangers with a direct, honest, confident approach and how they responded by holding their heads and shoulders up high, eager to interact with him. The watermelon man was willing to please us as he cut out a small square and held it up to display the red juicy pulp.

I thought to myself sobbingly, *Papà! Papà! Oh papà! Two years is too long,* I rushed into the exit on the right as it curved around a bend between two walls. The right wall rose above me, descended, and turned sharply, concaving as it bent to the left before leveling and turning right. I studied that wall's cement and stone construction and liked the occasional splash of pastel colors. I was fascinated by how the left wall embanked the piazza and mirrored the curvature of the opposite wall before it stretched across to host the top of a descending road flanked by homes that met the main avenue crossing at the bottom. The bar where I found my papá that night he carried me home is smack in the center of the crossroad.

I paused in front of the bar a moment before turning left and headed toward the smoke shop diagonally across my school and directly across the home of our former landlord, Doctor Itasca. The street narrowed significantly in this vicinity. It always felt cold, as if all shadows lived there.

I heard the voices of some school kids as I walked around the bend and saw my friends, Franco and Nino, playing a war game across from the school. Franco blew into a straw, and a paper missile launched out and barely missed Nino. Franco reloaded and ducked as Nino fired back and also missed. The two rushed to retrieve their missiles, and Nino was first to fire back and hit Franco in the leg. He shouted aloud, "I win! I win! I got you in the leg!"

I took a deep breath, hoping that all my words would come out smoothly in one breath, and shouted back, "*Aspetta.* Wait. Not so fast." They stopped and turned toward me. I took another deep breath to utter the following words: "A wound is not a kill." I paused again, and they turned toward me as I said, "Franco should be allowed to at least fire back once." Wide-eyed, Franco looked at me and said, "Bravo, Bianchi! I like how you think." I breathed and said to Nino, "Nino, because you are not wounded, you can move around as you shoot back. But Franco cannot move around while he shoots."

"Mi piace così anche a me! I like it that way, too," Nino responded as he fired his missile. It sagged to the ground while Franco shot him in the groin, and we all enjoyed hearty laughter. Nino then suggested, "Why don't we take Santino exploring in the countryside." Franco asked me, "Santino, would you like to go with us?"

"Sì andiamo"

"Allora Andiamo!" they both replied. We walked around the bend between buildings with the smoke shop to our right, and the midmorning sun hit our faces. We squinted briefly, and when we approached the Mayor's office, I turned my head to music playing from a window in the Mayor's office. "What! They have an orchestra inside this house here?" Surprised, Franco said, "No, Santino, that's a radio."

"A radio? What's that?"

"It's a special box with parts plugged into electricity. Then you turn it on to hear sounds from it."

"Who is making the music?"

"They are playing music from another city at the same time."

"Oh," I said, and then I noticed by the bar that the trench was all covered up now. *They worked pretty fast I thought.* From the corner of my eye diagonally across us, I also saw Mamma sitting on a chair and breastfeeding Enzo. My sisters and brother were seated on the steps to the basement area. Mamma shouted out at me. "Where are you running off to now?"

"We are going for a walk in the country."

"Did you go to church?"

"Ah, always with the church!"

"*Ah per davvero?* Is that so? Then get home early, and I'll have dinner ready for you on two dishes."

"*Come è possibile esso?* How is that possible? You don't even have two dishes to your name." She pulled Enzo away from her, leaned to her right, and lifted an olive stick at me. *"Vieni qui scostumato!* Come here,

[137]

Piccolo Santino

you immoral!" While shaking her stick, she angrily said, "I'll show you two dishes with this stick." I responded while chuckling with my friends, "There's no church today, Mamma. It's not Sunday."

"You have to go to church whenever I tell you to," she said as she lowered the stick, and my friends both exclaimed, "Your mamma is tough!" I looked at Mamma as we walked past and said to her, "Si! Si!" then I turned to my friends and said as I picked up my pace, "*Andiamo,* let's hurry, guys."

We rushed away and came to the last building in town to the right. As we walked farther down, there was a vast natural limestone mountainous wall with two huge caves. We kept walking toward another set of limestone caves that were a bit smaller with lower ceilings and climbed to the right of these caves into the countryside. At the first sound of rustling in the brush and trees, Nino and Franco reached into their back pockets for their slingshots and then selected stones for ammunition. Franco fired the first shot into a tall tree, and Nino followed suit. "Santino, you don't have your slingshot?" asked Franco. "No, I don't have one," I responded, then said, "I can throw stones while you guys shoot." Franco said, "No, Santino."

"Why don't we make him one?" Nino answered, "Yeah, my Papá has an old bicycle tube from which we can make the rubber strips."

"Good, and I can get string at my house," Franco said. "All right. Let's look for a wood frame while we head back." We looked around in the brush and on tree branches for a small "Y" shaped branch. Franco was quick to choose and broke one off from a low-lying branch. He then pulled out a pocket knife and began to trim the ends, and by the time we made it back to my house, Franco had all the bark removed.

Nino ran to his house, and Franco invited me to his place. I followed up the stairway. It felt strange since this was my first experience visiting a friend's home. "Franco, you're home!" exclaimed his mamma, "Come sit over here and eat,"

"No, Mamma. I came home to get some string to make a slingshot for my friend Santino. His papá left for America." Disappointed, his Mamma said, "Oh, Franco, but everybody is at the table."

Piccolo Santino

"I can eat later, Mamma. I need to find some string." I listened as Franco introduced me to his family. I liked how he explained everything, and I particularly liked the understanding and willingness to help that his family showed him. What also struck me was how the sense of strangeness from being in Franco's home was made familiar by serving cooked zucchini with Swiss chard and boiled potatoes prepared with olive oil and salt. A simple dish Mamma often made for us showed me a deep feeling of friendliness and understanding. I liked how the experience showed me that even though we were different, we could be very much alike by the food we shared.

"I have some string for you, son," his papá said, his voice filled with warmth. "Grazie, Papá! I'll be back later." His papá turned behind his chair, dug into a drawer, and passed the string through various family members seated at the table down to Franco's Mamma. The string, a simple object, was passed with such care and love, it touched me deeply. As we were leaving, I felt that there was intelligence in Franco's house. I thought that this incident might not have transpired in my house as smoothly or with the same presence of intelligence.

Back at my house, as we waited for Nino, Franco took out his pocketknife and asked me to hold the wood frame in my hand to customize the handle length to my grip. He made a notch while I had it tight and then trimmed the excess. "Hey, we'll need scissors to cut the strips," yelled out Nino as he walked over. "All right, I'll get them," I ran inside for the scissors, came right out, and Franco took charge. "Okay, Nino, you hold one end while I cut the first strip."

"Okay, but let's cut the length first," Nino said. "Bene," replied Franco, and Nino said, "Better cut it a little longer. We need some for the wrap-around on both ends." I watched closely as Franco cut two strips of tubing about a half-inch wide and a foot long. He then proceeded to hold the new wood frame up against his model and trim the frame accordingly. He then meticulously carved a groove in each of the frame's arms about a half-inch in from the ends. He wrapped one end of the rubber strip around the groove to one armature and pulled it tight. As he held it taut against his chest, Nino tied the end with string.

Piccolo Santino

"Make sure it's straight, Franco, before I make it tight." With a slight strain, Franco responded, "It's straight. Go on, tie it now!" Nino tied it, and Franco said, "Okay, Nino! Now let's do the other side."

"You got it straight, Franco?" "Yeah, go ahead and tie it, Nino," "Yeah, go ahead and tie it," Nino responded Franco. As my friends worked, I watched with excitement and gratitude after they secured the two strips to the frame. Franco held the wood frame in his left hand, pulled on the rubber strips and released them to test the elasticity. "Okay, now we need the saddle. Nino, did you bring an old shoe tongue?"

"No, I didn't have one."

"Santino, do you have an old shoe around?"

"No, we're lucky just to have shoes."

"That's all right. Let's go down to the shoemaker over there!" We walked across the street right next door to the mayor's office, and Franco walked down three steps below street level onto a small patio with a worker seated in a dirty smock and stitching a shoe as we waited from the top. Surprisingly, this was a shoemaker's shop I hadn't noticed before. It was a small, longish, skinny room tucked away from immediate view, and I watched as an older man in a filthy smock, seated inside behind a shoe anvil, banged away at the sole of a shoe. Behind him, deeper into the room, a skinny young man, also in a dirty smock, slowly rotated a shoe against his chest as he carefully trimmed the sole with a hook knife. He looked at Franco and asked, "What do you kids want?" I liked how Franco got to the point with his direct and free-spirited attitude, and the owner seemed to appreciate that approach. "We are putting a slingshot together and need a saddle. Do you have an old shoe tongue you can give us?"

The man paused briefly and said, "Let me see now." He put the shoe and knife down. I'm sure there's one lying around here somewhere!" Both men scrambled around, seemingly going out of their way to help us as they searched in a heap of scraps on a small table. "Here you go! How is this one?" said the older shoemaker, and the other man shouted, "Here's another one."

Oh, perfect! Grazie! Grazie," replied Franco. "*Prego*, you're

Piccolo Santino

welcome! Go on now, put that slingshot together." I felt numb by my inability to thank him as I clammed up with shyness and waited with Nino for Franco to come up the steps, and then we ran back home all excited.

Franco proceeded to cut the shoe tongue into the appropriate size and shape and then made two small slits on each end to slide the rubber strips through. He folded the short end of the strip between his right thumb and index finger while holding the shoe tongue by his left hand and pulled tight to stretch the rubber. Nino tied the one side and then the other. "And now to test it," exclaimed Franco. He reached into his pocket for a stone, placed it in the saddle, pulled back, and fired into the trees.

"Wow!" we all shouted. "It shoots really far!" I exclaimed, and then ran inside to return the scissors. Mamma saw me with them and asked, "What are you up to this time?"

"My friends are outside, and they made me a slingshot."

"Cosa devi sparare? Al tuo culo. What are you going to shoot? Your ass?" she shouted out, and my friends laughed as Franco handed me my new slingshot. I exclaimed, *"Grazie, ragazzi!* Thanks, guys!"

"Okay, let's go back out now," Nino said as I pulled on the bands back and forth and looked down for stones as we marched on.

I sensed Mamma's gaze as we walked away, and I was beginning to realize her purpose. There was no way that she would allow me to hang out with friends daily all summer long. On the farm, she could always keep an eye on me, but here in town, there was no telling what I could get into. I wondered what she was planning for me. Secretly, I always thought of my Papá, as I missed him and feared how that day would come for us to move to America. I kept my sanity by indulging in activities with my friends and school while leaving the departure date to fate.

I put my slingshot in my back pocket to be like my friends, and we resumed our journey, first stopping in the caves for a bathroom trip. We walked cautiously over the littered floor and looked for an individual area to squat down. I looked around on the cave walls and thought birds were pecking at the walls, but the chatter sounded strange, so I asked about it.

Piccolo Santino

"Hey guys, look at all those birds on the cave walls over there?"

"Santino, those are bats!"

"Bats?" I asked as Nino was pulling up his pants. We walked farther into the dark and I whispered, "Hey, guys, look inside over there. Wow!" There were bats covering the entire facade of the walls and ceiling of the cave. Their low chatter was frightening and eerie as it all felt in unison, not just to their mass, but also harmonious to the cave space and atmosphere as if forming a solid group of sound welded into the caves. "Oh my God!" I exclaimed. Nino blurted out, "*Che cazzo de miseria!* What fuck'n misery!" then he whispered, "Hey guys, let's shoot them!"

"Yeah, let's do it!" we responded.

"I need ammunition," said Franco as he searched for small stones on the littered floor. "Hey, you guys need any?" he asked. "Yeah, I need one," I whispered to Franco. "No, I have one," said Nino. We loaded our slingshots and took positions, thinking this was easy prey. We reared back and released our ammunition into the wall of bats, and the mass of darkness instantly swelled in front of us in a shrilling, piercing sound. Then individual bats flew out from the pack and poured total fear into us. With our breaths in our throats, we ran to the outside, ignoring what we might step onto, and Franco hollered out, "Okay, we're safe now we're in the sun, guys!"

We turned around and saw the bright sunlight act like a glass wall forcing the bats to fly upwards and then dive back down inside the caves. We scrambled to clean the bottom of our shoes by rubbing them on grass and dirt until we got all the poop off. Once we cleaned our shoes, we followed an existing path contrived between tall birch and oak trees with the wild brush. Throughout the countryside, we strolled with our slingshots cocked, and our heads lurched upward, turning left and right toward the trees and ready to fire at any sightings or slight sounds of birds. We walked for at least an hour, and on each occasion, when the trees dispersed and the sun beat down upon us, we welcomed the warm feeling on our shoulders and tuned our ears for possible sounds inside the brush, hoping we might score a rabbit.

Piccolo Santino

But what we truly hoped to score was war relics along the way, hidden behind bushes or in caves. Franco began telling us about Nello, this teenager whose family moved away after he finished fifth grade there in Jonadi. "Last time they came back to visit, Nello found a gun. He was afraid to pick it up, so he ran to the police and two *bersaglieri,* members of the elite military asked him to show them where he found it."

"Where did he find it?" asked Nino. "He took them down the hill right by your house, Santino! The bersaglieri told him it was a German Luger." He then told us that Nello would visit again next week, and some guys had planned a gathering to hear him talk about it. The trail got narrow again, and Franco kept in the lead as Nino and I followed along with our slingshots in hand. He kept talking, and I decided to eat my bread now.

Back at home, Mamma looked up from her chair and immediately recognized the man on the bicycle as Papá's former co-worker before he called out to her. "Signora Anna buongiorno! I came to tell Bartolo I have great news for him," he said as he dismounted from his bicycle. Seated in a chair in front of her house, Mamma looked up from nursing Enzo as her other children played in the dirt by the doorstep. "Ah ciao Gumbah Roberto!"

"Ciao, Signora."

"He is not here. He left for America already"

"Left for America? I thought he wasn't going until next month!"

"No, he left weeks ago."

"*Ah sporca a miseria!* Ah dirty misery, but I came to tell him he got the foreman's job on the new highway construction. Because of his military service, he's got the job ahead of all the others."

"He left on the Andrea Doria about two weeks ago. Had you come earlier, he probably would not have left."

"For real, you're saying it?"

"Sì, sì for real!"

Piccolo Santino

"But the Andrea Doria sunk. It's right here in the newspaper."

"What?" She leaned forward in her chair, interrupting Enzo from sucking, and he let out a short whimper as Anna cupped her breast with her right hand and clutched Enzo closer for him to resume. She firmly stared at Roberto and replied. "But I got a telegram from him saying all is well. What are you talking about?"

"No! No! Signora, if you got a telegram already, there is nothing to worry about. Here I got the newspaper right here it said it crashed with another ship on the return trip to Italy."

"Oh my God! *Che miseria,* what tragedy."

"Si signora! Si for real!"

"Did many people die?"

"They are not sure yet, but it seems like maybe fifty people or so died."

"Poor souls! Excuse me, Gumbah Roberto." She turned away from Roberto to yell at me as I returned with my friends. "*E dove cazzo ere?* And where the hell were you? Get over here right now, before I take a beating to you *vagabondo,* lazy good for nothing." I dejectedly turned to my friends and struggled slightly to speak two words. "Ciao, g-g-guys."

"Ciao, Santino." Franco and Nino looked at each other and continued on their way home. I walked over to my siblings playing on the ground by the front door and sat next to them.

"I'll leave the newspaper with you, Signora, I read it all. You don't have anything to worry about. Your husband is safe." said Gumbah Roberto.

"Grazie, Gumbah Roberto."

"You're welcome! I'm sorry I didn't get word sooner about the job for Bartolo I just found two days ago. I didn't even know you had moved into town. I rode to the farm first, and then they told me where to find you."

"Oh, I'm sorry you rode all over the place."

"Oh, that's all right, it's a beautiful day. I'll be going now, Signora, make sure you mention this to Bartolo when you write to him. Tell him I wish him the best and good luck to you and your children."

"Grazie, Don Roberto." He mounted his bicycle and then turned back and said, "Arrivedérci, Signora."

"Arrivedérci." Mamma turned to her children and singled me out. I was sitting in the doorway. "You made it back home?" My head sunk to my chest. "But don't worry, tomorrow we will make an adjustment!"

After Mamma's warning yesterday, I didn't know what to expect as she led Lillo and me by the hand and said, "You both come with me. Let's go." Her voice was firm but soft. I wondered about her kindness in holding my hand as much as where we were going. We didn't travel far; we just walked through a doorway at the end of our building. The door was opened wide on that warm, sunny day. A few clothes were on racks, and three mannequins were positioned close to each other. One was bare, one had an open shirt dangling from its bust, and the other had what looked like half a jacket with white lines drawn on it for the shoulders and arms. A young man in his early thirties had his sleeves rolled up with a yellow measuring tape dangling around his neck. He was leaning over a portable fire trough on the floor with his front to us.

He looked up and greeted Mamma, "Buongiorno, Donna Anna, excuse me for a moment."

"Of course, Mastro Giancarlo, please go ahead and finish what you're doing." He carefully emptied hot burning coals from a spatula into his iron, then closed the trap door to the iron and put it down on a flat marble stone on a table near the ironing board in front of us. "Signora, how can I help you today?" She pulled Lillo forward by his hand and said, "Mastro Giancarlo, I was hoping you would do me a big favor and take on my son Lillo here as your apprentice. As you know, we are to leave for America in two years, and I planned to have you make my children's outfits for the journey."

"Signora Anna, I would be more than happy to have your son Lillo here with me. How old is he?"

"He is six, but he can sweep up for you and do small errands."

"Why, of course. It will not be a problem at all."

Piccolo Santino

"Now please understand I will not be able to pay you all at once for the clothes, so I would appreciate it if you gave me some kind of estimate, and I will be glad to start giving you money on installment during the next two years."

"Of course. That's not a problem. We can certainly work that out."

"I certainly appreciate your kindness. When would you like Lillo to start?"

"Why, you can leave him here with me now if you like."

"I appreciate that as I have other errands today."

"Come on Lillo. When you are not working, you can sit over here on this little stool."

"Go ahead, son. Go with Mastro Giancarlo. He will tell you when to come home." Mastro Giancarlo pointed to the stool, and Lillo walked over and sat down. "Here you go, Lillo. You can always sit here anytime you're not working. We are going to get along fine together."

"Grazie, Mastro Giancarlo."

"*Prego,* you're welcome, Signora Anna, don't worry about Lillo. He will be safe here with me."

"Thank you again and Buongiorno, Mastro Giancarlo."

"Buongiorno Signora." Mamma tugged on my arm and said, "Come on, you, let's go."

We made a left out the door and headed toward the end of town in the direction my friends and I walked to explore the countryside. But this time, I was wondering where Mamma was taking me. At the end of town, Mamma led me up a ramp to the last house on the right. I detected the smell of sawdust and liked it immediately. At the bottom of the ramp was a large double door closed, and Mamma proceeded to the other end of the building as sounds of work alerted us. The door was open, and a medium, stocky man was feverishly shaving a board clamped to the vise built into his workbench. I looked at the vise and was immediately fascinated by its construction into the workbench. I liked how this man put his weight into his work, which shook the entire workbench, and how curly wood shavings flew off the plane and dropped to the floor, like hair flying off a

Piccolo Santino

barber's scissors. He pushed his plane down, drove it forward with solid and bold strokes, then stopped to inspect the evenness by sliding a square along the board's edge, and then resumed with a few fast, simple, and lighter strokes before putting down his plane. As if in one motion, he turned the handle counterclockwise on the vise, and as he lifted the small board, he noticed us outside the doorway. "*Perdonami Signora*, Forgive me signora."

"Don't worry, Mastro, you have your work to do." Mamma stepped forward. "My name is Bianchi Anna, my husband has left for America, and I am trying to find an apprenticeship for my son here. The tailor Mastro Giancarlo was kind enough to accept my youngest son, and I wondered if you would be able to take on my oldest boy here. Perhaps he can be helpful cleaning up or doing errands for you."

"Si, Signora Anna. You live down the street right here?"

"Si, the first house to the right toward town."

"Why I would be delighted to have a young apprentice here with me. Come in. Please come in, Signora." Mamma pulled me by her hand, and we walked inside. The carpenter stepped away from his workbench to face Mamma directly. "How old is the boy, and what's his name?"

"He is eight, and his name is Santino."

"*Ah mi chiamo anche Santino,* My name is Santino also. Why we are going to get along great together here."

"Grazie, Mastro Santino"

"My pleasure, Signora. You may leave him here. We can start now.

"I appreciate that Mastro Santino, and I want to assure you that I give you permission to hit my son if he is disrespectful in any way." My heart dropped like a tree falling. "Oh no, Signora! That won't be necessary. He looks like a good boy. He seems so quiet." With those words, Master Santino quickly reversed the damage and lifted me back up. "I will be going then, and I thank you again."

"I will send him home when we stop work around five o'clock."

"*Grazie e buona giornata Mastro Santino.* Thank you and have a good day, Master Santino."

"Buongiorno, Signora Bianchi." Mamma left. I waited for orders

Piccolo Santino

from the master carpenter. He ducked under the workbench and then resurfaced with a bucket full of used nails in one hand and a hammer in the other. "Santino, sit right there, son, on the step. This is going to be your first job." I sat down with my back propped against the doorframe. Master Santino knelt close by, giving me the impression of a friendly orangutan in baggy pants. He set the bucket down on the cement floor, removed a bent nail, and explained the work to me.

"Here. Hold the nail on the floor with your left hand. Bulging part of the nail facing up. Hold the hammer always by the end of the handle. Then, gently hit the bulged part of the nail until it becomes straight. This way, we can use them again." I watched with intensity as he held the nail by its head and banged it down in the center where the curve was. I understood the leverage gained by grabbing the hammer at the end of its handle. "*Bene,* good Santino! You got that?" I nodded my head, "Yes."

"Good, I will get you an empty can to put the good nails in." I took a giant nail bent in two places out from the bucket. I held it down from the pointy tip since the bulge was closer to the head of the nail and landed the hammer firmly on it several times until that bulge was level. I then held it from the head for the other bump closer to the tip and completed the task on my first nail. I figured there had to be several hundred nails in the bucket if not a thousand, so I felt my job was secure for a while.

Master Santino placed a large tin can next to the full one. "Here you go, Santino. Take it easy, and be careful not to hit your thumb with the hammer." His humor was kind and put me at ease, and since I would be spending less time with my friends, I realized Mamma's purpose. The sawdust smell reminded me of the sawmill. I became more settled and looked forward to placing the various scents on the actual wood I would get to meet and handle somehow. I thoroughly enjoyed this task of whacking nails and pursued the work at a joyful pace. I caught the master spying on me from the corner of my eye as I worked. Then he suddenly exclaimed, "Bravo, Santino!" He paused from working, walked over for a closer look, and continued praising me. "Bravo, Santino! Bravo!"

I liked it when the Master praised me in that manner, as it brought me back to the farm when I cleaned the walkway, and I heard that same

Piccolo Santino

praise for the first time from Doctor Itasca. "If you have something to say, Santino, you can say it! Don't be afraid. You can talk here!" I nodded a "Yes" and then realized I should say the word "Sì." I said it, and he walked back to resume his work. It became evident he could not get over my solitude.

The hammer began to feel lighter, and I continued banging nails with increased confidence as I pressed my lower back against the doorframe for a quick stretch. I started to look for nails with several complicated bends in them as they presented a more significant challenge, and the reward of success felt more gratifying.

Occasionally, I looked toward home to see if my brother and sisters were outside playing. I thought I should be coy about how I looked up so that the Master would not have a reason to scold me. I liked how the sun warmed my body in the doorway, and I figured the shadows would feel calm in the latter part of the afternoon when they arrived. I took solace in knowing that the change would be the signal for going home. I looked inside the bucket of bent nails and felt I could have done better with the remaining volume.

The sun had shifted slightly past the center of the sky, and the Master walked over and made me feel proud again as he greeted me. "Bravo, Santino! Santino, you can take a break from the nails for a while. I have another job for you, son." He held out two empty green liter-size glass bottles and waited for me to rise. I immediately understood the chore but waited for him to explain. "You know where the small stream is just before by the bridge across from the caves, right?" I answered, "Sì."

"Go and fill these two bottles with fresh water for me, and come right back." I welcomed the errand as relief from indoor entrapment. I walked out of the doorway and down a few steps from the dirt platform. Almost like a blink of an eye, I walked past the first set of caves. I continued past the second cave, where my friends and I disturbed the bats. I walked across the street and found the pathway leading me to the ravine's bottom. While I descended, I could hear women chattering while doing their laundry at the public wash pool. Twice, I accompanied

Piccolo Santino

Mamma there to help carry our clothes. I didn't mind assisting Mamma. But I got offended by the women's lewd conversations, so I sat down off to the side on the sloping embankment of bushes.

From there, I compared that pool to the one we had on the farm. Ours was much smaller and didn't have a roof to protect Mamma. Then I remembered seeing a man here once washing clothes, and the women quietly gossiped about him as he kept to himself. I looked away from the roof line and could still hear some of the women's dirty talk with loud laughter. But at least, in the brush, I felt isolated and was spared many of their details. They should've put those thoughts in their last *vucata* (the practice of boiling clothes to kill bacteria.)

The bridge covered a small section of the stream and was a short distance away from a rock formation hugged by a grassy slope, where water exuded and ran into a shallow stream. I carefully planted my feet on dry rocks so Mamma wouldn't scold me for getting my shoes dirty. I avoided the stones, sunken into the thick, wet carpet growing in the path of water running into the stream. I set the bottles down and leaned over for a cold drink. I pricked my left palm on a hidden thorn in the brush, and as I pulled back, I had to do a quick dance to regain my footing before I could hold my mouth to the cool gusher. The cold water rippled through my senses and sent me calm waves of relief. I reached down to get one bottle and held it to the gusher until it overflowed. The sun felt hot on my shoulders. I looked up at the sky and let the second bottle overfill so the coolness could travel up my arm and befriend my senses again before I headed back.

I held the bottles tight by their necks and was careful not to spill any water. I rushed back so that the water would remain cold. I made it up the four steps, and Master Santino greeted me from the doorway as I approached him. "Bravo Santino. You got back fast. Thank you very much! Why don't you go home now for lunch and return later?" I handed him the bottles, nodded, "Yes," and ran home.

The door was wide open, and I saw a pot on the stove with bubbling tomato sauce that made my mouth water. It was very unusual that

Piccolo Santino

Mamma had the means to cook like this on a weekday and in the middle of the day. Especially since it wasn't a holiday and we rarely had pasta on Sundays unless Aunt Isabella across the street gave us some. I stopped questioning my thoughts, rushed to the breadbox for a piece of bread, and furtively dunked it in the mouthwatering sauce. I looked around for Mamma, then dipped a more significant piece and quickly dashed outside. I gulped it down, feeling relieved and surprised by my success. I looked for someone to play with outside and hesitated to search beyond the vicinity.

Since the sauce was cooking, I figured pasta could be pretty close behind. I walked over to the tailor's and peered through the opened door for Lillo. I looked back and spotted him turning the corner of the house with my sisters following up the stairway from below. Anticipating a festive lunch, I doubled back and dejectedly stopped as I peered in the doorway. Mamma dumped all the pot contents into a large aluminum basin she had brought up from downstairs. They were the dirty dishes from a few nights ago when Aunt Isabella had given us spaghetti. Mamma had boiled them to soften the tomato crust on the plates. I secretly took comfort in feeling that the soaked bread tasted delicious, and I now regretted not having gone back for more since what I didn't know was not hurting me.

Upon returning to work, I saw Master Santino outside stirring a heavy bucket, hung by an unusually tall tripod, over a fire. Guilt ran through me like a burglar on a getaway. I automatically thought I was late and the boss was doing a job I thought would have been delegated to do. I watched him lift the dirty stick as steaming brown gooey stuff dripped. He set the stick back in and resumed stirring. He turned and greeted me, "Santino! This is called fish glue." I responded with a quick "Buongiorno."

"Si, buongiorno," he said as he used a thick rag to lift the hot bucket by its handle away from the fire and carried it with his arms extended slightly out. His voice straining slightly, he said, "Come with me, Santino." He hurried inside toward the other workbench away from the front door. I watched him set the hot bucket on the floor, scoop out some

Piccolo Santino

glue with a spoon, and pour it on a wide board about the width of his forearm and about as long as he was tall. He spread the glue evenly with a wooden squeegee, and after working several scoops, he repeated the process on another board. He moved the bucket away into a safe area before flipping one board over the other.

I immediately liked the reddish wood grain of the board. Moving quickly, he slipped three strips of wood underneath and three more on top to match positions. "Santino, hold this steady over here while I start a clamp." We repeated the process on the three strips of cross braces. Then he evenly balanced the pressure by turning the clamp's screw from end to end, each time, checking that the boards were flush before turning up the pressure to maximum on all six clamps. I took interest as glue squeezed from the sides onto cardboard strategically positioned to protect the workbench. "All right, Santino, while this dries, I will need your help by the other bench."

We walked over to the other bench, and I watched him disassemble clamps on two shorter boards previously assembled. I looked as he meticulously studied the edge by holding it out at eye level to check for any unevenness. He quickly locked the board in the vise and ran a plane over the edge several times. My eyes rolled to follow the wood shavings each time they flew off the plane onto the floor, and then, with a small square, he checked his work for evenness from end to end.

Then, he removed the board from the vice. "Santino, I need two pieces, each 65 centimeters from this here board. Now I need you to hold one end while I saw it in half." I moved into position while he locked it in the vice after he finished measuring and marking the pencil line with his unusually thick, wide, and flat carpenter's pencil, which had red and black stripes. Compared to the round pencils we used in school, this new pencil evoked a feeling of grandness and superiority. "Santino, now you hold the end of the board while I saw it." I held it firmly, and he looked at me stumped and said, "You don't have to hold it that tight. Wait until I get to the bottom with the saw. The purpose is not to let it fall and break off as I finish the cut."

Piccolo Santino

I responded by nodding, "Yes," after he cut two pieces from the same board, both the same size, he checked the sawed edge with a square. Immediately afterward, he locked one panel in the vice with the sawed edge upwards and slowly ran a small plane on top, careful not to run the plane off the edge. "You see, Santino if the plane runs off the edge, it will splinter the wood because I'm going against the grain." Then he grabbed the square and ran it along the edge end to end. "There we have it, Santino, a perfectly straight, smooth edge!" I showed a happy smile, and he smiled back. "Well, Santino, now you can resume your work with the nails!"

He placed the two containers next to me on the doorstep. I sat down and took the hammer out of the bucket. I resumed my position in the doorway as the afternoon sun moved west and now placed me in a cool shade. I began experimenting with holding the hammer in various places on the handle from close to the metal like a shoemaker and then moving my hand farther away to exemplify what Master Santino had explained. I looked up as he was beveling the edge of another board, and as the Master ran the plane off the edge, I noticed the wood did not splinter since he was going with the grain this time.

I looked out toward home and saw my family outside. Then, a man on a Vespa rode past them, continued down the street, and pulled up on the ramp here. As he turned off his motor, I held my breath to avoid inhaling the fumes. He was a short, thin man with a mustache and the same height as Master Santino. The stranger got off his Vespa, lifted a tool belt from the backseat area, and smiled at me as he walked inside. Master Santino shouted out, "Nicola, you're back?"

"We finished up early for the day, and I thought I would stop by."

"Glad you did."

"What do we have here, a new worker?"

"Oh, this is Santino. His mother asked if I could take him on as an apprentice to keep him off the streets." I kept on banging nails despite the interruption, and the Master shouted out to me, "Santino, this is Mastro Nicola. He is my cousin and also my partner!" I bashfully looked up and quickly said, "Buongiorno, Mastro," and I was glad it all came out

Piccolo Santino

without a stutter. "We have Another Santino now? What pleasure!" exclaimed Master Nicola. I liked him immediately and I responded, "Grazie, Mastro."

"Santino, why don't you stop a minute and go for freshwater? I'll get you the bottle," said Master Santino. I got up to take the bottle from him and walked down the steps as the men talked between themselves. "He seems very quiet!"

"Yeah, for some reason, he's afraid to talk. His father just left for America."

I thought about how Master Santino worked with his tools, used a square to check his work, and drew a line for sawing. I liked how he removed the metal blade from the plane. And how he then pushed a lever sideways to unlock the blade for removal or adjustment. And how the one screw controlled the locking. Unlocking allowed the edge to move for a deeper shave into the wood, which created thicker, heavier wood shavings; pulling the blade back for a shallower shave resulted in thinner, more delicate shavings. I particularly liked it when he removed the blade to sharpen it over a particular stone by moving it clockwise and then counterclockwise. He, of course, would first place a few drops of olive oil onto the dry stone. I felt I was gaining information from Master Santino I would have for the rest of my life.

Sunday arrived. Mamma was sick in bed, and my worries about how we would manage without Papá now required an answer. I could not provide one, so I walked out early in the morning to look for my friends. I found my friends Franco and Nino by the public water fountain located in the mini square just before the bend to the tabacchino by our school. I saw one woman washing a few garments in the pool around the fountain and another middle-aged woman filling a large, tall water jug. "*Scusa*, excuse me. Am I in your way, boys?"

"Oh no, Signora. You were here first. Finish filling your jug of water," Franco responded as Nino turned to find me while I walked up behind him. "Ciao, Santino!"

"Ciao, Nino, Ciao, Franco!" Franco turned around. "Ciao, Bianchi!"

Piccolo Santino

"Okay, boys, you can all drink now." Franco and Nino responded, "Grazie, Signora." Franco drank first, and I waited for Nino to drink before swallowing.

We headed back up the main street and stopped in front of the bar where my papá liked to play cards with his friends. To the side of the store, metal railings connected to three brick posts to form a fence that separated the street from a wide-open space and houses beyond it. Franco and Nino sat on the top railing while their feet rested on the bottom bar. With my back toward home, I stared at some bottle caps by my feet. I bent down to pick up the bottle cap with the Cinzano label.

On my way up, I was jolted by a man suddenly reaching from behind me and placing coins in my hands. I heard him say, "Santino! Here, this is for you." I recognized the voice, and he moved so fast that I could not turn around to place the voice to a face as I became tongue-tied. Before I could even call out to him, he was down the street, and with his jacket flying open, he turned and shouted, "I'm hurrying to catch the bus."

My mouth gasped, and my eyes swelled as my friends stared at the coins my hands held. Franco and Nino asked me, "Who was that, Santino?"

"That was my uncle Santino, and he gave me this!" I held out my hands, and they quickly jumped down and sifted the coins with their fingers as I was in disbelief. "Wow!" they both exclaimed at once. "150 lire."

"What can I get with this?" I exclaimed, and Franco said, "You can get something to eat in the store here."

"All right, let's go in and see what it can b-b-buy," I exclaimed. We ran inside the store and stopped short of a very high counter with a hidden platform behind its construction. Standing on the platform between two displays was a voluptuous woman with bulbous breasts that moved under her blouse like water balloons as she leaned forward. She was twirling two coins in her right hand and babbling at an old man in a worn-out grey jacket with matching pants and hat, waiting for his money.

Piccolo Santino

We used the time to read the menu high on the wall to her left. Since buying a sandwich felt foreign to me, I waited for Franco and Nino to absorb the menu. I turned to the older man seemingly bursting inside from the woman's well-known habitual twirling of coins. He wanted his change, but she kept on twirling it as if she owned all the space in time. Like a fox, the older man acutely kept his steam under wraps by rocking his head to the movements of the woman's blouse.

Nino and Franco debated ideas, and I turned to Franco as he said, "I think the mortadella would be good."

"Okay, let's get it," I said, and Nino commented, "That lady is still doodling with that man's change. She always does that!" Franco spoke up, "Signora, why don't you give the man his change? We would like to order something!" Startled, as if she came out of her stupor but still maintaining her habit, she leaned back with an attitude and looked toward the chef. The chef walked out from the refrigerated section, stared at us for a short spell, then looked at the woman, formed a frown, and squinted his eyes. They stared at each other, then the chef shrugged his shoulders, the woman turned to Franco and said, "What do you want?"

"This man has been waiting an infinity for his change that you have been doodling with." Alarmed, she turned to the old man, feigned incredulity, leaned over, and asked, "*Ah per davvero?* Oh! For real?" His stare was firmly transfixed on her chest. "Are you waiting for me?" she asked him. But his hypnotic state was too thick for her mundane voice, so she leaned in closer by resting her chest on the countertop, pushed her breasts further up, and he quickly swallowed hard with swelling eyes. She then looked down at her crowded cleavage, stopped doodling, pulled up her blouse, and snapped, *"Te scostumato*! Here, you pervert! Take your change." The man immediately came to life, reached for his change, and sarcastically said, "*Finalmente!* Finally!"

"*Va via va!* Go away, go! *Va caca*, go take a crap." The old man took his change and smiled at Franco as he left with a loaf of bread under his right arm. The woman turned to Franco and said, "Now, what do you want?" Franco looked at her and asked, "What kind of sandwich can my friend get with 150 lire?" She paused momentarily, "He can have the

Piccolo Santino

mortadella!" she snapped. "All right, the mortadella is good!" The woman extended her hand with an open palm and said, "Give me the 150 lire."

"No! When we get the sandwich, we will give you the money. Otherwise, we'll be here another half a day with your crazy habit!"

"*Intelligentone, ah.* Wise guy, huh." she blurted out, and Nino joined in and said. "I didn't hear what you just said," She quickly responded, "*Va bene! Va bene!* Very well! Very well!" She turned to the chef, standing by in a sagging posture, and said to him. "Go ahead, Chico, make the mortadella sandwich for them." He snapped into firmness, clicked his heals, and said, "Si. Pronto," We looked at him as he turned around and mimicked marching toward the refrigerated section, and we all said to him. "Grazie!"

"Prego." He proceeded to make the sandwich. Nino leaned into us and secretly pointed to the ceiling at hanging flypaper with hundreds of flies glued to it. Others swirled like satellites, and a few tried to kick themselves loose. Nino whispered, "I bet I could hit that thing with my slingshot from across the street." Franco smirked with eyes open, and I looked at Chico, the chef, handing the sandwich to the voluptuous woman. She held up the sandwich with one hand, reached out her other hand, and said, "Give me the 150 lire!" I took my hand out of my pocket, and Franco shouted. "Make sure you give him the sandwich at the same time!" I reached up with both hands and as she lowered the sandwich in my right hand, I dropped the three 50 lire coins into her right palm. She made it seem like the coins gravitated toward her as if her fingers were magnetic, and she instantly began twirling them.

We ran outside and assembled by the railing. Franco tore the sandwich into three pieces and purposely broke a more significant part for me. I relished the smell of store-bought bread and marveled at the sweet, light texture compared to the coarse, thick feel of homemade bread. I indulged in the slippery feel and aroma of the mortadella and decided to chew slowly to savor every bite. "What delicious mortadella! Thanks, Santino!" mumbled Nino with his mouth full. "It's great that your uncle Santino came by!"

"Wish I had an uncle like that," joined Franco. I responded, "He

Piccolo Santino

came up behind me out of nowhere and gave me 150 lire!"

Nino gulped down his last bite and said, "Oh my God, I was supposed to be home helping my papá by now!" He crumbled up the remaining wrapper in his hands, threw it down, and ran off while shouting back, "Gotta run, guys. Thanks again, Santino!"

"Ciao!" we shouted back, then swallowed our last bites, and Franco threw his wrapper away after he used it to wipe his mouth. I brushed mine with my hand as I had discarded my wrapper. Franco put his hand on my shoulder and said, "That was good, Bianchi! I have to go, too, and thanks a lot! See you later."

"Va bene, see you later!" His house was in the complex behind the square to the side of the deli. I watched him walk through the square down the side street as I strolled home with painful thoughts about Mamma and feeling very apprehensive as I walked through the doorway. I walked in with my head down and turned left into the main family room, and as I heard her voice, I looked up. My eyes widened with relief as I saw her standing in decent spirits.

"What did you do with the money your uncle gave you?" she asked in a slightly somber tone. I was startled as to how she even knew. "I was hungry, so I bought a sandwich," I responded, and she nodded her head and walked outside to Aunt Isabella's house across from us.

I stood there guilt-stricken and wondered if Uncle Santino had given me the money for Mamma because he might have been too embarrassed to give it to her directly. Then I thought, how was I to know since he ran off the way he did?

Piccolo Santino

Chapter 2 of Part Two, 1956
Getting used to the carpenter shop

I looked forward to my days at the carpenter shop even though I missed hanging out with my friends. I liked watching the Master use all the various tools for different applications, and I got excited at the results, whether it was sawing wood or smoothing out an edge with a plane. Then, there was a case where he used a rasp to grind down the edge of a wood board before using the wood plane for a smooth and fine finish. "The rasp," he exclaimed, "Is like a file." He showed me the two tools side by side. "See the difference?" I nodded a "Yes" and gave a slight "hmm" of amazement.

"But unlike the file, which has finer teeth to be used on metal, the rasp has protruding sharp, thicker teeth to dig into the wood surface and rough up the edge faster. Then, you can use a plane for a smooth, fine finish, but of course, always check the edge with a square afterward to make sure it's all squared! Check it sideways as well as long ways." And he held a square to the wood as he spoke and ended the lecture somberly. "If ever a mistake is made, this one would upset me because you can't put parts together on furniture if they are not squared!"

I especially liked it when he used the manual drill, which required multiple body motions. I liked how the hand drill worked. I observed how the Master coordinated the various movements to drill a hole in the wood. Rotating the armature, pressing down on it, and watching the wood shavings wrap themselves around the blade, like curly pasta, then seeing the shavings slide down onto the board like wet macaroni. I also liked how the drill bit loaded onto the bottom of the horseshoe frame by turning the locking nut clockwise and counterclockwise. But as much as I enjoyed watching the Master at work, I still preferred the tranquility of refurbishing nails on the stoop as it allowed me the freedom to daydream.

While I worked sitting on the step in the doorway, I thought back to a time Lola and I were passive in the grass and staring at clouds on a

Piccolo Santino

very still day. I stared so hard that I lost my sense of relation to gravity. Suddenly, I felt myself falling into the sky and quickly rolled over to regain my equilibrium.

"Ouch!" I exclaimed as I banged my thumb, then dropped the hammer and squeezed my thumb tight. "Santino, was that a thumbtack you found?"

"That nail was too small, Mastro."

"You're supposed to hit the nail." A stranger standing over me said while chuckling. I saw two boys in their late teens standing before me, one thick-built but not fat and the other thin but not weak. "Is the Master in?" the thick one asked. I released my thumb and pointed toward the second workbench deeper in the shop, away from the doorway. They walked past me to go inside and called out, "Buongiorno, Summastro." Master Santino stopped working to turn around, put down the sanding block, and said, "Good morning, and what do you fellas want?"

"We just got laid off from the sawmill after working there for two years, and we are now looking for work."

"I see."

"My name is Rocco, and this is Bruno." Mastro Santino reached out to shake hands. "I'm Santino Romanelli. What did you boys do at the Sawmill?" Rocco, the thinner boy, said, "We mostly worked inside, away from where they sawed the logs." Then Bruno said, "They have a shop inside the establishment." Master interrupted, "Sì, sì I am aware of that!"

"Well, they mostly make coffins at the Sawmill and minimal furniture. We stained and then polished the coffins," Rocco added. "We also cut parts with the handsaw or the combination power table saw and planer."

"I see!" expressed the Master and continued. "You, of course, made sure all the parts were cut straight and squared?" Both boys responded promptly, "Oh sì. Sì," and explained they were also responsible for sanding down the completed furniture for inspection before they were allowed to stain and polish to a finish."

"Well," the Master said in a reflective tone as he crossed his left arm across his chest and rested his hand under his right armpit while he rubbed his chin with his right hand. "But tell me. Were you allowed to do your own inspection?"

"Just before we got laid off, it was being considered."

"It sounds like you boys can handle some of the work here all right."

"Thank you," the boys quickly responded. "I will need to discuss this with my partner. Right now, he's on a job site and won't be back for a few days."

"We can check back with you if you like," Rocco said. Yeah! Why don't you boys come back in a week, and maybe my partner can be here as well."

"We are grateful. Thank you, Master Santino."

"You're welcome, guys. Oh, you boys have a way to get around?"

"Oh yes, we both have bicycles."

"Good! Good! Okay, then see you guys in a week!"

"Sì, arrivederci."

"Arrivederci."

Bruno walked past me as I held a nail down between my fingers and was about to hit it with my hammer. Rocco stopped for a beat as he looked down and said, "Don't hit your finger now!" I looked up at him and shook my head. "No," he rushed to catch up to his friend by the end of the building. Master Santino came out and watched them mount their bicycles and ride away. "Santino, it's time for a nice drink of cold water!" I put the hammer down as the Master handed me the bottle, and I couldn't wait to run my finger under the cold spring water.

When I returned, the Master gulped down almost half the bottle and then exclaimed, "The water is always cold when you come back! I used to have another boy here before, and he always brought back warm water." With that comment, I felt my self-esteem rise in two different ways. First, I felt a sense of superiority for doing a better job than my predecessor, and having just learned about a predecessor erased my guilty feelings about being here as a favor. His comment further cemented the idea that he needed me. The afternoon seemed to go by quickly, and

Piccolo Santino

before I could anticipate the Master's next move, he called out to me, "Santino, you can stop with the nails now. Put the tools away and sweep up."

I brought the nail buckets inside and removed all the tools from both workbenches. Some tools had their place on the bottom shelf of the workbenches. I hung pliers, screwdrivers, and saws in their designated areas on the pegboard. Then I brushed off the benches of sawdust and wood shavings before I swept the floor clean as expected. I put any nails I found into the bent nails bucket. Before sweeping, I splashed water on the cement floor. The Master stepped aside and watched my moves. Then he pulled some papers out of his drawer and sat down, looking studious. I stuck the broom under his bench, swept out a pencil, and laid it next to him. "Bravo, Santino, where did you find it?"

"There under your bench."

"Bravo! I can use it now." Upon finishing, I walked out the door. I looked down the street toward home and didn't see anybody outside. As I turned to go back inside, the Master looked at me and said, "Santino, go home! It's time!"

"Arrivederci," I dashed home and looked inside the bread box for a piece of bread since nobody was outside playing. I saw Mamma seated at the family table, writing a letter. She turned to me briefly and said, "There's some dried olives on the table. Have them with your bread." I sat down and ate bread and olives. "Are you writing a letter to Papá?"

"Sì. Why don't you eat some of the red pepper flakes in olive oil?"

"I like them for lunch, Mamma. But they burn my butt in the morning."

"There wasn't much cheese, and we ate it all."

"Does Papá think of us, Mamma?"

"Of course he does! Why wouldn't he?"

"He is so far away."

"Don't worry. We'll be with Papá soon."

"Where did everybody go, Mamma?"

"They went across to Aunt Isabella's. Why don't you go there?

Piccolo Santino

Maybe Eugenio can give you a piece of cheese?"

"No, that's okay."

"You know they called the doctor for that sick man down the hill from us earlier!"

"Mamma, is he going to die?"

"He might. He does have cancer of the throat."

"Is that bad?"

"Sì! Cancer could burst suddenly."

"I hope not in the middle of the night."

"Only God knows."

That sick man down the hill did not last the night. When the doctor gave his wife the news, her shrill cry sliced through my opened window and robbed me of my sleep. "*Cornuto! Figlio di puttana!* You cuckold! You son of a bitch! You left me all alone. All alone like a dog! You left me all alone!"

All night, I became glued to the sounds of the woman's wailing and family members struggling to pull her away from the corpse as they pleaded with her, and any success was short-lived as she dashed back to his bedside. Continually tortured by the thought of her man's death, she kept me awake as she repeated her outcry, "*Cornuto! Figlio di puttana!* You cuckold! You son of a bitch! You left me all alone. All alone like a dog! You left me all alone!"

This drama felt like it was bolted tight into the depths of midnight as it perpetually repeated itself. I was afraid to roll over in my bed, worrying that the reaper would see me moving and rush in through my window. In a paralyzed state, I prayed that exhaustion would soon overcome that poor woman as she fought off anyone trying to pry her away from her dead husband. I could hear voices, but none so clearly as the new widow. It sounded like a constant power cycle like the force of waves battering a cliff and retreating.

I listened to the woman lunge forward, slamming herself on his bedside, screaming. "*Mi hai lasciato sola!* You left me all alone!

Piccolo Santino

Cornuto! You cuckold!"

Then, there was a moment of quiet, and I could hear more clearly. "She's pulling on her hair again!" I heard a voice shout. Another voice cried out, "Stop her!" She screamed. "No! Noh! Leave me alone!"

"No, Gummah, enough already. Come get some rest." And again, quiet. I sensed that she finally yielded and must have sat down. I prayed this could be a pattern that would afford me some sleep, but the restful moments were short-lived, and when the tug of war resumed, I prayed that when they sat her down, away from the corpse, she would resign long enough to prime me into a dead sleep, so I could stop listening to this drama. Even worse, I began to fear the reaper was watching me while I held the covers over my eyes. Trying to regain my courage, I felt safe, having bolted the front door earlier. But my fear reminded me of the opened window and the reaper's ability to fly in and possibly scoop me up.

I woke up to the sound of the Death knell with the revelation that it was morning and that the night had passed. I hoped that the poor woman would find some comfort in believing that God had a purpose in recalling her man in such a sad way. For me, her painful wailing made me think that maybe I could avoid such pain in my life by being distant with everybody.

Piccolo Santino

Chapter 3, of Part 2
Exploring the old barracks

With our slingshots tucked into our back pockets, we walked out of church on a hot Sunday morning and decided to go exploring again. We looked at a small bulldozer parked in front of the large caves, and when we got to the smaller caves, Nino shouted, "Hey guys, I gotta take a dump. I'm going inside."

"I'll piss out here. There's no need to go inside!" answered Franco. "Me too," I added. "Hey, look, they cleaned it all up in here!" Shouted Nino. We saw where the bulldozer left its trail of chewed-up grass and how the new heap of refuse was left outside in the brush to decompose. "Hey guys, let's stay here a bit and explore inside since the grounds are all cleaned up, and maybe we can find a German Luger."

"No way!" responded Franco, and I followed with, "Did you forget about the b-b-bats?"

"Che cazzo! Oh, fuck!" Nino ran out, pulling up his pants, and exclaimed, "*Andiamo subito*, let's go quick!" He quickly led us up the ramp leading to the ground above the caves and into the countryside. Franco exclaimed, "Yeah, Nino, we are better off exploring the old barracks instead." Nino commented, "Yeah, I don't care what some people say. Those Germans could never have been able to use these caves as a secret radio outpost with all those bats inside."

We ventured into an area of birch and oak trees with light to medium brush on both sides of the trail. We speculated about finding a lost weapon along the way or other artifacts. We pulled out our slingshots at the sound of a few birds chirping, but the chirping stopped. We shot into the trees for sport and kept walking. I liked the sound of the stones cracking when they bounced off the tree trunks and ricocheted against branches, and the shaking of leaves made us think that possibly a bird got disturbed.

We walked until we came upon the wide-open field Franco and Nino had spoken of earlier, known as *il campo*. The wild perennial grass

Piccolo Santino

was up to our knees and taller, with the clear blue sky acting as a vast backdrop to an outdoor stage. The ground was getting softer under our feet on this natural stage as soothing croaking sounds directed us toward a pond. Nino and Franco ran ahead of me and started shooting at the croaking frogs. I became mesmerized by the enormous bullfrogs I had ever imagined. Thinking of the frogs as an easy target, I aimed. The instant I launched the missile, a cold chill settled in me like a tranquilizer, and the rock ricocheted off the frog and punctured a hole in the lily pad. The creature rolled into the water. Nino shouted out, "Great shot, Santino!" Franco joined in, "Wow, what a shot!"

But I was having difficulty listening to them as my heart sank in the pond with that frog. I felt relief as the frog leaped out into the thicket, and I heard my friends making sense. "We better stop," exclaimed Franco. "Yeah, we are hurting them!" responded Nino. "Where are the barracks anyway?" I asked. "Come, let's go," Franco said, and we followed him through the tall perennials speckled with white, yellow, purple, and occasionally orange that identified the poppies. The white dandelion tops flew in our faces as we kept toward the barracks. "They're all demolished!" I yelled out. "Bombs were dropped here during the war, Santino."

"*Che miseria*! What misery!" I softly said. "Look over here, guys," called out Nino, and we ran over to find scattered remnants of clothing under broken terracotta slates fallen from the roof among the debris of broken blocks that left holes in the wall. "I'm tired!" Nino said as he sat on a small heap of blocks. Franco and I leaned against the wall next to each other and slid down to sit on a semi-clean area, partially shaded from the sun. "Hey, look, I think this is part of a canteen," said Nino as he dug out the spout. "Hey," he continued, "You think maybe if we keep looking, we'll find an old gun?"

"I doubt it. The weapons were all cleared out long ago." Franco lifted the laced shoe part of a boot from its tongue after rummaging through dust and debris. I looked around and felt drawn to the streaks of light entering from holes in the wall. I looked at the guys. "Hey, I wonder if my Papá was here during the war!"

Piccolo Santino

"Everybody was stationed here at first, and then they were sent off!" Franco responded. I said, "The Russians captured my Papá, and Mamma told us he was in a concentration camp for five years." Nino and Franco both reacted. "*Cazzo!* Fuck! That is scary!" Franco said. Then he added, "My Papá was placed in a German concentration camp three months just before the war ended. Three months is not like five years at least!" He turned to Nino, "What about your papá, Nino?"

"They don't talk about it to me. But I heard talk about how they met in a hospital as my Mamma was nursing a leg wound on my papá."

"Per davvero? For real?" we both reacted, "Si!" Nino assured us. Franco asked, "Did you ever hear about where it happened?"

"Someplace up north, by Trieste. There might be some truth since Papá has a long scar on his right thigh."

"Do you ever ask him about the scar?" inquired Franco. "He just says he got it in the war."

"Guys, listen! Do you hear voices?" I said as I got up to look outside. They both got up and ran out. Nino pointed toward the sound and said, "It's coming from over there!"

"Sounds like playing of some kind!" I exclaimed. "Let's go see. Come on!" Franco said, Nino interrupted, "Wait a minute, I gotta piss!"

"Come on, piss while you're walking!"

"I don't want to get all wet!" He didn't even bother to unbutton his pants. He lifted one side of his shorts, let it hang out as he walked backward, and shouted back at us, "Just wait a minute, you guys!"

"We'll stroll until you catch up," Franco shouted back, and the voices ahead were getting more transparent. There was a group of guys possibly playing a game of soccer. "I'm gonna beat you guys over there!" shouted Nino as he ran past us and shouted, "There is a soccer game going on!" We followed as he kept ahead, and as we got closer, the grass was taller than we were for a short moment, so we pushed through with our hands, and those voices got louder. "Pass it here!"

"No, Paolo!" The voices reached their apex, we pushed ourselves through the thick hair grass and found ourselves in front of a large clearing. We could see older boys from sixteen to early twenties scrambling

Piccolo Santino

to take possession of the soccer ball.

"Over here now!"

"Pass it here!" shouted someone from the opposition.

"No! No! To me! To me!" Four boys converged close to the goalie area as one dribbled the ball with his feet, and the other attempted to steal it away. A thin player, tall with thick lips and a long face, positioned himself as the goalie, and I quickly recognized him. "That's Aldo," I said to Nino and Franco. "His Papá and Master Santino are cousins!"

"Dante, over here! I'm the goalie now!" shouted Aldo. Dante took his eyes off the ball to look at Aldo rushing forward. "Over here, Aldo!" Another player rushed in to intercept the ball, and sent it to the foul side of the goal area. Aldo ran and retrieved the ball with his hands, and the opposition shouted out, "Penalty!"

"No! No! I was also the goalie since we are short a player!"

"Yeah, but you didn't yell it out when you took over as goalie!"

"Yes, I did. Some of your guys were right here. They heard me. Didn't you Dante?"

"No! Dante doesn't count. He is on your team!"

"What do you mean he doesn't count?"

"He can say he heard you even if he didn't!"

"That's not right. We need another player then, or you lose a player!"

"Oh no, we can't lose a player!" Aldo shook his head in bewilderment and stopped shaking when he saw us sitting at the perimeter. "Wait a minute. Never mind, I found a goalie!" He ran over to me and shouted my name, "Santino! Where did you come from?" Startled that he even knew my name, I looked up as he rushed over, and I remembered Mamma saying that she would talk to Aldo about his being my sponsor when I made my confirmation. I guessed she must have spoken to him since he called my name. "Santino, come with me. We need a goalie!" I gave a bewildered look of terror, and Aldo read me instantly. "No, don't worry, I won't let anything happen to you. You just stand guard over here between these two rocks and block the ball. You

Piccolo Santino

can use your hands." I looked up at him and responded timidly, "*Va bene.* All right?"

"Don't worry! I'll run in front of you if some of the guys rush the ball here."

"What are you doing? He's just a kid," someone from the opposition shouted. "He can do it!" Then said. "I'll protect him. Agreed?"

"All right, agreed. Let's go then!" The players took the field, and my friends stood up as I took my place in front of the goal area and nervously waited to see if the ball would come to me. Luckily, a player kicked the ball to the opposite side of the field. I looked at my friends as they smiled at me with their fists pumped. Like a spark, four to five players positioned close by me readied themselves to fight for the ball. The ball appeared about six meters in front of me. Aldo dashed into position and kicked the ball back to the center of the field. He then leaned over slightly and pointed to me with a smile. Franco and Nino jumped up and down in excitement as they yelled toward me, "Santino, you're safe!"

"For now!" I yelled back, and the ball was kicked to the left. Then, the right, down the center for a quarter of the field, past the center, and toward the opposition. Aldo chased after it, and then he ran past center field to receive the ball. His teammate yelled out, "Aldo, pass it back to me. Hurry!" An opposition player got in front of him, but Aldo faked a turn and then passed the ball to his teammate, who faked kicking it to the right of the goal side. Instead, the ball landed in the left corner of the goal. The goalie tried to recover by jumping back to the left, but the ball flew past his outstretched body, and he fell to the ground.

"Bravo! Bravo, Filippo!" Four nearby teammates jumped all over Filippo, screaming, "Four-three, the score is four-three in our favor. We're close to the end now." The goalie ran out from inside the field of hair grass with the ball in his hands and called out, "All right, everybody get into position. The score is four to three!" He kicked the ball into the center field before my two defenders. Nino and Franco ran down the line as they yelled to me, "Santino, get ready for a goal!"

I spread my feet out in preparation to dive to either side of me, and like a swarm of bees, players rushed for the ball and smothered it like

Piccolo Santino

ants on a piece of *Perugina* chocolate. No one succeeded in taking control, and somebody kicked it foul between Franco and Nino into the tall grass. Two players yelled out together at Franco and Nino. "Hey, boys, can you get the ball for us?" No sooner said, Franco yelled back, "I found it! I found it!" He ran back and threw the ball to possibly the hairiest person in the world. He was of average height and wearing a white tank top, shouting out into the field. "It's our ball. You guys kicked it foul!"

"*Va bene!* All right! Let's go already, *brutto*, ugly." Aldo was inside the playing field as others took positions. I watched as it all felt too close for comfort and positioned myself again for a possible goal. My friends yelled out to me, "Get ready, Santino!"

What felt like a gang of bullies converging together to gain individual control suddenly changed to three players and then to one person. Like a flash of lightning, the ball smacked me on the left side of my face. With my face burning, I saw Aldo floating toward me. My cheek felt like the grooves of a soccer ball, and I saw it sail deep into the field of hair grass with loud shouting ringing in my ear. "Game over! Game Over!" followed by whispers of "Santino, you all right?"

"Santino, you all right?" I couldn't tell whose voices they were, as the burning on my cheek dulled any logic. I simply recalled bodies running onto the field after the ball, and then a mass of people converged around me. A flush ran through me. I turned my head left, right, up, and down, then slowly identified Franco and Nino appearing frozen next to me. Excited, Aldo held me by my shoulders, shouting, "Santino, you saved the game! We won! We won!" The other boys celebrated by jumping up and down in jubilation, their disbelief at the unexpected victory adding to the frenzy.

"Come on. We found the ball. Let's get to the bar!" someone shouted. Aldo, stopped as three other guys around me walked away, murmuring to each other about me being okay and not even hurt. Aldo looked down at me and said, "Santino, tell your mamma I'll be by to talk to her about being your sponsor for your confirmation." I looked into his eyes with a perplexed look as I nodded a "Yes" and softly said, "*Va bene,*

Piccolo Santino

that's good." Then he repeated, "I'll be happy to be your sponsor!"

"Aldo, come on already," a voice called out, and Aldo ran off with his friends to the opposite end of the soccer field. They all disappeared inside the perennials.

"Santino, we thought you were a goner the way the ball hit you in the face!" Nino took a close look and joked, "You look okay, but the black and white squares on your face might never go away."

"*Per davvero?* For real?" I said, in a panic, then rubbed it and felt the ball's thick texture on my skin. "He's just joking, Santino. Your cheek looks fine! It's just red, that's all." Nino exclaimed, "Come on, let's get a drink of water. There's a fountain near here.

We headed west after the big boys headed east, and both parties needed to head south toward opposite ends of town at some point. The sky to me felt doused with a deep sense of loneliness in its silence but alive with a vast volume of light blue. I felt a sense of emptiness as I thought about where my papá might be, as his time zone was six hours behind.

From the corner of my eye, I saw an old man with three white cows walking toward the same water fountain as we approached. Franco ran to the spout, and Nino and I waited our turn. I watched as the old man brought his cows to the overflowing large cement basin. His thoughts seemed to have been pantomimed by the quietness in the sky. I looked into his gaunt face. His glare radiated the field's depth and the lonely sky's vastness. Mamma's warnings about not muddying up my shoes came to mind as I slipped with my right foot on the wet grass and stepped into the mud.

The old man looked at me. I studied his worn-looking garbs. His jacket had holes with some patches sewn into it. His baggy pants were held up by a leather belt that had a knot tied and twisted out of shape. Under his wide-rimmed brown hat with a corner missing, he showed sorrowful eyes that made me wish I had a piece of bread for him. I regained my balance and bent down to drink from the gushing spout of cool water. I observed how the cows sank their long pink tongues into the water basin during their drinking moment. Then sucked them back into their mouths repeatedly at rapid speed, and I wondered if the amount of water spilling out from their mouths was equal to the amount they swallowed. I cupped my lips to the rushing water for one last swallow as its magical coolness rejuvenated my body for the long walk home.

    Nino and Franco returned to the fountain for seconds, and I watched the old man maneuver his cows away from the water trough. While we were joined by water for mutual need, I realized the old man never drank. Franco exclaimed, "That was good."

    "It got rid of that tired feeling in my legs completely," Nino answered, "Me too!" I added as Franco led the way home; I followed, looking back to glance at the old man as we became specks in each other's distance. It made me think of my sister, Martina, who always told me that God sometimes visited us on earth, and we never knew how.

    I was surprised when nobody answered my knock. I checked the key's hiding place at the bottom of the doorframe and didn't find it; the key was usually wrapped in a small towel or just placed under a rock inside the hole. I decided to go downstairs, thinking Mamma might be in the storage room, but that was also locked. Hoping to find her across the street, I quietly opened the door to Aunt Isabella's. I peeked in and spotted them seated next to each other. I bashfully made my way down the short hallway and saw Martina crocheting as usual, with cousin Bianca helping her and my other siblings seated on the wooden floor close to each other.

    I stopped by the end of the large dinner table to my right, and just then, Cousin Eugenio walked in from the kitchen and sat across from me. Mamma immediately shook her finger at me and shouted, "Where have you been all holy day?" Aunt Isabella told Mamma, "Don't be harsh with him, child. He is also feeling lost." Mamma changed her tone, asking me, "Did you eat anything?"

    "N-n-no!" I answered haltingly. "We already ate. I don't know what to do for you now." Sitting at the table across from me, Cousin Eugenio said, "Oh no! I'm sure I can find something for him." Cousin Eugenio was a tall, lanky gentleman in his late twenties who suffered from ulcers and was almost always dressed in brown clothing. He got up and returned from the kitchen with a large piece of homemade bread and a hunk of homemade cheese and said, "Mangia Santino! Mangia!"

"Gr-Gr-Grazie, Eugenio!" I said. Aunt Isabella said, "Eugenio, there should be some dried olives in the kitchen, too!" Eugenio returned and placed a handful of the black dried olives on top of the muslin tablecloth before me. "I also found a little bit of wine for you."

"G-g-grazie molto, Eugenio!"

"Mangia, mangia son, eat, and God bless you," said Aunt Isabella. I thanked her, but I stuttered, "G-g-Grazie, Zia!" Mamma then scolded me, "Why don't you say the words all at once with force? That way, you won't stutter." Aunt Isabella asked Mamma, "Does he always talk like that?"

"A lot of times, but mostly, he is okay."

"Most likely, he'll outgrow it," said Aunt Isabella. Mamma responded, "I think the doctors have to slit this part under his tongue." Mamma opened her mouth and pointed to the webbing on the under part of the tongue. "Oh my God! You believe that?" said Aunt Isabella. "Somebody told me that a doctor did it for someone, and that person spoke normally afterward."

"Oh God, I hope that's not true!"

"I don't know. When we get to America, they can do something. As they continued talking and shifting from topic to topic, I finished my food, only to drop my head down on the table with my eyes feeling heavy. Then Bianca said to Martina, "No! No! Martina, not like that!"

"I can't do it that way!" The voices felt like they were fading in and out. "Here, let me show you!" A different voice with a new topic interrupted my twilight, "That was right after the war ended," I thought that was Aunt Isabella speaking. Eugenio's voice woke me up, and I felt the long day quickly weighing heavy on me. I tried to sleep again, and Eugenio said, "Don't you remember we had to lead him around by the hand all over the place?"

Piccolo Santino

Voices continued floating around the space by my ears, "Oh, poor Bartolo! Five years trapped in that horrible Russian concentration camp!"

I thought I heard Martina say, "Mamma, look at Santino," in a whispered voice in the room, and it reverberated in and out of my mind. I tried to make sense of what was just said by my sister, and then Mamma's voice interjected, "His friend froze to death in his sleep right beside my husband." I tried to envision a man frozen to death, but my head slid off the table, and my arms reached out to catch my balance. I heard laughter and quickly asked, "Are we going home, Mamma?" I regained my balance, mumbled the exact words repeatedly with my head on my arms and craving the comfort of my bed. I then lost continuity as their talking bashed my subconscious.

"They were so malnourished, and all were sent home naked from Russia in the middle of winter."

"What horror!"

"Bianca, can you show that to me again? I'm having a hard time!" I felt myself sliding again but did not have the will to take control. The voices in the room kept competing with the comfort zone that I was trying to achieve. "They had to be led by the hand as they got off the train."

"I heard a lot of them were blind. Isn't that right, Eugenio?"

"I remember going to meet Bartolo. Anna, you didn't even believe he was alive!"

"I wasn't getting any letters from him for the longest time!"

"He was so blind I had to lead him by his hand from the bus stop." That sounded like Eugenio. I found the urge to call out with my head tucked in my arms on top of the table, "Mamma! Are we leaving now?"

"Just wait. Not now!" I lifted my head toward Mamma. "I want to go to bed!" I rudely said. "We are not leaving! If you are that tired, take the key and go home by yourself! Just leave the door open for us." I lay there simmering at the idea of going home by myself. I thought it would feel more natural if we all left together. I heard Stella whispering. I felt myself wobbling.

"Look, Lillo! Santino is going to fall again." I felt myself swaying amid more voices echoing inside my head. "But the war was horrible for

Piccolo Santino

us at home too!" Annoyed, I yelled out, "Mamma! Are we going now?" Laughter broke out as I stopped myself from rolling off the table and got up startled and dazed, causing Mamma to yell at me, "Here, take the key and go to bed. We'll be home later!" Unable to fight it any longer, I surrendered, "Sì." I said, "Here, make sure you leave the door unlocked!" Mamma said as I took the key from her and exited.

There was moonlight outside to guide me down the steps and across the street. I struggled for the keyhole like a drunk, and once I got inside, I closed the door behind me. I put the key down someplace, kicked my shoes off, unbuttoned my shorts, and let them slide independently. I lifted the covers and jumped right in with my eyes already closed.

Minutes later, I heard men talking outside as I lay in bed. Then, they stopped right by the door and continued talking loudly. I rolled over twice and then tried holding my ears tight long enough to fall asleep, but instead, one or possibly two other men joined them and talked even louder. Some of them walked closer to me behind the wall, their voices swelling. I hoped that they would go away, but instead, they debated a recent news item about an escaped convict who supposedly was on the loose and possibly headed south in our area. I jumped out of bed, bolted the door, and ran back to bed shaken, planning to open the door for Mamma as soon as they got home.

Soundly tucked in my warm bed, my eyes slowly brought into focus Mamma's image, patiently sitting in a chair with her hands resting in her lap. Gradually, my mind tried to process the information, and as we made eye contact, like a bolt of lightning, she leaped from her chair with her right hand high in the air and began pounding me through the covers with a thick olive stick. At first, it didn't feel too bad as the covers provided some protection, but then she ripped the covers off and poured it on as she vented her anger. Like flashes of lightning, the hits repeated on my body as I slithered out of bed in my underwear.

I raised my arms to cover my head, but Mamma was too creative as she maneuvered blows to my legs. I danced. She switched from leg to leg, then to my upper body. My eyes billowed, and tears poured out. My

Piccolo Santino

only defense was to cry out louder. During all this time, I tried to figure out what happened, as I never heard her come home and didn't know how she got into the house.

Mamma's blows were hard and eternal, and I thought back to when Papá used to protect us from her, but he could not hear my crying. So, I cried harder, hoping that it would make her stop. I listened to the sounds of a trowel tapping on stone and cement slapping on the wall, and from the corner of my eye, I partially saw a man peering inside from the bottom of the doorframe. Then another man's voice, working low to the ground, pleaded with Mamma, "Signora, it wasn't his fault!" I reached for my shirt on the floor as she turned to him. Then the other man joined in. "The kid just fell asleep, that's all. Signora!"

"Don't you mind, this one knows exactly what he did!" I sneaked my left arm into my shirtsleeve and turned my face away, hoping to slide my right arm into place before her next blow, but Mamma was shrewd. She went right for my shoulder, and it was too late as I pushed my arm through. It was all becoming clear to me as tears poured down my face. I realized the mason was here to reconstruct the stones he removed so the carpenter could disassemble the door frame from the wall to get the door opened. I didn't hear any of that during the night.

Blows rained down on my back as I bent down for my pants, and I turned to block Mamma, and I wished I were a spider with multiple arms, but then Mamma would have more places to swing at, so I sucked it up and quickly lifted my shorts as she also berated me. "*Mascalzone!* Scoundrel! Why did you lock us out?" I didn't think a response would help, so I slipped my left foot into my pants leg, and she zapped me on my right leg. I switched legs, and so did her stick. Then I thought I heard Eugenio's voice over my crying as Mamma chagrined me again with words, "You think you can just do as you please in this house?"

I buttoned my shorts quickly and lifted my hands to slip on my suspenders, but instead, I had to protect my head, and I caught one between both wrists. With my next scream, I sensed possible relief when Eugenio's voice rushed over from across the street, saying. "Anna, let him go. He is just a boy!" Eugenio stopped inside the doorway and made

Piccolo Santino

me feel that he might be my savior, but Mamma still had some more left in her, and I absorbed it all. "*Pezzo di merda.* You piece of shit. Why did you lock the door?"

"Anna, for goodness sake, let him alone. He's just a boy."

"Just a boy, nothing. This one does it on purpose, I tell you!" She raised the stick high in the air, and I could feel her thinking I locked her out on purpose. I shrugged and peeked between my forearms in front of my eyes as I tried to cover my head and turned my back to her to take her most brutal blow on my shoulders, but thankfully, Eugenio still had her attention. "He gets me so riled up with the stunts he pulls all the time." He distracted her long enough for me to slip on my suspenders with my shirttails out. "Go on, get dressed, and get out of this house right now!" Eugenio stepped inside, looked at me, and addressed Mamma. "Anna, what he did was innocent. Don't be so harsh on the boy!"

"Innocent, you say? This one is as cunning as a fox!"

"No! That can't be true."

"*Ti dico che è vero!* I tell you, it's true! He was being vengeful because we didn't leave last night when he wanted us to! He doesn't fool me!" She stared me down with piercing eyes, lifted her apron, and blew her nose into it. I looked for my socks and realized I never took them off going to bed, so I slipped into my shoes, ignoring the shoelaces to make haste past her. Mamma continued talking to Eugenio. "He's like the devil, I tell you!"

I rushed out the doorway, wondering how to spend my day, and ran down the block to the street with the long shadows at the top. I turned around the bend to be in seclusion and stopped to tie my shoes as I tried to control my sniffling. I peeked around the side of the building and watched the carpenter and mason work together to restore the door's integrity; I did not dare hang around by the house. I needed to freshen up, so I walked past the mayor's office and down to the public fountain. I splashed cold water on my face, and shivers traveled through me, but it was nothing compared to what I had just endured from Mamma. I heard the footsteps of people, but I didn't bother to look up. I held my mouth under the rushing water and took a long drink as I listened to the women

Piccolo Santino

talk. "There's no school in the summer. What is this little boy doing out so early?"

"I don't know. He must have done something bad. Look at the welts on his legs."

"Poor child, how bad could he have been?"

"Oh, the poor creature!"

I quickly rinsed my face, walked away, and ventured across from the fountain down a side street I had not yet explored. The road was so narrow it felt more like an alley of balconies, and neighbors could almost reach over and shake hands as some of them shared a laundry line across from each other. I looked at these heavy doors made of olive wood, the same as my house. Further down, I saw oak doors. I might not have paid any mind before, but since I had been at the carpenter shop, I had learned to appreciate such skill, and of course, this morning, I had witnessed the durability of olive wood.

The center of the street had odious smells in the gutter, either from urinal pots dumped from above or dirty dishwater. But there was one distinct foul odor I didn't wish to study further, so I rushed my steps and concentrated on the sharp sunlight ahead where the alley opened into the large market square. Water dripped on my head, and I looked up at beautiful red carnations around a balcony above me. These people were up early to water their plants, so I decided to move away to avoid getting drenched, and I marveled at the new view of the square. Two loud voices echoed from one of the surrounding houses. "Rosina, where did you put my fuck'n pants last night?"

"You're wearing them. You came home so fuck'n drunk you never even took them off!"

I looked to the left corner of the square at the very narrow entrance, fit primarily for pedestrians, across from the tabacchino. Further down from that passage, the church for Sunday mass was in the center. The street on the other side of the church I was not yet familiar with. Directly across from the church, in the center of the square, was a large pit area where they held markets on various days. Inside the pit was a maze-like area sectioned off by concrete walls about my height. Fishermen set up

Piccolo Santino

their stands inside the pit with many fish to sell on Fridays. I decided to walk across and check out that pit, but once I got a sniff of the lingering fish smell, I kept walking and explored the street ahead of me to the left.

The morning had started so hot that I was grateful for the shade between the buildings. I was particularly drawn to this side street because of its width, a stark contrast to the first narrow street I had explored. It was wide enough for a small car to maneuver, although it would have to navigate the various descending and ascending steps. I was amused by the thought of a car climbing over steps, a sight I had never seen before. "Hold still, you hairy thing. You savage! You stubborn brat!"

"Ahh! Nonna, you are pulling too hard!"

"Hold still before I smack you one!" I discreetly glanced up to a balcony at a little girl sitting in a chair as her grandmother combed her hair, but I tried to be discreet after that outburst. Then, a neighbor's voice abruptly called out. "What are you doing to that poor child?"

"Ma fatte le cazze tue! Mind your fuck'n business this morning!"

I reached the bottom of the street, followed its soft curves to the right, and climbed the first group of cobblestone steps. My ears became intrigued by a magical sound rattling about in this area. I climbed the street further up, and I thought the sound was coming from crickets or maybe the ticking of time, but it sounded so rigid, light, and graceful. I found its rhythm continuous and very haunting. From the highest step, I peered inside through slightly opened shutters. A woman was seated in a chair in front of a giant wooden contraption with armatures holding many strands of thread in a seemingly static position. I noticed her pedaling with her feet, and then with her hands, she fed an item left to right in between the lines of thread coming down from armatures on top, which seemed to converge in a straight line left to right. The sun landing on the strings almost looked like the sun rays were woven into a pristine white cloth. Then, a man asked her, "Teresina, what do we have to eat this morning?"

"Mario, I have to finish here before noon! Go find something!" I ducked away and continued my way up the street. I climbed eight steps, each about a meter in depth. I reached the top and turned left, with the

Piccolo Santino

sun beating down on my forehead no matter what side of the street I was on. I hugged the buildings to my right, hoping to get some shade from the overhang, and the rhythmic sounds of wood clanking escaped through an opened window, followed by an older woman's voice. "*Aspetta!* Wait! Let me get on top!"

"But if I can't make it going downhill? *Como faró a salire?* How am I gonna make it going uphill?" responded a male voice. I kicked a stone, and it ricocheted loudly off the wall, "Shhh! S*ilencio*, quiet," the woman said. I glanced back and saw the shutters closing. I quickly turned the corner at the next building to my right. My paternal grandfather Massimo was locking his door and was startled as he saw me. "What are you doing over here? Your father left for America. I already told your mother to stay away from here." Numbed in place, I stared at him for a pause. "Go on, get away from me." He waved with the back of his hand as he angrily shouted at me. "I have no more ties with all of you." He quipped as he walked away, and I never saw him again.

I made my way to the very top, where metal pipes supported by brick posts traveled horizontally, parallel to my house. As I approached a railing post, I heard arguing over a card game inside the bar. Feeling hungry, I leaned on the end railing post and furtively stared toward my house. And after a short spell, I decided to risk walking home.

I opened the door slowly and vigilantly walked inside the foyer and moved as quietly as dust, even though I didn't see anybody around. I reached for the breadbox, quickly grabbed a nice hunk of bread, and headed to the carpenter shop, kicking stones between bites.

Master Santino and his partner were supposed to be away working on location for the next two weeks, and Rocco and Bruno were in charge, but this morning, they had some personal business to settle. They were coming in late, so I hoped the place was open by now. I had been wandering the streets for at least two hours, and the sun was halfway toward the noon part of the sky. After eating half of the bread, I put the uneaten half in my pocket for later as I swallowed. I kicked one last stone down the street and walked up the ramp. I sidestepped their bicycles parked against the building, at first, I used to resent their presence as it made me feel they usurped the individual attention I was receiving from Mastro Santino. Still I got comfortable with them, and I liked the composure I gained, which empowered me to speak freely with them. The door was wide open. I saw them in the rear of the room. Rocco measured a longboard on the workbench while Bruno held it still, and I yelled out, "Ciao!"

"Ciao, Tino!" they both said and then Rocco added, "What! You always come to work in the middle of the day?"

"What? You told me to come late today!"

"No, we didn't." They both answered at once, and I blushed with embarrassment thinking the boss would find out and hold it against me somehow. I slowed down my walk and put my head down, and Rocco said, "No, no, we're teasing you!" I then responded back, *"Voi siete cazzi di buffoni!* You guys are fuck'n jokesters!" Both stared at me with startled faces, and Bruno quietly said, "Hey, you shouldn't talk like that. The boss's wife might hear you upstairs, and then we'll have to explain everything!"

" Si. Si b-b-Basta! Okay, stop it," I said. Feeling defeated. I lost my composure and continued, "I'll get the n-n-nail b-bucket and sit in the doorway."

"No! We need you here!" Rocco said as he reached for the handsaw lying on the bench. He looked at Bruno and said, "Bruno, you hold the board down, and Santino, you blow the sawdust off so I can see the pencil line."

Bruno pushed the board out from the bench as Rocco got into position to saw it length-wise, and I bent down. As Rocco began sawing, I wiped the sawdust off my face and continued looking for the pencil line. "He's looking on the bottom," Bruno said to Rocco." Why are you looking down there?" demanded Rocco as he stopped sawing, and I spit some sawdust, "Why are you looking at the bottom of the board?" He pensively said, "Hey, wait a minute. I know you from someplace!" I looked up at him, and he and Bruno began to look familiar to me also. "Hey Bruno, isn't he the one with the oranges?"

"What!"

Piccolo Santino

"Yeah, he's the one who gave us the rotten oranges at the Fontana Di Taccuni, remember? Last year."

"For real? Are you sure?"

"Don't you remember last year we were passing by and stopped there? He was sitting under the shade in their driveway with his sisters and brother. When we asked them for a couple of oranges." Bruno turned toward me for a closer look and said. "Hey, yeah, now I remember! We talked to him through the closed gates from the top of the driveway and asked them to pick the oranges off the tree, not from the ground."

I felt like shrinking as he continued berating me. "They looked good on the outside, but they were rotten after we left and peeled them." They both shouted out at once at me, "You fooled us!" Then Rocco interjected, "Tu sei il *imbroglione!* You're the cheater!" I defended myself. "Well, you didn't want to pay, so what did you expect?"

"So that's it. Now we know you are a real scammer," shouted out, Bruno and Rocco sarcastically said, "By the way, the pencil line is on the top of the board, not on the bottom!"

"Oh!" I responded quietly.

"Blow on top here so I can see the line as I saw!" I reacted with slightly more energy, "Oh! All right!" They looked at one another with contorted smiles, and Rocco put his weight on the board with his hands as he sawed. I blew the sawdust off on top but didn't see a line. A woman's brisk voice interrupted our tranquility. "*Buongiorno Ragazzi!* Good morning, guys!" Startled by a woman's voice, Rocco looked as if frozen stiff with the saw in his hand, and we all turned to face the boss's wife standing in the center of the room. "Buongiorno, Signora!"

"I just came down to introduce myself as my husband suggested." Rocco and Bruno responded to Mrs. Romanelli as she walked toward us. "It's a pleasure to meet you, Signora."

"And which of you boys is Rocco, and who is Bruno?" Rocco responded with a broad smile and then pointed to Bruno, who responded with the most superficial smile. Rocco said, "And, of course, you already know Santino, but we call him by his nickname Tino."

Piccolo Santino

"Of course. He has the same name as my husband, Santino!" She said the name with such emotion and flair that I let the sound slowly burn in my ears as she kept on talking, "He is so quiet, but Santino does everything he is told without any trouble at all. The master just loves having him here."

"Yes, he's very helpful to us, too," Rocco replied with a wry smile. "Well boys, I must go back upstairs, but please know that the master wants you to tell me if you have any difficulty with any of the work, and I will relay the information to him when he gets home at night."

"Grazie, we'll be glad to check with you before we leave, Mrs. Romanelli."

"You're welcome! All right then, I'll leave you, boys, to your work."

"Thank you again, signora, and arrivederci."

"Arrivederci!" We returned to work, Rocco exclaimed loudly, his head turned toward the sound of the boss's wife's footsteps going up the stairway, "All right, Bruno, slide the board out so I can saw it!" Bruno leaned in toward Rocco as he whispered, "Do you think she was there all that time?" Rocco quietly reacted with a dumb look as he shrugged his shoulders. Bruno continued whispering, "She came down to check on us. She is not fooling me!" Rocco turned to him with his eyes bulging and index finger up to his closed lips. I asked loudly, "Where's the line?"

Rocco lowered his hand from his mouth, pointed down at the board while he was still looking toward the stairway, and said, "Right there! Are you blind?" I looked closely and said, "It's not there. Maybe it blew off." He turned to Bruno while shaking his head and softly said, "This guy is either blind or *pazzo*. Crazy!"

"There it is. It's on the bottom!" I exclaimed, and Bruno turned the board over to reveal the pencil line. Dumbfounded, Bruno mimicked Mrs. Romanelli in a sotto voce, "He does everything he's told. The master just loves having him around." I looked over to him and said, "She's coming back! Quiet guys." They stared at me, and Rocco said, "Why don't you get out of here and go fill the water bottle for lunchtime." Eagerly, I responded, "Yeah? Okay!"

Piccolo Santino

I grabbed the two empty bottles and walked out the door down the dirt steps at the end of the landing, and as I turned right, I heard my name called from down the street. "Bianchi *aspetta,* wait up." I turned my head to Franco running and yelled out to him, "Ciao, Franco."

"Ciao, Bianchi."

"Come on I'm going to the stream for Water."

"Let's go. I can use a drink of water!" Franco stopped next to me and bent down to pick a couple of pebbles while talking and walking," I figured I'd find you here. I heard your boss was working in Vibo for a couple of weeks."

"Yeah, how'd you find out?"

"My big brother has a friend in Vibo who works at the same job site." He put the pebbles in his pocket and continued walking with me, "Oh wow! D-d-did your brother say what kind of work they are doing?"

"Yeah. They are putting a roof on this new building. It's some factory."

"I guess they will be there for a few weeks then."

"Come on, let's hurry. I'm thirsty."

"Okay, let's walk fast." We double-responded by timing past the first set of caves and the second caves; then, we slowed down to a regular walk as we turned left into the walkway behind the thicket on the side of the road. The downslope was steep enough to require some respect. We walked a single file until we reached the bottom, where the terrain was more tolerant. Franco ran fast ahead of me to the rustling spring. I caught up to him and scanned the area as Franco drank. I spotted a sparrow in the brush above us and whispered, "Franco, there's a bird inside that bush above us to the right." Franco slowly rose, pulled his slingshot from his back pocket, and whispered, "Is it still there?"

"Sì, he just moved inside the raspberry bush."

"Okay, I see him!" He slowly loaded his slingshot with a pebble and quietly took aim, and within the sound of the release, the missile reverberated inside the brush. "Wow! Franco, I think you got him!"

"Yeah, I think so. I'm gonna climb up there and see." He scrambled up on all fours, and once he reached the raspberry plant, he looked inside the underbrush for a minute and then said, "Sì, I see it!" He reached inside and came up holding the limp bird by its head and yelled out, *"Proprio Nella testa!* Right in the head!"

"Wow, Franco, what a shot!"

"I can't wait" to bring it home so my mamma can cook it for me." He carefully slid down the slope, and as he landed on flat ground, he brought the catch up closer for me to look at. "Look at this. It's a pretty good size bird too! Isn't it?"

"Veramente! For real! The one, my sister, caught last week with the mousetrap was really small compared to this one."

"Oh, my mamma won't believe her eyes. Come on, let's go!"

"Wait, I gotta fill this bottle yet!"

"Okay, I'll wait."

Franco and I talked in the street outside the shop before going inside. We were still admiring the bird. Then I overheard Rocco and Bruno talking, and I peeked inside, motioning for Franco to be quiet. Rocco locked one of the boards he cut into the vice, checked the sawed-off end with a square, and said to Bruno, "Do you think Tino got lost?" We leaned past their view slightly. "He's the boss's pet now. Watch what you say!" Rocco looked up at Bruno after running the square several times across the edge of the board and said, "Yeah, but when is he coming back already?" Rocco looked for the plane. Bruno understood Rocco's body language, grabbed it off the workbench, and handed it to him as Rocco continued talking, "Didn't you notice? He met his friend outside, and they left together!" He took the plane into his hands and checked the blade for depth, and began making a slight adjustment. "No wonder! He'll be gone for at least a year now." Said Bruno sarcastically, and Rocco reacted, "No, I don't think so, maybe a week or so."

"I'm hungry. Why don't we stop to eat anyway?" Rocco put down the plane after having adjusted the blade and said, "Yeah, why not. He's gotta come back soon." They both got their lunchboxes from a shelf in the rear of the room and pulled up stools across from each other at the

Piccolo Santino

end of the bench by the entrance.

"I'm going right home and see if my mamma is there." Franco said, I saw Bruno peek outside at the sound of Franco's voice. I nudged Franco forward, hoping Bruno hadn't seen me. He said to Rocco, "They're back, finally!" I walked with Franco down to the shallow part of the ramp at the other end of the shop so I could keep talking to him. "I hear them talking outside." Bruno said. Rocco asked, "Where is he going? He walked right past us!" Rocco stepped in the doorway, "Let me see."

"If my mamma is not home, maybe my sister can cook it for me." Franco said to me. "Enjoy the meal, Franco."

"Grazie. Ciao, Bianchi!"

"Ciao." I turned left up the ramp and stopped by Rocco standing in the doorway. "What took you so long?"

"Franco got a bird with his slingshot."

"Oh, he won't show it to us?"

"No, he went home so his mamma can cook it for him." We walked inside, and Bruno held his thumb slightly away from his index finger and commented, "What was it about this big?"

"Yeah? You should've seen it! Here's the water." I placed the bottles on the bench between their lunch boxes. I took out the hunk of bread, from the morning. I sat down on the door stoop. Rocco said to Bruno. "Why don't we go see a movie tonight? There's a new American cowboy movie playing with a *Jungle Jim* movie!"

"Wow, two good movies. We could go since we don't have to wait for the boss tonight."

"If he has anything new, he'll leave a note with his wife anyway."

"We should be done early today." Curious about where the movie was, I asked them, "Where is the feast?"

"There's no feast anywhere tonight," answered Rocco. "Then where are you going to see the movie?" I asked, "Movies are not shown just at a feast. You can go to a theater!" replied Rocco. "What's a theater?"

"It's a place where they show movies every night."

Piccolo Santino

"Can anybody go there?"

"Yeah! But you have to buy a ticket."

"Oh. Does it cost a lot?"

"No, just a few lire."

"Do they have a theater close to here anywhere?" Rocco responded, "No, we have to go to Vibo."

"Oh, that's far." Bruno raised his right hand to his chin and asked me, "You never went to a movie?"

"No! Who is Jungle Jim anyway?"

"He's like Tarzan of the Jungle," Bruno said. "I don't even know who that is." Then Rocco said, "We can bring you a comic book to look at tomorrow."

"Yeah, my papá got me a comic book when he went to Naples."

"Oh, which one did he get you?"

"He got one called, *Il Cavaliere Sensa Volto*."

"That comic book?"

"Yeah. With a masked man and an Indian?"

"That's right!" Rocco excitedly said, "Bring it tomorrow, and we'll bring ours."

"Okay." They slid their stools away from the bench and lit up cigarettes and began blowing smoke rings in the air. "How do you do that?" I asked, and Bruno replied, "Just by putting our tongue inside the smoke as we blow out." Then Rocco said, "Here, watch this one."

"Wow! That was a real big one!" Then they both looked each other in the eyes in agreement, then turned to me, and Bruno said, "We can also make the smoke come out of our ears."

"Really? Let me see you do it!" They looked at each other, and Bruno said to Rocco, "You show him. You can do it real good."

"All right, but it works a lot better if I sit down on the stoop." He got up from his stool and sat on the stoop with his back against the door frame and said to me, "All right, now get closer to me and put your right hand here against my chest. Keep staring at my ears." I leaned to rest my

Piccolo Santino

right hand against his chest and stared at both of his ears. "Okay, are you ready?"

"I'm ready."

"Okay, look hard while I inhale and hold the smoke in." I watched him take a long drag and then stared at his ears. Suddenly, I felt a burn on the back of my hand, and I screamed out. *"Che cazzo mi hai fatto?* What the fuck did you do?" They both laughed hard as I scrambled to my feet and blew on my hand. "That burned my hand. You tricked me!" They continued ridiculing me by laughing harder, and then Rocco said, "Come on, let's get back to work; otherwise, the boss's wife will have something to say!"

Bruno positioned himself at the end of the workbench and began sanding a rounded table leg. Then, at the sound of descending footsteps, Rocco scrambled to look busy, and Bruno switched from sandpaper to a thick piece of glass and began shaving the table leg with that glass. Never having seen a useless piece of glass recycled like that, I stared at the fine shavings that rolled down.

"Ciao, Ragazzi!" called out the voice of a shapely young woman as she turned by the stairway and continued into the center of the room. "Ciao, Signorina," responded Bruno and Rocco with lumps in their throats as the Signorina stopped beside me. She appeared taller than Master Santino and even taller than his wife. "My name is Filomena. I kept hearing noises down here and thought I'd come down to see what it was all about. Mamma just told me that Papá had two new workers." With a semi-nervous smile that slowly formed, Rocco replied, "Yes, he took us on recently."

"What are your names?"

"I'm Rocco, and that's Bruno." She looked at me and, with a cheerful face, said, "And you are Santino? Papá always talks about you!" She stretched out her arms and pulled me toward herself, as if I were a big rag doll, and began gently rocking me. I blushed as she said, "Oh, this kid is so cute. I just want to squeeze him."

Looking incredulous, Rocco and Bruno stared at each other as Filomena kept me glued to her body and said, "Oh, he is like a teddy

Piccolo Santino

bear." From the corner of my eye, I saw Bruno and Rocco blush as if smoke were escaping from their ears. Filomena spoke again, and I felt my head sink under her bosom while she continually rocked me. "And what are you guys working on right now!"

Bruno and Rocco shook their heads, and Bruno stammered out a response, "I'm uh smoothing out these table legs for a table here." He held up the one leg he was working on. Filomena leaned her head forward and asked, "What about you, Rocco? What are you working on?"

"W-w-weluh, I have been making the sides and backs to the drawers for this dresser here."

"Oh, you guys are busy. I better go and leave you to your work." She gently released me, looked down into my eyes, and said, "You are so cute, Santino, Ciao, Caro!" Flaunting her dress while she turned, she said to the guys, "Ciao, Ragazzi!" With eyes pulsating in both sockets and about to pop, the guys awkwardly responded, "Arrivederci, Signorina Filomena!"

Piccolo Santino

Chapter 4 of Part Two
Anguish befalls best friends

That day of the brutal beating Mamma gave me, we worked later than usual at the carpenter shop. I opened the door and carefully walked into the foyer, hearing my family's chatter. I sheepishly entered the main room. My siblings were playing cards at the table, so I sat on the bench away from everybody. Mamma was mending a garment and looked up at me with one eye. She looked mad, but not enough to chase me out of the house. After a quiet spell, I asked Lillo, "Who's winning?"

"I am," Stella said excitedly. Then, while sewing, Mamma, looking down and grumpy, blurted out, "There are two sardines left. Get yourself a piece of bread to eat with the sardines."

Since most of my free time now was spent at the carpenter shop, I could only see my friends regularly on Sundays. But Mamma never failed to remind me to go to church. Most of the time, I would meet Franco at his house, and then we would join up with Nino in church. I found the chanting chorus exciting and liked the outfits the clergy wore, but I always gazed at the artwork on the stained glass windows. I found it most refreshing when the sunlight shone through. At times, I found myself transfixed by the expressions of the saints carved on the marble statues, as they seemed so lifelike and more sincere than the priest himself and some of the people present.

The priest, Father Cinquemano, meaning five hands, went far back to a family of thieves. He was a stern-looking man with a broad, thick face and silver-rimmed glasses that personified his demeanor very well. Further, the white-laced fringed surplice on top of his black robe acted like a mirror that reflected but squarely framed and accentuated his austere character. He moved with complete authority and flaunted the framed image by his surplice without humility. He exhibited total conviction that his power over the people was a special gift from above.

Piccolo Santino

On Palm Sunday, during the enactment of Christ slapping a man before giving him the loaf of bread, Father Cinquemano slapped the church sextant, participating in the role. The slap was so loud its sound reverberated high in the rafters. It caused everyone to gasp and turn their heads. Smoldering whispers criticized the priest quickly and spread inside the church like fire on straw roofs. There were murmurings that this priest was not the type to make a gift without a price. Actual tears rolled on one side of the old man's face. His sad grin showed he was without teeth, and our hearts went to him. We all knew he accepted the role because of the absolute need for bread.

Mass felt somewhat lengthy today except when the priest spoke in Latin, making the mass feel like a foreign movie, and the sudden burst of thunder almost shook the entire church. As the thunder rolled into the distance, the thick raindrops sounded very soothing, bouncing off the slate roof for the duration of the mass. When we exited, the sun was out, as if no rain had ever occurred. We stopped at the bottom of the church steps, and Nino said, "Guys, I have to do an errand for my papá." I asked, "What do you have to do?"

"He told me to get a bottle of club soda on the way back." Nino said, Franco replied, "Okay, we can walk to the store with you, then I gotta get back. My Mamma is making pasta." We walked to the store and stopped to talk against the railing outside. Nino said, "It's late. I better go buy the club soda."

"Ciao, Nino,"

"Ciao, Santino." Then Franco said, "I'll walk to the store with you."

"I'll wait here," I said, sitting on the top railing. A young man pulled up, parked his bicycle near me, and ran inside the store. People in these parts could not afford bicycles or cars, and for me to see a real racing bike, this close was so exciting that I jumped down and leaned over to look closer at all the different sections. A manly voice sternly said, "Hey, what do you think you're doing?" Alarmed, I looked up, and he slapped me fast and furious across my face. The young man swung his bike away close to me while continuing to shout, "Get away from my bike."

Piccolo Santino

Startled and dumbfounded, I rubbed my cheek and wished my papá were here to teach this guy a lesson. But that was wishful thinking, and instead, Franco must have been coming out of the store right behind this guy because I heard Franco yell out, "Hey! Why'd you do that for?"

"He was trying to steal my bike!"

"He wouldn't do any such thing. Who the hell do you think you are?"

"What do you know, asshole?"

"Yeah? I'll go home and get my brother d*isgraziato.* You wretch."

"*Vai caca VA!* Go take a crap, go!"

"*Vai fa inculo! Testa di cazzo*. Go fuck yourself dickhead!" The guy spun the bike around toward Franco and said, "What did you say to me? You little piece of shit."

"I told you to go fuck yourself." The man started to dismount, and Franco urged him on as he yelled out, "Come on, *stronzo*! Asshole!" Franco had just spotted his brother Argento, a hulking young man, rushing over.

Franco's house was within voice distance around the corner from the store. For sure, word got to his brother from neighbor to neighbor faster than a modern telephone. The biker looked over his shoulder at the hulking young man rushing at him, and he jumped back on his bike and turned away. "Now you're not so big anymore, ha! You coward." Yelled out, Franco. The biker yelled at Franco as he started pedaling away, "*Va fa inculo.* Up yours!" Argento yelled back, "*A Mammata vigliacco,* up your mother's you coward." The biker skidded on the dirt as Argento was unrelenting, "Go on, get the hell out of here, you coward." I was still rubbing my cheek when Argento turned to us and said, "You guys okay?"

"Yeah, Santino's face is still all red, though."

"That'll go away. Come on, let's go home. Mamma has pasta ready." Franco turned to me and said, "Bianchi, you'll be okay?"

"Yeah, I'll be o-o-okay by the time I get home."

"Bene, ciao."

"Ciao e Grazie!"

Piccolo Santino

"Ciao."

As we parted company, I began to envy my friend going home to a Sunday dinner as it would not be the same for me, but it felt great experiencing his big brother coming to our rescue. I brought my hand down from my face, and the hot sun stung briefly. I ignored the sting by figuring out the time zone Papá was now in America. I tried to speculate at what he was possibly doing, but not knowing what his new surroundings looked like, I could only picture his mustachioed face and tried to compose an image of his surroundings with items from here. Then I stopped since it didn't feel foreign.

I recollected a dream I had months ago before Papá left. I saw my maternal grandfather and Eugenio helping Papá board a large rowboat high in the mountains. A thick fog made the body of water appear infinite, convincing me it was an ocean. After others boarded the rowboat with Papá, Eugenio, and Grandfather pushed their boat offshore. I sensed that the boat would navigate deep inside the fog where the ocean climbed beyond mountains and clouds high in the sky, past the mist on a strange path to America.

"You're here!" Mamma exclaimed as I walked in the door. "Go see Eugenio. He needs you to do another errand for him."

"Oh no, not again, Mamma!"

"*Perquè no?* Why not?"

"Because every morning he has me get milk for him all over town before I can go to school or the carpenter."

"So what?"

"No, I don't feel like it today. Today is Sunday."

"If you don't go, he'll come here looking for you." No sooner were Mamma's words uttered than I heard Eugenio speak. "Santino *per favore*! Please go and get codfish for me at the fish market."

"No!"

"Please, Santino! Please go for me."

"No, I don't want to do it." On days I made the milk trips, I showed up with a container, and since they expected me, I didn't have to talk. But

Piccolo Santino

at the fish market, I feared speaking and risking embarrassment in public. Much like the kerosene incident. Eugenio turned to Mamma and asked, "Why won't he go?"

"I don't know Eugenio. He says he doesn't want to go." I felt sorry for Eugenio as he turned away, and I went inside. Minutes later, I came out to sit by the stairway downstairs and checked the mousetrap my sister and I had placed, hoping to trap a bird. I saw Eugenio in his jacket rushing off from the corner of my eye. That evening, he brought a portion of codfish in tomato sauce with potatoes. The aroma was wonderful, but my guilt from refusing to do the errand for him prevented me from eating. And the remorse from my fear of having to speak to strangers further compounded the issue.

I quickly thought about going to the carpenter shop tomorrow to escape the pain of regret. Master Santino told us that he and his partner worked on location for two weeks and would arrive home too late for us to wait for him. The instructions about the work he left for Rocco and Bruno were clear. "Above all," he said, "Make sure everything you cut and finish is straight and squared. I don't mind if you leave stuff for the next day as long as what you finish is all squared."

The following morning, I heard splashing water outside the doorway as Mamma emptied the wash basin and shouted for me to get up. Knowing that there would be a more relaxed attitude at the shop, I must have overslept on purpose since Rocco and Bruno were not Master Santino. All dressed, I rummaged in the breadbox for a thick piece of bread. Mamma was sweeping the foyer as she usually did every morning. She looked over her shoulder and said, "Take whatever pieces you can find for now. I'll borrow some from Aunt Isabella until I make the bread tomorrow." I put two small pieces in my left pocket and a more significant chunk in my right. The minute I kicked stones outside, Mamma shouted, "You're going to ruin your shoes. Stop kicking stones before I whack you over the head with this broomstick."

I stopped kicking stones and rushed to avoid Mamma. I wondered how she would make bread since we didn't live on the farm with the brick oven anymore. Being away from Mamma by the shop, I kicked a stone

Piccolo Santino

and saw Bruno and Rocco walking from the opposite direction. I surmised they had made their morning trip to the caves since they both had rolled up newspaper from their back pockets. Without the boss around, we all settled into a very relaxed atmosphere with a sense of a mini-vacation, especially when Rocco and Bruno included me in a game of cards after lunch. At first, I could not understand why the game ended so fast with these two guys. At home, the game lasted much longer. And playing with my family, I'd occasionally win. But with these fellows, the game was over as fast as it started, preventing me from an opportunity to even hope for a win. It wasn't until the third game that I saw Bruno remove cards from the deck, and at that point, I threw my hand in.

As devious as the two guys were, I learned by watching them work and enjoyed the occasional laughter we mixed in with the work. The two weeks without the boss felt like they would never end, and then, as if he had never left, Master Santino was back in the shop discussing a new project with his partner. Then, their attention turned to Rocco and Bruno to explain what was expected of them. The master turned to me and said, "Santino, tomorrow don't come here; go directly to the worksite at the bottom of the street left of the church in the market square. We will all be working there for a few days." I responded, "Va bene."

I arrived at the worksite early and saw men I didn't know meandering inside. Two of the walls were complete, and what was to be the front and sidewall were utterly exposed but had thick beams erected to support the main beams on the roof. It was evident that more beams should be constructed before a roof could be installed.

Rocco and Bruno rode in on their bicycles just as I found a place to sit. They shouted out to me, "Ciao, Tino."

"Ciao," I said as they parked their bikes against a wall in the shade and walked past me toward the three men inside. They shook hands with the men. I got up as Master Santino and Master Nicola stepped up and shouted salutations with two other men. They coordinated the hoisting of two new support beams within a short time. My legs began to weaken as I watched a man scale his way to the top. Rocco and Bruno were

Piccolo Santino

designated to work on the floor, measuring and cutting boards. I became fascinated at how beams were placed across a wide span to support the roof later. I expressed my thoughts when the boys called me over by the sawhorses to help them. "So now I see how a roof is started by placing support beams across the main columns. That's simple to understand."

"Oh? Now we have a new Master Tino! Did you hear that, Rocco?"

"Yeah, do you think that you can build roofs now?" I felt embarrassed as they ridiculed me. I walked away when I saw my friend Franco walking inside. He said, "Ciao, Bianchi" I walked over to him as Bruno continued pestering me. "Rocco, maybe he can hire out soon." They both laughed so hard that other workers looked on and started talking. "What happened?"

"Leave the kid alone!" some workers yelled, and I turned to Franco. "Ciao, Franco!"

"Those two guys bothering you again?"

"Yeah, they can be real bullies." Master Santino shouted out from a beam high up. "Hey, Rocco, why don't you send Tino for water?"

"Yes, Master Santino, I will." Then, Master Santino called out to the group. "Hey, you guys want fresh water?"

"Yeah, it's getting hot already in this sun. Who's going for the water?"

"Rocco, get four bottles to give to Santino and his friend there so we can take the morning break." Rocco turned to Franco and asked," Do you mind, Franco?"

"No, come on, Bianchi, let's go." We walked into the shade up the cobblestone street with bottles in hand. Franco said, "I think I noticed a bird's nest on a wall back there."

"Yeah, where?"

"On the very top of the wall with that slanted platform."

"Really, how high up is it?"

"I'll show you when we get back. Maybe we can figure a way to pilfer it."

"Sure, okay!" The end of the street opened up into the market

Piccolo Santino

square, and as we walked past the church, Franco remarked, "Don't worry about making the sign of the cross. Both our hands are full."

"You know, but just thinking about it should be okay!"

"Yeah! Let's cut through here to come out by the smoke shop." We came out into the main avenue, turned left up the street to the fountain, waited for two younger boys to finish drinking, and observed a third kid standing in the pool with his bare feet. The first kid finished drinking, and the second lingered after coming up three times for air. He put his face back down, pretending to be drinking. Franco decided to let the kid know it. "Hey, get out of there already." The kid looked up and remarked, "Why should I?"

"Because I can kick your ass!"

"I'm gonna tell my mamma." Franco walked over and said, "Go ahead and get her." The kid moved to the opposite side and stood in the water with his bare feet. Franco filled his bottles, then took a quick drink and stepped aside to fill my bottles while he stared down the three kids. The kids returned to the fountain and splashed water by putting two hands under the spout as we walked away.

Our walk back was mainly in the shade except in the market square, so the bottles stayed pretty cool. That made the workers happy, as they had already started their morning break. "You guys aren't eating anything?" asked the tallest worker dressed in white carpenter drab. I shook my head, "No," Franco responded. "No, I'll be going back home in a little bit."

"What about you? Your name is Santino also. Right?"

"Si," I responded, and then he looked at me again. "You don't have anything to eat?" I shook my head. "No," and he reached over and handed me a piece of bread. I looked at it and hesitated, as it reminded me of Mamma's words about refusing first unless people insisted. He looked at me and pushed the bread up close. I took it and said, "Grazie."

"You're working with us, so eat!" Then, another worker with a square but kind-looking face handed me a piece of cheese, and I thanked him. Master Santino took a long drink of water from the bottle and remarked, "Santino, you always bring back the coldest water. *Grazie*

Piccolo Santino

Ragazzi. Thanks, kids."

"Yeah, thank you, kids," remarked the man in white, then he said to Bruno and Rocco, "You still don't believe I can make a bucket hang down from a nail lying flat on a table?"

"Without the nail being hammered down?" asked Bruno. "That's right, just lying flat from the end of the table."

"That's impossible."

"All right, I'll prove it to you right now. Get that empty bucket over there while I position the nail." Franco and I watched as the man in white dusted off an area with his bare hand by the edge of a plank on the sawhorses. Bruno handed him the bucket. "Okay, now I'll place the head of the nail so it hangs off the edge about two centimeters while the rest lays flat on the plank. Now watch!" He slowly placed the handle of the metal bucket on the hanging part of the nail, and we were all amazed as the bucket remained suspended with the nail staying in place. Bruno's eyes bulged out as Rocco looked on with an embarrassed grin and disbelief. Franco looked on and said, "But if the nail were farther out, it would never work, right?"

"That's right, kid. It has to do with leverage." Shamefaced, Bruno and Rocco stared at each other as Franco advanced toward the setup and experimented with different nail positions to reveal his point. When the bucket fell due to the nail being moved too far out, Bruno sarcastically turned away, and they all returned to work. Franco looked at me and turned his head to the bird's nest across the street, and we walked out for a closer look. "You know!" he said, "With a ladder, we can reach the top."

"No! No! I'm afraid to climb."

"I'm not afraid. We can put the ladder on the cement slope. If you hold it in place, I can climb up there."

"Yeah, I can do that!"

"All right, I'll come back just before they break for lunch, and then we'll go to my house to get the ladder."

"All right, I'll see you later, Franco, ciao!"

"Ciao," I said. Rocco, looking around, shouted out, "Hey Master

Piccolo Santino

Tino, we need you over here." I walked over and he said, "Blow on the line here while I saw" He glanced at Bruno holding down the board, then said to me, "Maybe after this, you can figure out how to install a roof since you already deciphered the support beams." Rocco was interrupted by Bruno's laughter and then looked at him and said, "Come on, stop it before the boss says something."

I blew on the line as Rocco sawed the board. I became anxious for Franco to return. Until lunchtime, Rocco and Bruno worked the same way, alternating between holding the end of the board and sawing. My job remained as usual, with some breaks in between. The two guys were called to help on the rafters.

Just around lunch break, Stefano, the man in white, whose name I learned, came over by the sawhorses, spread out a newspaper on the planks, and said, "Guys, it's hot up there, and I don't have a hat, so I am going to make me one from this newspaper." With that, he got our attention again, and we looked on as Franco arrived. Stefano also narrated every step as he made each fold. "First, you fold the one sheet in half. Then you fold the top two corners to meet in the middle." I watched with keen eyes. I wanted to remember everything. "Then you bring up the flaps at the triangle's base, one on each side." Bruno asked Rocco, "How is he going to do this?" Franco came back and abruptly said, "Just watch!"

"Then you open the triangle's base and combine the two ends to form a square. Once the square is complete, you fold up the two open corners to make a triangle again." Rocco asked me, "Did you get that master carpenter?" Then Bruno smirked and said, "Now you can make hats too, to go with rafters and roofs."

"Leave him alone!" Franco ordered as he walked up. "Now, notice that the triangle's base can be pulled open. You can squeeze the corners together in the middle to make the square again." He held it up to show us the completed square, then pulled the ends out to unfold a boat shape. "Sideways, it looks flat like a boat, but if you put your finger inside the bottom of the triangle and push it open, the middle expands, and by pinching, the top sides will open and remain expanded so that you can

Piccolo Santino

wear it. As a hat." He placed it on his head, and we all laughed; then he rocked it in both hands and exclaimed, "Or you can put it in water like a toy boat!"

"That's amazing." Rocco said, and a loud voice from up in the rafters shouted, "Lunchtime!"

"Come on, let's go to lunch," Rocco said, and everybody split in separate directions as Franco and I left to get the ladder.

Once we got to his house, Franco quietly opened the door to the storeroom with outside access. The ladder was right by the door. He held one end of the ladder, and I had the other as we quietly walked off. "Where are you going with that ladder?" asked his older sister, and Franco said, "I'll bring it right back. We need it for something!"

The work site looked deserted, so we felt comfortable not explaining anything to anybody as we lifted the ladder onto the sloping platform, climbed over, and propped it up against the wall. The severity of the slope away from the wall concerned me, and I remarked to Franco, "Franco, I think the ladder will slide down on this incline."

"No, it'll be okay as long as you hold it still." I held the ladder as tight as I could and watched Franco climb. He climbed the top and said, "I can't reach it."

"The ladder is too short, Franco!" I yelled, and he said, "No, I can get it. I just have to climb on the very top step."

"Be careful?"

"Hold the ladder really tight now."

"Okay, I got it!" With both feet on the very top step and his left hand leaning against the wall, he reached up with his right but could not maintain his balance and, in an instant, came crashing down head-first onto the cement platform. Blood splattered from his head. He's *dead*, I said to myself. I sensed a flashback to the night I heard Mamma tell Papá to dump Lillo in the ravine to kill him because he was ugly. *Oh no, not again!* I thought. That concept reverberated in my head like a bad storm. Followed by three more words, *run, quick, run,* more comments followed, *someone can see you and report you to the police.*

Piccolo Santino

Without any hesitation, I darted out of there, repeating the following words inside my head: *you killed him. He's dead! You're a murderer. Now you're a criminal. A refugee on the run! Just like the public enemy number one. Zarafino!* Fearing the Reaper's shadow, I began to feel the cutter's ugly presence swell inside me and taunt me with the thought that I was going to be arrested for murder. I hurried my steps and kept in the shade of alleyways and empty streets as my conscience continued taunting me with more words. *When they find you, they will send you to prison for life. Run! Run and keep to the side streets so the police can't see you.*

Consumed with fear and ignorance and wondering if I were indeed to be imprisoned. I hoped that by the time I became of age, then maybe, with good behavior, I could be freed and allowed to marry. I wandered from side street to side street, and as I sensed the day nearing its end, I became leery as I grew tired of hiding and now wished to get arrested.

I ventured out onto the main avenue right by my school and sat on the top step of a short stairway descending below street level into a shoemaker's shop. The discovery surprised me because it was a house or two next to my school and a few buildings from Dr. Itasca's home. Now, I wondered why I had never noticed this shoemaker before, and I decided this would be a good place to wait to get arrested.

I looked inside the shop and stared at a tall, skinny shoemaker, possibly the owner, with a dirty smock. He stood before a large machine, holding a shoe in his hands. We stared at one another for a long spell, creating mutual discomfort as he conspicuously waited for me to say something. But my fear of speaking felt so thick in my throat that it arrested my larynx.

Disturbed by my persistent silence, the shoemaker nodded at a young co-worker and said, "Who is this fella? Does anybody recognize him?" I thought to myself, *there you go. That's the right thing to say. Now, don't stop.* "No! We don't know him." Two of the young boys said. "He won't talk! I wonder what he wants. He keeps staring at me." Said the man holding the shoe.

Piccolo Santino

I prayed that somebody here would say *he was the son of Bartolo and Anna.* I continued thinking, *it is such an easy thing to guess. Somebody come on already. Guess! I need to be <u>revealed!</u>* "He won't stop staring at us."

"Who could he be?" I kept on thinking to myself, *what is wrong with you people? Here I am, the kid who works at Master Santino's shop. You know the carpenter at the opposite end of town.* "Ah, leave him alone. He'll go away." One of the kids said.

The evening had begun covering the sun when I sat on this stoop. The shade brought on such a chill in me that I wanted to move away. Since I believed it was the best place to be found by the police, I didn't dare move. These people all seemed clueless about who I was, and I wished for more daylight to offer the police another chance.

The shopkeeper signaled his workers to close the shop. They looked at me one last time as they gathered their paraphernalia and went inside. One pulled the shade from behind the glass to the closed door. Feeling like a dunce, I remained seated on the top step, wholly deflated, because not even one policeman walked past here to arrest me all this time. Riddled with deep guilt and fear, I wondered where else I could go. I wouldn't have to hide anymore if the police just came here.

I walked away, keeping to the main street, and again wondered what they would do to a young boy for committing murder. After thirty or so years, I hoped I would be freed to try to go to America and look for my family since they would have left without me by then. My mood thickened as the night got heavier, and I decided to visit the church of St. Rocco, two blocks down from home. I moved to the church at less than a snail's pace. I inhaled the incense as I cracked the door open, and a greater fear seared through me. I felt unworthy and let go of the door.

It must have been around ten o'clock when I decided to just go home and sneak into bed, hopefully without my family noticing me. Then, I could sneak out early in the morning to continue my wandering, hoping to get arrested. My heart kept pounding in the moonlight. And the light from the nearby homes shined enough to identify me. When I arrived home, I held the door handle and pushed it slowly and cautiously, but the weight of the door with its squeaky hinges gave me away. In a normal tone, Mamma blurted out. "Oh, you made it home. You know the police came here looking for you twice. You're lucky your friend came to and explained what happened; otherwise, you would be sleeping in jail right now!"

Somewhat relieved, I slithered into bed without uttering a word and thought about how I could ever face Franco again. I thought back to the night Mamma wanted Lillo killed. Tonight, Papá's words echoed in my head. *I couldn't do it! I couldn't do it! I was afraid someone would report me to the police.* He failed to throw Lillo into the ravine because he feared being arrested.

Today, having seen Franco bleeding like that jolted in me that same fear of death from that night. The threat was present in both instances and like a sinister mystery, the fear of death scrambled my logic in time of need. Both boys survived, and I could not understand why I felt so pinned down when Lillo and Franco needed me.

If Papá had said that he couldn't do it because he loved Lillo, perhaps my mind would have been cleared, and then I would at least have known how to help Franco.

Chapter 5 of Part Two, 1957
Last year of school in Italy

Filled with anticipation, I got up early and leaned against the house, waiting for the right time to leave for school. Mamma walked up to me. "Here's one hundred lire for your textbook."

"Oh, va bene, Mamma."

"Now, don't lose it because there is no more where that came from."

"Si." I said. She turned away and began sweeping the ground outside before the door. I contemplated not having to go to the carpenter shop until after school and felt happy about starting fourth grade. Next year would be my graduating year in school since there was no compulsory education beyond fifth grade. But how could that be? There was so much more in the world to learn. I might have to seek out newspapers or borrow books and pamphlets in church or wherever else I could find books. I need to read to keep on learning. So I could achieve my goal of becoming a famous Italian poet.

My fingers thought they were ripping useless paper as if in a trance. As my hands moved back and forth, my mind feebly attempted to interrupt the ripping action. I had already conceded that I was not making the fifth grade in Italy. The dream of becoming a famous Italian poet was fading, leaving a profound sense of loss. I worried about having to start anew with a strange language in America. Suddenly, I felt a tiny burn from my brain to my fingertips as I looked down at a trivial gathering of tiny clippings cupped in my hands.

I walked over to Mamma, who was still sweeping by the door. I said, "Mamma, look what I just did." She didn't even ask questions. I was even more surprised and disappointed that she didn't smack my face. I thought to myself, If only the pieces weren't so tiny, then somehow we could glue them together again. But who was I fooling? All we had was flour and water to make glue with. It was hopeless, then Mamma asked, "What do you want from me?" Ashamed I said, "I didn't even realize I was ripping the money until it was too late."

Piccolo Santino

"I told you there is no more where that came from. You'll have to make do without a textbook. Now you'd better hurry, or you'll be late for school." I thought, oh, why couldn't she have given me coins instead of paper money? And on my way to school, I hoped that maybe today the postman would bring a letter from Papá with a dollar inside. One American dollar would get Mamma six hundred lire that could pay for six textbooks. But that was wishful thinking. As I walked, I could not beat myself up enough. Even if Papá did send a dollar, Mamma would use it for more pressing things than to make up for my stupidity. Besides, I never heard Mamma brag about Papá sending any money, even on special occasions. I might have heard her mention it once that she got a dollar in one of his letters.

I stopped at the public fountain for a drink of water. From all those women waiting in line, I feared that it was later than usual, and I could very well be late for school. I stood still and stared at the five women in front of me and dreaded I was in for a long wait. Then one woman looked at me, turned to another woman, and said to her, "Is he waiting for us?" The second woman responded, "I think so." The third woman on line shouted out to the first lady, "Why don't you let him go ahead of us." Another woman looked at me, "Did you just want a drink of water, son?" I nodded "Yes," and the one woman filling her container stepped aside and said to me, "Come on, son." The second woman on line added, "Go ahead, son, go on."

I took a few quick swallows and hurried away, and when I reached the school, I opened the door slowly and felt relieved to find four students ahead of me on the morning inspection line for cleanliness. I looked at Franco without the bandages on his head. I had wondered how I was going to face him, and when I saw him walking up to me a few days later, all bandaged up, I was happy to hug him and know he was all right. I watched the teacher bend and twist the kid's ears, checking for any dirtiness, and I felt confident about myself since I was one of the smarter kids in class. I looked at the teacher and said to him, "Buongiorno, professore!"

"Buongiorno," he replied, and then I felt his fingers on my left ear

Piccolo Santino

and anticipated going to my seat. He pulled hard on my earlobe as I hoped to walk away. He shouted, "What filthy ears!" The red burning sensation he caused made my face blush as he continued criticizing me, "Go wash your ears, and then you may return to class!"

On the way back to the fountain, I was more relaxed since I didn't have to rush. Only two people were at the fountain: a woman and an older man. The woman finished filling her jug, and the older man stepped up, placed his hat on top of the fountain post, and began washing his hands and face, then the back of his neck, before he took his hat and walked away. I strode up and rubbed the back of both ears as hard as I could, and last, rubbed the inside of my ears with my pinky and thought mission accomplished.

I returned to class with a sense of relief, my face solemn. I observed Isabella receive her textbook and walk away as Cesare was about to pay for his. The teacher looked at me as I walked past his desk. He acknowledged my presence but did not stop me for another inspection, so I went over to my desk, dropped to my seat, and rested my head in my arms. I listened to the names he was calling out. *"Romano, Cafarelli, Conforti."* I watched Gianna and Vincenzo go up to pay for their books, and as Vincenzo was leaving with his book, the teacher called out two more names: *"Bianchi e Palumbo."* I saw Alina go up first, and I caught the teacher glancing at me, and he called out my name again, this time with force: "Bianchi!"

Timidly, I lifted my head toward the teacher, my voice barely above a whisper, *"Non ho i soldi,* I don't have money!" Mockingly, he said, *"Ma perchè no?* But why not? Your father is in America. You're rich!" (This was a widespread thought held by everyone in the region or the entire country.) I did not want to embarrass myself further with an explanation as everyone stared. The teacher had extra books reserved for the needy kids. Knowing it, I put my head back down into my folded arms. But I did not qualify since my papá was in America. The class was reading chapter one in the textbook. Moments later, the teacher got up to make his rounds. The scent of his cologne told me he was close to my area. Keeping my head buried, I rolled it away from the aisle. When the

Piccolo Santino

smell of his cologne was most potent, I felt his large hand slap the back of my head.

He yelled out *"Pigrone, vagabondo!* Lazy bum! Vagabond, you should be reading with the class!" That added to the humiliation and caused me to cry out loud as I thought of how Papá would smooth it out with a few oranges. After what felt like infinity or maybe less, I regained my composure and lifted myself. My neighbor, Donato, slid his book closer to me so we could share. It worked out perfectly since I read much faster than he. I always had lag time to review the subject matter. After a few weeks, the teacher softened up and began lending me his book

This year's textbook covered a lot of religion, and the teacher also instructed us about catechism class schedules and the separate locations for the boys and girls. Amazingly, as I grew older, I never shared the story about my ripping the money with Franco or, for that matter, any other personal events. Somehow, the episodes all felt unique and needed to be privately sealed inside me for safekeeping.

After school, soon after that day, I walked into the house and put down my notebook. Mamma immediately told me, "Get yourself a piece of bread, and you can eat it on the way." The urgency alarmed me, but I reached inside the bread box and grabbed a good chunk of bread that seemed to have been waiting for me. "Come on. You're going to Nao with me."

"Why?" I asked, as it had all the feeling of the day she sought apprenticeships for Lillo and me. "Because Master Santino will be away for a while, and you will not roam the streets every day."

We walked down the main avenue past the two familiar bars, the town fountain and Dr. Itasca. Past my school until we reached the bridge into Nao. Just before the bridge, to my left, I saw a brand new building with an unusually thick concrete foundation and cement walls resembling a fortress. The idea of a new school evoked some regret since we would not be here by the time they finished. We crossed the bridge and faced an uphill climb on this dirt road. I liked reaching the top of the hill because it hosted such a magnificent panoramic view of the countryside and, on

Piccolo Santino

a clear sunny day like today, you could see far. I liked looking out so I could pretend to see our old home. Mamma made the sign of the cross as we walked past a religious station, and then she stared down at me. I obeyed her stare and made the sign also.

A thick wheel of cheese, the size of a medium-sized dish, rolled between us on the street. A young man with a string dangling from his right wrist rushed from around the bend after it. The game was in full swing, and the anticipation of the outcome was palpable. The men were playing a game of skill and strategy, rolling the cheese wheel to see whose team could move it the farthest. They would then use a measuring tape to tally up the distance and usually resolve the game over a bottle of wine in a bar by choosing a boss and underboss to debate how to divide the cheese.

The man stopped running and saluted Mamma by lifting his right hand, the string dangling down in front of his face. He said, "Excuse me, Signora. Did you see the cheese wheel roll past here?"

"Sì, sì, it rolled past my son and me over that way." She pointed toward the religious station, "It probably rolled down there by now."
"Grazie," he said as he continued his search, and a few moments later, three other young men jogged past us as they called out to their friend up ahead of them, "Totó do you see it?"

As they sprinted past us, my eyes caught a familiar face—Aldo from the soccer game! I couldn't contain my excitement and blurted out to Mamma, "Mamma, that's Aldo!" Aldo stopped, turned his head, and said, "Buongiorno, Signora Anna." We stopped to face Aldo, and he said to Mamma, "*Perdonami*, Forgive me, Signora Anna. I didn't recognize you immediately."

"Don't worry, Gumbah Aldo. My son recognized you."

"Va bene, I plan to come by before the start of catechism classes for Santino."

"Si! Si Gumbah, come by whenever it's convenient for you."
"Grazie, Signora Anna. Ciao Santino," said Aldo as I watched him salute me with his hand to his forehead, and Mamma pulled me forward as she said, "Come on, let's go." We continued up ahead, and a short way up,

Piccolo Santino

buildings populated the landscape in the outskirts of town to the left. Just before the hard dirt road changed to cobblestone, a rotten smell from the olive oil refinery breached our nostrils as waste poured out of a pipe and flowed into a shallow groove crossing the street and emptying into a ravine. I looked up and said, "Mamma, you brought our olives here once, right?"

"Yes, you came with me." She cupped her left hand over her nose. "I remember that," I said, looking in as we passed by and marveled at the building's complete open frontage. Recalling the very soothing smell of olive oil inside, I observed the owner dipping a piece of bread in the fresh olive oil pouring from the spout. I was envious as I watched him and his customer chew on dipped bread while they lifted their heads to the heavens. I held my nose as we stepped over the trench with brown waste. A way down from the stench, we made the first right into the town piazza. The square was small compared to the two large piazzas in Jonadi. But then Nao is a suburb of Jonadi, so we technically had three piazzas. Mamma led me through an opened door at the bottom of the square to the right. And to no surprise, it was another carpenter shop. A short, thin man dropped his measuring ruler on the bench and rushed out to greet Mamma.

"Buongiorno, Signora Bianchi and this must be your son, Santino," he said in a thin voice. Mamma answered him, "Si and Buongiorno Mastro Buccino." The master carpenter looked at me and exclaimed, "Well, Santino, are you ready to work?" I answered with a simple word. "Si."

As they conversed, I found myself increasingly curious. It was evident that Mamma had already arranged this. While I would miss the familiarity of Mastro Santino's shop, I also felt a sense of comfort in being away from the unpredictable nature of Rocco and Bruno. I was intrigued by Mastro Buccino's work habits, given his delicate presence. The shop itself was a chaotic mess, starkly contrasting the organized professionalism of Mastro Santino's place. Cleaning up here may mean adding to the disorder, I mused. I noted that going for water was relatively easy here since I only needed to walk to that fountain in front of me, in

Piccolo Santino

complete view of his shop. I felt the master didn't need me for that since he could just walk over and get a drink. I was uncertain if they had caves here in Nao for bathroom purposes, and I already began to miss the idea of that personal comfort.

Mamma turned to me and said, "You'll stay here, and the Mastro will let you know when it's time to come home." Then Mamma put her hand on my shoulder and said, "Now you do as Mastro Buccino tells you, son." She turned away and said to the new Master, "Arrivederci, Mastro."

"Very well Signora, arrivederci." I felt her absence as I watched her walk away, and it made me withdraw like a plastered flower on the wall. I felt a heavy need to sketch my way out of loneliness, so I waited for Mastro Buccino's first directive. "Well, Santino, first thing, we need water. Go and fill this bottle over there at the fountain."

Just hearing him saying "water" was enough to catapult me down. I took the bottle from him and walked outside to the public fountain. As I filled the bottle, I longed for the warmth of Jonadi. I found this water a bit colder than the one in Jonadi. I returned and saw him at his workbench using a screwdriver. I walked over and handed him the bottle of water, and he took a long drink and said, "Bravo, Santino. The water is nice and cold here, more so than in Jonadi. What do you think?" I nodded, "Yes."

He placed the bottle on the bottom shelf of the workbench and rummaged through a large tin of old fasteners, and came up with a screw. He then held the screw down on a delineated section of a board and hammered the screw down halfway. Then, he used the screwdriver to drive it in place. Mastro Santino would have predrilled a hole and applied a bit of soap on the screw to screw it in tight. He would never have used a hammer on a screw.

"I have another job for you, Santino." He grabbed the container of mixed fasteners he had rummaged through and walked to the opposite end of the bench. Then he found two smaller containers from a shelf underneath and laid them next to the full one. "Santino, separate all the screws from the nails and put them in these containers." He pulled up a stool for me to sit on, but I quickly found it easier to sift through the box standing up. While I separated the items, I noticed his sign on the front

Piccolo Santino

wall, "Buccino Antonino, Falegname." The room was square-shaped with a back door in the far corner of the back wall, which might lead to a courtyard with access to his living quarters. He was quiet all the time, unlike Master Santino, who broke up the silence with shout-outs to try to get me to talk. Or he responded to shouts from his family upstairs, and then he would run up for a spell and return by wiping his mouth and adjusting his pants.

At first, I found the walk here somewhat adventurous as I always stopped atop the road for that panoramic view of the countryside. But not on the return trip home. At times, I hoped for a chance to encounter Lola during a possible visit by her. She did make the trip once, and we made eye contact a few times, but there was no way we could have sneaked off alone in a corner of the new house. I considered accompanying her to the outer skirts of town when she left. But people would've reported what they might have seen or imagined. I, therefore, abandoned that idea. I feared I would never see her again. I wondered why Mamma never visited Lola's family since it was a good walk.

I didn't know when my last day with Mastro Buccino would be, nor could I envision how it would occur. But one thing was for sure. His quietness was becoming an aggravating factor. He worked for hours on end without saying a word, and after I finished a chore, he left me lifeless like dust on the doorknob, as if waiting for a chance to be blown off. But he was like dust on a cathedral ceiling where I could not reach him with any of my usual subtleties. So, I waited for him to come down, and when he descended, his directive was short and to the point, which forced me to hope that the chore lasted longer than his elusiveness.

Then, one day, on my way to work, I saw kids from school hanging out in front of the new construction site, watching the men assemble the scaffolding. I stopped to look, and Franco approached me down the street. I also saw Nino and Giuseppi and then Roberto. I felt contented watching the progress on this site, and I figured I could be late for work today. After a short break, I walked over to the bridge. I leaned against the retaining wall and noticed my friends gathered around me as I gazed at the new building from this angle.

Piccolo Santino

Franco and Nino sat on the wall and discussed exploring the work site after the men left. At first, I thought about going to work, but then I became fixed there, so I lifted myself, sat with the others on the wall, and listened to them talk as I pondered my uncertain future with Mastro Buccino. I listened to my friends talking. "Does anybody know what time they stop work?"

"Yeah, around three, I think."

"What time is it now?"

"It's way past one-thirty." Two hours might pass when they go exploring inside, I thought, and the idea of playing hooky from work was growing on me. My friends kept talking. "Okay, guys, I think that's it. The last two workers are leaving now."

"All right, one of us goes in first to check around."

"Wait a little longer. Let's make sure," Franco suggested. Roberto, the son of a good friend and once a co-worker of Papá, then said, "Guys, I want to be the front guy." Franco said to him, "Just wait a little bit longer."

I could have gone to work, been late, and still have made a decent showing had I left an hour before. But to leave now, Buccino would indeed question me by the time I got there. Being at work for only two hours or less felt like a waste of time. Nino slapped me on my shoulder as he jumped down from the wall and walked down to the end of the bridge shouting, "I'm going to take a piss."

Giuseppi, a nerd type called the class dunce, walked across to the other side to seek recluse under the bridge and slowly said, "I'm going, too. I gotta take a crap." Franco looked at Roberto and said, "Okay, Roberto, you can check the place out now." Nino returned, and my decision to skip work became fortified. No one here knew about my apprenticeship in Nao, nor did I tell anybody, and they never asked anyway. Then Franco shouted out, "Okay, there's Roberto's signal. Let's go, guys." Nino yelled down to Giuseppi, "*Giuseppi cosa stai cacando serpi?* Giuseppi, what are you letting out, snakes? Andiamo!" Giuseppi shouted back, "I'm done, I'm coming!"

We rushed off the bridge and carefully walked over construction

Piccolo Santino

material until we reached a clearing by the front entrance. Franco and Nino followed Roberto inside. I looked around and felt drawn to the foundation, which seemed strong enough to support a dungeon. The cement walls to the first floor looked impenetrable. Then, I noticed metal rods sticking up inside the walls. Giuseppi caught up with us and sat on a pile of terracotta blocks. Roberto walked out first, followed by Nino and Franco.

Nino said, "There wasn't much to see; it's too dark inside," and after a short pause, he added, "This is gonna be some freaking school!" Roberto responded, "Yeah, all the classes are supposed to move here!" Then Roberto walked over by a set of sawhorses and set one of the horses up in a clearing, and Franco said, "Yeah, I heard that, but I don't think we will be coming here. They won't finish on time for us to come here." Hearing what Franco just said alleviated my guilt about not being able to finish school in Italy.

Roberto stepped aside from the sawhorse. "Yeah, for sure! All right now, let's see who can jump over this sawhorse."

"I can do it!" said Nino sarcastically as he set himself for a running start. His thin body cleared the horse quickly and he jubilantly shouted out, "I told you I could do it!" Roberto and Franco shouted back, "That was good! You cleared it by a lot!" Nino looked at Giuseppi and said, "Come on, Giuseppi, you try it next."

"Oh no! I can't do that, besides I'm too scared anyway," he said slowly and timidly. Roberto answered back, "Go on, and try at least!"

"No! No way, I'm too scared!"

"All right, I'll go next," said Roberto and he stepped back, raced forward, and barely cleared the top of the sawhorse. "Wow that was close!" Nino and Giuseppi exclaimed. "Yeah, I think I might have just touched the top on the last second."

"Go Ahead, Franco, you go next."

"No, let Bianchi try first. I can go after him."

"Yeah, come on, Santino!" Roberto said. I set myself a little bit farther back and took off hard and fast, and as I got near, I leaped, but once in flight, I felt I was doomed as my back leg was too low. I went down in

Piccolo Santino

excruciating pain with the horse on top of me and cried out, "Oh Noh! Ahhhh!"

"You all right, Santino?" everybody said. I lay there curled up and held on to my right shinbone as some laughter emerged around me. I continued crying for what I felt to be an eternity. I gripped my right leg and rocked back and forth on my hips. Franco reprimanded Roberto and Giuseppi both for laughing. "Okay, that's enough laughing, guys. He could've been hurt!" Roberto stopped laughing. Nino chuckled a little, and Giuseppi's laughter just kept growing as I lay there, thinking I was about to die. I cried again, and Franco fired back at Giuseppi, "It's not funny anymore; now stop laughing!" I slowly climbed to my feet and stared down at Giuseppi as he would not stop. I shouted angrily, "Nobody laughs at you in class when the teacher always calls you stupid. Do they?" I limped away from the sawhorse and sought a seat on several blocks. I continued firing back at Giuseppi. "Not so funny when the teacher refers to you as a class dunce! Is it Giuseppi?"

I watched him sulk, seemingly starting to boil, and I continued as my anger freed me from my speaking impediment, "You'll always be a dunce in life as you can barely read still and are in fourth grade!" His face sunk low into his chest, and I began to feel sorry for him as I realized his lack of intelligence was also matched by the poverty in their home, as Mamma once described his family to us. I stopped taunting him, and as I was turning around to sit, Giuseppi was in front of me, lifting his leg to kick me in the groin. I instantly raised my right foot and slammed the bottom of my shoe against his knee. The heel of my shoe caught his kneecap and dropped him to the ground. He screamed out in excruciating pain. I was stunned by my unexpected success. I had hoped only to blunt his kick by pushing down on his thigh with the bottom of my shoe. However, the angle of contact created a most unexpected result.

"Ah, Ohhhh, it hurts badly!" He cried out louder and more deeply than I had cried earlier, and I felt sorry to see him like that. I feared he was seriously hurt, and I could be in severe trouble again if he limped home. I imagined his family pursuing me to answer the doctor, his Mamma, and possibly the police. And now I thought perhaps I should have gone to work.

A roar overcame our presence, and we all turned to look into the street. Our eyes danced, and we raced out by jumping over mounds of debris as fast as our feet could leap. Giuseppi limped along, and within a blaze of time, we were all chasing a massive bus like wild hogs. The bus was not speeding but traveling faster than we were. But we knew we would catch up to it by the smoke shop. Everybody shouted out their comments. "How is that bus going to turn the corner?"

"No way will it make that turn!"

"It will never fit through there."

"It's going to have to turn around and go back."

Giuseppi trailed along without limping and, feeling relieved I asked him, "You okay?"

"Sì," he said, and I was elated as I felt fully exonerated of any guilt regarding this incident. In front of Dr. Itasca's house, we witnessed the driver stick his head out the window to look around as he maneuvered and tried a more direct angle into the passageway. We all laughed, knowing the driver would not make the turn. Other people began to congregate. The driver jockeyed the bus again. We could see others gathering on the opposite side. One man directed the driver with hand signals; others quibbled over the situation. An older man standing before us expressed his thoughts with very animated hand gestures and said, "He should turn the bus this way, not that way." Another man next to him offered, "He'll never make it that way!" Someone from the other side shouted out, "*Ma che cazzo?* What the fuck? Are you crazy? It's impossible that way!"

"This requires masons to rearrange the walls." A third man in the crowd shouted, and several women added, "That's for sure!" Laughter ensued as people continued shouting out opinions. "*Ma di dove cazzo è venuto questo autobus?* Where the fuck did this bus come from?" The driver tried another angle and slammed on his brakes as the right side of the bus scraped the building, and shouts continued. "This bus driver must be crazy."

"These walls have to be all rearranged."

Piccolo Santino

"Are you kidding? They must demolish an entire building to bring in these giant buses!"

"Yeah! Or stick to the smaller, older buses!" The driver then backed up as three masons signaled for him to move back. The masons laid down their bags of tools and began surveying the situation together. One mason with a thin body and a vast Roman nose, Mastro Puma, suggested. "First, we need to make room for the driver to drive the bus into the market square so he can turn around and go back."

Another mason with a short and muscular body, Mastro Lambiaso, wearing a thin tank t-shirt, walked up to the wall of Dr. Itasca's house and pointed out bricks that needed removing. A third mason, Mastro Luigi, a man of average height who looked more like a butcher with a thick, wide mustache and thick, stocky body, added, "You're right, Mastro Puma. We could remove bricks from both sides of the passageway so the driver can turn around inside the square." Mastro Puma said, *"Beh, ragazzi.* Since we all agree, guys, let's get to work!" In less than an hour, the masons removed enough bricks for the bus to squeeze between Dr. Itasca's and Roberto's houses to drive down into the piazza slowly. Instead of immediately turning around, the driver went to other possible exit points. He quickly realized that those streets were wide enough to enter but diminished farther in width. He backed up and circled inside the square like a wandering ladybug in a glass jar.

We dashed down into the square, eager to witness a real-life comical event that had us in stitches. The three masons, stationed at the top by the exit, kept signaling the driver to return. As the bus passed through, we followed closely, our excitement noticeable. The bus came to a stop just before our school, and the Mayor, flanked by two Bersaglieri, made their way to the front of the bus. The driver opened the door, and from our vantage point, we could see the Mayor engaging in a lively discussion with the three masons, a plan of action taking shape before our eyes.

The bus left town the way it came in. The smaller, older bus resumed the route for the next few weeks as the masons remained busy at work. The masons changed the doctor's house to facilitate the easement into the main square. It was primarily Roberto's house that

Piccolo Santino

needed streamlining, along with the corner of the smoke shop. In conclusion, the facelift gave the whole area a very avant-garde look with newly rounded corner-less walls. When the new bus drove through, it produced a surreal effect as the old seemed to mock the modern. The new modern bus was a testimony to the ensuing modern reality. However, it still had to maneuver around the corner slightly, and we liked watching the driver jockey back and forth as the whole affair still entertained us. It seemed the old was taunting the new for being forced to make way.

All this excitement made me forget I had been playing hooky at work for weeks. After coming home from school, I had to ensure that Mamma saw me leave the house and observed me walk down the main avenue toward Nao. It all felt too easy as Mamma had no idea, and since I didn't tell my friends what I was doing, it made me feel most secure.

However, one day, as I walked out the door, Mamma questioned me. "I got word from Mastro Buccino the other day that you're not going there anymore." I felt his dust fall from the cathedral ceiling like blocks of marble on top of me. I figured I better think fast and act like slick silence in a coffin. This way, Mamma won't question me again. I told her, "I don't know how he could say that. He hardly ever talks! I have been going."

"All right." She shrugged her shoulders in bewilderment. I also got the feeling that since I wasn't in any trouble, she wouldn't press. First, I made sure she saw the hunk of bread I was putting in my pocket, and then I started my walk toward Nao on the way to seemingly Buccino's Carpenter Shop. After much continued deceit, I figured this would all have to change. But there was no sign of when and how. If I were to end it myself, I would have to walk into Buccino's shop and endure whatever burden I face. But after playing hooky for such a long time, I didn't know how to deal with the uneasiness of returning almost as a stranger.

Then, one day, all my friends cleared out from our usual hangout earlier than expected. That left me feeling obligated to go home. I strolled along to kill time and stopped at the public fountain, moving slowly to freshen up. I walked with spirits of trepidation as if wanting to be caught. When I arrived at the Mayor's office, I saw a sign of hope. I spotted

Piccolo Santino

Rocco and Bruno riding from the direction of Mastro Santino and stopped in front of my house. I quickly hurried my walk. Mamma pointed toward me as both Rocco and Bruno waved me over.

I ran up to them. They were straddling their bicycles, and both said, "Ciao, Tino."

"Ciao, I said, "We were just telling your mamma that Master Santino is back." Said Rocco. Then Bruno added, "He said to come back to work tomorrow." I nodded my head excitedly and said, "Va bene!" Both responded, "We'll see you tomorrow at work then."

"Si, I'll be there for sure." They turned their handlebars straight to balance themselves and said, "Arrivederci, Signora! We've gotta get going."

"Sì, sì thank you for stopping by." I yelled back at them as they rode off, "Ciao. See you tomorrow."

"Ciao, Tino."

I returned to Master Santino the next day right after school, and on this hot day with a light breeze, the smell of fish carried halfway down the street to my home. I walked into the driveway and turned left, continuing up the ramp onto the front landing, unnoticed as the Master stirred the fish glue over a fire with a stick. This time, the bucket was suspended over a fire from a hook on a tall tripod made with three tall metal rods, unlike the typical short tripod I was used to seeing. I stopped by the doorway and said, "Buongiorno, Mastro." He quickly turned around and happily said. *"A bellezza del piccolo Santino.* Ah, the pleasure of little Santino! Buongiorno." I smiled with glee as I asked, "Should I go for water, Mastro?"

"Santino, you are just in time. Check with my cousin Mastro Nicola. I think he needs water, too." Rocco and Bruno were in the rear, sanding parts on the workbench. They looked over as I approached Master Nicola. I took a deep breath to make my words come out without stuttering. "I'm going for water, Mastro Nicola. Would you like some freshwater, too?"

"Si Santino! Grazie molto." Looking dazed, he said, "Now, where's that bottle?" He walked to the other end of his workbench, and Rocco interrupted him with a question: "Mastro Nicola, have you seen the new television invention yet?"

"Television? What is that? What are you talking about?"

"It's a new invention to show movies and programs almost like the radio, except you can actually see the people like in the movies."

"*Davvero?* For real? Where do they have this television? At the movie theaters?"

"No! Right now, Doctor Lumaca here in town is the first to buy it. He has it in his house."

"What does this television look like? How big is it? How did you know about it, anyway?"

"We heard about it in Vibo. Then we found out about the doctor. Now some of us go there at night to watch it."

"He lets people go in his house just like that?"

"No, the doctor keeps the sliding glass door open a bit for the sound, and we watch from outside." Mastro Santino walked in from outside and said to me, "Santino, you're still here?"

"Si Mastro, I'm going." Startled, Mastro Nicola said, "Oh Santino, you are waiting for me. Here's the bottle, son!"

"Cousin, did you hear about this new television invention Rocco is talking about?"

"Television? Oh yeah! Last night, my daughter told my wife about it, and then my son suggested we get one. I don't know how much it costs."

"What does this television actually do?" I listened to Mastro Santino ask as I strode out the door, hoping to get Rocco to tell me more about it later. I liked the idea of seeing movies in a box in your own house. But sadly, it sounded like something only for the rich. I still hoped to one day go and see what a movie was like in a theater. However, the distance between the locations and the ticket cost seemed insurmountable. To even think about crashing in on Dr. Lumaca was an even more ludicrous and frightening idea.

Piccolo Santino

I had recently overheard Mamma tell Aunt Ernestina how Mrs. Lumaca scolded her in front of her house one day to the level of not responding during that disagreement. The woman then became amazed at Mamma's calm demeanor and asked why she did not lash back. Mamma answered that it wasn't necessary because Mamma was doing it secretly in her mind. Mrs. Lumaca retorted that it was the same as lashing out openly since Mamma revealed her idea and then told her she was smart in thinking that way.

When I returned with the water, Rocco and Bruno described television shows they had already seen called *Rin-Tin-Tin, Jungle Jim,* and *Circus Boy*. Then, a ray of hope shone as they exclaimed rumors were spreading that Dr. Itasca was also purchasing a television. During such times, I wished that both masters were out of the shop. I wasn't comfortable engaging with Rocco and Bruno with the masters around. Work ended early, and the boys left while I was cleaning up. The Mastro dismissed me quickly, and as I was leaving, Mastro Santino walked up to his cousin. I walked out, and I overheard the word television. When I next saw my friend, Franco, I revealed what I learned about the new television invention, and he surprised me. "Yeah, Bianchi! We were at Doctor Lumaca's house two times already and watched *Rin-Tin Tin* Thursday night. Saturdays they show *Circus Boy* and *Jungle Jim*."

"Yeah, those are the ones Rocco and Bruno were talking about."

"I saw them all already."

"You mean you went inside their house to watch?"

"Oh no! Everybody stays outside and watches through the sliding glass doors. They keep the door open so we can hear the sound."

"Are there a lot of people?"

"Enough. The bigger guys and adults hog all the space, so we kind uh have to squat down and peek between people's legs sometimes."

"Why do they allow all those strangers outside their home like that?"

"It's a new invention. The doctor and his wife get excited, too. Say, how about you come with us this Thursday to Dr. Lumaca's?"

"No, I don't think so. Not to that doctor's house."

Piccolo Santino

"Then we can go Saturday night to Dr. Itasca's house. He is getting his television this week."

"Really? How do you know?"

"My papá found out when he walked past Dr. Itasca's house yesterday, and he heard him talking outside."

"Wow! Yeah, that would be really exciting!"

The following Saturday, we rushed to Dr. Itasca and arrived so early that the doors were closed, but the curtain was partially drawn. We peered inside. "We're early, Santino, but we can stay here. We'll be the first ones in front."

"I think I see it. Is that the television over there?" I pointed directly across to a big bright box with a talking head inside. "Yeah, that's it."

"What's that on the television now?"

"That's the news. The reporter reports about what goes on in Italy first and then what happens around the world." We excitedly watched through the glass door from outside as Signora Itasca sat on a white leather couch nursing her baby. Her mother-in-law was seated on the other end of the sofa, watching her two-year-old grandson. The child was sitting on the floor and playing with toys. The doctor's wife was a most beautiful buxom-looking woman, the conversation topic with many men in town. One man went as far as to vow never to marry unless he found the likes of the Signora Itasca. As we peered in, La Signora Itasca noticed us. She looked at her mother-in-law and said something to her. Then she signaled for us to go in. I timidly tried to open the glass door by pushing, and then Franco reached over and slid it enough for us to walk in as Mrs. Itasca spoke. *"Buonasera, ragazzi veniti dentro. Veniti.* Good evening, guys. Come in, come in." We both responded, "Buonasera, Signora. E Grazie." She then looked at me and said, "Excuse me but aren't you Anna's and Bartolo's son?"

"Si, Signora," I responded, and she continued. "Go ahead, sit on the floor next to my son. He loves to play." We sat beside the little boy and played with him, and he responded happily. Then Mrs. Itasca turned to

Piccolo Santino

her mother and said, "Madre, when Santino was born, he was given up for dead by both of our husbands."

"*Oh, Dio Mio. Benedica figlio.* Oh my God! Bless you, child."

"You remember his mother, Anna? She is waiting for Bartolo to send for them from America." She pulled the infant away from her right breast and switched him over to her left as she kept talking, "They used to live on our farm."

"Oh sì, sì Bartolo and Anna, why, of course!" Mrs. Itasca lifted her nipple into the infant's mouth, and he began sucking. She then said," Santino. When are you leaving for America?"

"Mamma says by June of next year."

"You are so lucky to be going there. America is very rich."

The toddler crawled over to me and stood up. I caught him before he could fall as he gave a burst of hearty laughter, and Franco asked, "What's the baby's name, Signora?"

"His name is Gino."

"And what's this little boy's name, Signora?"

"His name is Salvatore." Then Franco picked up the rattler toy from the floor and shook it before Salvatore. He continued laughing. I set him down on my lap. Franco continued shaking the toy in front of Salvatore, and I looked at Franco as the programming changed on the television. He said, "These are just commercials now, Bianchi." Mrs. Itasca explained further, "The news is over, so now they show a series of propaganda before the regular program starts." I nodded in response as I looked at Mrs. Itasca and then released Salvatore, who began squirming to free himself from my hold. He crawled away and then returned with a wide grin and a teddy bear clutched in his hand, and I said to him, "Oh Salvatore, you came back!"

Mrs. Itasca removed Gino from feeding, casually tucked away her exposed breast, and said, "Salvatore likes playing with you boys. I can tell he likes your company." She propped Gino against her left shoulder and patted him gently on his back for him to burp.

The commercials were almost over, and two men peered in from

Piccolo Santino

outside. Then, another younger man walked up to take a position. The *Circus Boy's* name came up on the screen, and when Circus Boy came on riding Bimbo the Elephant, our eyes swelled, and we grinned from ear to ear. I looked outside and saw a small crowd assembled, and Mrs. Itasca turned to her mother-in-law and said, "Madre, please slide the door open all the way so they can hear the sound better. It's all right."

Grandmother Itasca slid open the door, and Mrs. Itasca greeted the intruders as she readjusted the baby against her body. "Buonasera. Please come in, come in." The people stepped inside and formed a straight line before the doorway. In the middle, I saw Rocco and Bruno staring at me with surprised gazes. The crowd quickly bowed their heads at Mrs. Itasca and said, "Buonasera, Signora e Grazie."

"Buonasera e *prego*, you're welcome." Rocco coyly looked at me and then opened both hands as he pointed to the floor. Then, after a short pause looked at the television while Bruno just stared at me with his mouth open. A brawl broke out on the television. We all cheered as some of the actions involved the clown and the monkey with the elephant. Most of the time, Salvatore stayed close by Franco and me, but suddenly, his behavior took a turn, and he seemed agitated and hard to control. Mrs. Itasca turned to her mother and said, "Madre, I think Salvatore might need a change."

"*Si certo.* Yes, of course." Grandmother Itasca got up, walked across the television, and said, "*Scusate Ragazzi.* Excuse me, fellas."

"*Certo.* Of course, Signora." She walked over by us, lifted Salvatore, and took him into another room. As she walked away, people leaned from side to side to avoid missing a beat on the television, and, as *Circus Boy* concluded, the commercials came on. The number of people multiplied to a dense crowd whose presence had infiltrated three rows deep from inside the room into the darkness outside. Some people bobbed their heads up and down and ducked sideways, searching for a space to peer through. *Jungle Jim appeared* on-screen by attacking a tiger that was mauling a man. The crowd became astonished at the images of Jungle Jim's tenacious grip on the beast. As I watched Jungle Jim raise a knife and stab the tiger, I wondered how the action was put into that so-

Piccolo Santino

called television. The general belief was that it all was happening.

Simba appeared, and comic reliefs were always welcome. Everyone continued watching with eyes wide opened and disbelief at the unfolding adventure. In the end, the crowd looked into each other's eyes with complete excitement and filled with anticipation for the next program. Then as the people dispersed Rocco and Bruno turned to Mrs. Itasca and said, "Buonasera, Signora, e grazie molto." Others followed with more farewells, and Franco and I waited until everyone left. I turned to Mrs. Itasca and said, while Franco joined me, "Grazie e buonasera Signora."

"Buonasera, Santino, and say hello to your mother for me."

"Si! E Grazie, Signora."

We walked out into the dark. Most people had dispersed, and Rocco and Bruno were on their bikes out on the street as Franco and I walked home together up the main avenue. Franco started up a conversation. "*Jungle Jim* was great, wasn't it?"

"Yeah, *Circus Boy* was good, too!"

"Yeah! You think the Signora will let us sit inside again?"

"Oh, I don't know. That was kind of special."

"Yeah, it doesn't matter. We can still see and hear from outside pretty good."

"Yeah, that's true."

"We gotta go back Thursday night to see *Rin-Tin-Tin*."

"Oh yeah, for sure!" We parted company as Franco turned left inside the pitch black in the mini square toward his house, and I stayed the course. "Ciao, Bianchi." He shouted from inside the darkness. "Ciao, Franco." The street had many dark areas where the moonlight could not paint the spaces, and when some electric light or kerosene light spilled outside through the windows, it made for a calmer walk zone. I looked left down the street to my grandfather's house; that darkness was as dense as charcoal. Fearful of that dark, I quickly looked away and took comfort in the thought that my house was just a few doors down to the left. Thinking everybody was asleep, I opened the door slowly and heard Stella say, "Nonno said that when they see the scar on Tino's foot, they're

Piccolo Santino

not gonna let him go to America."

"Yeah, he'll have to live here with Nanna and Nonno," Martina interjected. Lillo asked, "Mamma! Will Tino really have to stay here?" Mamma responded, "What can we do?" Martina's voice was filled with disbelief, "If you have something wrong with you that they don't like, they won't let you board the ship?" Mamma's response was a solemn confirmation, "Your Grandfather saw it happen many times when he used to go to America."

I closed the door with a resounding thud, shattering the peace inside. I ascended the steps from the foyer to the family room. "You have returned," Mamma said, breaking the silence. I responded, "Si." Mamma continued interrogating me, "Where did you end up tonight?"

"We were watching television."

"Che cazzo di televisione? What fucking television?"

"The doctor's wife says, 'hi.'" In a disturbed tone, she asked, *"Quella puttana di Dottore Lumaca?* That bitch of Doctor Lumaca's? You went over there?"

"No Mamma, at Doctor Itasca's house."

"So now they also have a television?"

"Si! It's Mrs. Itasca who said, "Hi." In a subdued manner, she said, *"Va bene. Andiamo tutti a letto. È già tardi.* Very well, let's all go to bed. It's late."

In bed, I thought about what I had just overheard and what my life would be like living alone with my grandparents. I thought about finding reading material to continue my education beyond the fifth grade for my goal of becoming a poet. I felt a mix of excitement and apprehension about the possibilities that lay ahead. I wanted to know if I would do that here in Jonadi or Scaliti, where my grandparents lived. Or would I be learning a new language in America and graduating in fifth grade in English? To circumvent possible hysteria in Naples if I fail the medical inspection there. I now accepted the fact I could be left behind.

As an excuse, on Tuesday, I will pretend to visit Nanna in Scaliti to look for that little metal "C" clamp I saw at Antonio's carpenter shop the last time I visited. Nanna was away, and Antonio opened the door to his

Piccolo Santino

shop and invited me in. Afterward, he explained that my grandparents were also his aunt and uncle and were on the farm. Antonio had a one-room carpenter shop with a workbench that was almost the entire length and width of the room. His bench was littered entirely with randomly placed tools, remnants of wood boards, and some parts of a buffet he was working on. I sat in the rear of the room and studied the mess on top of the workbench. When I spotted a cute little metal "C" clamp, it caught my eye.

The next day, I described it to Rocco, and he promised to lend me two *Jungle Jim comic* books and one *Tarzan* comic book if I could steal that C clamp for him. At first, I was not too fond of the idea, but now that I saw my first *Jungle Jim* show on television, the temptation was wilting my better judgment, so I decided to make the trip and put myself to the test.

The twenty-or-so-minute walk to Scaliti felt endless as my mind swelled with anticipation, even on this perfect day for walking. I planned on going to Nanna's first and hoped she would not be home so that Antonio would invite me again. Then I could pretend to wait for her in his shop while I caroused the room, hoping the little "C" clamp would still be in that same spot. Upon arrival, I tried Nanna's door and found it locked. I knew about the key wrapped in a towel inside the hole in the wall at the base of the door frame, but there would be no point in using the key to enter an empty home. I looked across the street at Antonio's carpenter shop, and I didn't see any signs of life, but just the same, I gently tried to open that door and found it locked. I paced up and down the street for a few minutes, each step a reminder of the disappointment of not seeing Antonio, and each time, I strode toward home a bit farther out from the locked door. On each occasion, I thought, *just one more walk and then leave if Antonio did not show up*, then I assumed *it would be too troubling, or I might not muster the courage, to come back another day*.

On my final attempt, I decided to wait around the bend, four buildings away, out of sight, in case Antonio returned. As I circled back, I saw him unlocking his door. I hurried to my grandmother's house and knocked on her door. Standing in his doorway, Antonio greeted me with the news, "Santino, they are out on their farm again."

"Oh!"

"Come on over here if you want." I walked across and followed him inside. "Yeah, at least they will not be home until maybe five o'clock. They just left about an hour ago."

"Oh again?" I said, and Antonio reached up to open the shutters to the front window. I was glad, as the room felt so hot, and he resumed working on the buffet he had assembled. Antonio, now in the polishing stage, dipped a cloth dauber in linseed oil and then spread it on the top surface of the buffet. He began working it over with slow, intentional, clockwise circular motions. I roamed to the room's rear as Antonio seemed deep in concentration. I sat on the same stool as last time and leaned toward the bench, and, as if by magic, I saw the little clamp. My heart raced as I asked myself if he would notice me when I reached for it.

I glanced at him and wondered if he would ever miss it. Or even notice it is missing at all. Antonio had so much stuff piled up on this bench that he probably didn't even know it was there. I relaxed for a beat and reasoned that I would take from my family and give to a stranger. Then, my ego inflated me again, reminding me that I had promised Rocco I would do it, and I couldn't go back without it. I said I would do it, and now I had to do it. I came here just for that clamp, and it was right there before my eyes.

Still rapt in his work, I looked at Antonio and casually leaned forward while crossing my arms on the bench. With my eyes toward Antonio, I rested my head. He stopped polishing and cocked his head sideways to admire the glimmer. Coyly, I extended my left arm as he resumed polishing in circular motions. My fingers searched for the clamp with my arm and hand in position and soon felt its metal frame. I began to palm the little thing slowly, swung my left arm sideways, and lowered the clamp into my pocket. I then sat up straight and resumed the pretense of hoping that my grandparents would return home.

Piccolo Santino

Outside an old woman shouted out from a balcony to someone below, "Gumbah, you have a hole in your hat. I can see it from my balcony." The old man responded toothlessly, "Gummah, I think you also have one, but I just can't see it from here."

"*Che scostumato!* What pervert! You're bad again, Gumbah."

"*Si come te.*" Yes, just like you." Antonio stopped for a beat, lifted his head, and shouted toward the outside, "*Ancora?* Again? Come on now. I am trying to get some work done here."

"*Ma fate le cazzi tue.* Oh, mind your own fuck'n business."

"Maybe another day! Right now, there's a little boy here that's visiting me."

"*Mi dispiace! Scusati!* I'm sorry! Excuse us!" He returned to work as laughter ensued outside from the old couple, and I lifted my head and said, "Antonio, I'm not going to wait anymore." He paused from working as he lifted his head and turned toward me, "No, I told you they're not gonna be home till at least after five." He resumed working, and I responded, "I better go then."

"Yeah, go ahead." I got up and walked toward the exit, pushing the door open as he kept working. Ciao," I said. He responded the same, "Ciao." As I opened the door, I looked down so as not to trip on the doorframe. It seemed funny to step over a skinny doorframe from the inside to the outside. It made me think of Antonio's room as a secluded alley with a fancy exterior facade, all because his floor and the street shared the same cobblestone.

Outside, to my left, the old man was under a balcony. He quickly turned to me with a wry smile and watched me turn away. I rushed my walk back to meet Rocco at the shop in Jonadi. I thought about how the town of Scaliti appeared much different from Jonadi or Nao. Here, the streets weren't as spacious as in Jonadi or Nao. Nao had some rows of somewhat constricted buildings, but they also had a sense of individuality, whereas here, in Scaliti, the buildings seemed to gang up on you. However, the short length of the main street did allow some room for forgiveness. And yet, in Scaliti, the architecture seemed to speak so primly and properly. The close-knit construction of the buildings radiated

Piccolo Santino

an aura of a tightly woven, stuffy atmosphere as if robbing the streets of needed space.

Scaliti had one large public square occupied by a church for St. Peter, and as you walked out from any street into the open square, it could feel like somebody just propelled you through the stem of a funnel as you took a whiff in the open air. Notions of guilt temporarily surfaced in me to combat my ego's festivities for the success of my crime as I turned into the country path back to Jonadi. I kept justifying the evil act by telling myself Rocco would now lend me the *Jungle Jim* comic books, which would be all worth it. Then I absolved myself by believing that Antonio would never clean up his bench and, therefore, he would never notice the clamp missing. Furthermore, I was on a mission I had to accomplish and should enjoy my success.

When I returned to the shop, Bruno was sitting on the stoop smoking a cigarette, and he called out to Rocco inside as I approached, "Look here, Rocco, Tino is just now getting to work."

"He's here already?" Rocco stopped browsing his comic book and rushed over to the doorway, and Bruno said to him, "What do you mean?"

"You'll see." He shouted out to, "Tino, you made it." I looked up at Rocco with a wide grin and said, "Si!" Bruno looked at me and said, "What's going on? You look like you caught a bird with your fist." Rocco stepped back inside and said, "Guys, we better get inside. The boss should be getting back soon." Bruno quipped, "Oh shit, that's right! We better look busy then."

Inside, Rocco closed the comic book he was looking at, and I pulled out the little clamp from my pocket and held it up for Rocco to see. "Che, Bella!" He exclaimed as he reached for it, held it in front of his eyes, and then said, "The comic books are right here on the bench. Grazie, Tino." I reached over, gathered all three books, started reading *Jungle Jim* right from the front cover, and became completely immersed. Bruno then asked Rocco, "Hey Rocco, when the boss comes in, are we going to talk to him?"

"Oh yeah, the holiday is coming in two days, and tomorrow is the

Piccolo Santino

start of the celebration. We have to talk to the Master."

"Yeah, he should be coming back any time now. He said he would be out most of the day." I exclaimed, "Wow! Here is Skipper with Kaseem, and the monkey is funny. For how long can I borrow these, Rocco?"

"The boss is coming. I see him down the street," said Bruno from the doorway as he turned back inside, saying, "Come on, let's look busy." Rocco told me, "Tino, start putting the tools away. We're all done working."

"Can I take these home, Rocco?"

"Oh no! Let me have them. I'll return them for you next week when the boss is away."

"Okay," I said, then Bruno said, "Hey Rocco, this dresser door is still in the vice over here. Is it done?"

"Oh, *Dio Mio*, I forgot to check it. I'll do it now."

As I reached for the square, Rocco hurried to conceal another comic book and said, "Tino, start putting the tools away from the other bench." His voice carried a sense of urgency as if he was trying to divert attention. "Okay," I responded as I grabbed the saw and reached for the square. I need that square." Rocco grabbed the square from me and applied it to the top edge of the small dresser door in the vice to check for evenness. Bruno asked him, "Is it all square?" Before he could answer, the Mastro called out, "Buongiorno, Ragazzi." We all turned around at the master and said, "Buongiorno, Summastro."

"Well, Rocco, is it all squared?" asked the master. With a peal of bashful laughter, "Sì Mastro, it's all squared." Responded Rocco, a tinge of relief in his voice as the tension of the boss's presence lifted. "Bravo! Boys, I'm glad to tell you we have work for the next month."

"That is good news, Signore."

"But for this week, it's all over since tomorrow is the start of the Sacred Heart celebration." Bruno looked up as he stopped rubbing a blade to one of the planes on the sharpening stone and asked, "So we won't be working the rest of the week then?"

Piccolo Santino

"No, there's no work left for this week so you and Rocco can get ready to leave. Santino has to clean up yet."

With a mischievous glint in his eye, Bruno carefully set the blade down and motioned towards the master. A mere apprentice, I stepped forward, the blade feeling oily in my hand. I quickly wiped it with a cloth, and the blade was pristine once more, so I stowed it in the drawer.

Rocco and Bruno confronted the master at the workbench in front of the exit, and Rocco asked, "Summastro, we were wondering if you had planned to give us any kind of token for this holiday." Surprised, the master rested his hands on his hips while facing the guys and said, "Well, I hadn't planned on it. Why?"

"We reckon we've earned a little something, considering the hefty workload we've shouldered this month," Rocco asserted. Bruno chimed in, "And we've been here every single day, at your service."

"Well, let me think now. The work did get completed ahead of schedule." He brought his right hand up to his chin and pondered a moment. "Hmmm. All right! How about I give you three hundred lire to divide amongst yourselves?"

"That would only give us one hundred and fifty lire each." Rocco responded. Bruno interjected, "That's hardly much at all, Summastro!" Then he looked at Rocco, and they both turned to Mastro Santino as Rocco said, "At the Sawmill, we used to get a thousand lire, but with you, we were hoping maybe eight hundred lire apiece."

"No way, I'm not like the Sawmill. I'm sorry, but I can't afford that."

"But it is the holiday master, and we always work hard for you."

"Sì, sì, but I can't do eight hundred lire each!" They all paused, and I kept busy in the background. I was surprised at the discussion of money but hoped that some of it would come my way. Rocco and Bruno remained steadfast and stared at the master as he rubbed his chin and shook his head back and forth. Then he crossed his arms, looked at them, and said, "I tell you what, boys. Let me think."

Afraid to go near them, I stayed aloof by looking busy in the rear as the master, a man of considerable means, reached into his right pocket and pulled out a fat wallet. He turned his back to them and counted out

Piccolo Santino

six hundred lire (at that time, it was the equivalent of one US Dollar) on the workbench by creating two separate stacks of three bills each. He then put his wallet back in his pocket and stepped aside. He turned around, gestured towards the money with one hand, and said, "There you are, boys. That's the best I can do. Three hundred lire each if you want it to take it."

The two boys, their faces reflecting a mix of disappointment and resignation, exchanged a few silent moments of contemplation. They met each other's gaze, their eyes revealing the internal conflict they were experiencing. With a reluctant nod, they accepted the money, their heavy hearts a stark contrast to the master's casual tone. Their shoulders slumped, and they averted their eyes, a clear sign of their sadness. 'Glad we are in agreement,' he said. The boys, now visibly saddened, turned to the master and uttered a polite, "Thank you for your kindness, and have a nice holiday."

"You're welcome, and you have a nice holiday, too boys."

They walked out in silence. I advanced toward the other bench with the dust brush to dust it off, and the master said to me, "Santino, I'll be right down." I looked up and nodded "Yes" as he dashed upstairs, and I eagerly anticipated that he would get some money for me. I continued brushing the top of the workbench and realized there were more tools to put away that I had avoided earlier.

The master must have left the door open to the upstairs as I heard his wife seething. "A thousand lire? What gall! I hope you..." The upstairs door slammed shut, and I dashed away with a handsaw and a drill to hang on the rack across the room as the master briskly descended the stairway. I slowly hung the drill up and the handsaw and then resumed brushing off the benches as the master returned and sat at his workstation studying some drawings he laid out in front of him.

I then realized my usual time to go home was about an hour away or so, and since the guys left early for a holiday, I hoped I would get some consideration. I walked around splashing droplets of water on the floor with special care by the Mastro, hoping for a little financial acknowledgment, but he seemed oblivious. I swept the floor from one

Piccolo Santino

end to the other and even swept extra slowly by him, but he never lifted his head from his drawings. I made some noise with the dustpan as I gathered the clippings and dust, but he kept on ignoring me, so I emptied the dustpan in the barrel, leaned the broom in its corner, and planned to do "my desire to go home routine" from the doorway right in front of him.

Piccolo Santino

Chapter 6 of Part Two, 1957
Building a Baby Coffin

Filled with anticipation, I started toward the exit but stopped quickly in the center of the room. A short woman in black, sobbing, stood in the doorway, gathering her composure before she stepped forward to be noticed by Master Santino. "Excuse me, Mastro," she lamented. He looked up and immediately got up from his stool, startled as he spoke. "Signora, how can I help you?" I sensed a dark shadow that weighed down the air like a giant blanket of wet sawdust. As the room's atmosphere dampened, I thought the Master would now send me home. "Mastro, I need your services."

"Si Signora, how can I be of service?"

"My son of five died, and we need a small coffin for his burial."

"Oh, Dio Mio! I am so sorry. How old did you say your son was?"

"He was only five years old."

"Oh, my heart goes out to you."

I saw a lone hammer on the bench and slowly walked over to put it away as they talked. I wouldn't dare leave without the Master's permission, so I watched, hoping for his magic words. They talked for a long moment, and the Master made sketches in his workbook and showed them to her. The woman looked at the drawings with an approving sobbing nod. "Now, I'll be glad to show you some boards I have here for the construction."

"All right."

"This way, please, follow me!" He led her into the machine room past the other side of the stairway to the upper floor. I quickly walked onto the ramp to see if my siblings were playing outside. I was relieved that there was still plenty of sunlight left, and since Rocco and Bruno were gone, I figured the Master would be doing the job tonight by himself. After all, I was just a kid and didn't think I could be of much help. So, for sure, I felt he would dismiss me. I ran back inside, and the

Piccolo Santino

Master came out with several boards and laid them on his cousin's bench. The woman asked, "Mastro if you can reconsider your price, I would be grateful."

"I am very sorry, Signora, but please realize the kind of time I will have to put into this project to have it finished for the morning."

"Very well, we will be here tomorrow morning and pay you the balance." They shook hands, and I was happy to see her leave. I stared at the Master in anticipation as he looked at me and said, "Santino, come with me, son! Tonight, we have a lot of work to do."

Those were not the words I was hoping for. The Master grabbed the boards from the bench and led me back into the machine room. Dejected, I followed him as he held the wood boards tight against his chest like huge loaves of bread. He forged into the next room, and I followed, but my knees weakened in the doorway. I feared the big machine in the room, but even more so, the many coffins stacked against the back and side walls. Suddenly, I had visions of Master Santino secretly being the Reaper, posing as a carpenter. I imagined him going out nights with a coffin on his back in search of victims. I looked away from his collection of coffins to soothe my beating heart. My feet wanted to make tracks, but my commitment and loyalty kept me in the room.

The Master propped the boards to the side of the big machine and flipped on the switch. The shrilling sound of it pierced through my ears and rattled my skull, and I barely heard him shouting at me. "Santino, you go on the other side and pull on the boards as I feed them through." It all felt so intense and frightening as I grabbed the first board coming through the power sanding process. Sawdust flew in the air and littered my face and body. After sending seven boards through, the Master looked like a fat sandman waddling about. I was happy to hear the machine shut down. I listened to the Master spitting out sawdust and slapping his body as he walked over. He grabbed five boards in one swoop and said, "Santino, grab the other two boards and come with me." He didn't have to ask me twice to follow him out. My heart had already left long ago. I reached over and hugged the two boards against my body and liked how my feet rushed me out of that room.

Piccolo Santino

On the workbench, the Master measured according to the drawings he had laid out. I walked outside while he was beating his brain to see if my siblings were still outside. The Master said, "Santino, come over here and hold down this board while I saw." I immediately obeyed and held down the board while he sawed off a small section. I anticipated he needed to cut another board, so I stayed put, and sure enough, my prediction occurred. I felt a break, dashed outside again, and noticed the shadows had engulfed much of the light. I went back inside to help again. Once he finished sawing, I raced outside two more times, and on the last trip, he abruptly called out to me, "Santino bello! Come and hold this board down." I hurried inside and pressed down on the board with all my might as he worked, and then with a subdued and concerning tone, he said. "I'm sorry, but you can't go home yet, Tino. We have very important work tonight."

At that point, I was more disheartened that the volume of shadows outside had swallowed up all bright light. Feeling robbed of my playtime, I pressed down on the board as the Master worked furiously. The Master's working attitude was a trait in him whenever urgency was at hand. It all felt like a very tight mission as he worked like a raging bull the way he moved without a bite to either eat or drink or the idea of me letting my Mamma know that I would not be home for a while. The concentration was all about the project and getting it done. However, during the process, I felt the coolness of dusk, and I took the opportunity to peek outside a few times. Surprisingly, I noticed two of my sisters, with Lillo, looking in from the street to check on me. I figured Mamma was worried. As soon as they saw me assisting the Master, they left. I wondered how to let Mamma know of my whereabouts, and I was relieved.

After cutting all the necessary parts, the Master moved the longer boards over to his cousin's bench and joined them to form wider boards. His decision to use cold glue, a departure from his usual preference for hot fish glue, was a clear indication of the urgency of the situation. We got the usual clamps to hold the glued boards together, and once the clamps were fastened tight, he returned to his own station and prepared the smaller pieces. I watched as he continuously measured twice before

Piccolo Santino

cutting and always drew a line with a square to indicate how far he would need to plane down an edge. I liked how he checked his work two to three times to make sure it was done in a precise form.

Close to two hours had passed before the smaller pieces were completed, and then he checked the glued boards and, as he unscrewed the clamps. I was surprised to see how tight they had dried. The Master even had to use a mallet to bang some of the cross braces off, which kept the boards flat as the glue was drying.

We returned to the power room with the pre-assembled panels for fine sanding. The early evening darkness now magnified my fear of the coffins but not the piping sound of the machine. I figured the piercing noise was enough to frighten any ghosts lurking in the room, so I learned to befriend the shrilling noise as the Mastro fed the boards through.

I slowly pulled all of them out. The Master turned off the machine, and I quickly followed him outside. I now gained some confidence in my participation. He sifted through the container of nails I had hammered into reusable form. He couldn't find finishing nails, so he put the head of a regular nail on top of a metal surface and banged the head on four sides to minimize the top so he could drive the head below the wood surface with a center punch.

The little boy's coffin began to take form. I could feel the woman's pain and wondered how she or her family overcame such a tragedy, especially around a holiday—tomorrow had to be the day of the funeral. That is why the Master was rushing to finish tonight. I watched him assemble the baby coffin and then sand down the sides and the inside all by hand. Last, he placed the lid on top, and I was impressed with how the Master designed an inside border on the cover. The completed shape was a baby version of the giant coffins in his storage room. Wide at the shoulders and narrow in the head and feet area. It all felt so heartbreaking to be involved in this little boy's death instead of a happy life for him. The lid was a perfect fit, and he put down the sanding block and surprised me by assisting in brushing off the benches of wood shavings and sawdust and putting tools away.

Piccolo Santino

I sprinkled water on the floor so that the sweeping would not kick up any dust, and he surprised me again by taking the broom away from me And saying, "Go on, Tino, go home, son." He laid the broom down and applied a dark stain onto the raw wood. I looked at him and said, "Buonasera." I surmised he was now at a point where he could complete the coffin in time for tomorrow's funeral. "Buonasera *figlio,* son," he said.

I had never walked home in the dark from work. And thinking about the coffins in the power room hastened my steps. The idea of the master possibly being the reaper with a coffin on his back prevented me from looking back. I quickly concentrated on pushing open the front door to my house and jumping into bed. I pushed it open, and Mamma greeted me at the door in her nightgown. In a subdued voice, I said, "We had to m-m-make a baby coffin."

"Here, eat something." she said as she pointed to a small feast of bread and cheese with some dried olives she had arranged on a small stand right by the door. My eyes devoured the food before my mouth could taste it, and after my taste buds were freed, they now feasted on the sight of a glass of red wine. I was so exhausted, but Mamma's care and understanding rejuvenated me. "Didn't Master Santino realize it was really late?"

"They have to bury the little boy tomorrow."

"Oh, that's right, day after tomorrow is the feast of the Sacred Heart." I took another drink of the red wine, and it felt good, then I bit into more bread and cheese before finishing a few olives. "Go ahead, son, finish eating and get to bed. It's late."

I could hear sound bites of musical instruments right outside my window. The noises from musicians tuning their tuba and horns urged me to get up as the sound almost vibrated my bed. It felt late. But then, I should have heard the church bells and slept through them because now I heard Franco and Nino talking outside. I got up, slipped into my shorts and shoes fast while I put on a shirt, and lifted my suspenders into place while I walked outside into the warm sun. I called out to my friends.

Piccolo Santino

"Ciao, Franco! Nino!"

Nino responded first as Franco talked with one of the musicians, who was preoccupied with his tuba. It was rumored that the church couldn't spend much money for this year's festivities for the Sacred Heart, and thus not much was expected. The belief was that the church was hoarding money to support the other feast in the summer when it could enjoy better profits from the larger crowds it could draw from out-of-towners. This stark contrast between the two feasts, one for the Poor Madonna and the other for the Rich Madonna, awakened sympathy in me for the underprivileged. Franco called out to me. "Ciao, Bianchi"

"E Buongiorno," exclaimed the musician right after Franco saluted me, "Buongiorno," I replied, and Franco said, "Bianchi, the band is going to lead the funeral procession for a little boy this morning from here."

"Yeah, I know it's for a little boy who died yesterday."

"You know who it is?" Franco asked me as the two musicians and Nino looked on. "No, Mastro Santino made the coffin last night. I was helping." The news of the boy's death had spread quickly, and the community was visibly affected. The two musicians and Nino looked at me with a mix of sadness and concern.

"Really?" asked the tuba musician and then added. *"Que miseria! What misery!"* The other musician, a clarinet player, added, "That poor family!" The player hoisted his tuba by its strap and said, "Come on, Pasquale, we better go. We're g the reed and was quickly installing it on the clarinet as he said, supposed to be at the church soon." Pasquale had just finished cleaning "Va bene, Vincenzo andiamo." Vincenzo told us, "Don't worry, kids, we are a good band. Don't believe the rumors you heard." The two walked away, and Vincenzo looked back and said, "We're gonna tell the others about the little boy. This way, we can all play with feeling, boys."

"Mille Grazie!" exclaimed Franco. "You're welcome," they shouted back.

During the funeral march, the priest and two young boys carrying thuribles filled with incense led the crowd ahead of the pallbearers.

Piccolo Santino

Following right behind the casket were immediate family members, and to my surprise, Mrs. Romanelli was walking beside the mother of the deceased child, with Master Santino next to her. I studied the solemn face of Mrs. Romanelli as the other woman leaned on her for support. It gave the impression that this experience had made them best friends.

The band followed along and played somber tunes. I thought the music was to ease the pain, but as I watched the many faces, it acted more as a lubricant for the outpouring of extra tears. Many townspeople followed along. Of course, a group of kids, including my two friends and me, followed the procession into the top of town through the large square, past the rich Madonna's church. The procession turned left past the church and slowly climbed the uphill road lined with cypress trees that delineated a path to the cemetery, and by this time, the band stopped playing as it needed its energy for the uphill climb. The mausoleum building was to the left at the end of the road in a wide-open field.

Inside the columbarium was a dirt floor, and the smells of cement and plaster were prevalent as two masons prepared the niche while the procession arrived. The crowd parted, allowing the family to enter as the pallbearers and the priest led the way inside. The casket was gently placed on blocks in front of the little boy's final resting place, and, as if preordained, the gathering crowd formed a semi-circle that allowed ample space between it and the family for the band to regroup and play a few lasting notes.

I stared at some coffins protruding from niches and feared walking inside, so I watched from the doorway while Franco and Nino walked past me. The two altar boys raised their thuribles several times, and the smell of incense jammed my nostrils as if it were saying, "This is what death smells like. Beware of the Reaper." I stared at how pretty the white lace cloth looked against the dark walnut stain of the baby coffin while the priest showered it with holy water. I thought of the cold the little boy's body would bear in this room.

The altar boys and priest made way for the masons to slide the small box inside the niche, the music notes intensified, the priest sprinkled more holy water, and tears moistened veils on women's faces as the

Piccolo Santino

music came to a crescendo and stopped. Then silence and sobbing prevailed, replacing the somber melody. I looked outside as I rested against the doorframe. I was amazed to see a tall sunflower slowly turning toward the sun, which made me think the flower was observing the little boy's soul rising to heaven. The musicians slowly lowered their instruments, and I stepped outside, staring into the field and wondering how a flower could move like that.

Franco and Nino tapped me on my shoulder. We returned to town to the fading sounds of a hammer banging against a brick. And that of a metal trowel slapping cement and tapping against that brick with the end of its handle. All reverberating from inside the columbarium. We were joined by swooshing footsteps from the gloomy silence of people all in black.

The next day was a big celebration. The band had already put all rumors to rest about it being a lesser band as people continually raved about the musician's quality playing. By midday, Franco and I were meandering in the piazza of the rich Madonna's church. Since the Sacred Heart church was located in a congested area, it lacked room for a square. I observed people enjoying candy and pastries and some children being treated to toys and games. The anticipation of the celebration was palpable, but it was overshadowed by the memories it evoked. I tried to ignore the aroma of it all, but it was too thorny, and my memories brought me back to when Papá had treated me to watermelon here. Franco turned at the sound of his name from someone in the crowd. I saw his sister in the distance as she called him, "Franco! Where are you?"

"Santino, I think my sister is here looking for me."

"Sì, I just saw her over there."

"Where?" he asked.

"Over there, straight ahead in the crowd." He looked over, and I said, "She just saw us. Here she comes."

"I see her. Rosina, I'm over here!" She approached us and said, "Franco, you need to come home. The pasta will be ready soon."

"Oh, I didn't know we were eating this early."

Piccolo Santino

"Mamma and Papá sent me to look for you. We're having our celebration dinner now."

"Oh, okay."

"All right, let's go then."

"Ciao, Bianchi."

"Ciao, Franco." Franco walked into the crowd with his sister, and I felt envious. I turned away from them and saw a group of well-dressed people looking like they had just left church. In the center of that crowd, I saw Mastro Santino walking with his family, and even though his wife and daughter were about a head taller than him, his glowing pride certainly made him equally tall. Our eyes made contact, and Mastro pointed toward me, and they all stopped as Mastro Santino said, "Look, there is Santino." He looked at me and said, "Happy holiday, Santino."

"Happy holiday," I responded with gleeful eyes, hoping for a last chance he could dig in his pockets since I needed some money right now. After all, he gave Rocco and Bruno money, and I helped him with the coffin late into the night. I watched for any movement of his hands as he kept them in his pants. His wife and daughter to his sides held on to his arms. He turned to his left, pointed with his right shoulder, and said, "I present my wife, Mrs. Romanelli." She said, "Happy Holiday." Then the Master pointed with his left shoulder, "My daughter Filomena and my mother-in-law." They both said, "Happy Holiday."

I hoped he would've taken a hand out of his pocket and have me reach over for one coin at most negligible. So, I smiled at the women and nodded to them as I said, "Buongiorno and Happy Holiday." Looking sideways at me, Mastro Santino pushed forward. The women obeyed his motions, and my heart sank as the group casually walked away.

I wandered about with an aching heart and could not stop thinking of the time Papá got me watermelon in this spot. Feeling the pain of aloneness, I strolled about aimlessly, and when futility sunk in, I headed home, not expecting any celebration. At home, the door was locked, so I looked across the street at Aunt Isabella's house, and I wasn't sure if I caught a glimpse of two of my sisters.

Piccolo Santino

I walked downstairs to see if Mamma might be there. The doors to the storerooms were locked. Emptiness on the sloping terrain behind our house mirrored my feelings down to the street below. Dejected, I walked back up and climbed the steps to Aunt Isabella's. I found the door closed. I felt too shy about going inside. I stepped over to the security of the retaining wall, where I nestled in the corner and rested my hands on the ledge. I looked at the neighbor's courtyard and studied how the grass was stained with a thick brown color. My eyes followed the brown stain up the wall to an opened window. There was no need to guess what the brown color was. Since there were no indoor facilities, most everybody emptied their chamber pots out the window into a courtyard. In that window, I saw my cousin Simona stop to wave at me with a genuinely happy smile, but then I was quickly saddened by her mamma's cold stare as she pushed Simona aside and intentionally leaned out to close the shutters. I liked my cousin Simona very much; that was the last time I saw her, even though we lived across from each other. All because of a family dispute started by the mailman shouting our name, "Bianchi," when he delivered the mail one day.

Mamma was walking back from Aunt Isabella's, and the mailman reached out and handed her an envelope from America. Mamma opened it immediately and unfolded the letter without first reading the envelope. I heard Mamma read some words under her breath, "*Caro Fratello*, Dear brother, etc., etc., etc.," a few lines later. She quickly stopped reading when she realized the mailman had given her somebody else's mail. I had thought of advising her to burn the letter and pretend it never happened. But she was already at Aunt Isabella's house before I could approach her. That evening, Aunt Isabella tried to explain to Simona's papá and mamma how the mail had been mistakenly opened. They did not accept the explanation and accused Mamma of intentionally snooping, which was why Simona's family and mine stopped talking.

I inhaled the smell of pasta cooking all over town and wished I could have some. I became transfixed and pondered why my uncle didn't clean his courtyard. A hand abruptly tapped me on my shoulder, and a man's voice called my name from behind. It was Eugenio. "Santino, I've

Piccolo Santino

been talking to you, and you ignored me. What are you doing out here when we are all inside eating?" Seeing Eugenio, I became equally stunned by his presence and the idea of a dinner. In a trance-like mood, I looked up at him and felt confused by this man wearing a white shirt and black pants, as Eugenio always dressed in brown. I had to remind myself that it was Eugenio's voice. I felt most grateful as he took me by the hand and walked me inside.

I spotted Mamma in a chair by the balcony, holding Enzo. My sister Fabrizzia was seated on the floor. I thought back and realized that I must have been in a natural deep trance, as I remembered them playing outside at the base of the stairway a few minutes before, but I could not recall seeing them walk up the stairway. Then I remembered Eugenio calling me several times as I remained transfixed on my studies of the dirty courtyard. Since I was unresponsive, he tapped me on my shoulder. I concluded that we must have been invited here to the celebration. I just was not aware of it all.

The hot aroma of pasta filled the room as we were all served. I looked at Lillo and noticed his shoes were still tied with wire instead of a string. Lillo could never hold on to his shoelaces, and Eugenio got tired of providing an endless line for his shoes. Last week, he laced wire through the eyelets. I reveled in the intense aroma of the rural grated cheese as I waited anxiously for my turn with the cheese grater and savored every bite until the last morsel of pasta. The afternoon felt like speeding clouds at Aunt Isabella's, and before the night came, we were snacking on dried figs with nuts and fennel. Eugenio was cautious about what he put in his stomach so as not to aggravate his ulcers. I respected him tremendously, and despite his ulcers, he always showed kindness.

The evening also brought in Don Giancarlo, the tailor who always sported a suit jacket with matching pants and a white shirt but no tie. Giancarlo visited every night to call on Eugenio's sister, Bianca, a tall, beautiful woman with full, long hair and squared shoulders.

Chapter 7 of Part Two
The final preparations for America
First Communion and the last of Matilda

Enlightenment can come from the most unexpected places, even amid education. The most surprising revelation, one that caught me off guard, came during my catechism classes, which were conveniently held diagonally across from my home. I had always assumed that the strip of buildings across from us, down to the last building of Master Santino, were all homes for the average townspeople. But behind one of these plain exteriors, a rectory for the clergy was hidden. Aldo opened a plain wood door, and rich, heavy olive wood framed the entrance into the building. This unexpected discovery led to a deeply personal realization- the clergy possibly hides bigger skeletons than us. We entered a foyer through those doors, being the entranceway to a large standard hall room directly ahead. To the left and right were separate stairways that led upstairs to segregated living quarters for nuns and monks.

When we entered, dusk was lingering outside, and Aldo paused as two monks walked down the stairway from the right and greeted us, "Welcome, brothers, and good evening."

"Good evening, Brothers," Aldo said, allowing the monks to proceed ahead of us. The monk with a long, stringy beard held the door open for us, "Please enter." he said. The way these monks moved and spoke felt unreal and unlike other people. They seemed to have an aura, with a lightness in their steps, almost as if they were floating when they moved. I wondered if they were creatures sent down directly from God. We entered the large room practically filled with other children and their sponsors, seated at makeshift counters made of planks on bland white boxes and aged as if by a dusting of flour.

Aldo led me to the unoccupied section in the rear to the left. A stern voice spoke out, and I looked up and saw Father Cinquemano, the town priest in his silver-rimmed glasses, seated at a small table against the wall

Piccolo Santino

that housed the stairway to the nuns' quarters. To each side of Father Cinquemano stood two monks, each holding leaflets. "Brothers, you may hand out the leaflets. I think all the children are present now."

I realized that none of my classmates were present because these children were all fifth graders. I remembered Mamma saying that I was old enough to make the first communion, and since we were leaving for America, the church also agreed for me to make my confirmation. Two more children came in with their sponsors, and both sat down as the priest shouted out. "Brothers, start forming your groups so we can begin with the Ten Commandments."

We were about four groups of five kids, and the monk leading my group was the one with the long, wiry beard who had greeted us. He possessed a very gentle demeanor. We met each night in the same place for a couple of weeks, and I wondered if the other boys were feeling holier by these new religious exercises. I wondered if a halo might sprout above our heads as a reward for all the thoughts of purity extracted from us after we receive instructions for tomorrow's acceptance of the holy wafer.

On the last night of classes, the monks individually positioned themselves in confessional booths. At that point, I watched Father Cinquemano dash into a confession booth like a burglar with loot, and my insides rolled like tremors after an earthquake. I prayed to avoid his station and contemplated a strategy for confession with Cinquemano if I got him. Monks walked about recruiting us, and I focused on Father Cinquemano's booth, where I thought he must be drilling that little boy. I watched the kid rise from his knees after a long time and walk away, sulking, as another boy took his place.

I prayed to avoid that priest further as memories of the slap on the poor sextant's face echoed in my head. As more boys vacated their booths, monks recruited new boys. But Father Cinquemano seemed to be the only one working overtime. I feared that if I confessed to him, he would undoubtedly approach Mamma regarding any details about Lola I might divulge. If I avoided him, I could lump my experience with Lola into one well-rounded thought without disclosing any details.

Piccolo Santino

From behind me, a gentle, young-sounding voice entered my ear. "Child, you can come with me." I looked up and saw the monk with the long, wiry beard, and I gulped as I feared he would direct me to Father Cinquemano. Reluctantly, I walked alongside him, and he pointed me to a confession booth hidden between two other stalls. He led me to kneel on the kneeling step as he walked inside the booth. Relieved, I stooped and listened as he opened the porthole door, and I made the cross sign while repeating the words, "In the name of the Father, The Son, and The Holy Spirit." I lifted my eyes to the monk and watched him make the sign of the cross over me as he spoke. "Lord be with you." I timorously rushed my words. "Forgive me, Father, for I have sinned."

"Don't be afraid, my child. It is only your first confession."

"Sì."

"And do you obey your Father and Mother?"

"Sì."

"Did you upset your Father and Mother at any time?"

"Sì, I-I-I upset Mamma when I locked her out of the house one night."

"Don't be afraid, child. God loves all children. And why did you lock your mamma out of the house?"

"I fell asleep and couldn't u-u-unlock the d-d-door."

"And did you ever play doctor with girls?"

"No! But my friends in school tell me bad things about girls."

"And do you like hearing those things?"

"I don't think about it. We are leaving for America soon to be with my papá."

"Do you miss your papá?"

"Sì." I responded, and he said, "God will watch over you, child." I looked at him, and he said, "Go on, child, just say three Hail Marys." I made the sigh of the cross. "Lord be with you," he said, and I slowly walked away feeling humbled like never before, knowing he was making the sign of the cross behind me.

Unlike all other mornings, this morning felt very special because I

Piccolo Santino

had on a brand-new pair of long pants for the first time. The air began to feel brand new as I looked down my legs to check out the length of my pants. I felt tall and contemporary as the long trousers stirred untested feelings of adulthood. Mamma stared at Martina as Gummah Catolica fixed Martina's hair, all decked out in a white dress and ready for her big day, too. Aldo knocked at the front door, and Mamma shouted, "Come in! Come in, Godfather."

"Buongiorno Gumbah, Good morning Godmother." Aldo walked past the foyer into the large family room, then stopped and said, "Today, you look like a real gentleman Santino." Mamma said, "We're ready, Godfather Aldo, we can go."

"But first, I have a present for Santino." He turned to me as he took something from his jacket pocket and said, "But a gentleman has to wear a watch to go with the long pants, Santino." He held out a gold watch with a black leather strap. As he buckled it on my left arm, it seemed to fill me with an unknown humility that was elevating me further into euphoria. I wondered if that was where God lived. I was speechless, and Mamma said, "Grazie, Godfather Aldo."

"My pleasure, Godmother, and congratulations, Santino." The words felt heavy and thick in my throat as I responded slowly. "Thank you, Godfather." I wasn't used to walking to church with family, and today, Aldo felt like a father figure as he walked with us. Even more peculiar, I realized this was the first time I could remember going to church with my family members. The ceremony was held in the bigger church in the upper part of town to accommodate the high volume of children. "Godfather, it seems like the girls are going to the left and the boys to the right."

"Yes, Godmother, we have to bring the children inside."

"Martina, you come with me and your Godmother Catolica," Mamma said to Martina, Aldo, and me, "Santino, you go with your Godfather. Godfather, we'll meet up inside by the doors."

"Yes, Godmother, I'll find you. Come on, Santino." The girls were in white, and the boys in white shirts with a few white jackets and bright or dark blue pants. The sun was shining, and all the sprinkled colors of

Piccolo Santino

flowers on the children made it all feel ethereal as we walked down the aisle in separate lines across from each other. I studied the children ahead of me as they proceeded toward the altar and observed as the girls turned left and the boys turned right. After the first group vacated, another group of children advanced to the altar. The line was so long it felt endless, and I finally knelt at the altar. I anxiously awaited my turn to receive the holy wafer from the Bishop. I looked to my left and saw Martina and the other kids receive their host and blessing.

The Bishop arrived by the kid next to me. My heart was bursting. I looked up at the Bishop as he lifted the host from his cup. Feeling so foreign and rash, Father Cinquemano's hand in front of my mouth blocked the Bishop from placing the host on my tongue. Startled, the Bishop looked at Cinquemano, shaking his head. "No," and he moved on to the next boy as the priest stared me down as if infested with devilish lice. As the other kids were leaving in prayer, I was at a loss and wondered what else I was supposed to do. I walked over to a pew; Mamma looked at Aldo puzzlingly. "But why did the priest do that?"

"I don't know. That was not right!" On the way out, Aldo asked me, "Santino did he say anything to you?"

"He just said, No! No! Not him." Mamma staring at Aldo, "Maybe we should look for the priest and ask him."

"But the Bishop is finished now, Godmother." The crowd dispersed, and Aldo searched for Cinquemano, who had left for the rectory. However, Aldo discovered that the Bishop would perform the services in Nao the following Sunday. "Godmother, the priest left before I could talk with him. But we can go to Nao for Santino to make his communion there next Sunday."

"Va bene. Let's go then." I felt like a hollow space as other boys left with their parents and godfathers in celebratory fashion. At home, we celebrated Martina's success with cordials as Aldo and Mamma remained puzzled by Cinquemano's action. But we were confident that he would not be in Nao next Sunday and everything would go well. "Drink up, Santino. We'll get it done next Sunday in Nao. That priest is not going to be there because he's not from that church," he said. He lifted a toast to

Piccolo Santino

me, and I began to unstrap my watch. Aldo stopped me. "No, Santino, you keep the watch, and don't worry! By next week, this will all be straightened out."

In Nao, I really felt out of place as I now was to participate among complete strangers. At least in Jonadi, I was in familiar surroundings and at the convenience of our church. I lined up again among the other children and started the slow walk to the altar, all the time feeling myself hiding from the stares of different children's eyes. I felt like a green thumb in the crowd. I made my way to the altar, knelt between two other boys in a clandestine motion, and spotted the Bishop at the left end of the altar. I lowered my head in anticipation while praying that the Bishop would be swift.

Butterflies swirled inside me as I caught sight of his Closeness. I lifted my head to him. Father Cinquemano surged from behind again! He stuck his hand in front of my mouth, and the Bishop haltingly moved away. I felt singled out at this point and wondered what wrong I could have done. I stepped out with the other kids and knelt on the bench. Instead of praying, I sulked and wondered what I might have overlooked. I felt like a lost wheel as other kids rejoiced and left with their parents.

I felt Mamma's hand on my shoulder, and she took me behind the altar. There, I saw Aldo confronting Father Cinquemano as other monks and members of the clergy looked on. "You deliberately prevented Santino from making his communion twice." Father Cinquemano lifted his hands and lowered them to suggest that Aldo lower his voice as he turned his back to Mamma and me. At the same time, the priest put his hand on Aldo's shoulder to turn him around. Cinquemano turned and looked at me quickly, and then Aldo looked at me. A short pause followed, and both shook their heads in agreement. Aldo took me aside. "Santino, did you make your confession?"

"Sì!" I said firmly. "The priest thinks you didn't make your confession."

"But I did!"

Piccolo Santino

"Okay, wait here." He walked back to Father Cinquemano, and the two began talking again. The priest brought his hands together by his chest and quickly parted them while shaking them red-faced. Aldo returned and called Mamma over. "Gummah Anna, the priest believes Santino didn't make his confession."

"But how is that possible? He was at catechism class the last night."

"Yes, I was there, but I didn't see who confessed him, and now the priest wants to know who." Aldo turned to me, "Santino, who heard your confession?"

"It was one of the monks."

"Okay, I'll tell the priest that." Aldo spoke to Cinquemano, the gathering monks began shaking their heads. Bewildered, the group gathered in front of Aldo and me. "Santino, did one of these monks hear your confession?" Timidly, I responded, shaking my head, "No."

"Then who was it?" Cinquemano asked. "What was his name?" Father Cinquemano sternly demanded while lifting his head high into the clouds and repeated his question, "Tell me his name!" I answered timorously, "I don't know." Aldo asked me, "Do you remember what he looked like?" I struggled to piece together the monk's appearance in my mind, fearing that I might unintentionally mock him if I described his long, wiry beard. This struggle made me hesitate, but Cinquemano persisted. "Come now, tell me what he looked like." At the risk of sinning, I said, "He was thin and had a long wiry beard." Looking at all the monks present, I could feel the tension in the air.

"I don't know who that is. There is no such monk here," The priest stated firmly. A moment of silence passed, and they all looked at me, their expressions a mix of confusion and disbelief. Then, a voice cut through the tension, "*No é vero.* No, it's true," one of the monk insisted. The priest turned to him, his eyes narrowing in suspicion, and demanded, "Then who was it? Where is he?"

"That was Brother Vittorio," another monk said. "Go get him so we can verify. Where is he?" Cinquemano demanded. The monks huddled, and amongst their muttering, another voice spoke out. "I'm afraid that won't be possible. Brother Vittorio left to walk back to the monastery four

Piccolo Santino

o'clock this morning."

"There it is," responded the priest, and Mamma said, "What are we supposed to do now? My son was at your catechism classes every night, Father. You were there."

"Yes, but I didn't see him make his confession."

"Did you witness all the boys make theirs or just the ones that came to you?" He thought a moment and said, "Just a minute, wait here." He disappeared into a closed room for a short while and returned to Aldo, who then came over to Mamma and me and explained. "He said the Bishop has agreed to allow Santino to make his communion today as long as he makes his confession with Father Cinquemano."

"Va bene," exclaimed Mamma. Aldo turned to me and said, "Santino, do you want to make your confession again? This time with Father Cinquemano."

"Sì!" Aldo walked me to a corner where Cinquemano was seated. Cinquemano signaled for me to kneel. Aldo left us in private. Now I was convinced that this priest was primarily looking for dirt to gossip about. I decided to allow him to lead, and I would simply answer questions. I knelt down in front of him and made the sign of the cross while I held rosary beads in prayer. I kept my head bowed, and I could feel him making the sign of the cross over me, but I dared not look up, and when he finished muttering, he said, "Did you lie about your last confession?"

"No."

"Do you lie to your mother?"

"No."

"Do you go to church on Sundays?"

"Sì."

"Did you ever use curse words?"

"Sì."

"When?" he asked with higher interest.

"I hit my finger with the hammer at the carpenter shop once." I gulped. He leaned in slightly and said, "Did you ever do dirty things with girls?"

[252]

Piccolo Santino

"Dirty things?" I asked.

"Yes." He demanded.

"What are they?" I quickly asked. He cleared his throat. A short silence ensued. "Hmm, since you started catechism classes have you been saying your prayers?"

"Sì." Then he mumbled these words: "In the name of the Father, the Son, and the Holy Ghost." I made the sign of the cross, and he directed me to go with my sponsor. Finally, I received communion at the altar by the Bishop in the presence of the local priests and monks, Father Cinquemano, my mamma, and Aldo.

We went home to have a cordial together, and now I felt that I finally deserved the watch. From that day on, Mamma vowed never to set foot in the church again as long as Father Cinquemano performed mass. I still attended church most Sundays with my friends and ignored Father Cinquemano's stares at me. I was sure word got to him about Mamma's attitude toward him because whenever the two met by chance in town, Mamma would usually tell us of his icy stares and her responding with a cold shoulder.

From the very next day after the religious exercises, the slow waiting time toward America felt like it suddenly catapulted from a crawl to a speeding locomotive as each new day felt like yesterday before it was even over. I had a feeling something terrible was going to happen. At first, I liked the attention I got from all the new kids gathering at my house, including my closest friends. I was sweaty from a bad feeling as I watched Matilda panting from the heat. Mamma was waiting to hand me a rope she was holding. I thought about our dog and how Matilda made her way back to us the several times that Mamma tried to give her away. The final time, I even witnessed how this man put her in a burlap sack tied to the backseat of his Vespa while exclaiming in complete confidence that she would never be able to find her way back this time. But within a week, Matilda returned to amaze everyone who listened to the story.

"Tino, tie this rope around her neck and then go and get the marshal," Mamma said to me, and then Franco exclaimed, "There he is,

Piccolo Santino

Signora, he's coming." We looked down the street and saw the large-framed man with a shotgun over his shoulder sporting a white tank top with a parade of kids like flies on a rhino. As he approached, the shirt created a feeling of familiarity and quaintness in me, as it made me feel that a tank top shirt would be something one wore around their house but not in public. However, the openness of his shirt seemed to say, "See, I have nothing to hide," but instead, he was more of a threat to Matilda, like a giant mousetrap. The tall man's leather strap from the shotgun sunk diagonally across his barreled chest, pushing the salt and pepper hair out like soap suds and coal dust. The children paraded behind him to gaze at the shotgun dangled from his shoulders. He stopped and greeted Mamma as Franco and I looked at him. "Buongiorno, Signora, is everything ready?"

"Sì, Marashallo, everything is ready." He stopped, pulled a blemished handkerchief out of his pants pocket, and said, *"Fa molto caldo Oggi*. It's scorching hot today!"

"Sì, è molto caldo. Yes, it is scorching," responded Mamma as he wiped his brow and mumbled under his breath. *"Sporca a miseria.* Wretched misery." I watched him wipe his neck from side to side, and then I looked at Matilda, and she made me realize that we could not wipe off her heat of the moment by any means. I wondered what was going on in everybody's mind as mine felt numb. There seemed to be at least ten kids gathered in front of my house, waiting anxiously for the tall man to finish wiping his neck.

Mamma looked at me and said, "Here, son! *Tiene la corda.* Hold the leash." The big man looked at me, nodded his head toward the road, and said, "You walk ahead of us to the caves. I'll tell you when to stop." Franco got next to me as I took the leash from Mamma, and I looked at the marshal as he tucked his handkerchief in his back pocket, *"Va bene andiamo.* Well, let's go," he said.

I led Matilda by the leash, and she quickly raced forward on my right and kept pace with Franco and me as we led the small parade. In the atmosphere of feeling above the crowd, I also felt alone. We walked past the rectory, where a plain façade hid its rich doors, then past Master

Piccolo Santino

Santino's carpenter shop, and I glanced over at the closed doors since today was Sunday. We then walked past the first set of caves, and I turned my head back at the big man. "No, not yet. Keep walking." Once we passed the second set of caves, I stopped before the bridge to the next town and looked at the tall man. "Walk over there by that tree," he ordered, and I led the crowd into the thick field of perennials and brush by a low tree with some clearing in front. "Stop there and tie the dog to that tree." The gunman ordered.

Still feeling important from all the attention, I tugged on the rope, and Matilda came loyally and innocently. Within seconds a large knot flexed inside my stomach as I tied the rope around the tree. Feeling as if I were Judas. I recollected that vision of her walking past me with a dead puppy dangling from her mouth a day after Papá had buried her litter alive. I turned around to face the murmuring kids by the gunman, and a cold shiver ran through me. Franco must have sensed something and quickly put his arm around me.

The big man reached out with both arms and waved us back as he said, "Everybody, stand behind me." We watched the gunman lift his shotgun and take aim. Without a thought in-between the loud blast, Matilda dropped to the ground. The poor thing didn't even have a twitter of life to utter one last sound, as if a vacuum within her sucked all the reality out. Matilda was a real credit to her breed. Maremma sheepdogs were known to befriend you for life, and Matilda always found her way back no matter where she wandered off. But there was no coming back from this final journey.

On the way home, I thought about the many times I had walked across that bridge to Grandmother's house or walked past that same tree to meander in the countryside with my friends. And coming down to the base of the bridge for water. Now I wondered if Matilda would haunt me if I crossed this way again. Mamma later explained that Matilda would have hiked to Naples and died swimming in the ocean looking for us.

Chapter 8 of Part Two
Move to Nanna's and on to Naples

    Franco and Nino wondered out loud as we walked past Matilda's remains during a first excursion into the country after her mercy killing. I feared looking over, but compelled to peek, I saw Matilda's bones lying lifeless inside a latent image of her burnt into the grass with the empty rope. Flooded with guilt, I rushed along in complete trepidation. These feelings surfaced in me one last time the day we moved away from Jonadi. Although we took the shortcut through the countryside, the sound of the water trickling from the shallow stream turned my head toward the bridge where Matilda's remains lay directly across.

    I thought of her as caring for the family more than we did for her. We walked barefoot in the shallow water, and its coolness on my feet confirmed the laconic state hiding in me. We didn't have anything to carry with us to Nanna's. Mamma had already sold all the valuables along with the house. When we left, I thought about my co-worker, Rocco, expressing real disappointment when we said our last goodbyes. He revealed that Mamma didn't give him our accordion as promised, so he upset me by calling her two-faced. I asked Mamma about it, and she explained how she gave it to a little boy from an impoverished family that lived by Aunt Ernestina.

    I justified Mamma's decision by thinking how Rocco and Bruno always cheated me at cards and played cruel and perverted jokes on me. I was glad he did not get the accordion even if my Mamma "two-faced" him. I watched my sisters pick violets as we walked, and I listened to them repeat the words sì, no, sì, no, as they plucked the petals one at a time. We moved from an incredible ceiling of birch trees to an open, flat, rocky terrain with trails of water paths between stones protruding from a wet outdoor floor. I couldn't help comparing the sudden heat from the sun to the coolness from which we just left.

Piccolo Santino

Mamma continued to lead with two-year-old Enzo in her arms, forcing us to stop and rest several times. As we approached the outskirts of Scaliti, the terrain was slightly uphill. Located on the hilltop to our left was one of Nanna's farms, harboring olive trees and a few cherry trees that seemed to pierce the clouds as I looked up for the chestnut-sized ruby-red cherries.

We became alarmed at the sight of army tank-like tracks that forcibly reformed the width of the normal pathway as the machine broke through natural barriers of brush and branches. Mamma explained it was the wheat thresher that came through to go to Nanna's wheat field for the harvest. I observed the broken tree branches high up and felt a significant violation upon nature by that man-made machine that showed no mercy.

Upon walking through the town of Scaliti, we noticed several excavations that revealed new large pipelines in the ground. We entered Nanna's house and walked upstairs to find Nonno seated at the table in the main room, and he blurted out, "Ah, you all finally arrived."

"Buongiorno, Padre," Mamma said to Nonno. "I'm glad you are all here. We got a busy day tomorrow, kids." Lillo snapped back as he usually did, "Nonno, we didn't come to work. We're leaving for America."

"Not until all the wheat is harvested, boy."

"Oh no! We're only here for a little bit. We're going to America."

"Okay, we'll see about that tomorrow."

"Tomorrow, we're going to America, Nonno!"

"You better watch out when you get to America, boy!"

"Why?"

"Because there are tramps there with big sacks that steal little boys like you take them home and cook them."

"Really, Mamma?"

"I don't know."

"So you're better off coming to work in the field tomorrow," responded Nonno. Lillo turned to me and asked, "Tino is that true?"

"We're leaving for America in ten days, not tomorrow."

"See, you're wrong, Nonno. The bad man is not going to get me

Piccolo Santino

tomorrow."

Nanna came out from the kitchen, and Mamma asked," Madre, why is the main street all dug up?"

"The government is bringing water lines into our homes now."

"Well, that will be a real convenience."

"U cazzo in culo! Up their ass! They're doing it to get money from us. But I came up with a way to fool them."

"What are you talking about, Madre?" Nonno interrupted, "*Lascialo stare,* leave it alone, they're gonna make it like in America now." Nanna quickly responded, "*Sì dove il governo ruba da tutti.* Yes, where the government robs everybody."

"*Come dice tu.* Whatever you say."

"*Sì è come dico io cazzo.* Yes, it's like I say damn it. Come with me daughter, I'll show you."

We all followed downstairs, through the large room with the bed against the wall facing the street and then through a doorway into the courtyard outside. I was immediately seized by the scent of ruby red roses in her garden completely doused my senses. I watched Nanna show us the new basin installed in her courtyard. "Look over here, daughter. See, they placed a meter on the incoming water line so they can make me pay." Mamma said, "But they didn't take out the public fountains did they?"

"No, and everybody still goes there for their water instead of paying for it."

"And when do you use this water then?"

"Look here, see! I open the spout slightly, and water drips so slowly that the needle doesn't move. After a few days, the basin fills, and I can do the laundry."

"Really, you don't have to pay like this, Madre?"

"*Ancora no.* Not so far. They must think we are all stupid here."

"But it's progress, Madre."

"*Lo dici tu!* You say! M*a a me non mi fotteranno.* But they're not gonna screw me."

I stood by the rose bushes to take in the perfume as Nanna kept

Piccolo Santino

talking, and then I walked further into the rear of the courtyard and stopped between embankments of thick orange carnations. At the end of the walkway, for the first time, I noticed a locked solid wooden gate. It was as if I had just discovered remote access to Nanna's house from the rear. I peered through the cracks and gazed at the upheaved dirt with thick water pipes resting on top and waiting for installation. But no workers in sight. I tried to stretch my view further down the street through the crack between the post and gate, but to no avail. And as I tilted my head to lean on the post, I heard voices calling me. "What are you doing over there? Come on!"

"We're going back upstairs," shouted Martina and Stella. I snapped my head out of a trance and noticed everybody walking away. Then I realized Mamma had called out to me first, and then my sisters called me. I quickly ran back as Mamma waved me on by the door and yelling, "Hurry up, move it!"

Upstairs, Nonno was winding a typical alarm clock with two large bells when I approached him. "Nonno, what are you doing?"

"I'm winding the alarm clock. We have to get up before the rooster tomorrow. The wheat needs to be cut down, and we can't be late."

"But the clock is for upstairs. We're sleeping downstairs."

"Don't worry! Even the rooster will hear it, and if he doesn't wake you up, I will." With his large hands, he held the clock as if he were trapping time itself. A layer of sadness quietly emerged in his eyes. His youngest son had already moved north to Turin. His eldest daughter went to Argentina, and now we were going to America, where two of his other children migrated. There was a trend in this region in which people abandoned not just their parents but also their way of life. A change that left the aging parents to care for the land. Nonno feared that his land and way of life would perish when he passed.

As the night progressed, Nanna told us her grandfather and great-grandfather always said that the world would end when one-day people would tire of propagating. She then said that we live in the middle of the world with people living below and above us. I found it hard to imagine

Piccolo Santino

people living underground or floating in the clouds, so I concentrated on the clock ticking in the silence, making me feel that the heartbeat of time resided in Nanna's house. At night, the atmosphere of silence and time there felt strange compared to our house, where we didn't have the company of a loud alarm clock to remind us about the existence of time constantly—time echoed like eerie musical notes, loudly, one at a time. The silence slid by slowly like the quiet moments in music. Both with the thick, mysterious presence of a faraway conductor. A vast company that Nanna supported with a candle-lit religious arrangement on top of her mahogany bureau.

Back home in Jonadi, silence and time felt like two cozy, quiet partners lying on the pillow with you at bedtime when you surrendered. Then, in the morning, silence would mysteriously tap you on the inside of your head. You would rise and follow its lead throughout the time of day. You responded naturally to its every demand, whether at home, at work, or in school. And when you sat down to rest, time seemed to wait by your side as the silence rested within you.

It was difficult enough to fall asleep in a strange bed without the tick-tock reverberating through the floorboards from upstairs. Still, when sleep arrived, it felt like a pleasant transient moment into dawn when the melodic sound of hooves clattering on cobblestones outside Nanna's window replaced the ticking clock. I lay in bed listening to the subtle tugging and pulling of the oxen shift from side to side, and when it faded away down the street, I felt Mamma's hand on my shoulder. "Come on, get dressed. You are leaving early with me. The others are coming down later with Nanna."

"I didn't hear the alarm clock, Mamma."

"Nonno turned it off. He left early before us."

"What time is it now?"

"Here, put your pants on. It's six-thirty."

"All right."

"I brought you down a piece of bread. You can eat it on the way."

I stared across the street at Antonio's carpenter shop and hoped we would not run into each other these next ten days as I waited for Mamma

Piccolo Santino

to close the door behind us. She nudged me forward and said, "Come on, let's go." I kept pace with her as I juggled my steps on the cobblestones and couldn't wait to get on level ground. "We'll stop at the fountain. You can get a drink there and wash your face, too."

When we got to the field, the sun was not at its brightest yet, and it still felt cool compared to what it would be like when entirely in the sky. The men had started working early in the wheat field—much wheat laid on the ground from their cutting. An older man and a woman followed the three workers with short sickles and trimmed what they missed. Another woman was helping Nonno gather the loose wheat and tie bundles. When we met him, Nonno was standing some piles up and stacking them against each other into pyramid-like formations in groups of three or four bundles. He looked up at Mamma, "*Arrivasti!* You arrived!"

"Sì, where would you like me to start, Padre?"

"Let's get all this wheat picked up first, then you can help with the sickle."

"All right, Padre. Tino, you start picking up wheat over there by Rosaria and help make bundles."

"Okay." I said walking over by the woman picking up wheat and figured she had to be Rosaria. She stood with her feet straddled, lifted her long dress above her ankles, and smiled at me. It was odd that a water-splashing sound would be present. I quickly realized she was peeing, so I casually stepped farther away while pretending to be looking for fallen wheat elsewhere. I gathered some wheat into sizable heaps for bundling, and Nonno called out. "Tino, come here." I quickly ran over without hesitation, as expected, "Hold this bundle upright while I stack others around it."

"Sì," I said, and he leaned five other bundles around my one as a pyramid. Then he had me follow him around the field, stacking other bundles. The sun had been rising faster, and my shoulders complained to me. As I turned around to face the sun, Nonno stared at me and said, "Ah, you're starting to feel the sun already! This is not like being indoors at school, is it?"

"No," I said, and then I saw Lillo approaching us as Mamma was talking to Nanna and one other woman in front of the barn. I looked around and saw my sisters sitting in the shade of a large tree away from the barn. I surmised Nanna and the other woman walked my sisters down, and I wondered why they were leaving as Mamma turned away from them and walked toward us. "Padre? Madre said they are coming back by ten o'clock with the food."

"Va bene, let's gather all this wheat," he said. I followed Mamma's guidance in gathering and even tried my hand at bundling, but I did not have the coordination and strength to tie the bundle, so I called Mamma. We were moving faster than Nonno, but he eventually caught up to us and then called Lillo. "Hey, boy! Get me some long wheat threads to tie this bundle over here." Lillo ran around like a spinning top, wondering what to look for, but Nonno had already found what he needed. Still, he kept taunting Lillo. "Hurry up, boy, if you want to make it to America."

"Here, Nonno, here's some more!"

"Good boy." He proceeded to use the strands Lillo had gathered. "I'll get some more Nonno." Lillo came by me and said, "Nonno calls me 'boy' all the time, and I don't know what it means."

"When he lived in America, he learned some American words."

"Oh, I better go back by Nonno." Lillo ran to Nonno with long strands and seemed excited as Nonno kept using some American words on him. Leonardo stepped out of line and walked off. "Where are you going, Gumbah Leonardo?" shouted one of the women. "I have a private need, Gummah."

"But you can pee inside the wheat field right here. Nobody can see you there."

"Oh no, not for this one." The ladies looked at each other, and one whispered out loud, "*Ah, deva cacare*! Oh, he has to take a crap!" As Leonardo walked away, the women continued to taunt him. "Watch out for snakes when you squat, Gumbah!" Another woman interjected, "You heard about where the snake bit Gummah Lucia when she squatted on the

Piccolo Santino

grass, didn't you?" Hearty laughter broke out, and Leonardo responded, "Don't you worry none!" He disappeared into the heavy-foliated woods across the road from the field, and the women resumed chatter amongst themselves. "He just got married three weeks ago."

"He's gotta be thinking about his wife all day still."

"He wouldn't be normal if he wasn't."

"Let's see what he says when he comes back!"

"He went to take a crap, not for a hand job."

"How do you know?"

"Hey, let's watch ourselves. There are children present."

"Ah, they're too far away to hear us, and besides, they don't know what we're saying, anyway." The sound of the thresher screeched across the sky, jarring the women's absorption of perverted thoughts into screams. "AHHHHHH!"

"*Que spavento.* Ah, what fright!" Everyone looked at the thresher. And my stomach did such a summersault that left my body trembling. Leonardo ran out from across the way, mumbling under his breath, and then yelled, "*Ma Che cazzo è successo?* What the fuck happened?" He looked at the wheat thresher and returned to work, still mumbling. "What fucking noise that thresher makes when it starts up, heh!" He picked up his long sickle and hollered, "Back to work, everybody."

"Ah yes," responded the men, and Leonardo looked toward the women and said. "Back to work, ladies,"

"You're just fucking around now!"

"Careful ladies, there are children present."

"He's not saying anything this morning since he's happily married now."

"What did you expect?" The thresher pulled me away from this lewd conversation, and I watched the machine swallow bundles of wheat and spew out the kernels into a flue where, at the bottom, a man held a burlap sack. I turned back to the men with the long sickles, and the sound of the thresher seemed to awaken something in them as they resumed work in rhythmic unison. I liked the pace and enjoyed how they swung

Piccolo Santino

the long-handled sickle that continuously forced the wheat blades down like heavy rain in the wind. Four other men with long-handled sickles worked alongside Leonardo, spaced far enough apart to prevent the blades from accidentally meeting. Others followed behind with short sickles to slice wheat blades that the long sickles missed.

Leonardo continued to lead the men into the broad field, moving as smoothly as a shadow and with an aura of advancing soldiers. I sought cover from the hot sun under the big tree where my sisters were and called out to Martina. "What are you doing, Martina?"

"I'm knitting."

"What for?"

"Mamma says it's for my trousseau."

"*Che cazzo stai facendo?* What the hell are you doing over there?"

"Oh, oh!" said Martina. "Mamma is yelling at you. Better go back over there." I turned around, and Mamma seemed unhappy and waved me back as she yelled out, "Get back over here right now before I kill you!" There was no point in even thinking about debating the situation. It would only end up two against one since we were on Nonno's farm, so I moped over, and she demanded, "Get over here and get back to work."

"And you, Lillo, go fill a bottle of water by the stream." Shouted Nonno. "I can't go for water. It's too hot!"

"Go and get the bottle, boy."

"No! I'm too little for that."

"You're not too little to drink the water, right?"

"No, not for that," responded Lillo. Nonno reached over to grab Lillo, but Lillo was too fast and ran off. "Come back here, boy."

"No, I can't go. I'm too busy here!" Mamma turned to Nonno and said, "Padre, let him go. Just send Tino."

"Okay, boy, don't go, but don't come around later for a drink of water."

"I'm not thirsty anyway,"

"Okay, we'll see later."

"Tino, put that wheat down; you. You are going for water!" Nonno

Piccolo Santino

showed me a jug and a green bottle. "Here, go fill both of these, Tino."

"Mamma, where's the waterfall?"

"Just walk down the road till you see it."

At ten years old and feeling dwarfed by anything rising above my head, I decided to zigzag as I walked down the road. I looked at the trees for signs of animal life and spotted a large owl asleep on a low-lying branch. With the weight of the bottle in my right hand, I wiped my brow and quickly stepped away from the dried snakeskin, signaling a snake had traveled there. I continued down the dirt road as it curved to the left. As I obeyed its winding, the soft sound of rushing water slowly filled the air around me, and a gentle breeze combed through my hair. I wondered if it was for real. I followed the path to the bottom of the slope, and the draft here felt cooler and picked up slightly. As the roaring sound of the waterfall filled my ears, a gentle mist sprayed my face, and I rushed to the end of the slope onto soft and damp ground.

I looked up and saw a wide, tall waterfall emptying into a large shallow pool, where the water continued downstream through a small variety of channels. I marveled at the waterfall's tree-size height and welcomed its mist as it sprayed me from a distance. I accepted the cool embrace of misty water with deep breaths as I leaned against a boulder to remove my shoes and socks before I walked into the water to face a ledge in the center of the shallow pool.

The water was a bit warmer close to shore, but as the sandy floor gave way to flat rocks, I found myself deep in water up to my knees, and the coolness ultimately arrested my body as I walked closer to the rocky shelf up to my chest. I positioned the jug in the downpour. I held steady under the rush, and soon, the liquid world began to feel like a smooth, soft body snaking between my fingers as it made its way downstream through tributaries to eventually empty into the Mediterranean Sea.

The same sea Papá crossed two years ago, where we would soon follow. I thought of him still with his thick mustache and full head of dark hair, with his stoic body getting between Mamma and us kids when she chased us with the broom. Sometimes, Papá intentionally absorbed some of the blows himself. The flasks overflowed, and I pulled myself away

Piccolo Santino

from the rushing water in perpetual motion while God kept on pouring.

On the return trip, I kept dead center along the path to feel the sun drying my damp clothes. I spotted the sleeping owl again, and a few sparrows fluttered in the brush. When I reached the clearing into the wheat field, Nonno came rushing up, took the bottle from me for a fresh drink, and was pleased to find the water was still cold. "Bravo! Bravo *figlio,* son!" he said to me and then ushered me under the big tree where everyone had settled down for brunch as he lifted the jug from me. "Sit over here and eat," he said. He then sat against the oak tree and looked toward the group of workers. "Anybody that wants a drink of water, I have it over here," he announced. Then Lillo called out, "I need a drink."

"You can go down to the waterfall if you want to drink."

"Why? There's water right here."

"This water is mine, and you're not getting any!"

"Oh yeah? When you fall asleep, I'll sneak up and take it." Laughter broke out. "Yeah, you just try it," Nonno leaned back against the oak tree's thick bark with his left hand propped on the water jug. Lillo sat on the ground facing him from about ten feet away and said as he crossed his legs, "And I'm gonna sit right here and guard my water." Laughter broke out among the others, and Nonno slid his left foot toward him, bringing his left knee up to rest his hands on it.

Lillo's eyes keenly observed the older man's every move, waiting for his hands to wilt. Nonno's head slowly dropped to his chest, and Lillo leaned over with his head arched sideways, hoping to glimpse the old man's eyes from under his hat. Nonno's arms sagged and slowly sank to the ground. Lillo uncrossed his legs after waiting under the hot sun. From under the oak, soft snoring signaled Lillo to make his move. The boy quietly rose and tiptoed toward the water jug. We chuckled; Mamma put her finger to her lips and glared at us. Lillo closed in on the water jug and, with one swoop, reached down to drink and fled with the water jug like a panther while shouting, "I told you I'd get me a drink!"

Our laughter awoke other sleeping workers, and Nonno quickly rose to his feet and darted after Lillo in a fast, haphazard walk that was no match for those young legs. "Come back here, boy!" Lillo looked back

Piccolo Santino

while holding the jug of water and stopped to taunt Nonno. "See, I'm drinking."

"Now I'm gonna give you a real beating!"

"Here, I'm all done." Lillo put the bottle down and ran away. "Come back here, boy!"

"Aha, you can't catch me!" Lillo safely ran back for another gulp. Hearty laughter ensued by all, and the awakening workers rushed to their feet and shouted, "*Ma che cazzo c'è?* What the hell is going on?" Nonno bent down to retrieve his hat while returning with the water bottle. Laughter intensified, and the awakened workers shouted out, "*Andiamo*, let's go, let's get back to work!"

At the close of the day, I listened as a woman describe food plans for tomorrow's meals, the final day of harvest. Mamma quickly engaged Nanna for her approval, which evoked a sense of a tug of war for Nanna's attention. I decided to distance myself in case a tense conversation erupted. I walked about fifteen steps away. I turned around and saw the sky light up as if a switch had suddenly snapped. Blank-faced, I stared at the soft embrace of vivid orange light that formed silhouettes of those three women under the giant oak tree against this Calabrian wheat field.

Such pigment from a large body of a sudden color slid down from the sky in complete silence. The sight was now stirring my insides with such fresh insight it made me completely forget I was thinking of tension between women. This melting palette of nature's colors completely doused any misunderstanding in me; Mamma called out, "Tino, you'll stay here tonight with your cousins."

"Okay," I responded while transfixed by the newly colored landscape. I gawked straight ahead as the other woman said, "There's a bed in the barn you can all sleep in." I thought that must be what they were discussing when I walked away. "Your cousins should be back any minute," continued the other woman, and I realized she was another one of my aunts that I seldom met, and the cousins were her sons. Now, I do remember meeting them once a while back. My cousins arrived when the orange light changed into darker ambient light. I presumed the sun was

Piccolo Santino

on its way to America, where my papá was. Mamma didn't get enough letters from him, and she sometimes expressed her anger out loud. I never wrote him, and I wondered if we children could have.

Then I remembered Papá saying it was too heartbreaking for him to have direct correspondence with us children. I wondered what he did in America. All we knew was it would take two years for him to save enough money to send for us. America was indeed far away, and the two years had diminished to weeks, and once we boarded our ship, it would only take eight days to reach him. I speculated on the sun's appearance in America when it rose and set.

My favorite sunlight time was in the barn with Lola. Now, at Nanna's farm, the light from Lola's barn seemed to have arrived, pouring out and dissolving into one radiant dye of orange that mystically bound everything. You could never wash the orange color off your skin if you tried, but you could certainly walk away from it by crossing the border into the moonlight. I pledged to always remember my Nanna from the light of this sunset that emerged on her farm.

Before the final Sunday in Scaliti, Mamma insisted on one last confession and mass to receive the host. Martina and I walked to church to make one last confession in Italy, with Mamma's warning reverberating in my head. I wondered if the exact words were rummaging in Martina's mind as we walked inside the church. I wished Mamma had not insisted on this. I could not escape this one, so I reluctantly yielded to the emotional punishment. I felt somewhat relieved by the thought that Scaliti did not have Father Cinquemano and that I could now divulge my sins to an absolute stranger. We approached the confessional booth, and Martina said, "You want to go first?"

"No, you go." I sat in the pew and thought about what to say. I did not like what it was doing to me, so instead, I thought about this morning when a street vendor stopped his wagon in front of Nanna's house and how she secretly handed the vendor money for a comb. Then I gawked high up at the windows when, on a day like today, the light burned through the glass-stained colors with vivid vibrancy. "Okay, it's your turn

Piccolo Santino

now." I heard Martina say. I turned to face her and whispered, "Oh, you're done already?"

"Yeah." Then she looked real serious at me and whispered, "That priest in there looked like Father Cinquemano." My heart spilled through my clothes and splattered on the floor. I watched Martina bow her head and kneel in the pew before me. I stared at the brightly lit art in a window high up in solemn silence. A minute or more must have passed when a priest with glasses tapped life onto my shoulder and said, "Are you here for confession?"

"Sì," I said. The priest gestured with both hands toward the booth. I was relieved that he wasn't Father Cinquemano. I inhaled my heart back into place and walked toward the booth. I knelt on the step in front of the window covered in what looked like chicken write. I wondered what this priest would be like. It didn't seem fair that adults attending church never showed any improvement, and as children, we couldn't hold them to task. I hoped to get past this without much pain as he slid open the porthole door. I prayed timidly, and his question hit me like a lightning bolt after his blessing. You would think he would have allowed me to take a breath and swallow first, but no, he dove right in. In a sharp, whispering, monotone voice, he asked, "Did you do any nasty things with girls?" *Why didn't he ask me something else first?* I thought.

I realized now what Martina might have been thinking. Thoughts raced through me like a derailed bicycle wheel spinning rapidly on the side of the road. While I planned other things to confess, I kept the following secrets hidden in the back of my mind: The time in the barn, Lola showed me what adults do on their wedding night. Then, at work, after that short visit from Filomena, Bruno, and Rocco masturbated in the back corner while whispering her name. The following morning, I tried masturbating in my bed, and Mamma beat me more severely than the time I locked her out of the house.

As the priest cleared his throat, he rustled in his seat, waiting for my response. But fear startled my decision, and he repeated his question with firmness. "Well! Did you do any nasty things with girls? *Sì, oh no?*" I felt his words shake the air, and words rushed out of my mouth on their own, "Sì!" flowed out on its own, and I had to think fast. "I did a circle jerk once with friends." *I needed better mind control*, I thought. He quickly asked, "When did you do this?"

"A long time ago in Jonadi."
"You need to say ten Hail Marys' for that one."
"Do you obey your parents?
"Sì."
"Do you use curse words?"
"I did with my friends that time."
"Are you kind to your siblings?"
"I did a bad thing once."
"What did you do?"
"I hit my sister on her head with a hammer."
"You must say five Hail Marys' for that one. Was your sister okay?"
"Sì."
"Do you go to church regularly?"
"Sì."
"Do you say your prayers at night?
"Sì. I talk to God a lot."

"And when was your last confession?" I didn't dare tell him it was that time with Cinquemano, so I said, "Last month in Jonadi."

"Go my son and say twenty-five, Hail Marys." I made the sign of the cross as he said, "God bless you, my son." I walked to a pew wondering why he gave me twenty-five Hail Marys since I only counted fifteen while we were talking. Then I added five more anyway for good measure since I held back stuff.

The next day at church, my sister and I walked up to the altar for the host, and I became hopeful that in America since we won't know the language, I might be able to avoid all this stuff for a long while.

I didn't anticipate having to make a vow while in Naples, and we needed two limousines for the trip. I recall my first ride in a car when Mamma had me accompany her friend to the market. We walked for

Piccolo Santino

hours that day, and for the walk home, I didn't know if we would both survive it unless we stopped to rest for a couple of hours off the highway. We stopped under the shade of a large tree, and Pippa expressed an idea and then ordered me to stay put while she walked a slight distance and proceeded to flag a car in her dark clothes and hair rolled up in a bright red and yellow scarf. I wondered how she would arrange a ride since we had no money to bargain with. Pippa was not much older than Mamma, but she appeared aged and a bit older in her drabs.

A car stopped, and she stuck her head in through the opened window and talked away for a few minutes. She brought her head out, turned to me, and shouted for me to stay there as she got inside the car. A block of time passed, and I wondered when we could move on. Her voice suddenly pierced my tranquility and brought me to my feet. I looked as she held the car door open and pressed me to rush over there. I squeezed into the back seat with the few items from the market and felt relieved, but I also sensed something had happened between Pippa and this tall, broad-shouldered stranger in a grey fedora. Once they began speaking with familiarity. I became convinced it wasn't a money exchange in their privacy. No sooner were my thoughts completed than we arrived at the four corners toward Jonadi, and he let us out to continue our trip home on foot.

Nanna waited behind the black limo parked in front of her sister's house. One at a time, we walked up to her and kissed her goodbye, but it was her hands squeezing my face and her mouth pressing hard on both cheeks that told me she was hurting miserably. I could feel her emotions trembling under the soft skin of her face as I kissed her gently and she spoke her last words to me. *"Ciao Santino, Figlio bello!* Bye, Santino, beautiful Son!"

"Ciao, Nanna," I answered as I thought of the aches in her heart, although she kept repeating that she would be strong. She had already said goodbye to three of her children, the eldest daughter, Flavia, who had to immigrate to South America because the quota to the United States did not permit them. The other two children, Vito and Fabrizzia, lived

Piccolo Santino

close by Papá and were preparing for our arrival. I thought about the long distance between America and Italy and how insane it would feel for Nanna when we could no longer walk over to visit her. I watched her sob gently from the rear window and thought she would undoubtedly cry after we left.

In the front seat of one limo was Nonno with the driver, and Mamma was in the back seat with some of us kids. In the second limo, Papá's cousin, Eugenio, agreed to join Nonno in escorting us to Naples. I continued watching Nanna from the rear window, and as the cars began moving, her feelings spilled out, and she had to be held back by her other family members as she ran toward the car. I closed my eyes and thought of her back on her farm, lit in orange by that everlasting sunset.

The limos were to take us to the bus station, and the bus would then take us to the train for the long ride to Naples, where we would board a ship called the *SS Giulio Cesare*. Mamma carried a bottle of anisette in her purse to soothe our stomachs during motion sickness. I was too sick during the bus ride to enjoy a swig, and the scent encouraged Lillo to feign illness. His eagerness for more was no match for Mamma's keen perception.

I was relieved to find the train ride free of any motion sickness and happy that it allowed me to enjoy my first view of the ocean. I became mesmerized by the pure turquoise colors of the Mediterranean water and its magical blend into the distant horizon. The beach with its people was so new it made me envious of what it would be like to live in this part of Italy. Oh, to live by the ocean and be immersed with people of this region in their whole way of life. To learn to swim and not be afraid of the water!

The train sped along with its reverberating sounds, and my eyes roamed over buildings dug into sand that weaved the landscape between beach and highway. It was one thing to study Italy in schoolbooks, but to be stirred by the presence of new places? Places filled with new colors on homes against the ocean. It is spellbinding to witness tints seep from the sky during sunsets and blend a horizon between the spaces down to the sea. The possibilities jam-packed my heart with trembling emotions, and my eyes swelled in ways I had never known.

Piccolo Santino

    Having enjoyed a window seat for well over an hour, I got up so we could alternate since there were nine of us traveling, and seating had become scarce after each stop. Lillo and I moved into the aisle outside our cabin and listened to the shifting train sounds as it exited and entered short tunnels. Every sudden blast of air in the gaps between tunnels felt like musical bursts, and I liked the longer-lasting, snug sound of the lengthier tunnels. The night approached seamlessly and with a heavy imposition as strangers crowded the aisle, and I fell asleep on the floor between stranger's shoes. Later in the night, each stop became increasingly comforting as more passengers were leaving than boarding. I noticed that Nonno had settled in the cabin with Mamma and my sisters. Mamma looked tired, holding Enzo in her arms. Fabrizzia was seated next to her, followed by Angelina. Martina sat next to Nonno, directly across from Mamma. While dozing on the floor, I thought I heard voices from inside the cabin urging me to join them. I was surprised to see Nonno seated since he had been sporting the aura of a world traveler who had engaged Eugenio in his ways. I then noticed Eugenio standing by a window away from me, gazing into the night.

    "Martina, call your brothers to come in here. Tell him there's some room to sit in here now."

    "Tino! Lillo! Come on back!" said Martina from inside. Lillo raced over first and squatted on the floor in the far corner by Angelina, and Mamma said to me, "Sit there by the pretty young lady."

    "Grazie, signora," said the pretty lady. I carefully positioned my body so as not to disturb the lady. She graciously shifted her body to make room for me and said, "Come sit here, join us." It felt strange being spoken to by a beautiful woman this way. Yet a stranger as well, and spoken to familiarly. All in new surroundings and the presence of family. Something in me felt like melting. Although, I also felt the need to hold back. I sat quietly and observed Stella as she carefully picked up a skinny, colorful stick from a pile of a board propped on the pretty young lady's lap. "We're playing pick-up sticks," Stella said to me.

    The pretty lady finished her turn, looked at me, and said, "Would you like to play with us?" With my eyes darting, I shook my head. "Yes,"

Piccolo Santino

and Mamma said, "This is Signorina Madalena. She has taught your sisters how to play this game." Stella picked up the last few sticks without moving any others, and Madalena said, "You won this game, Stella. Brava!"

"You must pick up one stick without moving another, or you lose your turn!" Stella said to me, all excited. Madalena asked my name in the plural sense, "How are you called?" Feeling all flustered, I felt clogged in my throat as I debated between saying my nickname, Tino, or my full name, Santino. Assuming my stuttering, Mamma quickly said, "His name is Santino."

"È Bellissimo nome, It's a beautiful name," she said, looking at me. Then, she dispersed the sticks from her hand on the board while continuing to speak to me in the plural sense. Santino, you go can first. Try picking up your first stick without moving any others." She wore a bright summery dress that covered her below her knees.

She turned her knees toward me slightly with care as I reached over, and I could lift three sticks on my first try successfully. That extracted a frown from Stella. "Bravo! Santino. Bravo!" exclaimed Madalena. I looked at her with eyes wide open, and she smiled back. A glow radiated through me. "Signorina, if we weren't leaving for America, perhaps you could have waited for Santino to get older, and fate might have arranged for you two to get married." Mamma expressed. *"Davvero! Perchè no?* For real! Why not?" Madalena delightfully exclaimed. I was overrun with emotion as I secretly gloated inside with a runaway fantasy about Madalena.

We arrived in Naples late in the night, possibly midnight. Tired and weary, we walked off the train into darkness lit by spaced-out lampposts in the railway yard. Nonno spotted a conductor and ran to him while shouting for his attention. Eugenio followed. We gathered on the walkway between the tracks, waiting for directions as other passengers got off the train and walked about their destinations. Despite feeling tired, the structure of the place made me feel privileged to see such an extensive display. Artistry occupied this vastness, with huge locomotives that felt

Piccolo Santino

so heavy and solid, yet ample space willing to be dominated by massive trains and the ferrous odors of locomotives.

Nonno and Eugenio returned and led us out into the central station, putting my nostrils to rest. People were scattered and walked fast to leave the place rapidly. The central station had me gazing at the high ceilings in wonder, and the woodwork inside the arched windows and framed wall sections had me thinking of Master Santino and how much I could enjoy watching him craft such designs.

Once outside, the air felt thinner and not as stuffy. Nonno and Eugenio led us through the night streets of Naples on the way to the hotel. The hotel was not home, but it felt good to sleep in a bed. In the morning, we experienced a continental breakfast for the first time and then prepared for the trip to the customs office for our medical examinations and passes.

We were separated at the customs agency by gender. A uniformed guide directed Lillo and me to one area, and Mamma, with two-year-old Enzo and my sisters, went another way. We met other young boys in that same room, and I found it pleasant as they asked us where we were from. I liked hearing the other boys mention the different places in Italy they came from. Hearing the names of new areas of Italy reinforced my faith in the geography lessons in school, as I witnessed Italy's idea and felt genuine remorse that I would no longer be part of it.

A nurse entered the room and advised us to remove our clothing except for our underwear, and I braced myself for when they would render me unfit to go to America because of the burn-induced scar on my right foot. Mamma had reminded me that I might have to return home with Nonno. The door opened like a sudden wind, and a doctor entered the room. He was an older man in an oversized, widely open suit jacket, whose elder age reminded me of Dr. Itasca. He was tall and broad-shouldered, which made me feel that his frame was too large for him as he wobbled while he walked. I feared he was going to fall.

He sat down quickly, and as soon as he held his stethoscope, he became magically steady. I worried about my foot and what he would

Piccolo Santino

examine first, as he seemed oblivious. The nurse got me on the scale and then asked me to step down in front of the doctor. I braced myself as he positioned his hand by my groin and asked me to cough. I turned my head from one side to the other while my pupils looked downward. I finished coughing and the nurse ordered me to dress and leave. I was astounded as the doctor never even looked down at my foot. I felt relieved, but also there was something in me that grieved at the missed opportunity to remain in Italy and experience the possibility of cultivating my own life, that of a self-made Italian poet.

We spent most of the afternoon at the customs agency and finally regrouped in the main lobby. Mamma was surprised when I told her the doctor never even asked about my foot.

Eating at a restaurant for the first time was a new experience. I liked the atmosphere of the harbor in Naples as I looked at it from the restaurant window. We listened to the waiter read off parts of the menu, and when he said pasta marinara. I did not hesitate as the sound of it brought me back to the Mediterranean Sea I had seen in Vibo Valentia. That sea had arrested my heart, and what better way to experience the bay in Naples and Vibo Valentia than with pasta and seafood in Italy?

The next day, we checked out of the hotel. Two shoe-shine boys walked past us with boxes containing paraphernalia, and I noticed the metal form of a foot protruding from their shoeboxes, which looked like they were carrying tiny toy coffins. On our way to the bay, we could spot Mt. Vesuvius from blocks away, and thoughts of it spewing lava ran through my mind. The panoramic view had my soul running ahead of me as it rushed forward to smell the salty air in the bay. The Bay of Naples was all new to my senses. The groomed grassy areas in the bay were taboo for anybody to walk on, and Nonno warned of trouble should we trespass. All this was a total contrast to the expansive fields we once had trouble-free access to.

Everybody sat on the public benches to await the boarding time. Lillo and I raced to the bay's perimeter and peered over the railing. We gazed out into the distance, and I pointed to Mt. Vesuvius as I explained

Piccolo Santino

to Lillo that this was the volcano that destroyed Pompeii a long time ago. We then compared the ships and tried to guess which ship we would be boarding as they all seemed too small. Before this moment, we were counting the years, months, and weeks, and now we were down to the hour that we would be boarding before the minutes came. Then, after we boarded, we would begin the countdown by the day until we met up with Papá. I kept imagining his mustachioed face to identify him once we met, as I could not envision him in any other way.

Lillo kept walking back and forth to the family and joined them for a drink of water at the public fountain. On his last visit, he informed me that I should rejoin the family since we were preparing to board. As we walked toward the ship, I began feeling the demise of Italy in me, the end of everything I knew! I thought of my last night in Jonadi. In a flash, my senses wanted to uncoil and run wildly in front of my eyes. I feared losing control so much that it made me want to turn my head back to look for my friends.

Scared to turn around, I instead recollected the night Franco came for me for the last time, which made me think we were meeting up with Pino as usual. Another classmate showed up, and then a few more arrived, and they led the way to a hangout with more boys. I didn't make anything more memorable of it than just being in the company of friends until they led the way into the piazza, where another large group of boys waited. I had never met many of these boys, yet they made it all feel real festive. Then, we split into two groups after choosing sides and began playing a game of tag. I didn't know that this game even existed.

There were imaginary holding cells to the left and right center, and we lined up facing each other on the opposing sides. The forwards advanced to tag an opposing player and place him in the holding cell as a prisoner. The only way out was for another team member to come and tag him out without being tagged himself and put into prison by an advancing opponent. I found myself in both predicaments once or twice and felt thrilled to be participating.

Slowly, I began to realize that this moment was my farewell party. This gathering sprung up as a big surprise. It all blossomed on its own. I

Piccolo Santino

didn't ever remember having so much fun and feeling free-spirited and loving. Feeling freed was a complete contrast to my generally feeling contained and suspicious. The game lingered, and I thought it would continue forever until I detected that night had arrived in the square. The boys gathered around me, and one by one, all wished me farewell. I felt grateful and could not understand how such a good time was a one-time event. Franco and Nino accompanied me home up to my door and said goodbye. Feeling somber as they walked away, and with a heavy hollowness, I watched them sink into the black of the night for a long moment before I could go inside my house.

Sensing that paranoia would swallow me entirely if I turned and looked behind me, I said to myself, *never look back and keep walking straight ahead.* Then, I made a secret vow with the following words. *From this moment on, think only of America; forget Italy, for it will no longer be your guide. Once you set foot in America, it is only essential to learn English. You must learn to think American, for that will be your future. When you reach home, gather the memorabilia you brought and throw it away.* I felt the weight of saying goodbye to Nonno and Eugenio lessen as the secret vow curled up inside me.

I reciprocated Eugenio's and Nonno's goodbye kisses. I walked up the ramp with Lillo following along. Once on deck with the family, we waved goodbye to Nonno and Eugenio. They turned around, and I watched them slowly sink into a folding past of Italy with the crowd.

Chapter 9 of Part Two
Eight days on board the *MS Giulio Cesa*re, June 1958

On board the ship, everyone spoke Italian, and popular Italian songs like *"Volare," "Lazzarella," "Arrivederci Roma," "Maruzella,"* and many others played over the public speakers on deck. As the songs blasted, it was reminiscent of when the music played during religious feasts at home, and although it made me feel that we were still in Italy, I felt the ship's haste during these eight days of travel was sealing my Italian past like a slow burn.

Mamma thought it best to spend much time on the deck away from our cabin, next to the boiler room. And enjoy the music and soft drinks while observing the goings-on by the poolside. None of us could swim, so we took an interest in watching the lifeguard shout out rules about using the pool. Then the lifeguard scolded three young boys for not wearing lifejackets, and one chubby kid yelled back with the conviction that he knew how to swim and didn't need a life jacket. The lifeguard enforced the rule, and the kids had to abide. Three adults in their twenties approached the diving board. The lead guy was being instructed on diving by his two friends. We watched him sink into the water, and when he tried to float helplessly, he screamed out, "*Aiuto! Aiuto!* Help! Help!" as he also shouted that he didn't know how to swim.

People yelled out to the lifeguard. "He can't swim! He can't swim! Somebody help him!" The two friends jumped in after him, but the lifeguard rescued the young man and brought him to the poolside. The young boys could not contain their laughter, and the lifeguard ordered them out of the pool. The non-swimmer was given a lifejacket and allowed to return to the pool, and his two friends gave him lessons.

By the third day, we all began feeling queasy, and Mamma led us all up on deck, thinking the fresh air would help. We sipped some lime soda, and despite the boat's ability to fiercely slice through the waves, the ship's rocking seemed to have allied with the sea to sour our stomachs.

Piccolo Santino

Our trip to the deck was hopeless, and we haphazardly raced back. When we returned to our cabin, an orderly approached Mamma. "Buongiorno, Signora." Mamma meekly replied with lifeless eyes. "Buongiorno, Signore."

"Signora, your daughter, has scarlet fever, and I'm here to take you both to sickbay where you will be quarantined."

"Just me and my daughter?"

"Sì, Signora."

"But I have seven children!"

"Seven Children?" he asked while shaking his head. "*Sì Signore*. Yes, Sir." With his surprised look, he informed Mamma, "Very well then, you must all be placed in quarantine."

"When are we moving, Signore?"

"Right now, Signora." Mamma turned to us and said, "All right, kids get all your stuff, and let's go." Stella yelled out, "We're moving!"

"Martina, go get my bag on the bed with the anisette." Lillo asked, "Wow, we're moving again?" Angelina turned to Martina and asked," Are we going on another boat?"

"No! We're going to the hospital room because of Fabrizzia!" Mamma turned, looked around, and asked, "Is everybody ready?"

"Sì! Sì! Sì!" Mamma turned to the orderly and said, "We can leave now, Signore!"

"All right, everybody. Stay together and follow me." We followed single file down the hall, up to two flights, down a hallway, and finally into the infirmary, where we occupied two cabins next to each other. "You will be in quarantine here, so please don't go out on deck. If there is anything you need, just ask."

"Grazie, Signore."

"You're welcome! And arrivederci!"

"Arrivederci, Signore." Then Mamma said, "Oh, thank God we're away from that boiler room."

"Maybe we should thank Fabrizzia for this," Stella said. "Tino, you and Lillo sleep in there. Martina, there's room in here for all of us."

Piccolo Santino

Mamma said. "This sure is better!" Lillo said. "Yeah. At least there's a doctor close by here." Martina said. "I gotta lay down, kids," Mamma said, not looking good as she laid down after placing Enzo on the bed close to the wall.

The next day, Lillo and I decided to go back on deck to see if the salty air would lessen the constant nausea. The weather was grey and damp. It was hard to tell if the heavy mist was from the waves splashing against the ship. We sat on chairs under an overhang, but the nausea persisted, so we got up and joined the sightseeing people by the railing. I rested my elbows on the deck railing. My stomach lifted, and I opened my mouth, thinking that in this grey atmosphere, no one could see me launching vomit overboard. I tried several times, and nothing surged. I wondered if Lillo was even seasick since he moved about quite sober, but he complained like the rest of us when we spoke of the problem. There was no point in bathing in the grey, cold, salty soup any longer. I turned to Lillo and said, "This is not good. Let's go back."

"The weather is lousy, that's why," he said, and we looked for the doorway back to sickbay after our first effort led us in the wrong direction. We got our bearings straight, raced over to the last entrance to our destination, and were confronted by a custodian mopping the floor. "Hey, where do you boys think you're going?" Worried, we looked up at him and hesitated momentarily, and Lillo quickly said, "We're going back to our room!"

"You are not allowed down there."

"Our Mamma is down there!" Lillo said to him, and I responded timidly, "That's our room down there!"

"That can't be! No, not down there!" I shouted back, almost teary-eyed, as I feared we were doomed. "Yes, it is!"

"That area is quarantined. Now get out of here, the both of you." We retreated under a nearby stairwell and furtively watched him mop past our entrance. We removed our shoes as he worked farther away and began tiptoeing toward the door. With trembling hearts, we heard his mop bang against his bucket, and the bucket screeched on the floor. I grabbed the door handle, slowly turned it to open, and allowed Lillo to duck inside

Piccolo Santino

first as the custodial noise got louder. I dashed inside, and we ran to tell everybody what had happened.

"Oh, I don't feel good," cried Angelina, and then Stella joined in: "Me, too!" Then we heard four-year-old Fabrizzia's comment as she sat next to Mamma on the bed: "Mamma, my tummy is squeezing me."

"It's the seasickness. Just lay down again."

Lillo and I had been listening by the door, unsure if the ship's crew had missed us and would be in trouble for leaving without permission. But we had yet to be mentioned. Finally, I said something. "We're back, Mamma," and I saw her looking pale and lying on the bed. Mamma looked up and asked, "Did the fresh air help you two?"

"Not really. The custodian stopped us on our way back here," my sisters laughed. "Yeah, we had to take our shoes off to sneak back in," Lillo added, and the laughter surged. "He kept saying we weren't allowed in the quarantine section." The clicking of the doorknob and the orderly's voice got our attention. "Buongiorno, Signora!" The orderly entered inside with a boisterous-looking young boy about my age. "This is Armando, everybody. He is also sick and must stay in quarantine for a few days." Mamma looked up from her bed and said, "Of course, Signore." He looked at Mamma lying down and said, "How are you feeling today, Signora?"

"If it weren't for the seasickness, I would be fine."

"I'm sorry, Signora." He turned to Armando while he said to Mamma, "Scusa, Signora."

"Sì, go right ahead, Signore."

"Bene Armando," said the orderly. He showed him the bunk beds, and Armando quickly chose an upper bunk in the room with Lillo and me. "Make yourself comfortable with these other boys here for the next few days, and then you'll be out of here."

"Sì! Grazie," said Armando. After the orderly left, we resumed a food fight using a banana we had tried eating earlier for the first time. We found its taste too unfamiliar. Armando quickly knocked on us and said, "Hey, you are not supposed to throw food around!" Lillo shouted back at him, "This is no good!"

Piccolo Santino

"*Quella è una banana.* That's a banana," Armando responded in grammatical Italian, and I shouted back at Armando. "We can't eat that thing." Then Stella joined in, smirking and turning her nose up. "It tastes bad!"

"Using the banana for food fighting is a sin." Armando retorted, his accent was different from our part of the country, and he sounded almost comical, which brought us to stitches, and he could not understand when we laughed. Just how he used an unfamiliar word to us and its pronunciation with the funny regional accent brought out the heartiest laughter from us all. *"Neshi in coppa o lettu!* Get down from the top of the bed!" he shouted to Lillo that evening, and we all laughed. After that, Lillo climbed on Armando's bed to hear him repeat those words, and we jubilated as Armando looked stupefied.

During the three days Armando was in quarantine with us, Lillo and I ventured out onto the deck twice and were stopped once by the custodian, so we repeated our routine to get back inside. Amazingly, Armando was not affected by the sea, and he made us jealous every time he ate his meals as the food smelled delicious.

Sadly, even the aroma was enough to disturb our equilibrium. We tried looking out the porthole for relief, but as we tried to get up, the sickness forced us back to bed only to resume the countdown from a prone position. Mamma was still not taking it very well. She could not walk around and hardly ate anything. It wasn't until one day after Armando left that we began to sense some relief as the ship was getting closer to land, and we got all excited as the countdown was now down to one more day. Seeing Mamma rise out of bed and get dressed was a real treat. "You all stay here. I'll be back soon," she told us. "I have to get a telegram to your papá of our arrival time."

It was early morning when we woke up as the *MS Giulio Cesare* cruised up the Hudson River. We heard the door open, and the orderly shouted as he entered, "We have arrived in America!" We all cheered, "But I am sorry to tell you that everybody must stay on board until tomorrow. The Fourth of July is a national holiday in America, so we are forced to disembark tomorrow." That was a real letdown, but as it turned

Piccolo Santino

out, we all needed to rest from the seasickness, especially Mamma. If we hadn't had that day of rest, Mamma probably would not have been able to walk off the boat of her own accord. As the ship cruised along the New York skyline, we competed for space and viewing time by the portholes to gaze at the tall buildings, and we shouted out, "Those are the skyscrapers! Look over there!"

"Oh no, those are it over there!" We kept observing the moving landscape in wonder and exclaimed about the skyline. "No way, that one is too low. Look over there!"

"*Quello sì*. That one, yes," I said as I tried to make sense of the Italian word *grattacieli*, skyscrapers. In that word, the root word *gratta* means to scratch, and *cieli* means heavens. I thought we were looking for large cats scratching the sky from the rooftops. Then, when I didn't see any cats, I thought that maybe they were hiding. I didn't dare share my thoughts, so I kept going along with the flow as I secretly looked for cats on the rooflines. I chose a tall building and said, "That one over there is as high as the sky. Look, everybody!" Lillo interrupted, "Look over there; that one is even higher!"

"*Per davvero.* For real," said Stella. Then Martina said, "Oh look, small boats are approaching the ship." What used to be a countdown of months to weeks and days now came down to hours and a series of steps before we could head down the walkway to the customs area. It all felt eerie as we left the ship. It was all becoming clear. Italy onboard the boat was just a temporary replacement Italy, a pretend atmosphere that was now flushing out of me as the presence of the Italian language around us was diminishing and replaced by occasional American chatter I tried to make sense of. But Italian sounds still outnumbered the Americans in the immediate surroundings as we followed Mamma, holding each other's hands. Four-year-old Angelina held on to Mamma's dress as she carried two-year-old Enzo. Martina walked in the middle, holding Fabrizzia's and Stella's hands. Lillo and I followed hand in hand.

I kept Papá's image in the forefront of my mind. I thought the photo image of Papa Mamma kept on the dresser would be what I would find, and I never dreamed of what was to come. It all felt unnatural as a stocky, grey-haired, average-height man with a bouquet walked toward us with three other men and two women following behind. He walked to Mamma and greeted her with roses, a long hug, and a kiss. I figured he had to be Papá, but he wasn't the picture I had been holding in my mind for the past two years. Then, other people greeted us with kisses.

The two-year wait ended as Papá said my name and kissed me. The young, lean, tall figure with a mustache and sympathetic face of two years ago was not about. In his place was this short, stocky, salt-and-pepper-haired man with tattered silver glasses, in dark dress pants and a white shirt with elastics above his elbows to hold up his sleeves. His image made me wonder what happened to my Papá, the real Papá I once knew.

All kinds of questions were racing through my head. Did he drown on the *Andrea Doria* and abandon us? Was this a substitute to maintain sanity in the family? If this were the case, this guy must have a lot of courage to take on a woman with seven strange children. Furthermore, everyone who knew us would have to be in on it. Without any direct evidence or further logic to support my theory, I carefully yielded to learning about this new Papá, who was seemingly responsible for our move to America.

I studied the other two men beside Papá, sporting rubber bands above their elbows. One of them, I later learned, was Eugenio's brother and I listened to them speak in cut-up Italian and chopped-up English. It wasn't fair since it sounded so cheap and presented little of a challenging language for me to learn. I wished to turn back, but it was too late, so I finally abandoned any hope of ever completing fifth grade in Italy. I was foolish in thinking there would be a chance of returning to Italy once we landed here. I let my ears wander farther away and listened to others speak as they loaded things into their cars. I speculated they might be German. I heard another group beside them sounding the same but different, and I got scared, thinking I might have an impossible task to accomplish if that were the English language.

We didn't know that Papá had already been interviewed earlier by an Italian newspaper regarding the successful immigration story of his

Piccolo Santino

wife and family of seven children under the provisions of the Refugee Relief Act of 1953.

We were soon gathered and lined up straight along the dock for pictures. The photography didn't take long, and everyone commented on how worn Mamma looked during the photo session. Everyone was surprised at how seasick we all were during the trip. As we waited to leave for our new home, I didn't realize the cause of the delay until we saw one of our uncles walking our oldest sister, Martina, by the hand and realized she had wandered off. We split up into three different cars for the trip home, and I continued observing how Eugenio's brother mixed English words with Italian. I wondered about their accuracy as I still felt the weight of the English language I heard earlier. That now convinced me we were on foreign soil, and I shuddered at the thought of the arduous task ahead.

Piccolo Santino

Chapter 10 of Part Two
Our new home in America

Papá had set up a home for us in a crowded two-bedroom apartment on the second floor of a two-story walk-up, multi-family dwelling in a New York suburban town. Our neighbor across the hall was a single mother of four named Sheila. Even though there was a language barrier, we managed to communicate somewhat and liked learning from them.

Life in America seemed very festive, with many relatives and friends around our table overflowing with food, a scene we were only used to in Italy on holidays and then only at Nanna's or Aunt Isabella's house. This excessive display of food lasted for several weeks to accommodate visitors. But what attracted me was the television. It was hard to conceive such an expensive item back in Italy, and now it was in our home in America. I was surprised to see a baseball game but no soccer. When some of the visiting adults adjusted the picture on the TV, I watched and listened to what they were doing so that I could learn.

As visiting relatives became less frequent, I was still amazed to see Mamma set the table for dinner every night. We never did this back home, and thus, I asked Papá if, in America, every day was a holiday. Bursting with glee, Papá raced to tell everybody about my comment. The next night at dinner, I chose to have a beer instead of soda and quickly received icy stares from Mamma and Papá and everybody while I insisted. As I pressed down with the can opener, thoughts of beer being more expensive than soda made me feel guilty. But I also felt superior to my siblings while I took a sip.

During that entire time at dinner, I felt ashamed as the beer taste became earthy and less desirable to my taste buds, and I could not finish the whole cand (*spelling for can in that period*). After dinner, I helped clear the table and volunteered to take out the trash so I could hide the unfinished cand of beer. I admitted to myself it was wasteful and thought

Piccolo Santino

about the financial concern on Papá's face when he stared me down earlier. From the next day on, I drank soda like everyone else.

The telephone became an absolute novelty for us, and when it rang, we all raced to be the first to answer it before handing it to Mamma. Eventually, we were tired of it and no longer wanted to answer it. Usually, someone called first to inform us they were planning to visit. Once Papá got the news, he expressed frustration over the sudden inconvenience. Grudgingly, he reached into his wallet and sent Martina and me to the deli to pick up an Entenmann's coffee and soda. Papá usually also had us get him a carton of milk and cigarettes. He would give us his empty pack to show the clerk the brand. We anxiously placed the items we gathered on the counter and hoped that just showing Chesterfield's label would avoid a conversation.

The clerk understood, and we relaxed as he reached into the display case for the cigarettes, then immediately slapped down a large paper bag on the counter and whipped out a pencil from behind his ear. He quickly itemized each item and totaled it right on the paper bag. He then bagged everything, swept the money from us, and made change as if all in one swoop. As he gave us the chance, he probably said, "Thank you," but we were afraid to respond, thinking it could lead to a conversation. We raced to return home before the company arrived, our fear of a potential discussion lingering.

During the guest's visiting time, we sat close to the television, away from the company where Papá and his friends drank *Gallo Wine* and cracked mixed nuts for snacks. Mamma and her friend drank soda and also snacked on the mixed nuts. It was vital to Papá to serve guests ample refreshments and snacks to avoid social gossip about them being stingy. As the guests got up, I kept looking at the Entenmann's coffee cake's remains. I deliberately ventured over to sneak a small piece while they were busy saying goodbye. The farewells lingered longer than anticipated. By the time I retrieved a morsel from the Entenmann's box, Daddy, as we started addressing him now by the American version, shot me a clandestine stare as his guests continued talking.

Piccolo Santino

I felt a sigh of relief when the couple finally made their way down the long hallway as Mamma and Daddy escorted them out. I turned my back to the hallway and reached for a better piece of cake, but before I could turn around, I felt the loud sting of Daddy's belt across my shoulders while he shouted out, "I told you not to touch any of the snacks while the company was here!" Mamma watched in agreement as Daddy, his strictness evident, continued his tirade. "I told everybody before not to go near the food while the company was present."

The other siblings silently lowered their heads to their chests, but Lillo rose and raced for a piece of cake. "Now it's all right? I can eat all I want?" asked Lillo, but nobody laughed as I put down my uneaten piece of cake and shrugged my shoulders back and forth. The thought of this Daddy being an impostor for who used to be my papá surfaced fast and stung me as sharp as the sting of his belt. This new Daddy was not like the one in Italy, but if he were the same Papá, I sensed a tyrant secretly simmering in Daddy. The tyrant showed himself by openly beating my youngest brother Enzo and sister Fabrizzia with his belt on constant occasions, seemingly without cause.

Now, there were those visitors we didn't care much for, and we figured they had to pay the price for imposing upon us. So, while they stood around reiterating their goodbyes, we coyly planted clothespins on their jacket tails. But there was one visitor we were always glad to see: Uncle Vito. He always came with two large bags of groceries, which included big boxes of cereal with milk and cookies. We had just finished dinner when we heard a knock on the door. Mamma said, "Stella, go open the door!" Stella and Lillo ran to the door and yelled, "Uncle Vito is here, everybody!"

"Uncle Vito!" we repeated, "Hello, kids!" he said as he walked in and turned to Daddy, who was seated sideways in his chair at the dining room table, holding a glass of wine, his right arm resting on the table. Uncle Vito laid the bags on the table away from Daddy, and Mamma said, "What did you do, Vito?"

"It's a little something for the kids." We liked it when he came with treats because it introduced us to new things, and Mamma then learned to add some of those items to her grocery list. Uncle turned to Daddy and said, "Bartolo, how are you?"

"Hah, what can I say? All seems good. And you?"

"I'll be working here next week. I got a chimney to do."

"Yeah! Where about?"

"Down by the canal area. Mr. Greenberg just built a new house there and needs a chimney done."

"You want a glass of wine?"

"Yeah, just one, though." Mamma pointed to the empty chair by the window at the end of the table and said to him, "Sit over here, Vito." He sat by the window at the end of the table, and we settled onto the futon next to Mamma, close by Uncle Vito. Mamma said, "Martina, put down your needlepoint. Put those groceries in the kitchen and bring out a glass for your uncle. Stella, help your sister."

After he lit a cigarette, Uncle slammed the lighter lid shut, turned toward Lillo and me, and said, "How would you two boys like to come to work with me next week." Mamma turned to him and asked, "What do you mean?" Uncle looked around for the ashtray, and Daddy pushed the one he had been using toward Uncle. He continued, "I can take them to work with me for a few days if it's okay."

"For real, you're saying it?"

"Sì, for real!"

"By all means, take them away!"

"Va bene!" he said to Mamma and looked at me. "On Monday, I'll stop by around nine o'clock."

"Okay!" I said, then he turned to Lillo, "You too, Lillo."

"All right, but are we getting paid?" Laughter broke out, and Uncle Vito blushed and jokingly said, "People are saying that you are bad kids already. I am only trying to keep you from getting arrested." Mamma turned to Uncle Vito and asked, "Who is saying those things? What are you talking about?"

"When people visit here, your kids hang clothespins on their coattails." We all laughed loudly, and Uncle Vito said, "After visiting here

Piccolo Santino

Last week, *Il Barbiere,* the barber, got scared when a guy tried to approach Him down Main Street. He started running away so fast he tripped and almost fell. When he got home, he found three clothespins stuck to his coat." Laughter broke out, and Stella yelled from the kitchen, "That was Gumbah Pernozzo. I snuck one clothespin on him!" Lillo laughed and said, "Angelina and I did the other two!" We all laughed together again. Daddy put down his glass with a chuckle and a smirk, and Mamma joined in our laughter.

Martina and Stella ran out of the kitchen and asked, "What happened? What happened?"

"You guys shouldn't be laughing!" exclaimed Uncle Vito, but Mamma could not contain her laughter, "Ahhhh! HAAHH! HAHAHA!"

"Come on, Vito, they're just kids," Daddy said. Uncle Vito interrupted, "Kids, you say? (It was customary in our culture to refer to other people by making fun of any noticeable physical feature about them). *Culo Grosso,* big ass, and his wife were looking at handkerchiefs in Woolworth after leaving here the other day, and they thought they were in trouble when an employee started talking to them. They couldn't understand English, so they dropped the handkerchief and ran out of the store, fearing they'd be arrested for stealing."

"Are you serious?" said Mamma, and we laughed harder. Then Martina said, "That had to be Gumbah Tomaselli and his wife." Stella and I said, "Oh yeah!" then Lillo pranced about by sticking his butt out, repeating the words "Culo Grosso. Culo Grosso."

"AHHH! AAAH! HAHA!!!!" Looking agitated, Uncle put his glass of wine down and said, "Why, these kids know everybody already." He looked at Daddy, who was chuckling heartily, then shook his head as Mamma joined in our laughter again. Uncle took a long drag, exhaled a lot of smoke through his nostrils, and then turned to Mamma. "Go on, laugh, Anna! But you should know that people are afraid to visit here now."

"Good, we'll save money that way," exclaimed Mamma. Uncle Vito turned to Daddy, who was grinning and chuckling. Exasperated, Uncle responded by getting up and saying, "Well, I better get going."

Piccolo Santino

"Why are you leaving? Stay for coffee at least, Vito," said Mamma. "No, that's okay. I have places to go," said Uncle Vito, sounding disappointed. "All right then, thanks for the groceries," Uncle Vito looked at Lillo and me and exclaimed, "I'll be back for you two rascals Monday morning early, and you better be ready!"

"Okay, Uncle Vito," said Lillo as he ran down the long hallway. Mamma got up to walk Uncle out. I tagged along, and as Uncle opened the door, Lillo looked like he was palming something and dashed out of the bathroom by the exit. Uncle Vito noticed Lillo's clutched fists and said, "*Mascalzone a mia non me cazzo fotte!* You rascal, you're not going to fuck and fool me! I see you're hiding a clothespin in your hand." Lillo started laughing, and Mamma turned to him and said, "Basta! Get out of here." At that moment, I planted a clothespin on his coattail as he spun to exit. Lillo and I then sneaked around Mamma, holding the door open, and yelled down to Uncle Vito from the top landing as he descended the stairway, "Goodbye, Uncle Vito!"

"Just be ready when I get here, you rascals," he said, lifting his coattail and yelling back while shaking the clothespin at us, "I told you. You can't fool me!"

I liked living among American kids because it hastened my English learning. Whenever we could gather some loose change, we would go outside and look for Butch, a school dropout with a slight attitude, or his red-haired, freckled younger sister, Jenny. We would show them coins in our hands and then mimic chewing to communicate bubble gum. They would then return from the store with single pieces of *Bazooka Joe* chewing gum, and we would share them.

We ventured by the canal behind the house, where at first, Butch and Jenny showed us where to cut down a branch from the tall hedges growing on the perimeter by the garage. They showed Lillo and me how to make a bow and arrows. Such ventures helped me increase my English vocabulary. We then tested the bows by shooting arrows, and when we played cowboys and Indians, Jenny and her friend made feathers from colored paper and rigged them on my head. Lillo became frustrated when

Piccolo Santino

he could not launch his arrow from his bow. "Jenny, no good, no good! See!" He showed what he was saying, and Jenny took the bow from him, wiggled the string, and said, "Look, Leelo, too loose! Too loose. See!" I made mental notes of those new words and their meanings as we walked around to the front of the house and saw Mamma seated on the front stoop with my sisters. I immediately sensed that interrogation was coming.

Mamma looked at me in a curdled tone and said, "What kind of mischief have you been up to now?" Butch and Jenny blushed as they looked at me. "*Niente,* nothing," I said, and Mamma responded curtly, "*Aspetta tu.* You wait until your father gets home from work." Jenny and Butch looked intimidated by Mamma's tone, and Lillo wiggled on the string as he held up his bow towards Mamma and shouted, "See! Too Loose! Too loose!" Everyone burst out laughing, but Butch kept staring at my sister Martina. Mamma jokingly said to Lillo in Italian, "Bring it here. I'll fix it for you!"

Lillo held the bow against his chest as Jenny and Butch turned their heads back and forth to read the facial expressions. "No, you'll break it." answered Lillo in Italian, and Mamma said, I'll break it over your head!" Wide grinned and smiling even though Butch kind of understood what had transpired and, in a laughing manner, said to Mamma, "Anna. I want to kiss Martina." He blew kisses toward Martina. Martina, concerned, said to Mamma, "He says he wants to kiss me, Mamma." Startled, Mamma shouted, "Whaahh! *Ma tu sei pazzo!* Yoo crazy! I gotta broomma for you!" she yelled at Butch as she reached behind for the broom she had on the stoop. Butch quickly backed away and said, "Anna! I wanna kiss Martina. I no wanah the broomma." Mamma raised her broom again and said, "Yoo no Kissa Martina Boochee."

"I love Martina. I wanna kiss Martina." Mamma shook her broom in the air and shouted back, "You lova this broomma." Laughter swelled as she continued. "Boochee, *va! Va!* Butch, go! Go!"

Jenny looked up at Mamma, fully blushed with color, and then shouted to her brother, "Butch, you better stop it now, or I'll tell Mother!" I listened to how Jenny pronounced Butch and compared it to how I said boo-ch, as I watched him back away, and then I called out to him,

Piccolo Santino

"Booch! We go to the park now?" I thought I said it right as I watched him back away, but I realized I needed to practice more. "Yeah, Sonny, let's go," he said, standing by the tall hedges near the sidewalk. "Come on, you too, Leelo."

"I'm coming, too," said Jenny as she walked over and rubbed shoulders with me. "Come on," said Butch as he led the way.

We looked for raspberries and wild grapes in the empty lot a few houses down from ours, sandwiched between a place where a man had a famed pet monkey. Jenny and her younger friend didn't care for the sour grapes, but they did like the raspberries. The park was diagonal across from the house with the monkey. In the park, we went directly to the activity center and played floor shuffleboard, and I wondered about Jenny as she kept rubbing shoulders with me. The park attendant called out for the equipment as the rain started, and we went inside to play the table version of the shuffleboard.

One day, we went there with the whole family, Daddy's cousin, Giorgio, and Eugenio's brother, who were back in Italy. We arrived during a pie-eating contest, and since it involved food, Lillo ran over to participate with all the other contestants. I felt very self-conscious about getting my face soiled in public among strangers and declined to participate. When we returned home that day, as cousin Giorgio was upstairs with the family, I wanted to show my gratitude for his driving us to the park. So, it was a good idea to clean the inside of his car for him. After I finished, I ran upstairs to tell him the good news. "You did what?"

"I cleaned the inside of your car. And even peeled off all those papers inside the windows for you."

"What?" he shouted, "Come show me what you did?" I showed him the left side of the windshield, where I peeled off the papers, and with grave concern, he asked, "Where did you put the papers afterward?"

"In the garbage." With a serious tone, he continued, "Where, Tino? Show me where you put them." We walked to the back by the garage where the garbage cans were, and I asked, "Were those papers necessary?"

"Yeah, they are the inspection and registration of the car." I didn't know what that meant, but I figured they had to be necessary since it worried cousin Giorgio. "There, I put them in this garbage can." I lifted the lid off the garbage, and his face dropped after it turned red while he sifted the little pieces of paper through his fingers. "Okay, I better go to Motor Vehicle tomorrow and see if I can get new ones."

"I just wanted to clean the inside of your car for you."

"Yes, okay, Tino, yeah," he mumbled under his breath as he hurried to lock his car before returning upstairs. I stayed on the front stoop hoping for either Butch or Jenny to show up. From that day, whenever anybody visited, they locked their car.

That same summer, Butch took us to see a movie called *Shane*, and I was mesmerized by the vivid colors and rich sound, which made me feel as if I could almost smell the smoke from Shane's gun. Despite the language barrier, the action was easy to follow, and I understood the essential good versus evil storyline.

The introduction to popcorn and soda at the movies was an absolute novelty, and never did I think that the blow dryer in the bathroom would be a frightening experience. Lillo and I had dried our hands with a paper towel, and Butch was still in the stall when I inquisitively pressed down on the shiny button, and the motor roared so loud that I thought something was about to come through the wall. I immediately called out for Butch. "Butch! Butch! Waah!"

"Sonny! What happened?" Butch called out from inside the stall as I wailed, "Butch! Butch! Wah! Wah!" I shouted while circling in place, and Lillo backed away from me. Butch raced out as the dryer silenced, and I was able to calm down. "Sonny, it's nothing. Look!" He turned on the dryer again, quickly rinsed his hands in the sink, and rubbed them together under the blower. Lillo laughed at me as I looked dumbfounded. "Look! He repeatedly turned on the blower by slapping the "on" button and said, "See? Nothing bad happens."

"Oh!" I replied from a distance away, and he waved us on and said, "Come on, let's go."

Piccolo Santino

On our way home, Butch decided we could hitchhike instead of walking. He stuck his left arm out, made a loose fist with his thumb up, and started walking backward on the street. "Sonny! Do this." I didn't respond since I wasn't sure what he was saying, so he called me again. "Sonny!" He held his arm up to show me, and I stepped down from the sidewalk onto the street and imitated him. After a short moment, a car slowed down as it passed us, and the three of us ran over. Butch tilted the front seat for Lillo and me to sit in the back, and he sat in the front. The driver, a young man in his early twenties, said, "Where are you guys going?"

"We just saw a movie and are going home. We live down by the park."

"Oh, that's farther than I'm going. I can let you off on Atlantic Road, where I turn off."

"Yeah, that's good, thanks."

"My name is Bob. What's yours?"

"I'm Butch. These are my friends. They're from Italy and can't understand English yet."

"Oh, they're wops?"

"I don't call them that. They live across from me."

"Well, I think I'll turn here a couple of blocks sooner and cut across if you don't mind."

"Yeah, that's okay. Thanks for the ride."

"Yeah! Now, I gotta go home and clean the backseat of my car." As the car sped off, Butch waved his middle finger in the air. "What you do, Butch?"

"I do 'fuck you' to that man!"

"What that for?"

"He bad man Sonny, so I do Fuck You!" He held up his middle finger again, and as the confusion on my face bulged, he said, "Sonny, see, look." With his left hand, he made a ring with his thumb and index finger and went back and forth with his right index finger into the ring and repeated the words "fuck you" several times as he laughed. "Butch in Italia do lika this." I lifted my left arm and quickly slapped the left bicep with my right hand, Lillo laughed, and Butch started laughing with him, and then he imitated what I just did by also imitating my words several times. "Lika, this? Lika this?"

Lillo and I held our stomachs and bent over laughing as his antics brought us to stitches. "You funny Butch!" I said, and Lillo shouted out, "Funny, Booch." And he did it again real fast. "Lika, this! Lika this! Lika this!"

We turned onto the sidewalk between the tall hedges that fenced the surrounding perimeter of our home. Immediately, I noticed a small crowd in front of the house. Seated on the top step of a five-step porch leading to the entrance of the building was Danny, a thirty or so-year-old chubby man in a white t-shirt and blue jeans with cuffs folded up four inches above his ankles. Scattered on the lower steps were three younger kids, and standing against the cement post that completed a curved wall on the right side of the cement stoop were Butch's twelve-year-old sister Jenny and a younger girl.

Danny was holding a guitar with a harmonica harnessed around his neck. Although nervous around such congregations, I still welcomed them as another opportunity to learn new American words. Butch called out to his sister, "Hi, Jenny,"

"Hi, Butch! Where did you guys go?"

"We went to the movies to see Shane."

"Sonny, did you like it?" she asked with a broad smile that seemed to stretch and gather her freckles. I looked up at her and smiled back. I shook my head eagerly as I said, "Yes! Yes!"

"Danny, you got a match?" shouted out Butch. "Here you are." Danny snatched a matchbook from his T-shirt pocket and tossed it. Butch lit his cigarette. I refrained from asking him for one, knowing he would give it to me as he had done a few other times. Then Danny started playing his guitar and sang. When he played the harmonica simultaneously, everybody's faces lit up.

Piccolo Santino

Since television was still a novelty, we had yet to learn how those people got inside the television, nor did we know anything about production. It was something that was occurring somewhere, somehow, at that time. We were especially fascinated by a commercial for *Chock Full o' Nuts Coffee*. The rhythmic chanting of those musical beats, "TAH! TA TAH TA TAH!" in synch with the percolating coffee, seen through the glass bubble on top of the percolator, had us believing that with this brand of coffee, our pot would sing as it percolated. We convinced Daddy, and he took Stella to the store to identify the label. When they returned, we all stood around the stove and waited anxiously for what felt like an eternity for the water to boil. Angelina asked, "When is it going to sing?"

"It has to boil first," said Martina.

"Is it going to sing, kids?" asked Daddy.

"Yeah, Daddy. The water has to boil first," said Stella. Then I said, "Yeah, we saw it on the television,"

"It's not happening!" said Lillo.

"Wait until we see it bubble; then, the singing music should start," I said. Fabrizzia added, "It's bubbling, and it's not happening!" Daddy turned from rinsing a dish by the sink and came over with a naturally puzzled look. He bent sideways and said, "Forget it, kids. It's not going to do anything."

"Yeah! It's not gonna sing," said Martina. "I don't think it's ever going to sing!" said Stella, and we all walked away. I, most of all, felt dumb as I realized that coffee and a pot couldn't sing, and it had to be television secrets of some kind. Daddy made another frowning face and then poured himself a fresh cup of coffee. "It's good," he remarked.

Uncle Vito drove his blue '57 Chevy pickup over the raw landscape of the work site, and it felt like the waves at sea of a few months ago except more choppy and hard on the rump. By the time he parked in the rear of the house, I had thought I would be seasick. On-site was his worker, John, a tall, muscular African man, referred to here in America as colored, which was something for us to learn about in the American culture. I had already met John before Uncle Vito brought Lillo and me here on the first day.

We got out of the truck, and he called out to John. "Dida, you fixa the scaffold on top? Because I don't wanna fall from up there!" John walked toward us and said, "Yeah, it's done. You're not gonna fall, Vito. Did you bring back coffee, at least?"

"Oh shit, I musta forgot!"

"How can you forget coffee?"

"I'm sorry, John, I go to the banka first, and after I pick up ma nephew, I forgot to pass by the diner."

"All right, give me the keys. I'll go!"

"No! No! You no supposa to drive!"

"So you'll go?"

"No, I senda my nephew."

"How is he going to ask for coffee? He can't speak English for God's sake."

"No worry, I teach him."

"What? I think you're wasting your time."

"What you mean? He can do it," answered Uncle. He then switched to Italian and said, "Tino, do you remember the diner where I took you and Lillo for coffee last time?"

"Sì, I remember." John looked on as Uncle explained how to ask for coffee. "*Bene,* Good. Now repeat these words exactly the way I say them." I looked at how his lips moved to form the words. "Tree coffees, regular and tree donats."

"Now you say it."

"The coffees reguloo ah a dona."

"No, No! Listen to me again," he said in English. "Vito, this is not gonna work. Just give me the damn keys," John said, and Uncle Vito replied, "No, I no want you to geta no trouble." He looked at me with a serious face and said, "Now listen hard." I stared straight into his face as he spoke, "Tree coffees, regular and tree donats!" I repeated the words, "Tree coffees regula and tree donats."

Piccolo Santino

"Bravo!" he exclaimed, and I felt relieved. He reached into his back pocket and pulled out the fattest wallet I had ever seen, and as he combed his fingers through the thick folds of bills, I noticed his fingers looked yellow, and I could even smell the scent of cigarettes as he handed me two dollars. "Now you remember the way, right?" I shook my head. "Yes," I repeated the words to form a rhythm in my mind so that I would not be interrupted by stuttering when I arrived.

"I sure hope you know what you're doing," John said as he carried bricks toward the scaffold. "Don't you worry, he gonna do it?"

"I sure hope so."

"Come on, I help you with the bricks."

I dreaded going to stores asking for things, primarily if they were behind counters, as my fear of stuttering always lingered. Now, I tried harder to drown that fear by repeatedly saying the words "Tree coffees, regular, and tree donats" under my breath while reviewing the direction of travel in my mind. Going three blocks straight to the end, make a left at the street with the canal next to it, and then go four blocks to the end, and the diner is on the right at the corner.

As I approached the diner, tension from the language barrier and my fear of stuttering ballooned. I repeated the words to a varied rhythm, hoping to time my presence at the beginning of my sentence when I had to face the person in the diner. I pulled the door open, turned to my left, timed my steps toward the counter, and met this tall, thick man, forty or so, with thinning disheveled hair, sporting a tattoo on one bicep, and wearing a dirty white, greasy smock that made him look more like a confused sailor than a chef. I looked at him as he looked at me, and as he was about to speak, I stopped him by blurting out, "Tree coffees, regular and tree donats."

Like magic, I was instantly relieved he did not start a conversation and walked away to get the coffee and doughnuts. Then I saw something behind a glass display right in front of me on top of the counter. They were little *Tootsie Rolls* candies. I wished I could reach over and take what I wanted. I already knew that they were a penny each. I had twelve

Piccolo Santino

cents in my pocket, and then I thought that if I could only read the label, I could ask for them by name. I studied the brand and tried to figure out how to pronounce the words; I thought the "s" in Tootsie must have been misplaced. In Italian, this placement of the "s" would not make sense. The "s" should be before the "t," I believed. Someone must have made a mistake.

As the man bagged the coffees and doughnuts, he turned to me and said something, so I just thought now was the time to ask. With complete confidence, I proudly blurted out and took pride that I didn't stutter. "Twelve tostee rolls." He didn't give a dumb look that generally came from not understanding. He turned away and walked to the grill, so I felt I did great again. I looked at the Tootsie Roll display and wondered what happened. He was slicing bread rolls and putting them on the grill one at a time. What could I do? I didn't know the words to stop him. I thought of just running out the door, but then I would have to explain why I returned empty-handed to Uncle Vito.

I quickly waved my hands in the air and shouted, "No! No! No!" He was already bagging three toasted rolls and had the grill covered with more. I laid twelve cents on the counter and pointed to the *Tootsie Rolls*, and he shouted, "What!"

After removing the remaining rolls from the grill, he slammed down the spatula, advanced with bulging eyes, and snorted like a charging bull. Angrily, he grabbed a handful of the *Tootsie Rolls*, placed them down, picked one up, and slammed it down in front of me, yelling, "One! Grr!" I gulped, and he repeated the action twelve times and growled the number out each time, "Two ghrr! Three! Fouruhhrr. Etc." As he continued counting, I wished that twelve came faster, so instead, in my mind, I used the opportunity to check my knowledge of counting against his English by anticipating each count. I was proud to have been correct every time. Once I got back, I didn't dare explain what happened. I learned something new and now had a pocket full of misspelled Tootsie Rolls.

Piccolo Santino

Late one Saturday morning, after a rainfall, I stared out the window at smoky grey clouds with an eggshell border clinging to a wet pastel blue sky. I longed for that Mediterranean horizon in Italy, which I remembered seeing during our trip to Naples. Still, I realized I was trying to fool myself as I flipped through my Italian comic book, *The Lone Ranger*. Daddy was on an errand to the store and took my sisters with him, and Mamma was outside with the other kids doing something. I found it quaint being inside alone and wondered why Mamma didn't chase me out of the house, as usual, every morning.

I stared out the window onto the short rooftop and then angrily tossed the comic book out the opened window. I looked at the wristwatch that Aldo had given me. Its meaning was downright lost in America. I angrily removed it from my wrist, tossed it on the tar-shingled roof, and trembled as it landed within inches of the comic book. I had no desire to retrieve that memorabilia, even though I looked out onto the rooftop weeks later with slight remorse. The abandoned memorabilia was reminiscent of Matilda's remains. American rain and wind had already decomposed the comic book and watch beyond recovery.

Butch's sudden appearance, after what seemed like an eternity, left me in a state of wonder. It was a few weeks later, while Lillo and I were scavenging in a vacant lot for empty soda bottles, that he unexpectedly reappeared. "Sonny, what are you doing here?"

"High Butch! I lookee for soda bottle." Jenny showed me how to pronounce his name, and I felt good when I said it. "Oh yeah?" Then his friend asked Butch, "How come he talks funny?"

"They came from Italy and don't know English yet."

"Oh." exclaimed his friend, and Butch said, "Sonny, this is my friend Artie." Artie was about a head taller than Butch, and as we shook hands, Butch said to me, "Sonny, I hear you took over my job at the butcher after I quit."

"Yeah, me go there one week already."

"Sonny, don't go no more okay!"

"Yeah, why?"

Piccolo Santino

"That man no good, Sonny. Here, I give you money not to go anymore, okay?" I felt enriched as he instantly put half a dollar in my right hand. I quickly put it in my pocket and said, "Gee, thanks, Butch! Okay, me no go no more." I noticed he was smoking something different now, so I said to him, "Butch, you gotta one cigarette for me?" and he held up a skinny brown cigar about the same size as a long cigarette and said, "No, Sonny, I smoke these now!"

"Okay, can I try one?" I said, and he lit me up. As he handed Lillo an empty bottle to put into the paper bag, I took a drag, inhaled, and within a minute, the world started spinning. "Oh. Ohhhh." I began wailing, and Butch said, "Sonny, you not supposed to swallow this smoke." His words echoed in my head, but the spinning world and my moaning drowned them out. I continued moaning, "Ohh...hhh!" and from the corner of my eye, I saw Artie chuckling.

I got the urge to throw up and quickly ran to the side of a building and rested my head on my right arm as I pressed against the wall. The convulsions were strong and felt terrifying, and then the heaves came up dry, one after another. Questions raced through my mind about why people smoked if this is how sick it could make them. I kept thinking people have to be crazy to put up with this sickness, and as the last dry heaves diminished, I swore never to smoke again. I slowly regained my balance and haphazardly made my way back to the guys. "Sonny, you feel better now."

"Yeah, and I no wanna smoke no mo." Artie was growing impatient and turned to Butch and said, "Come on, Butch, let's go." Butch turned to me and said, "See yah Sonny, we gotta go now."

"Bye, Butch."

"See ya." I felt a sense of loyalty to him, so I never returned to work at the butcher shop, although a few times after that, I did come to regret it as I realized I could have had a good thing going. The owner had me slicing cold cuts with the electric slicer, and he was impressed with my youthful coordination and expertise of the machine even though I never handled one before. I liked that part of the job and handling meats, but I

Piccolo Santino

was bashful with him and the customers, and when Butch gave the half dollar, I saw it as an easy way out.

Lillo and I took the empty bottles to the grocery store and got a soda and a two-pack *Drakes* cupcake, each with the refund money, and surprisingly never saw or heard of Butch ever again after that day.

Piccolo Santino

Chapter 11 of Part Two, 1958
School in America

I listened to Mamma rummage in the kitchen while waiting to get up. I thought I heard Daddy leave for work earlier as butterflies vacillated in my stomach for the first day of school in America. I tried to prepare myself by reminiscing about what I had already learned and how, in Italy, I would've been going into fifth grade instead of now being placed in third grade.

Last night, Jenny and her mom, Sheila, came over to explain the morning school bus schedule. Daddy knew some English, and as Sheila and Jenny repeated themselves, we felt secure once we understood that Jenny was taking the same bus as my oldest sister and me. The younger siblings were going on the second bus a few minutes later. Jenny also helped us organize our school supplies, and her mom had been beneficial in finding a store for the school uniforms.

When we arrived, other kids were waiting at the bus stop, and Stella, Lillo, and Angelina stayed close to Mamma. Sheila kept some distance from her daughter as Jenny wanted space to roam. Martina and I stayed close together, clutching our notebooks, and all the while, I thought I should be in the fifth grade, but then I sensed that being placed with younger kids would be more advantageous for learning English. Ironically, by previous standards, Martina had already completed her education but would now be obligated for eight more years. Once we arrived at school, Jenny was in the forefront advising a teacher of Martina and me, and they thanked her. I was glad when the teacher looked our way while nodding as Jenny spoke to her, and I felt a sense of assurance. We gathered in the auditorium and soon realized that students walked over to a teacher who led them to their respective classrooms as another teacher called names. Look, see, and follow became my first lesson, and it worked, for the most part, all day.

Once in the classroom, I anticipated segregated seating between the

Piccolo Santino

sexes and was perplexed by the newly random seating arrangements. I looked around and became quietly rattled as I compared how the girls dressed paralleled to the girls back in Italy, who wore very conservative dresses way below the knees. It became hard to participate in any classwork or readily absorb directions from the teacher, so I applied my first lesson of "monkey see, monkey do" as much as possible.

I watched the other kids grasp and follow their routines whenever the bell rang. The line to the bathroom was usually long, as kids from different classes joined in, and I became overwhelmed by a strong odor emanating from the perimeter. I held my breath near the urinal and quickly saw the source of the pungent chlorine smell. At first, I felt uncomfortable being in the presence of other kids in the bathroom. Thus, I reminisced about my comfort back home in the privacy of the wide-open sky to relieve myself instead of feeling confined in this new way of life. I wished for when I could see the butterflies skedaddle in the open air with Lola.

At lunchtime, my sister and I spotted each other as we entered the cafeteria among a sea of children, and we sat down as others did but quickly discovered we needed to do as they did. We opened our brown bags the same as others, but the contents were vastly different. Instead of the usual American lunch, we had Italian bread, salami, and provolone. The unfamiliar smell turned heads and lifted noses in frozen stares in our direction. With total intimidation, we watched the frozen faces dissolve into ugly sneers and pull away from us as we cracked our hard-boiled eggs. As we tried to fit in by sipping milk through our straws, the children's Laughter and pointed fingers made us feel even more isolated. The desperate need for acceptance was real as we shrank in our chairs, Martina whispering, "Tonight, we'll have to tell Daddy to buy American bread for our lunch from now on."

Despite the challenges, I was determined to adapt. "We have to eat like the American kids now," I told Martina. That night, when we approached Daddy, it was surprising and sad to learn that our younger sisters and brother had the same experience. But we were determined to overcome these obstacles and integrate into our new environment.

Piccolo Santino

One day in the classroom, when I tried to communicate my thoughts using hand motions and cryptic American words, the butterflies felt more like swarming bees. Miss Manor, a very pretty young woman with short dark hair, showed us a slide-strip presentation. When the illustration of a farmer plowing his field with an ox-pulled plow came on, I immediately felt compelled to say something, so I raised both hands and pointed to the screen while saying, "Me this! Me this!" But my attempt to participate was met with confusion and silence, further isolating me in this new environment. Inquisitive faces stared and commented, "What is he doing?" Miss Manor looked at me and said, "Yes, Sonny, what is it?"

"Me this, Italy." Some students looked to my neighbors at my left and my right and asked, "What is he saying?"

"I don't know." Maybe he needs to go to the bathroom!"

"What's he trying to say?

"Quiet class! He is trying to tell us something," said Miss Manor as she walked over. I continued to point at the screen and say, "Me this Italy. Me this!" The blank looks on my classmates' faces and Miss Manor convinced me that my efforts were in vain. I had so much to tell about the English language, and it all felt so impossible. Thus, I settled back and watched the rest of the presentation in silence, secretly reveling after noticing the prettiest girl in class smiling at me. I had already made a point of listening to her name whenever I heard it to learn it. At first, I secretly sounded it out in Italian the way I heard it, Chanis, and then I changed it to Giannis until I saw her name on one of her book covers and learned how to spell Janice.

She was looking and smiling at me as I had tried to express myself. My head pointed to the screen, my eyes floated toward her. And I rejoiced in knowing that she was looking at me. The bell rang during the last slide, and everybody became jubilant as they rushed to clear their desks. I tilted my head to look at Janice again as I lifted my desktop to put away my books and pencils.

"Quiet class! As soon as your desks are cleared, you may line up by the door." Five boys got up with seven girls and formed separate lines, it felt strange seeing different lines, but then it took me a while to learn that

Piccolo Santino

the random seating was arranged alphabetically. Two of the boys asked, "Miss Manor can I go to the boy's room please?"

"Yes, go ahead, Neil. But what did you say?

"May I please go to the bathroom?"

"That's better!"

"I need to go to," said Charles.

"All right but two at a time, please, and come right back."

"Do any of you girls need to go?"

"I do," said Irene, and then Janice followed, and another girl followed her, and the teacher called her name, "Gretchen! Two at a time, please!" I got up to join the guys on line. "Yes, Miss Manor," replied the girl. "All right, class, is everyone ready?"

"Yes, Miss Manor," they all replied. Miss Manor entered the coatroom, two more boys raced to the bathroom, and two other girls returned. Miss Manor left the coatroom and handed me a large red ball. "A kickball!" exclaimed a boy, and other boys added, "Righto!"

"That's boss!" said another, and Miss Manor asked, "Is everybody here?"

"Yes!"

"All right, let's go."

Outside, the girls went to the opposite end of the playground, where some played hopscotch. The boys chose two captains, and as the captains made their selections, the team members gathered to the right and the left, behind their captain by home plate. Not knowing formalities, I watched as events unfolded, and I was one of the last picked on a team.

The two captains faced a finger battle of odds or even for first-ups. I wasn't fully aware of the proceedings, so I watched and waited, and when the face-off was over, four of my teammates escorted me into the outfield, and they signaled with their hands to spread out. Their first man was up, and our pitcher rolled the ball home. The kicker quickly ran up to it and sent it sailing over my head, running from one base to another. "Sonny, go get the ball! Get the ball," my teammates shouted as the other

Piccolo Santino

two outfielders ran for the ball, and I figured I was supposed to chase after the ball, too. The opposing team was already cheering the scoring run when we retrieved the ball. My fellow outfielders tried to explain to me, and I just kept nodding my head yes. Then several kickers followed, and we were down by three runs with bases loaded and two outs.

The next guy kicked the ball high toward me again, and my teammate to my left was running toward me. In the excitement of catching it on the fly, I panicked, and the ball bounced off my chest right into my teammate's arms to make the final out.

While I waited for the kickball to be pitched to me, I reminisced about playing soccer back in Italy, and it was getting close to the end of recess time. We were down nine to seven with two men on base. My teammates were hoping for another hard kick as I had done my last time up. This time, I felt more ready than before since I now had a better feel for the ball, and as the pitcher rolled it home, my right foot met it with a good running start and a dead-on kick that sent the ball bouncing three times after the first landing into the girls' court in the opposite end of the field. Mark and Jay chased after it. "Hey, boys are not allowed on this side!" shouted out Janice at Mark. He responded, "We have to get the ball."

"Yeah, your boyfriend kicked the ball over here."

"What?" Some girls commented, and Janice's close friend Geena joked, "Oh, Janice, I think he really likes you!"

"Shut up, Geena!" Mark and Jay retrieved the ball and threw it back into the infield, everyone swarmed me at home base as the bell rang, signaling the end of recess. For the moment, the pang of being out of place and not fully belonging in this new environment became replaced with jubilation and complete euphoria.

Once inside, Miss Manor handed out a multiple-choice test. I found myself in a predicament, not understanding what I read, and arbitrarily checked off some of the choices. I noticed that my neighbor Jeffrey left himself wide open, and I tried to copy him. To avoid any suspicion, I also glanced behind me to my left a few rows back at Janice, hoping to catch her looking up so I could sneak a smile. Miss Manor saw my wandering

Piccolo Santino

eyes and very politely said while pointing down at my desk, "Sonny! Look down at your own paper, please!" I didn't understand all of her words, but I felt her message, and Janice did look up long enough to catch my smile. During all that eye probing, I was able to also copy one answer from Jeff. The test was a struggle, a battle I felt ill-equipped to fight. "Children, you have forty minutes left before lunchtime."

I did understand minutes and lunch and looked up at the clock, and then I looked to my right, and Chris quickly put his left arm over his test paper. To ease the frustration, I reminded myself that I could do really well on math tests since back in Italy, I was up to fifth-grade level math, but these written word tests seemed impossible for me. I longed for the familiarity of my old school, where I was confident in my abilities.

"Okay, children, if you are done, raise your hand, and I'll come by to collect your papers. The rest of you have ten minutes left." She walked around, stopped by me, and took my test paper as she said, "That's okay, Sonny."

During such disappointments, I looked forward to days of art class. Art relaxed me and disclosed endless possibilities in the American education system as it revealed an abundance we did not have back in Italy. The Italian curriculum did not include art, sports, or music. As much as I liked art class, I disliked music class since I could not visualize sounds from the music scale. However, my reserve or snobbery made it impossible for me to sing along with the class. I slowly conceded to crack the door open from within myself and participated by mouthing some words I understood.

Chapter 12 of Part Two
Outside and playing Damsel in Distress

After that first day of school, my lunch bag was now in conformity with everyone else's. However, I still felt stupid in class when others interacted with Miss Manor's questions, and I had to keep my thoughts in check as I waited for time to shift more of the English language into me.

Everyone got up to the sound of the lunch bell, and I followed as I was eager to go outside after eating. I meandered in the playground, looking for my friends, and watched as some boys tossed a weird-shaped brown ball around. At first, I did not understand how anybody could play with such an odd-shaped item. In my mind, that type of ball was useless for rolling or bouncing, and if you dribbled it with your hand or on your head, the pointed end would not only hurt, but you could not direct it like a soccer ball.

I waited outside by the diamond court to watch the fourth graders play kickball. I usually waited against the corner from the doorway so my friends Gary and Billy could find me on their way out. I was lifting my left foot to rest it against the building when this kid came up and spoke to me slowly and condescendingly. "Hey, kid! Are you a wop?"

By now, I was very familiar with the term "wop" since it was not the first time I was called that, but this was the first such bold ridicule I encountered. I stared directly into his wise guy eyes. He swayed with messy light brown hair from side to side, and I kept staring at him silently. He lifted his shoulders to his ears, then dropped them fast with stiff arms and clutched fists, leaned into my face, and said, "Well, are you a 'wop' or a 'guinea'?" I stood straight and stared directly at him as I crossed my arms. "Well! What are you?"

Another kid in a *Levis jacket* with matching pants walked over and said, "Bruce! What are you doing?" Bruce turned to him and said, "Hi, Randy! This kid here won't tell me if he's a 'wop' or a 'guinea.'" Looking pensive, Randy snapped and said, "Hey, I remember this kid from the lunchroom. He's the one with the smelly food. He put his right hand on Bruce's shoulder to clear some space between us and said, "Watch me."

Randy tilted his head sideways at me and said, "Hey kid, are you strong?" Since he didn't call me any of those names, I sensed they might go away if I played along. "Yeah!" He stared at me for half a second, then reached back in his mouth, spat on the ground, and, with an obnoxious tone, said, "Okay, let's see you pick that up." I remembered how that turned out for my friend Butch when he tried it on Artie once, so I pushed away from the wall and wiped the wet pavement with the bottom of my shoe, and lifted it to show him the damp sole. I said to him, "There! I picke rup!" He looked insulted and said, "Pick it up with your hands."

"No, you picke rup with you ass!" I answered back, and they looked at each other perplexed. In a severe tone, Bruce said, "Oh, you said a curse word. You can get into trouble for that!" Then Randy looked spitefully at me and said, "We're gonna go tell Mr. Johnson on you!" Bruce turned to Randy while moving away and said, "Come on, let's go tell Mr. Johnson."

I looked away and thought of them as stupid Americans and decided to go and look for my friends Gary and Billy around the corner, but I did not find them, so I returned to the same spot to wait there again.

Last month, Gary and Billy went as far as introducing me to a fourth grader named Ernesto, hoping we could converse in Italian. Unfortunately, Ernesto only spoke English, and from that day on, Ernesto would occasionally search me out in the playground or say, "hi" during any chance meeting in the hallway.

"Sonny! Hey Sonny!" I thought I heard Billy and Gary, so I looked around. "Hey, Sonny over here!" I turned around and saw both of my friends waving me over. I walked toward them, and we stopped to talk. "Hi Billy, hi Gary."

"Hey Sonny, Ernesto is over there. Look!" Gary said. "Come, we're playing tag."

"Okay, yeah," I said, and as we ran over, I noticed that the game had shifted over to the girl's side of the playground among a group with Janice, and my heart began pumping. Within the group was Allen, an

Piccolo Santino

obnoxious classmate known for taunting the girls. We got closer, and I noticed Allen walking closer to Janice; then Billy shouted, "Ernesto, we found Sonny."

"Hi, Sonny!" I caught sight of Allen from the corner of my eye, teasing Janice as Ernesto and I prepared to shake hands amid girls screaming, "Hey, give that back!"

"Allen, you better give it back to her." Allen interrupted our handshake by running between us. Then he turned and taunted Janice by waving a small purse. "Come and take it if you can!" Janice's friends yelled back at him, "You better give it back, Allen!"

Allen kept taunting the girls by mimicking their words as he waved the purse, "You better give it back." The girls counteracted as Janice looked on in dismay. "We'll tell Miss Manor if you don't give it back!" Allen then said sarcastically, "Oh, I'm scared." Then he sidestepped Ernesto and ducked Billy as they attempted to retrieve the purse. I coyly advanced between other kids and got close to Allen, and with a surprise attack, I lunged at him and was able to put my arms around his ribcage and squeeze him. "Stop! Stop!" he shouted, and the guys started laughing. "Here! Here, take it!" he said, and the girls cheered me on as Allen dropped the purse.

I pushed Allen away, quickly retrieving the purse. As I walked it over to Janice, I couldn't help but feel a surge of emotion. Her face lit up, her gratitude palpable. "Thank you, Sonny," she said, her voice a melody. I feared blushing within her closeness, so I quickly turned, my response a hurried, "You're welcome." Billy and Gary called me over and said, "Come on, Sonny, let's go play tag."

"Sonny, help!" I turned around and saw Allen reaching for Janice's purse again. I rushed over and chased him by zigzagging between other kids as Janice and her friends started clapping and jumping up and down. When I caught up to Allen, we wrestled to the ground. Ernesto and my friends cheered, and in the joyous atmosphere, Allen shouted, "I give up! I give up!" Ernesto helped me up, and as Allen walked away, I saw Gary and Billy talking to Janice. Then Ernesto said, "You won, Sonny, you won!" Gary said, "Come on, guys, let's play tag now."

Piccolo Santino

We walked away about ten feet, and as Billy came over, we were joined by three other boys. Then Billy said, "Sonny, Allen is over there again. Look!"

As the routine continued, I found myself growing more confident. The staged confrontations had become a game, a ritual in the playground. I knew they were staged for entertainment, but I enjoyed the feigning. The guys cheered, Janice and her friends looked on, and I basked in the attention. These games, this attention, it all contributed to a swelling of my self-esteem, a show of emotion one day on the school bus.

I was always too shy to sit near Janice on the school bus, and when I saw the empty seat behind her, I was immediately drawn and sat down. I then found that being so close to her and not having the language skills necessary to convey sweet thoughts disturbed my newly found confidence. She was sitting with her friend Geena, and the two kept whispering words I could not understand, but as they looked back at me during each whispering, I felt cupid arrows darting at my chest. Then Geena asked me, "Sonny, do you love Janice?" I understood that and quickly nodded, "Yeah!"

Just as fast as I blushed, they sank into their seat. Then Janice looked up and, with vibrant blue eyes, showed me her innocent smile. This was the closest I ever looked into her face, and I began feeling trapped by my lack of words and confined since we weren't able to play our usual game of damsel in distress here on the bus. I kept staring into her eyes, and the blue of the Mediterranean flashed inside my head. I heard the Italian songs on the deck of the *MS Giulio Cesare*. Suddenly, without warning, the power of music took over me, and I found myself singing *Volare*. "Volare, oh, cantare, oh. *Volare, oh, cantare, oh.* I'm flying, oh, singing, oh." Geena turned to Janice and said, "He's singing in Italian to you, Janice!"

"Oh no, wow!"

"*Volare, oh.*" I'm flying, oh." Since the aisle seat had been vacated earlier, I slid over to be at a better angle to face Janice as she pressed her body against the window, lowered her head, and lifted her eyes to me.

Piccolo Santino

Then I heard the bus driver. "Quiet down, you!" He was mad, but I was encouraged by Janice's smile, and so I continued. "*Volare! Oh, cantare, oh, nel blu dipinto di blu, felice de stare lassù.* I'm flying! Oh, singing, oh, in the blue, painted with blue, happy to stay so high up."

The driver yelled out again, "Stop it already!" Janice's eyes widened as she blushed, and it spurred me on. Then I heard someone shout back at the bus driver, "He can't understand you!" Then, another kid said to the driver, "He just came here from Italy." In complete euphoria, I continued singing. "*E volavo felice piu n'alto del sole.* I was flying, flying happily higher than the sun."

"Stop it, or I'll throw you off the bus!" Janice looked straight at me with eyes moistened and a grin from ear to ear, and her friend Geena whispered to me, "Sonny, she really likes it!" At that moment, I found new courage and let it all out. "*Volare! Cantare!* I'm flying! I'm singing!" I felt the bus stop fast, and the driver's voice got up close. "That's it!" The driver put his hand on my shoulder while shouting in my ear, "You're off the bus! Get out!" He lifted me off my seat, escorted me to the exit, and shut the door behind me. From outside, I watched Janice's smiling face ride away as I collected my bearings for the walk home.

Valentine's Day was an unknown holiday to me back in Italy, and that year, in third grade, I received almost as many cards as the girls in the room. Of course, when I saw how they all signed their cards, I thought all the girls were in love with me. Janice was the one who loved me the most. I saved all the cards for about a month. During the first week, I looked at them every night. After a month or so, I began to trash them selectively.

A short time afterward, one night while we were all watching television, the phone rang, and Ma, since we now were becoming Americanized, we no longer called her Mamma, but amongst us siblings, we referred to her as "ma" or "Mom," ran to answer the phone. "Allo?" Ma said, and the voice on the other end spoke English. Ma could not understand, so she kept repeating herself, hoping the other person would start speaking Italian. "Allo? Allo?" Feeling defeated, after a short

Piccolo Santino

silence, she called Martina and said: "Martina, come here and see who it is." Martina took the phone as she whispered to Ma, "*Chi è?* Who is it?"

"*Una Americana.* An American girl," responded Ma as Martina placed the phone in her ear and spoke, "Hello?"

"Hello, can I speak to Sonny?"

"Okay." Martina let the phone hang by the cord, came over to me by the couch, and said, "It's for you. It's a girl!" I was taken by total surprise, and everybody's eyes turned from the television toward me. I walked into the kitchen, raised the phone to my ear, and said, "Hello."

I listened with curiosity and trepidation as the girl said, "Hi Sonny, this is Janice. Would you like to come to my birthday party on Saturday?" I thought to myself, *"Now what?"* I completely blushed inside, thinking that everybody would make fun of me. My entire family, sisters and brothers, will have a field day laughing at me. They will all tease me forever. I feared Ma and Daddy would even tell their friends, and I'd never hear the end of it. This could be the same as if I had confessed to Father Cinquemano about Lola in Italy. Now, my family could divulge my secret to the whole world. Feeling trapped, worried, and scared, I quickly hung up.

The weather was cold, and we weren't outside as much anymore. The fight games were gone like dust in yesterday's wind by springtime. After that phone call, my feelings encased themselves like a cocoon. I tucked in a duffel bag that dragged alongside me for a while. Since I was gaining a better understanding of English, I decided to improve my grades. One Day, Miss Manor gave an example of where to place the stress when saying the word "Because." She explained that if one emphasizes the wrong syllable, it would sound foreign, and she sounded it out as Beka ŌŌ se. My ears widened as it sounded Italian, and from that day on, I began to make significant improvements on spelling tests, a personal growth that I am proud of.

Some guys tried resurfacing the fight games when the weather warmed up without mentioning Janice's name. But it all had lost meaning for me, and I walked away. At the end of the school year, my report card

Piccolo Santino

showed a significant disappointment in most subjects, except math and Spelling. Despite the weight of these disappointments, the perseverance and grit I developed kept me steadfast, motivating me to continue my improvement journey.

Piccolo Santino

Chapter 13 of Part Two
Going to work early in life

In the summer of '59, Uncle Vito took me to work with him almost daily. Although I was eleven, according to Daddy, I was twelve. Martina explained that traditional Italian customs considered the time of conception as well. Therefore, Uncle Vito saw an opportunity to test my value for his possible gain. After completing work early, we stopped in the contractor's office to pick up his check, and I witnessed how the contractor questioned Uncle Vito about his asking price for an upcoming job. "Vito, why are you asking so much this time around?"

"Well, I gotta pay my worka, Mr. Geensbur."

"What do you mean?"

"I needa help to mixa the cement and to carry the bricks on the scaffold."

"Yeah, but you've done this kind of job before by yourself."
I could sense that Uncle Vito was feeling challenged. "But I gotta a helpara with me now."

"You got a kid with you, for Christ's sake. Vito! Don't tell me you're paying him a full salary!" Then he opened up, probably because he believed I would not understand what he was saying. "Would you, Mr. Gheensbur? He's ma sister's boy; she's got seven kids."

"I can't believe it, but…"

"Wooda, you do-a that to-a yoo family?"

"Okay! Okay! Just this one time."

"Thank you, Mista Greensburg."

The summer flew by, and of course, I never saw any pay from Uncle Vito, but I did gain a little bulk and muscle for a kid of eleven, and about two weeks into the fourth grade, Daddy arranged for me to go and work with him on Saturday. Daddy didn't drive, but since he was considered the most reliable by his fellow workers, someone always had a ride for

Piccolo Santino

him. It was Saturday morning before eight, and there was no pressure to be at work at any specific time. Then, a horn sounded outside, and Daddy led the way. I carried the brown lunch bag Ma had packed for us earlier, and Daddy brought his carpenter's hammer.

We boarded a red Ford pickup that was waiting outside. The driver exclaimed, "Hey Santino, you're going to work, too?"

"Yup!" I exclaimed as I smiled and slid into the middle of the seat. Sonny was Daddy's best friend, with the same name as mine. He was a thin man of average height with two spiked teeth in front and looked in his early forties. I had met him a few times before, once when Sonny helped us move and a few times when he dropped Daddy home from work. He spoke English to me now, but he and Daddy always spoke Italian. "Wait until you see the yard, Bart!"

"Why, when I left yesterday, it wasn't bad."

"They came in with two more loads after that."

"Where did they dump it all?"

"Right up to the gates, then Leo made me go back for another load."

"Another load! What you do with it?"

"I dumped it between the gates, and it's all sticking out onto the sidewalk."

"How we gonna work?"

"We'll get it done. We got Santino here with us, and the two uncles are coming."

"They're not much help."

"Yeah! Alice said he's coming too, but not until after ten. He probably went out drinking last night." I turned toward Sonny and asked him, "Ellis, the Sicilian guy?" Sonny shouted with laughter as I avoided stuttering, "He carried our trunk up the steps all by himself!"

"Sicilian? Bart, he's making the colored guy Italian now!" He rubbed my head, "Mom said he was a Sicilian!" They laughed as he pulled up alongside the curb to number 99 on a small corner building with a fence around the yard. Shocked at the amount of lumber dumped between the gates, Daddy exclaimed, "Olee Shettah! How are we going

Piccolo Santino

to get inside?

"We gotta work our way in, that's all," exclaimed Sonny as he and Daddy got out of the truck. I followed, and then Daddy said to Sonny, "You got an extra hammer for my son? I didn't have one home." Sonny flipped the seat forward, showed me two hammers, and said, "Which one?" I pointed to the bigger one and said, "That one."

"What?" he exclaimed loudly, and Daddy turned around as Sonny told him. "Hey Bart, your son says he wants the big hammer."

"Give it to him. We need the help."

"Now, I gotta make my way to the shanty for another hammer."

"Be careful," Daddy said as Sonny carefully climbed over the heap of lumber littered with dried cement and various nails sticking out. Amongst other debris, such as tarps, buckets, and other miscellaneous construction items, I could not identify. I couldn't see over the top to get a view of the inside part of the yard. Daddy told me in Italian, "Son, you work over here and start banging out nails. Remember, you don't have to kill yourself."

As I made my first extraction, I felt a surge of accomplishment. I placed the head of a thick nail in the hammer's teeth, yanked the hammer toward me, and heard the nail land on the sidewalk as it flew off my hammer. From then on, I became very focused and moved along with a total commitment and indiscriminate attitude about which boards to pick up. "Look out, kid!" yelled Sonny from the considerable heap. He threw down two crowbars and another hammer and then carefully descended. "Bart, there's a little room inside to snake around and put away the clean stuff once we break through."

"Va bene." Daddy said, and then Sonny pulled a sawhorse from on top of the heap, placed it by me, and said, "This is yours, kid!"

"Thanks, Sonny." I grabbed a pine board about six feet long and eight inches wide, then laid the part with the nails on the sawhorse for leverage. I carefully whacked down the sharp points of three nails, flipped them over and yanked them out, checked the rest of the board, and threw it down on the sidewalk behind me. I used three blows to drive another nail through a two-by-four, flipped the wood over, and yanked

Piccolo Santino

the nail out by the hammer's teeth. In one fast, hard pull of the hammer, another nail flew in the air on top of Sonny's truck, and he yelled, "Hey, watch it, kid!"

"I didn't mean that!"

"Okay, otherwise you'll have to walk home!" Sonny yelled in a kidding tone. The next nail was bent flat on the wood, so I positioned the nail between the hammer's teeth toward me and pulled down on the handle. The nail lifted halfway enough for me to trap it in my hammer's teeth sideways and bend it straight up. I whacked it through with a couple of hard hits. I flipped the board over and extracted the nail with another fast yank. It all became reminiscent of my first experience refurbishing nails for Master Santino. Those memories, so deeply personal and connected to my journey, began to enhance my excitement. I compared how I banged nails out of the wood and discarded them here in America to picking nails from a bucket and slamming them into reusable form back in Italy.

As I moved on to other boards, the excitement swirled and climbed to newer heights, surpassed by a growing clearing between the cyclone gates that enabled us to snake our way inside and carry the cleaned lumber to its proper bin area. Then Sonny stopped me as I was about to move a few clean boards through the clearing. "No, no. You keep working here. I'll put stuff away."

"Oh, okay." I returned to extracting nails, and resorted to using a crowbar on a stubborn nail. The sun had been growing beyond warm since the uncles had arrived. One of the uncles looked over to me, and the heavyset named Basilio asked me, "Is there another sawhorse here?"

"I don't know."

"Where did you find that one?" I said, "Sonny found it."

"Where?" I pointed behind both brothers into the pile of lumber and said, "Look there." The other uncle, Ciro, responded while throwing his left hand up in the air, said, "Yeah, but we gotta do a sack-full of work to get it." I grabbed a clean, long two-by-four, and, afraid of stuttering, I kept choosing a few short words and said, "Look here." I then carefully propped the two-by-four inside the heap by the trapped sawhorse and said

Piccolo Santino

to Basilio, "Push up!" I pulled on the protruding leg of the horse but could hardly budge it. Then Ciro helped, and with a few tugs and Basilio pushing up some more, we freed the sawhorse. "Bravo! Bravo, Tino." they both exclaimed as Daddy and Sonny returned from inside, and both asked, "What happened?"

"*Niente.* Nothing, we just pulled out this horse from the bottom." Ciro responded in a much-wilted tone, Daddy jokingly said, "Did he bite you?" Ciro laughed and said, "Now, how can a sawhorse bite?" Sonny quickly snapped, "With sharp nails!" We all laughed. In their forties, the fat and skinny duo arrived earlier while we were sipping coffee and chewing on buttered rolls. We hoped to have the first load cleared out before our coffee break, but Sonny insisted on going for coffee as he got a thrill from the work rhythm I had developed and even teased me several times by asking me if I wanted a bigger hammer. I grabbed lumber without prejudice, cleaned it, and chucked it behind me into the heap, where Sonny collected it and hauled it away. The uncles worked close to each other and were very selective as they moved, worked very deliberately, and made strict use of their sawhorse.

Basilio sometimes came to me and used my sawhorse when he saw I was primarily working by holding the lumber upright and propping it to the ground. Daddy kept to his reputation, steady as always, never shirking from his work and stopping only for a nature break. I turned around and saw a tall man and a shorter, stocky guy walking in, and I said to Daddy, "Daddy, there is somebody over there."

"They're the bosses, Leo and Frank." Leo and Sonny made eye contact, and then Leo shouted out, "All right, get to work. The boss is here!" We turned around as Frank said, "Come on guys, come get a cold soda." Leo walked up to the uncles, and they each took a soda. Daddy told me, "Go on and get yourself a soda." I walked over, and Leo handed me a Coke, and Sonny said, "We need beer, not soda." Leo jokingly said, "There's no drinking on the job here!" Then Frank said, "Hey, Sonny. Did Ellis show up yet?"

"No, I didn't see him."

"He was supposed to come by with another load."

Piccolo Santino

"Another load? I thought he was coming to help."

"No, there was more stuff around the back of the building." Leo said, adding, "Yeah, I spoke to Larry before I left the site yesterday, and he didn't think they could finish loading everything." Frank said, "I guess he'll be here Monday morning."

"That's better," Sonny said. "This way, we'll have most of this cleared up today." Leo paced to his left, then looked over the remaining work and said, "Not bad. Looks like there's a lot of room now for the new load." Sonny looked at Leo. "We did all this since eight this morning." I saw Frank looking over my way from the corner of my eye. He said, "Hey, who's the new guy?" Sonny responded, "That's Bart's kid."

"Look at that kid swing that hammer, Leo." Frank said, and Sonny added, "Bart told me he punched his friend the other day, and the kid rolled backward halfway down his hallway in three tumbles." Both brothers were taken aback, "What?" Leo continued, "I guess they're not friends anymore."

"Yeah! Bart said if he hadn't seen it with his own eyes, he would not have believed it." Leo asked Daddy, "Bart, that's your son?"

"Sì, this is Santino." Daddy answered in Italian, Frank looked at Daddy and said, "Looks like your son already knows how to work!"

"Yeah, my wife told me he was an apprentice at a carpenter shop back in Italy." Leo kept staring keenly and said to his brother, "Maybe we should put him on to work here in the yard, Frank. What do you think? Maybe yeah!" Before Frank could answer, Leo turned to Sonny and asked, "Sonny, you think the kid wants a job?"

"Why not? But he's got school, you know." Leo responded, "It doesn't matter. He can work after school for a couple hours a day." Then Sonny exclaimed, "He would be good for making the spreaders for us." Frank looked at his brother Leo and said, "Yeah! That's right. That way, there'll always be a steady supply of the stuff." Sonny added, "And he could work on Saturdays too, right?"

"Yeah, why not?" both bosses exclaimed simultaneously, and then Leo called out to Daddy, "Bart!" Daddy didn't hear, so Leo called out, "Bart!" Daddy looked over to the three men, and Leo waved him over.

[323]

Piccolo Santino

"Come here a minute, Bart." Leo switched to Italian for Daddy, "Would your son like a job here?"

"*Per davvero?* For real?" Surprised, Daddy asked. Sonny looked at Daddy and exclaimed, "Why not? The kid really knows how to work!" Daddy turned his attention to Leo and Frank and said, "Sì! Why not then?"

"Yeah, he can make the spreaders for us after school," Frank said. "Sì? Okay, I'll talk to him." Daddy said. Frank asked, "How old is he?"

"He's twelve." Frank shook his head in disbelief. "Twelve?" Sonny chuckled, "So far, he's outdone both of your uncles." The casual banter lightened the mood. "That's all right, Frank. We can pay him off the books." Leo responded. Daddy went back to work as Leo calculated out loud, "Let's see, two hours a day and then eight hours on Saturday at a dollar an hour, that's eighteen dollars a week. What you think, Frank?"

"Yeah." Sonny interjected, "Why don't you just give the kid an even twenty?" Leo and Frank looked at each other, their agreement evident, and both said, "Yeah! I guess so."

"All right, when we come back later, I'll show the kid how to handle the table saw and explain about the spreaders." Leo said casually. Leo and Frank walked away to their car, and Sonny shouted out, "Don't forget the beer when you come back."

On the way home in the truck, Sonny said, "And they're gonna pay you twenty dollars a week, kid." He slapped me on my left knee, and Daddy smiled with pride, knowing that his son was stepping into the world of work.

Piccolo Santino

Chapter 14 of Part Two
Trouble can follow good work, too

As fourth grade unfolded with a new purpose, I couldn't wait to ride my bicycle to work. The bike, a girl's bike I acquired for cleaning out a relative's basement, was transformed into a boy's bike with my newfound resources. I installed a thick wooden dowel across the center, found some paint at work, and painted the crossbar to match the frame. Lillo rode on the crossbar on Saturdays as I took him to work with me. Sonny had suggested we rake up all the loose nails on the ground to prevent trucks from getting flat tires, and he also offered to bring the filled kegs to the scrap yard for a possible sale.

On Saturdays, Leo always came by around four to pay me, and since he saw Lillo raking the grounds, he gave him two dollars. When we got home, Lillo jubilantly waved his money in the air, which made Ma laugh heartedly. Daddy suggested I give my pay to Ma every Saturday, and in turn, he always made sure I had lunch money. Twenty dollars was a lot for a kid, and I figured Ma could put it to use better, so I gladly gave it. This growing independence and responsibility made me feel proud and mature.

Working began lifting my spirits to new heights, and once I established an ambiance inside myself, it became a silent language that spoke to those familiar with such vibes. This sense of fulfillment was a beacon, guiding me towards my future.

I was in class when Mr. Johnson called out to Miss Melnick as he held the door open, "Hi, Miss Melnick. You know why I'm here, right?" Mr. Johnson, in a grey uniform, was the school custodian with salt-and-pepper hair, a thick frame, and a chiseled friendly face. "Yes, Mr. Johnson. How many boys do you need today?" asked Miss Melnick. "I was able to round up four boys from the other classes, and I need three more." Miss Melnick looked around and pointed to Douglas, a husky boy in the class.

Piccolo Santino

Mr. Johnson abruptly interrupted her, pointed directly at me, and said, "I want him first." Surprised, Miss Melnick responded, "Well, Mr. Johnson! All right, Sonny, you, Douglas, and Johnny can go. No, wait, Johnny! You need to finish. Jimmy, you can go instead."

"All right, boys, come on, let's go." He waved us on and then turned to the teacher and said, "Thank you, Miss Melnick."

"You're welcome, Mr. Johnson," she said, and we followed Mr. Johnson into the hallway.

He led us downstairs into an empty cafeteria with all the tables folded and stacked in the rear, many chairs folded up and leaned against the wall or on dollies. "Okay, boys, I need you to set up the chairs here, make an aisle in the middle, and set them up straight down that way."

He motioned by holding his hands apart in front of his head and quickly cast them forward. I understood what he was saying compared to last year when I first had to learn by watching. Once I knew what to do, I zoned in and used my peripheral vision to move like a tornado. He liked watching me work last year as I outpaced all the other kids, and from that day on, whenever chairs needed a set up for our school assembly, he always made it a point of asking for me.

I saw students sitting in the front rows with teachers guiding other students down the aisle. I switched to hyper gear and worked on finishing up the last few rows around the other boys.

We finished just in time so we could sit down ourselves. In the process, I caught sight of Janice, and for a short moment, I reflected on our games of last year. The principal, Mrs. O'Rourke, turned to Mr. Johnson and said, "I'm sorry, Mr. Johnson. We didn't check with you first and waited until you boys were done."

"That's okay. I wasn't watching the clock." Then Mr. Johnson turned to us boys and said, "Thank you, boys, you did a good job!"

"Yes, boys, thank you. You did a great job!" said the principal.

After the assembly, we didn't have to rush and a couple of the boys from the chair crew introduced me to the skill of shooting paper clips with a rubber band, which I likened to shooting stones with my slingshot back in Italy. Since the school bus was late one day, I decided to use that

Piccolo Santino

opportunity to indulge in the newly discovered pastime. I kept a rubber band with a few paper clips in my pocket, and I figured I could always find more in school later. I aimed across the street with my first shot to see if it would go that far, but it only traveled halfway into the first lane. For my second shot, I decided to use two rubber bands, and that one carried over the yellow line. I figured I would aim higher for my next try, and just as I was about to shoot my last paper clip, I noticed unfriendly stares from two girls waiting for the bus as it was pulling up. I quickly put the rubber band in my pocket, picked my books up off the sidewalk, and boarded the bus.

The bus ride to school felt rushed as the driver sought to make time. We arrived behind the other buses at school, and everyone got to class on time. It was Friday, and I couldn't wait to settle into class since we were doing art in the morning. As soon as I sat down and lifted my desktop, I noticed the usual morning traffic to the teacher's desk and thought nothing of it, so I put my books on my desk and closed the top. I looked around to see what supplies other students placed on their desks so that I could do the same, and with my peripheral vision, I could tell the teacher was walking toward me.

I listened to her say my name. "Sonny!" This new teacher never seemed considerate of my situation like Miss Manor. Miss Melnick treated me like the other kids in class, making me feel expected to perform to their level. I had significantly improved from last year, but I wasn't equal to my classmates yet. Then, one day, I accidentally saw the test score of a classmate across from me. Although I had yet to receive a passing grade in history or English, I felt relieved that he had a 40% score on a test, and mine was 50%.

I turned my attention to Miss Melnick, who was standing next to me. She said, "Sonny, you have been called into the principal's office."

"Oh, okay."

"Here is your pass."

"Thank you."

"You need to go now."

Piccolo Santino

"Okay." I took the pass from her. On the way to the office, I wondered if my low grades attracted the principal's attention. The wooden door to the office is made of pine and stained to look like walnut. The top half of the door frame was a typical frosted glass panel with chicken wire embedded inside, which made it difficult to see clearly, but you could see blurred silhouettes of people moving like clouds in the ocean. I grabbed the doorknob and turned it slowly, and listened to the sound of the retracting latch as it clicked away from the striking plate screwed into the door frame.

Slowly, I pushed the door open, stepped inside, and turned my head back to close the door. I released my grip on the knob so the spindle inside would turn back and release the latch into the hole of the striking metal plate so it could rest inside the carved opening in the wood frame. I watched Master Santino once install a lock on a door, and I paid close attention to his every move and how he tested each step for the perfect function of the lock. I listened to the final click of the latch as it settled into place, and then I turned my head back and faced the older woman with grey hair standing behind a tall counter.

I timidly walked over, and she said, "Do you have your pass, young man?" I gave her the pass. She read it and sternly said, "Oh yes! Follow me." She walked out from behind the counter and said, "Come this way, please." I followed her down a short walk through an opened door and stopped at the principal's desk, "This is Mrs. O'Rourke, our Principal." She said. Mrs. O'Rourke inhaled while Mrs. Walker introduced me. "Mrs. O'Rourke, this is Sonny, the boy shooting paper clips by the bus stop this morning." I froze instantly. "Oh yes, thank you, Mrs. Walker." Mrs. Walker left and closed the door.

The principal got up from behind her desk and stared directly into my eyes with an apparent deliberate attitude as she walked over. Instantly, the pounds of red lipstick on her thin lips mentally set me in the wrong direction. It reminded me of the stories I had heard back home, where boys with older brothers in the military often talked about the days of the Roman Empire. The red lipstick, a symbol of power and seduction, the women used on their lips to signal the soldiers of their services from

Piccolo Santino

their balconies for the soldiers to visit after their victory parade.

Mrs. O'Rourke was a short, blonde, fair-skinned woman with a reddish tone to her complexion, either from her heritage or blood boiling this morning. She stopped less than arm's length before me, looked into my face head-on, and shouted without hesitation, "Do you like to ride in cars?"

I quickly realized one of the kids by the bus stop must have reported me to the office, and this was the first time I ever had to face the principal for anything. She didn't seem to know about my background. I began wondering if I could convince her that I didn't understand English and be able to walk away from this without a scathing. But then she talked to me like I was any other student in the school. Having been in America for only one year and made such an accomplishment, I fully understood what she said. To pretend otherwise would have been insulting. So, since riding in cars gave me motion sickness, I had to be completely honest, and I proudly answered, "No!"

She leaned into me with glaring eyes and shouted, "Well, I do!" This was in response to my confession that I didn't particularly enjoy riding in cars. She pointed to herself with vivid energy and stared me down as she waved her finger in my face, "And I don't want to get a flat tire while I'm driving because people like you shoot paper clips at cars!"

Perplexed by what my honesty had brought on, I wondered if I should have lied and said that I did like riding in cars to appease her, but then it might have gotten more complicated. I thought it better "this way" and to get it over with. "Furthermore!" She began poking at my chest with her index finger. "You could've hit someone in the face and poked an eye out."

My face remained sullen the entire time, and as she put her finger away, I looked down. "Do you understand?" I shook my head "Yes."
"What?"
"Yes."
"Yes, what?"
"Yes, Mrs. O'Rourke"

Piccolo Santino

"That's better! You may return to class now, and don't let me catch you shooting paper clips again!"

"Yes, Mrs. O'Rourke."

I left with my tail between my legs, returning upstairs to class. After the phone call from Janice last year, I was relieved that she was not in my fourth-grade class, but instead, I now had a secret crush on Miss Melnick and thought about her long, beautiful, dark hair hanging below her shoulders. She wasn't tall like Miss Manor, but she was more attractive in a different way. Miss Melnick told us about the American West or American folklore heroes such as Paul Bunyan and Pecos Bill. I secretly fantasized about her being a damsel in distress in the Old West in places like Dodge City or Tombstone, and I, as the hero, would rush to her rescue. I liked how she unknowingly mitigated my feelings for her by treating me with indifference about my handicap in the English language. Even though I was embarrassed when she scolded me for getting 50% on a social studies test, it compelled me to study harder.

I welcomed work as a means of escape from failures in school regardless of the fear I endured from the roaring motor sound of the DeWalt tabletop saw that I worked with. The fear was comparable to what I had encountered in Master Santino's machine room with the coffins. I thought I had control of this situation by holding my breath to avoid inhaling the hot smoke every time the blade met the stiff resistance of the knotty pine boards. I had to pull the carriage forward extra slowly since the blade was dull, and its fast revolutions melted the sap in the knots, which released hot smoke. Even though I held my breath, the heat still burned my nostrils.

"Aspettate! Aspettate! (He spoke to me in the plural sense) Wait! Wait!" Leo broke through the smoke as he walked into the doorway, and I quickly turned off the power saw with Leo shouting over the grinding halt. "The blade has to be changed." He waved his hands to clear the smoke before his eyes and said, "Anytime you need the blade changed, come inside the office and get one of us."

I didn't know how to tell him that it was difficult for me to go into

Piccolo Santino

the office, face those people in higher places, and then find the courage to speak. It all felt hopeless to me. It was easier for me to face the fear in this hut, accept the shrilling noise, inhale the smoke, and think the problem could be solved serendipitously.

Leo leaned over the bench with his tall frame and long arms. He grabbed a fresh blade hanging from a nail on the wall and went for the wrench. With his fingers, Leo gently examined the tips of the teeth and got another one instead. After a brief inspection, he chose it. He picked a blade with teeth designed with smaller gaps than the other saw. Made with prominent claw-like teeth and wider gaps. He unplugged the DeWalt unit and swiveled the motor carriage sideways for access to the blade.

Then he wedged a block of wood between the protective fender-like cover to hold the blade still so he could safely use the wrench to turn the locking bolt counterclockwise. Having removed the bolt, he maneuvered the old blade off and then guided the new one into place before screwing the bolt tightly in position. Last, he swiveled the carriage back to its original position. During his every movement, to avoid going inside the office for the next time. I took careful notice of all the steps, planning to do it myself.

"Basta! Tutto a posto! Finished! All set!" he exclaimed, adding, "I forgot to pay you Saturday." He handed me a twenty-dollar bill from his wallet, and I said, "Thank you."

"I was coming to tell you they need nine-inch spreaders for tomorrow."

"Okay, I-I-I'll make them."

"Just make a good batch today. You don't have to keep making them like the others. This batch is for a special job for tomorrow only."

"All right, Leo!"

"Let's see where you can put them so they can find them in the morning." I followed him down the wooden ramp from the hut to the three storage areas sectioned off by cinder blocks along the fence to the right. "Did you make those signs on the wall for the different sizes?"

"Yeah."

"How come nobody thought of that before?"

Piccolo Santino

"I don't know."

"All right, we have six, seven, and eight-inch. We don't have another bin section, but we don't need one. Why don't you dump the wheelbarrow in front of the six inch spreaders by the gate? They need to distinguish nine inches from six. Just leave enough space between the two piles." "Okay," I said, and he followed me back into the hut for the old blades he had set aside and said, "I'll get these sharpened for you."

"Thanks!"

As he left, I realized I liked speaking English better because I could learn more than if he spoke Italian. Besides, I started to understand most of what he said. I also noticed a nervous tick in his voice when he spoke Italian, no doubt due to his lack of vocabulary. But then he didn't know that I was afraid of talking to people, especially people in higher places; I could not see myself as equal to their level, so I looked down whenever I spoke and tried not to stutter.

I admired the workbench, with its thirty-inch width and an eight-foot stretch to the left for longboards, and a six-foot span to the right. I took the ruler, measured nine inches from the blade to the right, and nailed a wood block onto the tabletop. I then went outside, retrieved a mixture of used three-quarter-inch thick pine boards, and ensured they were free of any nails. Daddy explained why each spreader I cut had to always be uniform in size because they used them as wedges between wooden boards that formed the curb between the street and the sidewalk. He then explained that after the concrete sits inside the forms, the spreaders got removed, and if they were not uniform in size, the curb would have waves in its final shape. That was why I decided to nail down a block on the bench's surface away from the blade for quality control. Instead of just using a nail for a marker like the others had suggested.

With an empty wheelbarrow positioned to my right and a good supply of boards on hand, I slid the saw carriage back behind the cutting area, plugged the unit in, and set up my board on the bench, flush against the backsplash. I safely turned on the power, grabbed the saw carriage by its handle, and pulled it forward. The piranha-like teeth of this new blade erased all my fears, and the buzzing sound, like a swarm of angry bees,

Piccolo Santino

sliced the wood as if it were Papier-Mache. It was a powerful and exhilarating experience."

For starters, I cut off a half-inch piece from the raw end of the board because it wasn't straight. I slid the board up against the nine-inch control block and sawed my way through to the end of the board. The board had several splits down the center, and some spreaders split off lengthways, but it didn't matter because they only used part of the width. They always split them with an ax into one-to-two-inch widths anyway.

As I cut each piece, I threw it in the wheelbarrow and let the pieces overflow onto the floor until I was ready to bring them outside. Since I got paid tonight and lost some time changing the blade and listening to Leo, I felt obligated to stay a little later and fill two wheelbarrows.

Leo saw me coming out around six thirty, looked with approval at the hefty pile of spreaders, and commented that there were more than enough. During my bike ride home, I thought about a quote from Larry, a foreman I met recently: "Always give your boss a little extra. That way, if you leave, he'll always take you back should you ever need the job again."

I reflected on last year in third grade, when I was always overlooked for baseball unless they were desperate since I could not hit a baseball, and every time I swung the bat, I kept wishing it was kickball instead. Classwork was a series of continued failures in Social Studies, English, Science, and occasionally spelling tests. This year, however, during the final marking period, I had begun to climb out from the red zone on most tests and liked the encouragement from Miss Melnick, especially the day she brought in a guest art teacher who taught us to work in Cray-Pas.

I created a seascape with a giant marlin fish leaping against the horizon. She praised me for my silvery look around the fish and on the caps of waves. But then she scolded me after I let the praise go to my head and overworked the fish with unpleasant lines around it that spoiled its silvery look and the sea. I felt insulted by her scolding even though I still harbored secret feelings for her. But then, at the end of the school year, Miss Melnick announced that she was marrying the art teacher, and all my feelings for her disappeared.

[333]

Piccolo Santino

I stared at my final report card with satisfaction, as the two failing grades were by less than five points. I decided I could now look toward the fifth grade in America with better awareness.

In the summer of '59, seeing a parade pass in front of our house seemed fitting. President Eisenhower signed the statehood bill that made Hawaii our fiftieth state. As people gathered to the sound of the parade, I recollected some of the lessons about different states in America from Miss Melnick's class. That summer, I was now twelve, and it was also a busy time at the construction yard. The pay remained the same even though the work schedule was six days a week from 8:00 am to 4:30 pm. But as September arrived, I was filled with anticipation and hope, looking forward to the familiar routine of school.

Chapter 15 of Part Two
Fifth grade in America

Feeling freed from any emotional distractions, I thought I could learn in Miss Moran's fifth-grade class, and I started to enjoy the best confidence I'd had thus far in America. Art was quickly becoming an outlet of self-expression for me. I began to realize the potential from the abundance of supplies, courses, and opportunities readily available in the American school system. However, the culture shock was still a reality that posed some stiff challenges. I compared life at home to examples on television shows like *Leave It to Beaver* or *The Donna Reed Show*. I became envious of seeing children in America portrayed as able to consult their parents for guidance and have the freedom to express themselves. Regardless of television portraying an ideal situation, I understood the message.

However, I still felt bound by personal hang-ups and old ways that traditions and my father imposed upon me. His ongoing comments about education were that it was unnecessary for my sisters and that I should be out working at fourteen. Thankfully, his wishes were restrained by legal bounds that prohibited him from short-circuiting our education until we reached sixteen. His stance compelled me to try and absorb at whatever speed my teachers disseminated knowledge.

But school was not the sole dividing factor between Daddy and me. Along with learning to speak fluent English, a completely new culture devoured me and all the youth of America. A new movement was rising in the United States, guided by uncontrollable waves from television, music, and Hollywood, and a new political movement encouraged by the most charismatic political face in modern times, John F. Kennedy, further inspired by Martin Luther King Jr. and later Robert Kennedy.

Adults couldn't try to control or filter out any of their ideas from the new political minds. Kennedy's campaign slogan, "We can do better,"

Piccolo Santino

was not just a slogan to attract attention. He outlined ways the country could improve in foreign affairs, and we listened and became better educated. He didn't just talk words. He backed his words about civil rights with a phone call to Mrs. Coretta Scott King and pledged his support after her husband was arrested.

We were learning to think for ourselves with unbelievable energy stoked by John F. Kennedy. After the historic Kennedy-Nixon debates, record numbers of young people became interested in politics. Unlike today's mud-slinging, simple-minded political atmosphere, the political atmosphere forces us to look down on politicians. The 1960 presidential election created campaign teams in the fifth-grade classes. I needed help understanding a lot of what the candidates said on television. Still, our class discussions helped me better understand the energy and serious debates between Kennedy and Nixon. There was an undeniable aura about Kennedy. It was an atmosphere that portrayed real strength and quiet intellectual calm, stirring all existence with such youthful energy and charisma unmatched by anybody on television, in movies, or anywhere else.

In class, I joined the Kennedy election team and enjoyed doing various posters and signs to help promote J.F. Kennedy for president. I was elated when he won the school election, even if it was by a slim margin. Although I didn't pick Richard Nixon, I respected him for saying he would not accept the presidency if he won the Electoral College without getting the popular vote.

During the time we spent working on the campaign, I made a new friend, Klaus. He was a nerdy kid that others didn't want to hang around, but I liked learning from him. He appeared very forthcoming about not just politics but the cultural patterns that were surrounding us. Maybe others felt he was voicing mundane and trivial opinions, but I needed information to mold my artistic education. Then Klaus, who eventually became my best friend after school, told me about the PT 109 song by Jimmy Dean, and after I saw it on the news, I rushed to the store and bought my first record.

Piccolo Santino

Along with Miss Moran's teaching methods, I also appreciated the intellectual attitude of my classmates. I especially liked the response from Mark, a bright, quiet kid who sat behind me. One day, I surprised myself when I raised my hand to volunteer the answer to the teacher's question. However, I was more surprised that I didn't stutter. When she said my answer was wrong, a kid named Scott sat across from me and said, "Ah-ha! You said the wrong answer." Mark then came to my defense by saying, "So what? You didn't say anything." I wasn't disturbed by any of it. Instead, I smiled at Mark as other kids nearby chuckled, and when the teacher revealed the correct answer, I felt rewarded by the actual outcome.

Later that week, Miss Moran called on me to read out loud, but it was then that my stuttering and nervousness returned, causing her to choose another person to read and curtail my session. However, the school also had a particular reading class for students below their grade level. That class was held in the lunchroom or the gymnasium twice a month by a specific visiting instructor, Mr. Davis. It surprised me that so many students attended that course, including two other students from my class, Mary Jane and Scott. The session addressed proper pronunciation and reading comprehension, and after two lessons, Mr. Davis spoke to me individually about my stuttering. "Sonny, I think you would benefit greatly if your parents took you to see a specialist for your stuttering problem."

"Where would I go?"

"There is a specialist I could recommend to your parents. They would need to drive you there."

"My parents don't speak English, and we don't have a car."

"All right, I will speak with the school principal about it."

When we returned to class, Miss Moran explained a particular assignment requiring us to choose a state in America and write to its chamber of commerce for information on their state flower or state bird. We were to write a special report about it. I was excited when I saw my name on a big envelope the day it arrived from Maine. I loved the idea of corresponding by mail, and since it was all free and the address to the

Piccolo Santino

chamber of commerce in any state was easy to figure out, I decided to write to other states just for fun.

I liked going to *F. W. Woolworths* for all my school supplies since it was easy to find things in that store, and everything was affordable. I also enjoyed stopping at the lunch counter for an ice cream soda. For my report, I purchased various sheets of colored construction paper and some colored pencils I wanted to use with crayons I already had. I drew a pine cone hanging from a branch and rendered the brownish-white pine cone with green pine needles against a light beige sheet of construction paper for the cover sheet. Although it's the state flower, it is technically not a flower but instead called a strobilus. Maine is the only state to have an official state strobilus.

After lunch, many of us boys usually hung around the bicycle racks. Some guys watched or talked to the girls returning from lunch at home. But mostly, it was a place to hang out or trade baseball cards. "I got two of Moose Skowron to trade." Then I said, "Wow! I have three Tom Tresh cards and two of Yogi Berra."

"I'll take Yogi Berra. I don't want Tresh."

"Okay, what will you give me?"

"I'll give you Willie McCovey."

"Is he good?" I asked since I was not familiar with many players. Suddenly, a kickball landed on me, and I felt my head sink. "Are you all right, Sony?" everyone shouted. I shook my head in bewilderment and said, "Yeah, it didn't really hurt."

"What?" Everyone shouted in disbelief. "It didn't hurt?"

"No!" I repeated. Klaus exclaimed, "Sonny, your head sunk below your shoulders!"

"I don't know, I feel okay!"

"Wow," everyone responded, and we returned to trading cards.

"Ricky, you sure you don't want Tom Tresh and wait? Here's an extra Bobby Richardson?" I said, and Ricky responded, "No, I already have them both." A voice called out as a kid walked over a short distance from us. "Hey, you guys wanna play dodgeball. We can use more people."

Piccolo Santino

"Yeah, we'll play," three of the guys said.

"Come on, Sonny, you can throw hard!" said Klaus, and I agreed as Klaus continued talking. "Yeah, I'm in, man."

Three others followed Klaus and me as we raced to the playing field and took sides. "Klaus, you play on this site. We need people. You too, Tommy, and we need one other guy. Sonny, you and Ricky go on the other side." Klaus spoke out. "When Sonny throws the ball, my arms burn badly when I try to catch it. I'm moving back some more, man!"

"Okay, let's start," shouted Bruce as he readied and threw the ball toward me. I wondered what would happen if I punched the ball instead of catching it. Hence, as the ball came toward me, I poised myself to punch it back at a slight angle from the side to avoid jamming my wrist, and upon impact, the ball sailed back and caught a kid by surprise on the side of his shoulder, and he had to dance to stop from falling. "You all right?" I yelled out. "Wow! How'd you do that?"

"Man! How does he do that?"

"I told you guys he can throw hard, man," said Klaus as he turned to his teammates with his arms stretched out to his sides and bobbing his head up and down. "He didn't throw the ball that time. He punched it."

"Yeah, I know that, but I'm just saying that was hard too!" The warning bell rang, and everyone scattered to rush back inside.

After school, I replaced a worn-out baseball card with a new Tommy Tresh card on my bicycle and attached it to the clothespin on the front tire frame. I listened to the slow rattle as I walked my bike out of the parking lot. A voice yelled at Klaus, "Hey kid, walk your bicycle in the school lot!" I turned to Klaus and said, "Hey, Klaus, the safety patrol guy is talking to you."

"I don't see anybody."

"He's coming over here."

"Hey, kid, get off your bike now!"

"Oh, beat it, man. I'm riding slowly. Can you dig it?" The patrol kid raised his voice, "Get off, or I'll report you to the principal's office."

"Yeah! Yeah! I dig it, man." Klaus got off, and walked alongside me

Piccolo Santino

and mumbled, "Man, what a dick!"

"What did you say, kid?"

"Nothing, Clyde, I'm hip, man, I'm hip."

"My name is not Clyde! You watch it, or I will report you!"

"Okay, beat it, man. I was joking!"

"You better shut up, Klaus," I said as a car slowly drove past us. "Hey, you're supposed to walk your car out of the school lot," I said, and the safety patrol kid walked away with contained laughter. But Klaus couldn't hold back and let out a hardy laugh as we followed the car out, then rode our bikes with the rattle of baseball cards against the spinning bicycle spokes on our way home. Klaus called over the rattling baseball cards, "Sonny, are you sure you're okay from before? When that kickball landed on your head?"

"Yeah, I don't feel anything wrong."

I began hanging out with Klaus at his house, and we would play games like *Monopoly, Life,* a card game of war, or shoot darts in his basement. One day, he had the screwy idea of shooting his BB gun at cars from his basement window. I refused to participate, and after he hit a vehicle, the driver stopped and came knocking at the door. Klaus did a song and dance and convinced his dad a pellet ricocheted outside, off the metal target through an open window in the basement. It took a long time and a lot of tough-talking, but the driver finally convinced his wife to leave. But not without much griping and hesitation, as she kept insisting she was looking right at Klaus, aiming his gun at their car.

Despite some isolated peculiar ideas, Klaus did help me see the value of patience as we hung out together. "You have to follow the directions exactly."

"Oh, I just look at the picture and glue pieces together as I go."

"That's why your model doesn't look right," he told me as I showed him my 1956 *Austin Healy* model car assembly. "I get confused with the directions."

"You have to follow step by step."

Piccolo Santino

"Can you help me? I have another one that I bought."

"Let me see!" I reached up into the closet and showed him the unopened box. "Oh, keen! You got the *57' T-Bird?*"

"Yeah, I liked the picture on the box. That's why I bought it."

"I gotta leave, or my mother will worry. Come on back with me. We can put it together at my house."

"All right." As he explained the words I didn't understand, I was then able to follow the instructions on my own and set aside the glued pieces to dry before assembling sections. "Keep your head back when you use the glue."

"What for?"

"It's not good to inhale airplane glue."

"What does inhale mean?"

"To breathe in."

"Why?"

"It's bad for you. It can make you sick."

"Really?"

"Yeah, that's how addicts get started."

"Addicts?"

"Yeah, you can become addicted and can't stop."

"So that means you need it all the time?"

"Yeah, some people get evil and end up in jail."

"I only put my head down so I could look closer."

"You can look close after the parts dry, or you might turn into a beatnik."

"A beatnik?"

"Yeah, a bum, with a long beard and dirty clothes, on the streets. They live in a village in New York City."

"They're called beatniks?"

"Yeah! Some have long beards and are also called winos."

"Mary Jane ducks her head under her desktop a lot and licks a tube like this. When she was absent and the teacher showed a slide show, I sat at her desk to see the screen better. I lifted her desktop and saw three

Piccolo Santino

tubes of airplane glue all used up."

"Did you tell Miss Moran?"

"No!"

"We should. Mary Jane hasn't been to school for a while."

"Maybe that's why, you think?"

"Could be."

I liked being patient by following the step-by-step assembly directions, especially since they became more evident. I also became attracted to comic books and discovered new ways of corresponding through the various advertisements. To make money, I enrolled in a vegetable and flower seed-selling plan. I tried going door to door, but the sales could have been better.

To my amazement, Ma's Italian friends were all buying up my supply, and I got the bonus with my third order of seeds, an 8mm plastic crank-type movie projector. The prize included small cartoon reels and two of the Three Stooges. Once I exhausted the third supply, I sold a healing salve. I could not believe how easy it was to get a response from ads in comic books, and when I saw an opportunity to get a bunch of books for joining a club, I responded.

My first book was *Treasure Island*, and after I started reading it, I got frustrated and tried reading it out loud, hoping it would help me understand it better. I discontinued corresponding, but more books arrived, followed by new bills. Thinking that ignoring them would stop the bills, I tore them up as fast as they came until I received a threatening letter.

I showed it to Klaus, and he explained that he did the same thing once, and his father wrote back, threatening to sue them for dealing with a minor. Since such a letter was beyond Daddy's capacity, I decided to send their letter back with cash in the envelope, and luckily, I have yet to hear from them again. In the future, I will be cautious with any other correspondence.

The class asked Miss Moran about putting on a school play one day.

Piccolo Santino

A play about the Puritans would be produced. At first, I shunned the idea of participation, but I felt at ease when I learned I could be an Indian without any speaking parts. On the day of the play, Ms. Moran made a band of feathers from colored paper to wear around my head. Some kids suggested I should have stripes painted on my body and face. So, while Miss Moran was doing the painting, I spoke. "Miss Moran, I started selling vegetable and flower seeds from something I found in my comic book."

"That's nice, Sonny. Did you come up with the idea?"

"Yeah!" And she stopped me short. "The word is yes!"

"I mean, yes. When I saw that I could get an 8mm movie projector, I sent away for the kit."

"You mean you sent away for the kit."

"Oh yes, right. Past tense."

"That's right, Sonny. You are learning." She completed painting two red stripes on my face and one on my forehead. "And how many packs of seeds will you have to sell for the projector?"

"I don't remember, but I sold a lot already."

"Okay, this might feel cold on your chest." She painted three red stripes across my chest. "Oh, that's okay. I'm going door to door after school to sell more today."

"Well, good luck to you, Sonny." I looked down as she painted three vertical stripes on my chest and stomach. "Thank you," I said. "There you are, looking like a real Indian."

"Since I am Italian, should I say 'ciao' instead of how?"

"That's funny, Sonny!" she exclaimed with heavy laughter, and the few other kids spread the joke among each other. "You don't have a speaking part in the play, Sonny. Remember?"

"Oh yeah." She looked at me. "I mean, yes!" My role was to walk on stage as a friendly Indian among the gathering Pilgrims, and I was glad others had all the speaking parts. Mr. Eisenberg, the teacher across the hall, stepped into the doorway and yelled, "Ciao, Pilgrims." We burst out in laughter as we turned toward him. "Word travels fast, Miss Moran.

Piccolo Santino

The rest of your class is already downstairs."

"Thanks, Mr. Eisenberg. We've just finished. Come on, kids."

I had already learned to sign Mom's name at home so I could sign my report card since it had all culminated into a meaningless formality, and it hurt to hear my parents refer to my artwork as *"scarabocchi"* scribbles. But when their friends visited and inquired about my progress, they readily expressed interest and called on me to show my work as they conversed in Italian. "And are you going to let him finish school?"

"Oh, no, Gummah. He should go to work and make money."

"In this country, they could end up in school well beyond the age of marriage."

"Especially girls."

"Ah, sì!"

"For real!" Laughter broke out among the two visitors. And Daddy said, "They are better off quitting school at sixteen." I interrupted as I retrieved my work, "But Daddy! Why should I do that? You brought us into this country so we could do better." Daddy responded, "Yes, and isn't being a truck driver better than farm life?"

"But in America, I can do what I want." Arrogantly, Daddy said, "Then I'm gonna do what I want, too." All laughed heartily, and then Daddy continued, "Tomorrow, I'll just take strolls, go into bars, and come home when I want." I looked toward my sister for help. "Daddy, that's not what he means. He means in America, there are better opportunities than working in construction. After all, you did bring us here for better opportunities." They all stared at each other in interrupted thought, and one of the visitors said. "Your children make a valid point, Gumbah." Daddy thought momentarily and said, "In that case, we'll have to wait and see."

Mr. Davis informed me that instead of attending his class, I would be going to the speech therapist he recommended to the school. The school arranged payments for the therapist as well as the taxi rides. On those days, an hour before school ended, Miss Moran would send me to the office where the taxi driver met me, and we would make the twenty-minute trip to the speech therapist. I usually got carsick, so I remained still in the backseat during a short ride that felt like forever. Once we reached the destination, the driver came in with me and presented papers from the school. Then, as I was shown into another room, the driver said, "Go on, Sonny, I'll be waiting for you outside in the taxi when you finish."

"Okay," I said to the driver while he turned away. I entered the small room and saw a man in his mid-to-late thirties with glasses and a friendly face sitting behind a small desk lamp at a mahogany desk. He pointed to the chair with a wide armrest in front of his desk and said, "Sit right there, Sonny." I sat down and looked at the small brown leather couch to my right, which had a corner table occupied by a few magazines and a lamp. Next to that was a small upholstered beige chair. I turned to him as he put the papers down and introduced himself: "Hi, Sonny. My name is Mr. Perry. I am a speech counselor, and I understand that your school has arranged for you to come here."

"Yes, and they pay for the taxi, too."

"Well, that's convenient, right?"

"Yeah."

"I should tell you that Mr. Davis has told me about you, but I would like to know what you experienced in the class that made him feel you could benefit from me."

"Yeah, it's just that I think because every time I read out loud, I always get stuck on a word."

"I see. And does that happen only when you read?"

"Sometimes no."

"When are some of the other times you get stuck on words?"

"When I talk to certain people, I get scared."

"What about at home?"

"Yeah, when I get mad and stop talking."

"What about with your friends?"

"No. With my friends, I'm mostly okay, especially now that I know more English."

"You say most of the time. What about the other times?"

Piccolo Santino

"I stop to breathe, and then I'm okay."

"All right, I tell you what I want you to try. You will read for me, and what I want you to do when you get stuck on a word, as you say, I don't want you to try to stop the stuttering. Instead, I want you to continue stuttering on purpose. Then you will come to feel you don't have to stutter anymore. At that point, you can switch and continue reading normally. Okay?"

"Yeah, okay."

"All right. Here's a book. Start reading on any page; remember if you get stuck. Do it on purpose until you have control, and then stop it when you feel ready."

I started reading, and I could not fool myself or the therapist when I got stuck. I felt my face blushing, and the more I tried to stop it, the worse it got. The therapist was wise: "No, Sonny, don't try to stop it. I want you to continue stuttering on purpose, and then you will gain control. Go on." The second time, I felt even more self-conscious, and my lack of comfort did not allow me to intentionally stutter.

Mr. Perry advised, "Sonny, let's try this. I want you to practice stuttering on purpose right from the beginning, then switch to normal reading, right?"

"Yeah, okay."

"Now do that a few times, and if the stutter happens naturally, take control by stuttering on purpose, okay?"

"Okay." I had to overcome the self-consciousness of stuttering intentionally, and listening to myself made me want to blush just the same. But I had to learn to ignore that initial feeling of shame so that I could now have the courage to stutter on purpose. As he advised, I began reading with an intentional stutter. "That's it, Sonny. You are in charge. Now stop it and read normally." I liked his encouragement, and at that very moment, I stumbled naturally. He said, "Keep it going, Sonny. Take over and do it on purpose. You will see that you can stop it when you want."

I was amazed at how right he was and sensed an internal glow with my success. Still, it was just as challenging to remember to switch from

Piccolo Santino

the natural stutter to an intentional one. During the half-hour session, I soon became anxious for each new trial to apply Mr. Perry's theory. I slowly got used to the novel idea of stuttering on purpose and was ecstatic over how well the speech therapist's technique worked. "Okay, Sonny, I think this is enough for today."

"Okay, I'm hip." He laughed and said, "That's funny! You're hip. Are you trying to be a beatnik?"

"No, I hear kids in school talk like that."

"All right, Sonny. Remember to take over and stutter on purpose until you are ready to let go, even if you stutter when you talk. All right?"

"All right."

"Okay, Sonny, I'll see you next week."

"Okay, bye, Mr. Perry."

I left his office and saw the taxi driver seated in the waiting room. "Hi, Sonny! I got bored sitting in the car. You all finished for the day, buddy?"

"Yeah!"

During the ride home, I didn't dare to put his theory to the test at home or school. It felt embarrassing enough to blush during a natural stutter, but intentionally stuttering with a voluntary blush felt too demeaning, so I considered trying it in private. But then I remembered when I read parts of *Treasure Island* in private, I didn't stutter even once. So, I resigned to a "wait and see" attitude, feeling that I could best achieve success with Mr. Perry, so I looked forward to my next session.

"Hi, Sonny! Come in and sit down."

"Hi, Mr. Perry."

"Did you practice what you learned during our last session?"

"I tried when I stuttered while I was talking. But I got scared in front of people."

"Why were you afraid?"

"They laugh at me or tell me what to do about it."

"Who is it that laughs at you?"

Piccolo Santino

"My aunt does mostly."

"What about at home?"

"My mother teased me in Italy and said the doctor had to cut something on the bottom of my tongue."

"And does she still tell you that?"

"Not anymore because at home, I don't stutter like I used to unless I get furious."

"I see. Don't believe what your mother told you because we won't do anything like that to you."

"That's good!"

"Would it help if I talked with your mother and aunt?"

"My mom won't come. We have eight kids at home, and she has another b-b-baby."

"Sonny, do it on purpose now, and then let go."

"B-b-b--bay-bee, but I could ask her about my aunt."

"Do you see how well that works?"

"Yeah! I think my aunt. She is not an aunt but very close to the family. Sh-sh- Sh-She might come through."

"That was good, Sonny! Before you leave here, I will give you the information so your aunt can call me, and I will explain if she has any questions for me."

"All right, I'll tell my mom, and she'll tell my aunt."

"Okay then. Today, we will continue with the reading sessions, and remember, Sonny, don't be afraid to stutter on purpose when you get stuck on a word."

"Okay." I read for the remainder of the half-hour session and gained new confidence, as I always remembered to stutter on purpose. I couldn't wait to get home with my newfound courage. When I entered the door, Ma was sitting on the couch, reading a letter. She then looked at me and said, "Father Cinquemano died."

"Who told you?"

"This letter arrived today from Eugenio."

"What happened, Ma?"

Piccolo Santino

"Pneumonia."

"Was he sick for a long time?"

"He didn't know he had it, and by the time they got the doctor, it was too late."

"When did he die?"

"About two months ago."

I thought to myself, *He finally met his end, and this time, he could not cheat Death, but there had to be some good in him since he did serve the church for a long time.* But the name Cinquemano (Five hands) was most fitting, for he would give with one hand and slap you in the face with his other four, thus robbing you of any meaning in the occasion. Maybe somehow, he was innocent of the pain he caused some people.

"Ma, the specialist asked me if Gummah Antonia would come with me next week."

"Gummah, Antonia? Why?"

"I told the specialist she makes fun of me when I can't talk right." Ma frowned as she looked at me. "You can't understand what he says, and I thought m-m-m- (I switched to intentional stutter) m-mm-maybe she could come." I was enlightened by the success and encouraged by the new technique. "But what is he going to say?"

"He wants to explain what he is doing with me and why I might have this problem. Then she can explain it to you."

"I don't know if she would go."

"The specialist said the doctors don't have to cut the bottom of my tongue."

"That's good."

"The same taxi will take us there and back, and the school pays."

"All right, I'll call her."

"Here, he gave me his card if she wants to call him first."

"All right, I'll call her."

Gummah Antonia brought her beautiful daughter Liliana, a high school graduate in her early twenties, with her. Mr. Perry explained why

Piccolo Santino

it was important for people not to criticize anybody with such a hindrance. He further explained the work he was doing with me. Liliana's presence was an added morale booster and affirmation that now Ma would receive a proper report.

The subsequent two sessions fortified enough confidence to instill a composure that allowed me to stutter whenever needed. In my final lesson Mr. Perry was interested in my comic book. "Well, Sonny, you know today is our last session together, right?"

"Yes, and I'm glad I came here."

"I'm happy to have had the pleasure of working with you. Sonny. Have things improved for you after having your aunt here?"

"Yes! And I was glad she brought her daughter Liliana with her. Because she explained things to my mom."

"Good! I'm glad. Is that a comic book you have there?"

"It's the new Superman comic book."

"You like Superman?"

"Oh yeah."

"Can I see it?" I got up in front of his desk, and he reached for it. Mr. Perry looked through it and stopped at a page. "What's this you filled in here?"

"Where?" He held up the comic book, "Right here on this advertisement for an art school."

"Oh yeah, I was thinking about sending away for those lessons."

"This is for a correspondence course, Sonny."

"What does that mean?"

"It means you study from home."

"Oh yeah. I'll have to. I couldn't go there, anyway."

"This is very ambitious. It's not only art but animation, too! Sonny, this is serious stuff. It's from an art school in California, Continental Schools, Inc."

"Yeah. I wanted to figure out if I could pay the seven dollars monthly. My sister said she would sometimes help me if I need money."

"Are you going to do it then?"

Piccolo Santino

"I filled the information in. I think I could pay for it without my sister's help."

"Well, you should do it then. But realize it's a real commitment."

"What does that mean?"

"It means to keep your promise and finish the course."

"Oh, I will, once I send it in."

"Good for you, and I wish you lots of luck, Sonny. Now, for today's session, you can read from your comic book if you like."

"Sure!" I breezed through the reading exercise without any hindrances and was no longer afraid of stuttering at home or school.

I became elated when Miss Moran announced that my oral reading had greatly improved, resulting in my looking forward to reading in class. Finally, in fifth grade, I received the end-of-year report card with all passing grades. However, it recommended that I attend summer school for reading since my passing grade in reading was based on a fourth-grade level.

Summer school felt almost quaint without the usual atmosphere of a complete curriculum. At the same time, I felt enticed by the ambiance of only one class to concentrate. By noon, I was home for lunch. Miss Magnani was fluent in Italian, and I was very comfortable with her. A great satisfying benefit of a short school schedule was a shortened workday at the construction yard, and the pay remained the same. I began to like the pace so much that I looked forward to Mondays for the start of each new week.

We were given a book report assignment for the end of the course, and while rummaging through the class collection of books, I chose Ernest Hemingway's *The Old Man and the Sea.* The writing style was most absorbing, and the old man's indomitable spirit clung to me like water on cement. As more school days unfolded and the horizon approached faster, I longed for even more school days. When I walked into the house from work, Ma and Daddy were seated on the futon, and Ma called out to me, "Your friends from the carpenter shop got arrested at the sawmill."

Piccolo Santino

"What? Who told you that?"

"Don Carlo came back from Italy and said it's all over Jonadi."

"What happened?"

"They were caught stealing money by the boss's daughter at the *sigaria,* sawmill. Then they threatened her."

I felt a gripping silence in me as the news brought me back to days at the carpenter shop when they expressed lewd ideas about Filomena. Then I asked Ma, "How did they get arrested?"

"Three Barsaglieri were at the four corners, and one of the workers ran over and got them."

"Franco was always leery of them, Ma."

"And you never said anything."

"I d-d-." (I now applied Mr. Perry's technique.) I d-d-d-didn't think there was anything to say, Ma."

"That's a good thing, then." Daddy said, "Son, you should have told your mother just the same."

"I wanted to tell you! But you weren't there, Daddy." He looked at me momentarily, lowered his head, and I said, "I have a letter from my teacher for you. It's in Italian." Daddy asked, "The teacher can write in Italian?"

Sì, she's Italian." I came back from my bedroom, handed the envelope to Daddy, stood in front of him, and said, "Today was the last day of summer school, and my teacher wanted to tell you how I did." Daddy read the letter, and his eyes widened. He then made a face of approval with expressive sounds. "Hum huh...." I went back to my bedroom to remove my work shoes. Ma then asked inquisitively, "Bartolo, what does it say?"

"His teacher says he can read American well and is her best student." Daddy called me back and said, "Tino, the teacher says you can read American well. Come here and read something to us so we can hear you read."

"All right," I read from a page in my social studies book. As I dug deeper, pride began to radiate from me as I realized that I was awakening my parents' attention to education in America. When I stopped, I almost blushed as I saw my parents glowing with pride, and then Daddy exclaimed, "You like school! Huh?"

"Sì." I also said it, nodding, "Yes."

"I tell you what. You keep working like you have been, and we'll see what happens. Your sisters stopping school at sixteen may be enough."

"Okay," I responded, feeling assured that my education was being considered.

As for Rocco and Bruno, I was glad they got arrested. I recalled my honest friend, Franco, whom I regretted saying goodbye to the most. After moving into town, Franco was like a window into the new frontier of Italy and the world for me. Regrettably, I would never see him again. With all this behind me, I still feared the presence of a dark shadow lurking inside that made me feel that something was missing in my life. I tried to put a face to that shadow by reflecting on the time I burned my foot, then changed my thoughts to those times with Lola and thought maybe it was a face of some guilt I could not admit to.

But the void remained. I wondered about the night Mamma desperately pleaded for Papá to ditch Lillo in the ravine, which led me to believe that I would never talk again, but I came around. Without a face to pin onto the lurking shadow, I succumbed to a negative image of humanity as that of the Reaper, waiting for Death's knell to beckon and call the way it does for us all.

If I am to find the answer to what is missing in my life, I wonder if it is hidden in Papá's words when he said to Mamma, "I couldn't do it! I was afraid that I would be seen and somebody would call the police on me." I often repeat Papá's words, only to feel the weight of my struggle each time. And I always find myself confronted by a solid wall, a barrier I can't break through.

But I always resort to the image of Nanna under the giant oak tree, inside the melting sunset in Calabria. With its warm embrace and golden hues, this memory is the source of light to my future in a time of need.

Piccolo Santino

I held open the flap to the mailbox and read the address on the envelope to the art school in California. Satisfied, I dropped it in and listened to the slamming of the flap before I turned away.

Chapter 16 of Part Two
Return to Fontana Di Taccuni

I got off the airplane and rode a taxi to what once used to be The Fontana Di Taccuni. The cab made its way around the bend past the house I was born in. The basic structure is there with renovations and additions. The gates have changed, but the design is the same. New people live here now. They are the owners of what was once a simple home in a poverty-stricken area. We ride past it down to where the orange groves used to be, and the taxi pulls into a new entrance to the parking lot of a beautiful bed and breakfast place. We park in the shade of two large olive trees, and as I step out of the car. I pause and feel my heart stop at the realization that not even in a dream could I have envisioned such a beautiful transformation. I take a deep breath as my eyes continue to feast and drop quiet tears in, wishing that we could have had the means to realize such splendor so that we would never have had to move away.

After I check in, I will roam this place and see what I can piece together in my mind. After all, I am here for the Piccolo Santino in me, for him to feel his way through what yesterday has become after some sixty-plus years. As I look from here, where I remember the orange groves once to be, I can now see the newly transformed original house in the distance on the hilltop. The embankment on the right that was once all wild brush and trees below the highway is now all contained with a very long, white retaining wall.

In the past, you could not see the house or the barn from here. The wild barrier of trees and brush made it feel like the house was on the other side of the world. Now, the barn is missing, and the top of the long retaining wall is formed with wide red bricks and decorated with large and small pots containing flowers and various palm trees. I can't believe this massive spectacle as the wall runs from the parking lot to the house, descending and ascending at multiple heights, and the walkway I once cleared is now paved with a colored stone. There is another ascending white retaining wall to the left as the walkway climbs to meet the

Piccolo Santino

driveway and a renewed patio in front of the house. Below the patio and walkway is a leveled ground area decorated with large palm trees planted in colossal wine barrels cut in half. This new spectacle is too much to absorb all in one day. After tomorrow, I will think about other places to visit in the main town of Jonadi. I will need a few days here to catch my breath, hiding behind my newly grown beard to avoid being recognized.

I want Piccolo Santino to feel his way, undisturbed by the risk of my being detected, through the places he once wandered about looking for Papá. Places he roamed with his friends, Franco and Nino, seeking solace in the comfort of their company and the splendor of the country fields where they had once roamed together. It's all for the little boy who stayed in me to tell all those stories he wanted to see written.

The End

Piccolo Santino

Acknowledgments:

Ernest Hemmingway
His book, *The Old Man and the Sea*, made a natural imprint on my soul.

Aesthetic Realism Foundation.
I am grateful to the Aesthetic Realism of Eli Siegel for teaching this landmark principle: "The World, Art, and Self-explain each other: each is the aesthetic oneness of opposites."

In memory of Barbara Probst Solomon
An award-winning author known for documenting life during and after the regime of General Francisco Franco. For encouraging me to keep writing. During our meetings throughout the production of her film. *When the War Was Over*, in which I have been credited.

In memory of Aunt Pat
For her numerous interviews and love of family.

In memory of Mamma and Papá
For their courage and foresight.

A special thanks to:
Skip P.
(With, Reedsy.com)
For his professional editing, which brought the story to a new level and really made it flow seamlessly.

Piccolo Santino

About the author

Sal Mallimo immigrated to America from Calabria, Italy, with his six siblings and their mother in 1958 to reunite with their father after a two-year separation. Sal was the first in his family to graduate high school and graduate college from The School of Visual Arts, Film School in NYC.

The very first writing for *Piccolo Santino* was the ghost story his mamma experienced. Sal wrote it as a short story for an English class assignment in high school. However, Sal first wrote about the birth of his sister when he was in second grade back in Italy.

Sal enjoyed a 35-year film animation career in NYC. Which included the formation of his film animation company, Mimondo Productions, Ltd.

Piccolo Santino, is his second book. His first book was, *A Walk in Time, Poetry from real-life About Love and Death*. To illustrate the poems, Sal employed his various animation talents. Both books are available on Amazon.

Piccolo Santino

Please visit: www.piccolosantino.com

Printed in the USA
CPSIA information can be obtained
at www.ICGtesting.com
JSHW081638230924
70170JS00001B/10